YOUR LIFE in CHRIST

FOUNDATIONS OF CATHOLIC MORALITY

Michael Pennock

ave maria press notre dame, indiana

I DEDICATE THIS BOOK

TO MY WIFE CAROL,

WITH LOVE,

AND TO OUR CHILDREN

AND THEIR SPOUSES.

ENGAGING MINDS, HEARTS, AND HANDS

An education that is complete is one in which the hands and heart are engaged as much as the mind. We want to let our students try their learning in the world and so make prayers of their education.

BL. BASILE MOREAU,
FOUNDER OF THE CONGREGATION OF HOLY CROSS

IN THIS TEXT, YOU WILL FIND:

 a comprehensive survey of Catholic morality that involves the quest to be responsible, both as individuals and communities.

 encouragement toward a prayerful attitude of adoration, praise, thanksgiving, confidence, supplication, and awe for God's story.

 communion with the Lord Jesus through projects and assignments that promote right action.

CONTENTS

CHAPTER OVERVIEW

Hearing God's Voice

In a world with many distracting messages, we must listen to God's voice. Only God can tell us how to find happiness in this world and in the next.

What Is Morality?

Morality is much more than labeling actions as "right" or "wrong." Morality is knowing what ought to be done.

Living a Moral Life

Choosing "the good" and uniting ourselves with God's will is the essence of living a moral life. Making good choices moves us toward God and happiness with him.

Character and Virtue

Our free choices and actions shape character—who we are and who we are becoming. Virtues are healthy, good habits that dispose us to make good and moral choices.

Nine Steps for Living a Moral Life

Appreciating our humanity, using our intellect, letting the law guide us, and imitating Jesus are among the nine steps to a moral life presented in the text. Following these steps will help us live moral, virtuous—and happy—lives.

INTRODUCTION

What Is Life in Christ?

Put on, then, as God's chosen ones, holy and beloved, heartfelt compassion, kindness, humility, gentleness, and patience, bearing with one another and forgiving one another, if one has a grievance against another; as the Lord has forgiven you, so must you also do. And over all these put on love, that is, the bond of perfection.

Colossians 3:12–17

Samuel Johnson

morality

Knowledge based on human experience, reason, and God's revelation that discovers what we ought to be and what we ought to do to live fully human lives.

What Will You Do?

For each of the following cases, decide what you would do. Then explain whether your choice is morally right or not.

- *You are involved in an accident with a parked car late at night in a known crime area. The damage done to the other car is slight. No one saw the accident. What will you do?*
- *You meet a homeless person on a city street corner. He asks you for some money for lunch. You also smell wine on his breath. What will you do?*

Hearing God's Voice

Asking questions is typically a human thing to do. Eighteenth-century English author and lexicographer Samuel Johnson noted that curiosity is the sign of a vigorous intellect. He observed, "Curiosity is, in great and generous minds, the first passion and the last."

One thing most people are curious about is how to be happy. We want to recognize true happiness, and we want to do what we need to do in order to achieve it.

The Gospel of Mark records a poignant example of a rich youth who sensed that Jesus Christ was the source and key to a happy life. The young man approached Jesus and asked him a question that echoes down through the ages, "Good teacher, what must I do to inherit eternal life?" (Mk 10:17). The young man was interested not simply in being happy in this life, but in being happy for eternity.

We can learn something important from this wealthy youth, namely, his intelligence to approach Jesus and ask *him* for his teaching. For Christians and others who want to know the secret to happiness, the essential first step is to draw near to Jesus the Teacher and learn from him. In a world with so many voices barking conflicting messages at us about how to achieve happiness, we absolutely must go to the Master and hear his voice.

But this is only the first step. The second step is also essential: We must adhere to his instruction—we must do what Jesus says—or we will not attain happiness. We must *put into practice* his example and his teaching by using the many graces he bestows on us.

Attending to and following Jesus' teaching will help us lead moral and virtuous lives, the key to lasting happiness. With the Lord at our side, and armed with the many graces of the Holy Spirit, we can begin to experience in this life the happiness God intends for us for eternity.

As you study and apply the truths of Christian morality in the chapters that follow, know full well that the Lord Jesus walks the journey with you and seeks for you the happiness that you desire.

What Is Morality?

The words **morality** and *morals* conjure up various reactions from people. For example, the American satirist H. L. Mencken claimed that morality is "the theory that every human act must be either right or wrong, and that 99 percent of them are wrong." The famous novelist Ernest Hemingway was less negative about morality when he wrote, "About morals, I know only that what is moral is what you feel good after and what is immoral is what you feel bad after." The German philosopher Friedrich Nietzsche, who once cynically proclaimed the death of God, concluded, "Morality is the herd-instinct in the individual."

Do these statements have anything to do with a definition of morality? Is morality simply a matter of labeling most human acts as wrong? Is morality simply a matter of monitoring your feelings after you do something? Is morality simply a matter of following the crowd?

Authentic morality is much richer than any of the above statements. Morality has been described as a special kind of knowing—a "knowing of what ought to be done." Humans—both as individuals and societies—are constantly confronted with decisions and choices that demand answers and a course of action. For example, take a student who must decide which course to take, a young person trying to decide whether or not to accept a date with someone he or she barely knows, or a society that is trying to decide whether or not to permit homeless people to sleep in the city park. Each of

What's Right? What's Wrong?

In today's pluralistic society, it is very difficult to get people to agree on what is right and what is wrong, what is moral and what is immoral. Judge where you stand on each statement according to the scale below.

1=strongly agree; 2=agree; 3=not sure; 4=disagree; 5=strongly disagree

STATEMENTS	1	2	3	4	5
1. There is never a good reason to lie.					
2. Cheating on tests or quizzes, even if the teacher is unfair and everyone else is doing it, is always wrong.					
3. Abortion is a great assault on innocent human life and can never be justified.					
4. It is wrong for a rich country to engage vigorously in an arms race when it has so many poor people in its midst.					
5. Outside of marriage, it is wrong to engage in sexual intercourse and the actions leading up to it.					
6. People have an obligation to worship God even if they don't feel like it.					
7. Given the efficiency of today's justice systems, it is virtually impossible to justify capital punishment.					
8. It would be dangerous and imprudent to lower the age for legalized drinking of alcohol.					
9. It is wrong to assess or judge people by the color of their skin.					
10. Pornography—both soft and hard—debases human sexuality. It should be outlawed.					

- Why did you choose as you did?
- Would your parents agree with your choices?
- Choose a particular opinion-influencing group (for example, music moguls, Hollywood tycoons, Washington lawmakers). Predict how the majority in that group would rate each statement. Offer evidence for your view.

---

these decisions and many more like them involve answering the basic questions, "What must I do?" or "What must we do?"

A traditional definition of morality calls it "the science of what humans ought to do by reason of who they are." This definition has held up well over the years. By terming morality a science, we are saying that we can acquire knowledge about a particular subject, in this case, the subject of how we should act as humans. Catholic morality draws on three main sources of knowledge to reach conclusions about how we should act: *human reason* (our God-given intellects), *human experience* (the collective wisdom of others, living and dead), and *divine revelation* (the teachings of God as found in the scriptures and the teachings of the Church).

Note that the second major feature of this definition holds that human behavior should flow "by reason of who they are." This means that morality hinges on a correct view of the human person. Only if humans are understood as precious children of God who have incalculable dignity can they be expected to act with freedom, dignity, and responsibility. As we will see in the next chapter, a proper view of the human person—derived from reason, experience, and divine revelation—is the

1. What do you think it means to be happy?

2. How do you think you can best achieve happiness?

3. Review the advertisements in a popular magazine. Choose several that depict what the advertisers are promoting to achieve a happy life. Share and discuss these advertised messages with your classmates.

The Gifts of the Holy Spirit (*CCC*, 1830–1832; 1845)

To live the moral life, the Holy Spirit gives us seven gifts that help us follow the Spirit's prompting to live good lives. These seven **gifts of the Holy Spirit** are wisdom, understanding, counsel, fortitude, knowledge, piety, and fear of the Lord. They complete and perfect the virtues in Christians who receive them.

In addition, the Holy Spirit allows us to partake in the firstfruits of eternal glory. Twelve in number, the **fruits of the Holy Spirit** are evident in a person who is living a Christ-like, moral, and upright life: charity, joy, peace, patience, kindness, goodness, generosity, gentleness, faithfulness, modesty, self-control, and chastity.

gifts of the Holy Spirit

God-given abilities that help us live a Christian life with God's help. Jesus promised and bestows these gifts through the Holy Spirit, especially in the Sacrament of Confirmation. The seven gifts are wisdom, understanding, knowledge, counsel (right judgment), fortitude, piety (reverence), and fear of the Lord (wonder and awe).

fruits of the Holy Spirit

Described as the firstfruits of eternal glory, they are charity, joy, peace, patience, kindness, goodness, generosity, gentleness, faithfulness, modesty, self-control, and chastity.

Magisterium

The official teaching authority of the Church. The Lord bestowed the right and power to teach in his name on Peter and the apostles and their successors, that is, the pope and the college of bishops.

critically important starting point in deciding what is the moral way to respond.

MORALITY AS A RESPONSE TO GOD

Another helpful way to understand Catholic morality involves our quest to become responsible, both as individuals and communities. The key word here is *responsible*. Applied to persons, the word means having the "ability" to "respond." Responsibility requires freedom and intelligence. Freedom and intelligence are two human qualities that enable us (give us the ability) to become good persons, to make right choices and engage in right actions, and to do our part to help build a more humane world.

But to what do we respond? The better question is to *Whom* do we respond? From a Catholic point of view, morality is a response to a loving God and a continuing venture to become fully the persons God wants us to be. As the *Catechism of the Catholic Church* [1691–98] teaches, we are able to respond to God because of the following:

- *Intelligence and freedom.* God has given us intelligence to know the truth. God has also created us as free beings with dignity, creatures who share in God's own life. With God's help and grace, we

can determine our own lives through our decisions and actions.

- *Help of the Holy Spirit.* Humans are also sinners, prone to make bad choices and to engage in evil. However, because of Jesus' self-sacrificing death on the cross, God gave to us yet another gift—the Holy Spirit. Through Baptism, the Holy Spirit comes to us and bestows on us his many gifts. These gifts enable us to follow the way of Christ, to walk on a path that leads first to a fully human and moral life and eventually to eternal happiness. The Holy Spirit allows Christ Jesus to live in and work through us. The Holy Spirit enables us to participate in God's own divine life, makes us holy, and gives us the ability to make Christ-like, loving choices. The Holy Spirit gives us the gifts and graces we need to engage in actions that are pleasing to our loving Father.

- *Support of the Church* [*CCC*, 2030–31; 2047]. The Church is both a mother and a teacher. Through the Church we receive God's Word, which contains Christ's law. The Church also confers the graces of the sacraments, especially the Eucharist, through which Jesus himself comes to us and empowers us to worship the Father through upright, loving lives. Further, the Christian community provides the example and inspiration of many Christian heroes who have lived faithful lives, for example, our Blessed Mother, the disciple of Christ par excellence.

• *Help of the Magisterium* [*CCC*, 2032–2040; 2049–2051]. Catholics also believe that the pope and the bishops are the authentic teachers in the Church, possessing Christ's own authority to teach in his name the truths of salvation that pertain to faith and morals. This official teaching office is called the **Magisterium**. All people have the right to instruction in the way of life and truth. The official pastors of the Church have a corresponding duty to teach this truth. Other competent teachers (like theologians) and ministers should also share their gifts to help pastors explain God's truth to the people.

The teaching authority of the Magisterium also extends to the specific precepts of the natural law, reminding people of who they should be before God. So serious is this responsibility to teach and guide faithful Christians that Jesus has left the gift of *infallibility* to the pope and the bishops united to him. This gift of being preserved from error

> *extends to all those elements of doctrine, including morals, without which the saving truths of the faith cannot be preserved, explained, or observed (CCC, 2035).*

Guided by Christ-appointed teachers who have our best interest at heart, Christ's Church is a powerful help in learning how to respond in a fully human way to God. The Magisterium continually reminds us that we need to conform our actions to God's divine and eternal law, that is, his wise and loving plan for humans. As we shall see in subsequent chapters, this plan can be discovered in the natural law and through God's revelation of the Ten Commandments and his law of love. For our part, we must form our consciences and develop our intellects in cooperation with the moral law and the teaching of Christ's Church.

• *Help of Jesus Christ, God's own Son and our Savior.* Jesus is our model and norm of what a fully human life should be. To be moral is to imitate Jesus, to be Christ-like, to allow him into our lives.

In summary, then, morality is a kind of knowledge based on human experience, reason, and God's revelation that discovers who we ought to be and to do to live fully human lives.

REVIEW AND REFLECTION

1. Define the term *morality*. Explain the various elements of the definition.

2. List three sources of knowledge Catholics use to reach conclusions on how we should act.

3. In what way is morality a response to God?

4. What enables us to respond to God and live good lives?

5. List the gifts of the Holy Spirit.

6. Who is the *Magisterium*?

FOR YOUR JOURNAL

Write a short profile of a Christian, alive or in heaven, who is for *you* an inspiration on how to live a faithful life. Discuss several examples of the person's fidelity and goodness.

Living a Moral Life

[CCC, 2044-2046]

◆ What are some factors that keep people from doing the right thing?

◆ How would you describe someone who is fully human?

Living a moral life means to decide and then act according to God's plan for us. It means being responsible and cooperating with God's grace to live a fully human life.

Living a moral life by "choosing good" unites us with God's will and gives us a taste of true happiness. Making good choices allows us to walk down the path that will eventually lead to a final destiny of union with our loving God. On the other hand, when we choose evil over good we misuse the gifts that God has given us. We walk down a path that will ultimately lead to the opposite of happiness because we are acting contrary to God's will for us.

People do not always see the truth of these statements: "being good" leads to happiness; "being bad" leads to unhappiness. In the short term, sometimes it is hard to be good, that is, to do the right thing. We pay a price, and it sometimes hurts. Take, for example, Karen, who refuses to join in the mockery of an unpopular classmate. Karen might, in turn, be teased for siding with a "loser." But she does the good and moral thing by treating her classmate with respect. Karen can live with herself and hold her head high because she shows respect for another human being. An upright conscience does lead to happiness. As the popular saying goes, "If you want a rainbow, you have to put up with the rain." And the Quaker founder of Pennsylvania, William Penn, reminds us, "No pain, no palm; no thorns, no throne; no gall, no glory; no cross, no crown."

In the short term, "being bad" sometimes seems to bring satisfaction. But how illusory and temporary this pleasure turns out to be because our acts do not mesh with how God intends for us to be. Take, for example, the college freshman who goes out to party every weekend, getting drunk each time. Unfortunately, the immediate gratification of alcohol so often leads to a lifetime of misery and wasted talents. Whenever we act contrary to what God has in mind for us, we are at odds with our true selves and will ultimately be unhappy.

In brief, living a moral life is living in the presence of God. Being good is responding to God and God's incredible love. In addition to bringing us ultimate happiness, living a moral life:

- allows the Holy Spirit to work in us, making us like Jesus;
- strengthens our friendship with the Lord;
- makes us persons of integrity who are responding to our God-given vocation to be fully human;
- attracts other people to God and to the Christian faith, helping to build up Christ's body, which is the Church;
- and helps bring about God's reign on earth, "a kingdom of justice, love, and peace."

A GOSPEL EXAMPLE OF LIVING A MORAL LIFE

As he was setting out on a journey, a man ran up, knelt down before him, and asked him, "Good teacher, what must I do to inherit eternal life?" Jesus answered him, "Why do you call me good? No one is good but God alone. You know the commandments: 'You shall not kill; you shall not commit adultery; you shall not steal; you shall not bear false witness; you shall not defraud; honor your father and your mother.'" He replied and said to him, "Teacher, all of these I have observed from my youth." Jesus, looking at him, loved him and said to him, "You are lacking in one thing. Go, sell what you have, and give to [the] poor and you will have treasure in heaven; then come, follow me." At that statement his face fell, and he went away sad, for he had many possessions.

Jesus looked around and said to his disciples, "How hard it is for those who have wealth to enter the kingdom of God!"

—Mark 10:17–23

The dialogue between the young man and Jesus teaches us much about what it means to be good. Note how the young man wants to live a life of meaning and value, one that will merit eternal life and happiness. We are all like this youth; we all sense a connection between doing good and our eternal destiny.

In his answer to the young man, Jesus first points out that the goodness to which the young man is attracted has its source in God. God is good because God is love, so loving that he gave his only Son to the world so we may live (cf. Jn 3:16). God gives the definitive answer to our human existence. This good and loving God implanted in the young man, and in us, a desire to be good, loving, and moral. This same desire leads all people to approach Jesus, God incarnate. Jesus' own goodness bears witness to God.

Made in God's image and likeness, the young man is attracted to the good and wants to know how to achieve it. Jesus immediately lists some of the commandments. These commandments—do not kill, do not commit adultery, honor your parents, and so forth—are part of God's covenant with all of humanity. They are the essential ingredients for living a fully human and moral life. These commandments find their fulfillment in the gospel, in the Sermon on the Mount, and in Christ's commandment to love.

By linking the commandments and eternal life, Jesus teaches of the necessity to obey God's word. When we ignore God's will for us, we act in a way that is contrary to our own good. In this gospel story, Jesus teaches us that

The commandments . . . are meant to safeguard the good of the person, the image of God, by protecting his goods.

Addressing the youth of the world, the late Pope John Paul II wrote:

"Jesus, looking at him, loved him." May you experience a look like that! May you experience the truth that he, Christ, looks upon you with love! . . . Man needs this loving look. He needs to know that he is loved, loved eternally and chosen from eternity.[1]

- Write of a time when you felt Jesus' love.

"How hard it is for those who have wealth to enter the kingdom of God!" What do you think Jesus means by these words?

- Read Mk 10:24–31.

- Then answer the following: What comparison does Jesus use to drive home his point? How do the apostles react? How does Jesus reassure them?

"You shall not murder; You shall not commit adultery; You shall not steal; You shall not bear false witness" are moral rules formulated in terms of prohibitions. These negative precepts express with particular force the ever urgent need to protect human life, the communion of persons in marriage, private property, truthfulness and people's good name.

The commandments thus represent the basic condition for love of neighbor; at the same time they are the proof of that love. They are the first necessary step on the journey towards freedom, its starting-point. (Splendor of Truth, 13)

The young man assured Jesus that he observed the commandments. In Matthew's account of this same dialogue, the young man asks, "What do I still lack?" (Mt 19:20). Jesus sensed that this young man's heart yearned for greatness, that he wished to do more. And, with great love in his heart, Jesus invited him to sell his belongings and come and follow him.

This invitation of Jesus to be perfect as his heavenly Father is perfect, to love as Jesus loves, is the heart of the dialogue with the rich young man. Its message is meant for all followers of Christ. We are to "let go and let God" into our lives by clinging to the very person of Christ, to make him the foremost priority in our lives.

REVIEW AND REFLECTION

1. Who is the greatest help in living a moral, responsible life? Why?

2. What does it mean to "be good"?

3. In his dialogue with the rich young man on the good life, what does Jesus say is essential for gaining eternal life?

4. What more does Jesus ask of the rich young man in Mark 10:17–23?

FOR YOUR JOURNAL

"Measure your wealth by who you are rather than by what you have." Briefly discuss how wealthy you are based on who *you* are. Also, discuss the strength of your current relationship with Jesus Christ. Is it great? Good and getting better each day? Or just OK?

Character and Virtue

Various surveys reveal some disturbing realities concerning the moral state found in Britain and America today. For example:

- The British are forgetting the Ten Commandments. Less than half of those surveyed could recall the commandments forbidding theft, murder, or adultery. Only 9 percent recalled the commandment not to lie. And only 4 percent remembered the commandment to "keep the Sabbath day holy."[2]

- In a recent study of almost 25,000 high school students, nearly two-thirds (62 percent) said they cheated on exams and more than one in four (27 percent) stole from a store within the past year. Additionally, 40 percent admit they "sometimes lie to save money."

- In this same study, 42 percent of the teens surveyed believe that "a person has to lie or cheat sometimes in order to succeed," and 22 percent believe that "people who are willing to lie, cheat or break the rules are more likely to succeed than people who do not."[3]

- Retail losses to shoplifting annually now amount to over $33 billion with the average shoplifting case amounting to $30.[4]

- "Pornography has grown into a $10 billion business—bigger than the NFL, the NBA, and Major League Baseball combined—and some of the nation's best-known corporations are quietly sharing the profits."[5]

- Almost 1.5 million babies were born to unmarried women in the United States in 2004. This set a record. Fifty-five percent of the births for mothers ages twenty to twenty-four were to unmarried women.[6]

It is impossible to reconcile these responses to Jesus' instruction to the rich young man to obey and put into practice the values of all the commandments, including telling the truth and not killing

others. These findings point out that our society is lacking in morality. How can we improve? Two ways, discussed below, involve building one's character and cultivating virtues.

Character is what a person is in the dark.

—Anonymous

CHARACTER

Our free choices and our actions, which are outward expressions of our choices, form who we are. Our character is at the very heart of our self-chosen moral identity.

Our character is how we respond to the divine invitation to love God, self, and neighbor. Character is our "yes" or "no" to Christ's invitation to friendship. *Character is who we really are and who we are becoming through our choices and actions.* It is the part of us that does good or chooses evil.

Have you ever watched the formation of an icicle? As each drop of water freezes, the icicle gradually grows, sometimes to well over three feet. If the water droplets are clean, the icicle that results is crystal clear and sparkles in the sun like a diamond. But if some droplets are dirty, the icicle that forms is murky, marred by the turbid water. It is like this with our character. Our good thoughts and decisions—important as well as trivial—help to form us. Everything we process—experiences,

- ◆ If you found a wallet containing $1000, would you return it to its owner?

- ◆ If you were an employer, would you hire yourself?

- ◆ If you were a parent, would you be proud to have a child like you?

images, words—helps create our character. Each of our freely chosen actions forms us as a person and strengthens or weakens our character.

The important lesson here is to take note of the droplets that form our lives. "Small" lies, arrogant attitudes toward others, evil intentions—all contribute to the defiling of a good character. Conversely, each seemingly insignificant act of kindness, truth-telling, and love forms us into people with Christ-like characters.

Here is one way to summarize character:[7]

1. Persons with good moral characters are *loving.* They love God above all. They love themselves. And, following Jesus, they recognize, respect, and respond in love to all other human beings.

2. People with good moral characters are *fully human* persons. They are free, intelligent, responsible, open to growth, social, and spiritual.

3. Good people are *virtuous* people. Virtues are the building blocks of a good character.

VIRTUES *(CCC, 1803–1829; 1833–1844)*

Virtues are the heart of the moral life. Virtues are healthy, good habits that help us do good and empower us to become what God wants us to be. These personal qualities emphasize that who we are greatly affects what we do. Virtues form our character and make us Christ-like. Virtues are moral skills for Christian living that help us act naturally. They equip us to face both internal and external obstacles on our journey to God.

The Catechism of the Catholic Church defines virtue this way:

> *A virtue is an habitual and firm disposition to do the good. . . . Human virtues are firm attitudes, stable dispositions, habitual perfections of intellect and will that govern our actions, order our passions, and guide our conduct according to reason and faith. They make possible ease, self-mastery, and joy in leading a morally good life. (CCC, 1803–4)*

Church teaching lists two major categories of virtues: theological and cardinal.

Theological Virtues *(CCC, 1812–1828)*

The theological virtues are gifts from God that empower us to be good so that we may do good. Infused by God into our souls, the three **theological virtues** of faith, hope, and charity (love) enable us to live in relationship to the Blessed Trinity. Their origin, motive, and object is the one, Triune God. These virtues serve as the basis of a Christian moral life. The theological virtues will be covered in more detail in Chapter 7. What follows is a brief definition of each:

- *Faith.* This theological virtue enables us to believe in God, all that God has said and revealed to us, and all that the Church proposes for our belief because

virtues

"Firm attitudes, stable dispositions, habitual perfections of intellect and will that govern our actions, order our passions, and guide our conduct according to reason and faith" (*CCC,* 1804).

theological virtues

Three important virtues bestowed on us at baptism that relate us to God: faith, or belief in and personal knowledge of God; hope, or trust in God's salvation and his bestowal of the graces needed to attain it; and charity, or love of God and love of neighbor as one loves oneself.

God is truth itself. Christians must cultivate their faith, but also proclaim it, bear witness to it, and spread it to others.

- *Hope.* Hope enables us to desire heaven and eternal life, trusting in Christ's promises and relying on the help of the Holy Spirit and his graces. Hope keeps us from getting discouraged as we live the Christian life and keeps us going when times get tough and lonely. It makes it possible for us to strive for true happiness and live the life of Jesus' Beatitudes.

- *Charity (Love).* This greatest virtue of all empowers us to "love God above all things for his own sake, and our neighbor as ourselves for the love of God" (*CCC*, 1822). Charity enables us to observe the commandments and love everyone, even our enemies. This key virtue helps us practice all the other virtues and uplifts our human ability to love, raising it to the perfection of divine love.

Cardinal Virtues (*CCC*, 1805–1811)

Prudence, justice, fortitude, and temperance are the **cardinal virtues**, from the Latin *cardo*, which means "hinge." The cardinal virtues are the source of all other good habits. Even non-Christians have recognized the cardinal virtues as the "natural virtues." We can gain these virtues through education and repeated practice in using them. Like anything worth doing, it takes effort to grow in the virtues, especially for humans who are weakened by sin and are prone to be lazy. But with God's help and the graces he gives us through the Holy Spirit, it is possible to strengthen these "spiritual muscles" that are necessary for robust Christian moral living.

What follows is a brief description of the four cardinal virtues. Later chapters will discuss them in greater detail.

Prudence. St. Thomas Aquinas called prudence "right reason in action." Prudence is practical wisdom, the virtue of responsible decision-making. Prudence uses memory, foresight, imagination, and openness to learning to help our intellects discover what is good in every situation. Prudence also helps us select the right means of achieving what is good. Prudence permeates all the other cardinal virtues, giving them direction and control as we make conscientious decisions. Prudence, in short, helps us take the moral principles we have learned and apply them to concrete cases.

Justice. Justice involves relationships with others and our life in community. Justice gives both God and neighbor what is their due by right. Justice, for example, requires us to worship and adore God since he is our all-loving Creator. And it helps us respect the rights of all other humans.

Fortitude. Fortitude gives us the strength and courage to stand firm with our own convictions and do the right and moral thing. Fortitude helps us to resist temptation and to overcome obstacles to living a good life. It helps us make sacrifices and overcome fears of criticism, failure, rejection, and disappointment as we pursue the good. Fortitude gives us the "spiritual guts" to resist peer pressure which might tempt us to conform to evil practices.

Temperance. Temperance is the virtue of moderation that brings balance to our life. It helps regulate our appetite for the good things God has given to us, such as food, drink, sex, and possessions. Temperance assists us in counteracting the vices of greed, gluttony, and lust by helping us master the appetites of our senses and indulge them within honorable limits.

St. Thomas Aquinas

The shrewd man does everything with prudence, but the fool peddles folly.

—PROVERBS 13:16

cardinal virtues

The four hinge virtues that support moral living: prudence, or "right reason in action," concerning the best way to live morally; justice, or giving God and each person his or her due by right; fortitude, or courage to persist in living a Christian life; and temperance, or moderation in controlling our desires for physical pleasures.

A Self-Examination on the Cardinal Virtues

How well do you practice the following virtues? Check the appropriate box.

CARDINAL VIRTUES	Very Well	Well	Needs Work
PRUDENCE (SOUND JUDGMENT)			
I respect learning and am open to new ideas.			
I reflect on past mistakes before acting.			
I can recognize goodness, truth, and beauty when I see it, and I can pick out what is evil, false, and ugly.			
JUSTICE (FAIRNESS TOWARD OTHERS)			
I both acknowledge and respect the rights of others.			
I do my duty, honor my promises, and follow through on my commitments.			
I respect the reputation of others, refrain from gossip and rash judgment, and give others the benefit of the doubt.			
FORTITUDE (COURAGE)			
I am able to put up with inconvenience, disappointments, and setbacks.			
I am willing to face problems and obstacles and refuse to run away from them.			
I am my own person and make strong efforts to overcome peer pressure, especially when others want me to do wrong.			
TEMPERANCE (SELF-CONTROL)			
I can say "no" to myself and wait for rewards and gratification.			
I enjoy in moderation the pleasures of food, drink, entertainment, sports, and the like.			
I am an actor rather than a reactor. For example, I respect rude people rather than returning nastiness to them.			

Nine Steps for Living a Moral Life

This introduction has provided some key terms—morality, character, and virtue—that are important in the overall study of Christian morality. From a Christian point of view, this material has also briefly reflected on what it means to "be good." The remaining chapters of the text will focus on nine steps necessary for living a good moral life. Briefly, the steps are:

1. Appreciating the gift of being human.

We respond to God in a responsible way when we act as the beautiful creatures God made us to be, that is, in the divine image and possessing tremendous dignity.

2. Using your intellect.

God endowed us with intellects that can systematically search out the right course of behavior when confronted with various options. When we use our God-given intellects we can discover the right thing to do. Chapter 2 presents a "STOP Sign" method of moral decision-making, which is an organized technique of applying our intellects to moral issues.

3. Looking to the law to guide your freedom.

Possessing freedom enables us to be responsible. However, misusing freedom is morally hazardous. Thankfully, to help guide our conduct, we have objective norms—laws—which are based on the wisdom of past ages.

4. Imitating Jesus.

Jesus is the preeminent norm and guide for Christians who want to live a moral life. Learning from his example, heeding his teaching, and allowing him to live in us are all profound helps in living a Christian life of virtue for God and others.

5. Forming, informing, and following your conscience.

Through our consciences, God's voice calls us to be who he created us to be. As a practical judgment in discerning right from wrong, we must develop an upright and truthful conscience and then have the fortitude to follow it.

6. Repenting and seeking forgiveness when you sin.

Unfortunately, at times, we do not take the moral and virtuous course of action. We violate the dictates of God's law and our own consciences. We sin. When this happens, we need to repent, reform our lives, and gratefully accept the mercy of our loving and merciful Savior.

7. Loving God above all.

As our loving Creator who is the source of all our gifts, God deserves us to love him with all our hearts, souls, and minds (Mt 22:37). God has first loved us. By observing the first three commandments and exercising the virtues of faith, hope, and love, we can begin to return God's love.

8. Loving yourself.

Without a healthy love of self, it is very difficult to love others and God. We must love ourselves by practicing virtues like gratitude, humility, and temperance and by sharing the many gifts God has given us. We also show love of self by observing the commandments.

9. Loving your neighbor.

We prove our love of God by loving our neighbor, including our enemies. We love others by exercising virtues like justice, kindness, and respect and by following the commandments, especially the fourth through the tenth of the Decalogue.

Following these nine steps of moral living is intended to help Christians to live moral and virtuous lives. They will help us attain happiness in this life and in a life of eternity with our Triune God.

- Add two personal statements under each virtue.

- Which virtue needs the most work in your life right now? State a plan of action for how you can improve in this area of your life.

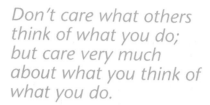

A Study in Character: "Have It Your Way"

The fast-food Burger King franchise is known for its advertising motto, "Have it your way." This true story happened at a Burger King in Deltona, Florida, when Henry Snowden drove up to the take-out window and was given two bags. One contained the sandwiches and fries that he and his friend ordered. The other had the day's receipts of $4,170 in it. The clerk at the window mistakenly handed Henry the money bag that the manager inadvertently plopped down next to Henry's food order. The policy of this particular Burger King was to place the day's earnings in a regular food bag rather than in a bank-deposit bag in order to fool potential robbers.

When Henry got home and discovered the mistake, he concluded that he should take the money back. But he admitted he was tempted to keep it since it would help him with his Internet provider company. The next morning he did in fact return the misplaced receipts. He was rewarded with tears of thanks and a free lunch.

Restaurant workers told him that he would probably get a reward. But Henry said he received something much better than any monetary reward—a clear conscience. He said, "I'm not a glory hound. I'm glad I was able to do the right thing. And I feel better than I've ever felt."[8]

- Do you think Henry was obligated to return the money, especially knowing that the restaurant manager engaged in the unwise practice of placing receipts in a regular food bag?
- What do you think you would do in a similar situation?
- What kind of character does Henry have?

Don't care what others think of what you do; but care very much about what you think of what you do.

—St. Francis de Sales

REVIEW AND REFLECTION

1. What is *character*? Describe some qualities of a person with character.

2. What is a *virtue*? How does it help us live a moral life?

3. What are the theological virtues? The cardinal virtues?

4. Briefly describe what each cardinal virtue does.

5. List and briefly discuss nine steps to living a moral life.

FOR YOUR JOURNAL

Ask your parents which of the four cardinal virtues they think is most absent in today's world. Discuss the reasons for their choices and compare their answers to your own view.

Catholic Life in Action

Exercise the gifts of the Holy Spirit, the seven gifts that He bestows on us to help us live good lives. Put into practice one or more of these in the coming two weeks. Write a journal entry on what you did and what you learned about yourself.

- Wisdom: Seek the advice of a person you respect and admire on an issue you are struggling with or a decision you are trying to make.
- Understanding: Listen carefully to a friend or parent the next time he or she is talking to you. Try to understand not only what he or she is saying, but feeling, as well.
- Right Judgment (counsel): Before making your next decision that involves right and wrong, consider the alternatives and consequences of each approach. Pray for guidance.
- Fortitude (courage): Dare to speak up when a classmate is being verbally attacked. Express your displeasure at prejudicial remarks made in your presence.
- Knowledge: Read about one of the saints, persons of heroic character, at one of these websites:
    Catholics Online: www.catholic.org/saints/
    Catholic Forum: www.catholic-forum.com/saints/indexsnt.htm
    Theology Library: www.shc.edu/theolibrary/saints2.htm
- Fear of the Lord (awe and wonder): Take a nature walk and notice the beauty of God's wondrous creation. Write a prayer of thanksgiving for the awesome gifts God has given to you, including the gift of your own life, which is made in his image and likeness.
- Piety (reverence): Show your respect to God by being especially attentive and prayerful at next Sunday's liturgy. Study the Sunday readings ahead of time so you can derive greater benefit from them. You can find the readings at the United States Catholic Bishops' website: www.usccb.org/nab/.

Summary Points

- There is a strong link between living a moral life and being happy. Christians believe that we need to hear the teaching of Jesus and then put it into practice as steps on the road to happiness in this life and unending joy in eternity.

- Morality draws on human reason, human experience, and divine revelation in searching out what we ought to do.

- Morality is a response to a loving God and a continuing venture to become fully the person God wants us to be.

- We can respond to God morally because God has endowed us with intelligence and freedom, gives us the gifts and graces of the Holy Spirit who lives within, supports us with the witness of fellow believers, and guides us through the official teachers in the Church. Jesus Christ, our Lord and Savior, is the greatest help of all in living a moral life.

- A good person lives morally, deciding on and then acting according to God's plan for him or her. In his dialogue with the rich young man, Jesus teaches that keeping the commandments and observing his law of love are essentials to being good. Jesus also teaches that we must "let go and let God" into our lives by making friendship with Jesus our top priority.

- Our character is who we really are and who we are becoming through our choices and actions. Character is the heart of a self-chosen moral identity. Persons with good moral characters are loving, fully human, and virtuous.

- Virtues help form a good character. A virtue is a habitual and firm disposition to do good. The theological virtues—faith, hope, and love—relate us to God and enable us to live Christ-like lives. Charity is the greatest virtue of all. The cardinal ("hinge") virtues can be gained through education and repeated practice and strengthened with the graces of the Holy Spirit. They are prudence (right reason in action), justice (fairness), fortitude (courage), and temperance (moderation).

- The steps to living a moral life are appreciating and using your human gifts, using your intellect, seeking guidance from the law, imitating Jesus, forming and following your conscience, repenting and seeking forgiveness for your sins, and loving God above all things and your neighbor as yourself.

or this reason, I kneel before the Father, from whom every family in heaven and on earth is named, that he may grant you in accord with the riches of his glory to be strengthened with power through his Spirit in the inner self, and that Christ may dwell in your hearts through faith; that you, rooted and grounded in love, may have strength to comprehend with all the holy ones what is the breadth and length and height and depth, and to know the love of Christ that surpasses knowledge, so that you may be filled with all the fullness of God.

Now to him who is able to accomplish far more than all we ask or imagine, by the power at work within us, to him be glory in the church and in Christ Jesus to all generations, forever and ever. Amen.

—Ephesians 3:14–21

- Describe a time when you have most felt the "breadth and length and height and depth" of Christ's love for you.
- Write your own brief prayer of thanksgiving to God.

NOTES

1. Apostolic Letter *Dilecti Amici* of Pope John Paul II to the Youth of the World on the Occasion of International Youth Year, No. 7, April 1, 1985 <www.ewtn.com/library/PAPALDOC/JP2YOUT.HTM> (9 August 2006).

2. ASSIST News Service, Jeremy Reynalds, "The (Forgot) Ten Commandments: Survey Indicates British are Forgetting Commandments," September 17, 2004 <across.co.nz/TheForgotTenCommandments.html> (9 August 2006).

3. Josephson Institute of Ethics, The Ethics of American Youth—2004 Report Card: Press Release and Data Summary <www.josephsoninstitute.org/Survey2004/2004reportcard_pressrelease.htm> (9 August 2006).

4. Jack L. Hayes International, Inc., "Theft Surveys: Shoplifting" <www.hayesinternational.com/thft_srvys.html> (9 August 2006).

5. abcNews.com, "Corporate America Is Profiting From Porn — Quietly," January 28, 2003 <www.churchsermon.org/sermons/reports/Porn_profits.htm> (9 August 2006).

6. Sharon Jayson, "Births to Unmarried Women Hit Record," *USA Today,* October 30, 2005 <www.usatoday.com/news/health/2005-10-28-unwed-moms_x.htm?POE=NEWISVA> (9 August 2006).

7. This summary comes from Russell B. Connors, Jr., and Patrick T. McCormick, *Character, Choices & Community: The Three Faces of Christian Ethics* (New York: Paulist Press, 1998), 24–33. We will develop the theme of being fully human in Chapter 1 and what it means to be loving in chapters 4 and 7–10.

8. "Worker Mistakenly Gives Bank Bag to Honest Customer," *Northwest Florida Daily News,* June 24, 1998, 6C. Accessed online from the *Daily News* archives <www.nwfdailynews.com/archive/kid's_corner/980624newskid2. html> (9 August 2006).

CHAPTER OVERVIEW

Act Human
To live a moral life we must first act like humans and be ourselves.

Humans Are Made in the Divine Image
God made human beings—male and female—in his own image and gave them stewardship over creation and other creatures.

Human Dignity
Since we are made in God's image, all human beings have inherent dignity and value.

Our Spiritual Nature
Having immortal souls and called to live eternally with God, human beings are spiritual beings who think, love, choose, grow, and have free will.

The Social Nature of Humans
Like God, a community of love in the Father, Son, and Holy Spirit, human beings are social and meant to live with each other.

Humans Are Wounded by Sin
Infected by the Original Sin of Adam and Eve, humanity is wounded by sin, inclined to evil and weakness, and in need of a Savior.

CHAPTER ONE

The Gift of Being Human

What are humans that you are mindful of them, mere mortals that you care for them? Yet you have made them little less than a god, crowned them with glory and honor.

Psalm 8:5–6

Act Human

When we cooperate with the way God made us, then we are on the right road that leads to living a moral life, doing right, and living virtuously. The message of this chapter is to act like a human.

The starting point for this endeavor is to be yourself. But experience teaches that individuality is difficult. Pressures from many different directions work against us. Advertisements tell us what we must buy to be acceptable, peer pressure tugs at us to conform, false beliefs distort our thinking about what will really make us happy. All these contribute to presenting a false self to the world.

You have probably heard someone say that "stinking thinking" **contributes to the failure to be our true selves**. To counteract this bad mindset, Canfield compiled the following set of helps—"I Try to Remember"—to help us be true to ourselves:[1]

1. *Everyone doesn't have to like us.*

It is nice being liked and loved, but we are still okay if someone doesn't like or love us. After all, we probably don't like *all* the people we meet each day. The approval of others does not make us who we are. Herbert Bayard Swope said it well, "I can give you a formula for failure: try to please everyone all the time."

2. *It's okay to make mistakes.*

We don't have to be perfect. In fact, we can't be. Humans make mistakes. It is inevitable that you will also make **mistakes**—just like everyone does. The American poet Nikki Giovanni observed that "Mistakes are a fact of life. It is the response to error that counts." This is similar to the saying that the only mistake is the one from which we fail to learn.

3. *Other people are okay; so are you.*

Just because people do things that we don't care for does not necessarily make them bad people. People do pretty much what they want to do. But they still deserve respect. So do you! The Presbyterian minister William J.H. Boetcker (1873–1962) gave some good advice when he wrote, "That you may retain your self-respect, it is better to displease the people by doing what you know is right, than to temporarily please them by doing what you know is wrong."[2]

4. *You don't have to control everything.*

Little good comes from getting upset about things we can't change. Besides, it is impossible to control everything anyhow. We all must learn to deal with reality as it is, not as we would like it to be. And we must learn to accept other people and even ourselves, with all our limitations. Reinhold Niebuhr's famous "Serenity Prayer" puts it brilliantly:

> God grant me the serenity
> to accept the things I cannot change,
> the courage to change the things I
>   can,
> and the wisdom to know the
>   difference.

5. *We are responsible for how we feel and what we do.*

We must take responsibility for our own lives. If the day is going poorly, maybe we let it get that way. If the day is going great, we probably deserve some of the credit. In short, we don't have to react negatively to a bad situation. Other people do not have to change to make us feel good. We can control our own lives and reactions. We can be actors, rather than reactors; owners, rather than blamers.

6. It is important to try.

Tough situations usually don't go away by themselves. So we might as well try to meet them head on rather than avoid them. In life, the things that are most worthwhile most often take considerable effort. Reflect on the words of the American hero General Colin Powell: "There are no secrets to success. It is the result of preparation, hard work, and learning from failure."[3] We need to use our God-given talents.

7. We are capable and can change. The same is true of others.

God gave us the ability to think and make decisions. We can stand on our own feet. Our past does not force us to be a certain way today. We can change. Other people also have God-given abilities. They have the ability to take charge of their own lives. We can help them and love them, but they must also learn to do things for themselves.

8. We can be flexible.

Typically, there is more than one way to do something. There are many ways to tackle problems and live our lives. We can often learn from the ideas of others. Therefore, it is worth seeking out wise people for advice when we are having a tough time of it.

This chapter will try to build on these suggestions by offering a perspective on them from the eyes of faith. Listening to the great news God reveals about human beings, and living according to these magnificent truths, can greatly guide us in living a moral life.

Search out an adult you admire who has talents similar to yours. Ask the person to serve as a mentor for you during your high school years and beyond. Seek his or her advice on how to best develop your skills and gifts, especially in a way to serve others and create a livelihood for yourself.

How Do You View Humanity?

Your philosophy of life—how you view humanity—usually provides you with some principles for making decisions large and small and determining what is right and wrong.

Rank the life philosophies from 1 to 8 with 1 being the one most like you and 8 being the one least like you.

_____ "We are all angels with only one wing. We can only fly while embracing each other" (Luciano De Crescenzo).

_____ "If it feels good, do it; if it feels bad, don't do it."

_____ "The foundation of morality is to have done, once and for all, with lying" (Thomas Henry Huxley).

_____ "Morality begins at the point of a gun" (Mao Tse-Tung).

_____ "The meaning of life is that nobody knows the meaning of life" (Woody Allen).

_____ "Do to others as you would have them do to you" (Jesus of Nazareth, Lk 6:31).

_____ "Look out for number one. I am number one."

_____ "Life is a place of service, and in that service one has to suffer a great deal that is hard to bear, but more often to experience a great deal of joy. But that joy can be real only if people look upon their lives as a service and have a definite object in life outside themselves and their personal happiness" (Count Leo Tolstoy).

- Which philosophies are compatible with Christianity? Which are not?
- In two sentences or less, summarize your own life philosophy.

1. What is the starting point for being human?

2. Give an example of how a particular philosophy of life affects how a person would judge a moral issue.

FOR YOUR JOURNAL

Write three rules to truly guide you in being yourself.

Humans Are Made in the Divine Image

(CCC, 355–384; 1701–1703)

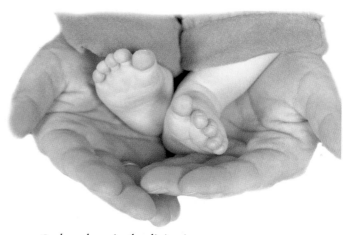

Then God said: "Let us make man in our image, after our likeness. Let them have dominion over the fish of the sea, the birds of the air, and the cattle, and over all the wild animals and all the creatures that crawl on the ground." God created man in his image; in the divine image he created him; male and female he created them. God blessed them, saying: "Be fertile and multiply; fill the earth and subdue it. Have dominion over the fish of the sea, the birds of the air, and all the living things that move on the earth." God also said: "See, I give you every seed-bearing plant all over the earth and every tree that has seed-bearing fruit on it to be your food; and to all the animals of the land, all the birds of the air, and all the living creatures that crawl on the ground, I give all the green plants for food." And so it happened. God looked at everything he had made, and he found it very good. Evening came, and morning followed—the sixth day.

—*Genesis 1:26–31*

The Genesis passage offers some powerful insights about what it means to be human. Also note these further Christian beliefs about creation:

- God freely created humans out of love. God is the Creator; we are not. We are God's creatures.
- However, we are magnificent creatures, the summit of God's creative activity. God has put humans in charge of the rest of creation, commanding us to lovingly care for and use it for human betterment.

- God made us in the divine image.
- God made us male and female.
- God saw all that he made, and found it very good.

Let's briefly analyze each of these important truths.

GOD IS THE CREATOR

In commenting on Psalm 136 (which praises God for creation), Pope Benedict XVI said, "The signs of God's love are seen in the marvels of creation and in the great gifts he has given to his people. The Fathers of the Church teach us to recognize in created things the greatness of God and his merciful love toward us."[4]

Out of his goodness and love, God did create us. God remains our Creator whether we think about God or not. God keeps us in existence whether we think about this truth or not. History has shown time and again that when humans forget about God, or make themselves into gods, they bring on trouble and wreak havoc on the rest of creation. A starting point for morality is to admit that we are creatures. We are not God. We should therefore know our place and acknowledge God's Lordship over all his creation.

Psalm 100 also instructs us to praise this great creator God for his goodness:

Shout joyfully to the Lord, all you lands; worship the Lord with cries of gladness; come before him with joyful song. Know that the Lord is God, our maker to whom we belong, whose people we are, God's well-tended flock. Enter the temple gates with praise, its courts with thanksgiving. Give thanks to God, bless his name; good indeed is the Lord, Whose love endures forever, whose faithfulness lasts through every age.

HUMANS' PLACE IN CREATION

Humans are unique, the only creatures on earth that God willed for their own sake. God created everything for humans and put us in charge of the rest of creation. For our part, humans are created to return God's love and to serve him. One way we do this is by responsibly using the beautiful gift of creation to benefit all of God's children, and by gratefully offering these gifts back to God. When humans fail to be responsible caretakers of God's good

Time Out Quiz

Q: Since 1950, Americans alone have used more resources than
a. everyone who ever lived before them
b. the combined Third World populations
c. the Romans at the height of the Roman Empire
d. all of the above
Answer: Since 1950 Americans alone have used more resources than everyone who ever lived before them. Each American individual uses up twenty tons of basic raw materials annually. Americans throw away seven million cars a year, two million plastic bottles an hour, and enough aluminum cans annually to make 6,000 DC-10 airplanes. [5]

gifts, harm results. We have seen this in our own day through the abuse of the environment and over consumption of the limited goods of the earth. This over consumption has led to deforestation, air and water pollution, and other environmental disasters.

GOD MAKES US IN THE DIVINE IMAGE

We humans are unique because God made us in the divine image, enabling us to share in God's own life. God is pure Spirit, a being without physical or material qualities. God is a supreme being who possesses infinite knowledge and truth. God is all-good, a Trinitarian community of

perfect love: Father, Son, and Holy Spirit. By making us in the divine image, God endowed us with godlike qualities, the abilities to think, choose, love, and relate to others in community. These traits enable us to share, through knowledge and love, in God's own life.

Because we are made in God's image, we are spiritual beings who possess incomparable dignity, value, and worth. We are not just *somethings,* but *someones.* We are persons who can know and give ourselves in relationships to others and to God.

Because we are made in God's image, we were made out of love, for love, and to love. Through God's special

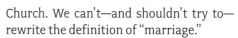

grace, we can also enter into a covenant, a love-relationship with our Creator, and respond to God in faith and in love. No other creature can do this.

GOD MADE US MALE AND FEMALE

Scripture reveals how God created us as complementary beings, male and female. Several truths flow from this. First, *complementary* means "making up for what is lacking in another." In his encyclical *God is Love*, Pope Benedict XVI writes:

The idea is certainly present [in the Bible] that man is somehow incomplete, driven by nature to seek in another the part that can make him whole, the idea that only in communion with the opposite sex can he become "complete." The biblical account thus concludes with a prophecy about Adam: "Therefore a man leaves his father and mother and cleaves to his wife and they become one flesh" (Gn 2:24).[6]

It is clear that humans need each other. We complete and fulfill each other. God builds interdependence into our very nature, creating man and woman to be helpmates, a communion of persons (*CCC*, 372).

In recent years, the promotion of same-sex unions as marriage has confused many people. Marriage has always been regulated by both civil and Church laws and has been understood as a legal union between a man and a woman. Now, some groups want to redefine "marriage." They advocate expanding the meaning of "marriage" to include a legal union for committed same-sex couples. But, as the Book of Genesis reminds us, the nature and purpose of marriage comes from God—not from civil law or even from the

> "Man and woman are both with one and the same dignity 'in the image of God.' In their 'being-man' and 'being-woman,' they reflect the Creator's wisdom and goodness" (CCC, 369).

Church. We can't—and shouldn't try to—rewrite the definition of "marriage."

The union of a male and female in marriage is an intrinsic part of God's creation plan. Only through the committed and sacramental union of husband and wife in marriage can the natural procreation and education of children take place in a setting that is secure, nurturing, and consistent with God's wise plan. In addition, the married union and life of a husband and wife is a great good for themselves, their family, communities, and society.

Second, God made us equal in dignity. Genesis does not teach that males are superior to females or that females are inferior to males. Males and females are *both* beautiful creatures of God. We need and complete each other.

Third, we humans are sexual beings, and God declares that what he made, including our sexual nature, is very good. Being sexual creatures draws attention to the fact that humans are composite creatures, beings with a body and a soul.

Unique among God's creatures, humans have a spiritual nature (soul). This spiritual nature gives us the ability to think, to make choices, and to love. But humans also have bodies. The way we exist in the world is as *spiritual-material* beings.

Because we have bodies, we are part of God's material universe. We are and become human through our bodies. We gain knowledge through the five senses. We express our humanity and experience reality through our emotions and feelings, passions and drives, preferences and dislikes. Along with our unique genetic makeup, these all help us live as a one-of-a-kind human being, male or female, an unrepeatable creation of a gracious God.

CREATION IS GOOD

Some philosophies of life take a very dim view of reality, creation, and the human person. An example is **nihilism**, which claims there is no meaning to existence, rejects all positive values, and believes in nothing. One form of nihilism holds that we are born alone, die alone, and that there is nothing of significance or meaning between these two cardinal events. The only thing that comes after life is nothingness, annihilation.

Contrast this negative and pessimistic view of the human condition with the scriptural account. Here we find the firm declaration that creation and human existence are good. In fact, in the second creation account (Gn 2:4–25), we discover that humans are not only created in God's image, but that the first humans—called Adam and Eve—were in harmony with God, each other, and the rest of creation.

Adam and Eve were in an original state of holiness and justice, sharing in divine life. An important sign of human familiarity with God was that God placed our first parents in the garden "to cultivate and care for it" (Gn 2:15). Work was not toil but a collaborative effort with the Creator in perfecting God's good creation.

The point of this second creation account is to assert the fundamental goodness of human beings who were created for friendship with God. Though, through the *Original Sin* of Adam and Eve, the harmony of original justice was lost, and humans became subject to suffering and death, we remain basically good because the supremely good God created us in his image to share his divine life and friendship with us.

The proof of our fundamental goodness is that God so loved us that "he gave his only Son, so that everyone who believes in him might not perish but have eternal life" (Jn 3:16). Any view of humans that would treat us as worthless and unworthy of respect profoundly disregards the love of a good God, who sees us as so precious that his only Son would die for us.

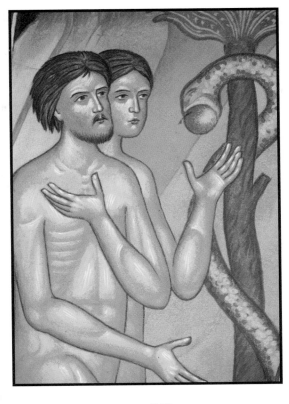

nihilism

A philosophy that denies there's any meaning in existence or in religious beliefs. Nihilists maintain that the only thing that comes after life is nothingness, annihilation.

REVIEW AND REFLECTION

1. Why did God create humans?

2. Why are humans the masterpiece of creation?

3. What does it mean to say that we are created in God's image and likeness?

4. Why did God make us sexual beings?

5. Is creation basically good or evil? How do we know?

IN THE NEWS: "SAME-SEX UNIONS"

How should God's people respond to the movement of some in our society to make same-sex unions equivalent to marriage?

To frame the debate, read the United States Catholic Bishops' clearly written statement *Between Man and Woman: Questions and Answers About Marriage and Same-Sex Unions.* You can find it at the United States Conference of Catholic Bishops website: www.usccb.org/laity/manandwoman.shtml (link still active on August 9, 2006).

After reading the bishops' statement, briefly respond in your own words to these questions:

1. Why can a true marriage exist only between a male and a female?
2. Are you being prejudiced, old-fashioned, or uncharitable if you do not support same-sex unions?

Human Dignity

Because God made us in the divine image, endows us with a spiritual nature, shares his very life with us, and calls us to himself for a life of eternal happiness, each and every human being—from the first moment of conception—possesses profound **dignity**. Dignity is a quality of being worthy of esteem and respect. Having dignity means that we have worth and value.

No one has to earn dignity and worth. Human dignity is **inherent**, inviolable, and inalienable. Dignity is inherent because it is an essential characteristic of being human. It is inviolable because no one has the right to violate or profane it. It is inalienable because it cannot be taken away by anyone. Even our own sinfulness, which distorts God's image in us, cannot destroy our basic dignity. God's love and grace can always call us back to be the beautiful creatures he made us to be. God's image always remains in us, despite our sins.

Also, we have dignity despite our personal accomplishments or lack thereof. We have dignity despite our station in life—rich or poor, very smart or less so, athletic or not. Our dignity comes from our relationship to a loving God who made each of us worthwhile. My role ("I'm a star athlete"), my possessions ("I own seven sports cars"), my productivity ("I get straight As"), my talents ("I have perfect pitch") do not give me dignity. Rather, God gives us dignity by creating us out of love. And God so loved us that he sent his Son to us, even though, compared in size to the rest of our vast universe, we are mere blips on the screen. Every human being has dignity, value, and worth because he or she is a human being, created by a loving God.

dignity

The quality of being worthy of esteem or respect. Every human person has worth and value because each person is made in God's image.

inherent

inborn or inherited, something that does not need to be earned or acquired.

How Jesus Treated Others

Read and summarize the following New Testament passages to learn how Jesus treated others.

Jesus' Actions
Mark 5:1–20
Mark 9:36–37
Luke 23:32–34

Jesus' Teachings
Matthew 5:38–48
Matthew 7:1–5
Matthew 25:31–46

Human dignity means, simply, that everyone is a someone, not a something. Respect for human dignity is the cornerstone of morality and Christian ethics. Because every human being is a someone, every person deserves respect, regardless of social status, accomplishments, education, skin color, sex, religion, nationality, ethnic background, education, contribution to society, or whatever.

The beginning of morality is to respect every human being, even if they lack self-respect. Respect means never manipulating, humiliating, exploiting, or being violent toward others. We respect others when we refrain from using people as a means to an end, as objects rather than people.

More positively, we respect others when we acknowledge their existence by greeting and listening to them, treating them with consideration and courtesy, and accepting them as precious creations of God. We show respect when we accept others as individuals despite how they differ from us, when we refrain from prejudice, and when we affirm their essential goodness by relating to them as brothers and sisters (which they are under God, our common Father, with Jesus as our brother). Treating self and others with respect is the basis of all morality.

Our Spiritual Nature

(*CCC*, 1701; 1704–1706; 1711–1713)

God has created us with both a body and a spiritual and immortal soul. "It is in Christ, 'the image of the invisible God,' that man has been created 'in the image and likeness' of the Creator" (*CCC*, 1701). The human soul, restored to its original beauty and ennobled by God's grace through Christ, includes our spiritual nature. It gives us incomparable dignity.

Our souls give us a share in God's life. Our spiritual nature makes us unsatisfied with living merely a physical existence in the here-and-now. It tugs at our hearts, leading us to ask ultimate questions like, "What *am* I here for? Why *do* I exist? What *does* it all mean?" In the depths of our souls we are restless; we thirst for an ultimate happiness that only God can quench. Church father St. Augustine knew this "holy hunger" for more when he penned his famous lines, "You have made us for yourself, O God, and so our hearts are restless until they rest in you."

By giving us a soul, a spiritual nature, God endowed humans with some awesome capacities that separate us from any

"The truth is not always the same as the majority decision."[7]

—Pope John Paul II
(1920–2005)

other earthly creature. These include our intellects and **free will** and our ability to love, to be responsible, and to grow. More information on these gifts follows.

Ability to think. Humans are rational beings. We have intellects. Being made in God's image, we can think and reason. Our intellectual nature enables us to figure out problems, discover how the universe works, and reflect on the meaning of life and death. As the only earthly creature that "knows that it knows," humans can reflect on what they have learned, master their environment, and pass on their knowledge to subsequent generations.

Moreover, because we can think, we can discover truth. When it comes to living a moral life, searching for truth will lead us to the highest norm of human life which is the divine law. By means of this eternal, objective, and universal law, "God orders, directs and governs the entire universe and all the ways of the human community according to a plan conceived in wisdom and love" (*Declaration on Religious Freedom*, 3). God has made us to participate in this law; humans have the duty to seek this truth.

Human reason enables us to recognize God's voice, which urges us to do good and avoid what is evil. We must follow this law, which we hear in our conscience, by

loving God and neighbor. To do this makes us moral people and witnesses to our tremendous dignity. (Conscience will be discussed in more detail in Chapter 5.)

Free will. Free will means we have the capacity to choose from among alternatives. Free will is "the power, rooted in reason and will . . . to perform deliberate actions on one's own responsibility" (*CCC*, 1731). Contrast this to the instinct that binds animals. A dog or cat or monkey cannot be morally good or evil. Free choice helps humans make themselves to be the kind of persons God calls them to be. We can make ourselves good or bad by our choices. These choices are always exercised in relationship to others; therefore, they carry with them responsibility.

Free choices help us determine our own lives and our futures. For example, just because I was born into a highly prejudiced family does not mean I have to remain prejudiced my whole life. I can choose to change. Or just because as a youth I made fun of a person with a disability does not mean I cannot change. I can be more loving and accepting now that I have grown to understand that all humans have dignity and are worthy of respect.

The Church teaches that the power of "authentic freedom is an exceptional sign

free will

"The power, rooted in reason and will [that enables a person], to perform deliberate actions on one's own responsibility" (CCC, 1731).

of the divine image within man" (*Pastoral Constitution on the Church in the Modern World*, 17). Free will enables us to rise above heredity and environment. Free will enables us to exercise some control over our lives by using our God-given talents and by cooperating with the many graces God provides.

Ability to love. Choosing to do good for other people, even to the point of personal sacrifice, describes love. Love of God above everything, and our neighbor as ourselves, is the highest choice humans can make. Blessed Mother Teresa (1910–1997) exemplified love when she freely chose to take a dying leper into her arms to comfort him. An onlooker recoiled in horror and said, "I wouldn't touch that person for a million dollars." The saintly Mother Teresa responded, "Neither would I." When we choose to love we are being godlike in imitation of the Triune God who is a perfect community of love.

Responsible beings. Free choices make us who we are. By our choices we determine if we want to live a life dedicated to God and truth. We are responsible beings.

We are accountable for our choices because they result in actions that express and determine the goodness or the evil of the person performing them. If our actions come from free and deliberate choices, they help to form us and define who we are. When we exercise our freedom according to God's eternal law, we are being moral. When we freely choose to ignore God's will for humans, that choice translates to evil and sin.

What we do, or fail to do, matters. Choices have consequences. They either build up or tear down our character. Freedom involves responsibility and accountability. Virtues like honesty, integrity, self-control, and consideration for others help make us responsible for our actions.

Capacity to grow. Humans can think, choose, and love in a responsible way. All of these abilities mean that humans—both individually and collectively—can grow in positive ways. In more concrete terms, we can learn from our sins and mistakes.

For example, for centuries even Christians tolerated slavery as an acceptable institution. However, the Gospel message that every human being is a person of incomparable worth finally started to take root. It helped to change the thinking of individuals and societies to conclude that slavery is an intolerable evil that destroys human dignity. All civilized societies ban it today.

Maturing individuals also grow, for example, by rejecting childish self-centeredness and looking more to the welfare of others. Perhaps you have experienced this type of growth by becoming more sensitive and responsive to a lonely classmate or by thinking of the feelings of others before blurting out potentially hurtful remarks.

Responding to Challenges

Question: If it is true that God gave us the great gift of freedom, then can't we decide for ourselves what is right and what is wrong?

Answer:

Freedom is indeed a great gift from God. But as with all gifts, we must know what it is and how to use it responsibly.

Freedom can be external as in being free from hunger, or being free to drive a car, or being free from physical constraint.

But the type of freedom that concerns morality is *internal*. Its source is in the human will, one of the powers of the human soul or spirit. (The other power of the human soul is the intellect which enables us to think.) The freedom that comes from the human will is a God-given power that enables us to choose what is true, what is right, what is good and beautiful. It helps us to act in a responsible way and in conformity with the universal laws and truths that God has implanted in creation and in our hearts to help guide us to live responsibly.

True freedom is not *license*, that is, "unbridled" freedom to do what *we* want to do whenever *we* want to do it, regardless of the consequences. Actions that do not conform to God's truth are morally wrong. In fact, they diminish freedom. Pope John Paul II warned: "When freedom does not have a purpose, when it does not wish to know anything about the rule of law engraved in the hearts of men and women, when it does not listen to the voice of conscience, it turns against humanity and society."[8]

A tragic example troubling today's world is the so-called freedom of a woman to choose. We all know that this "freedom" is really the choice to abort the life of an innocent human being. Note how this choice results in the destruction of the most fundamental freedom of all—the freedom to live. The pope is right: freedom that is not exercised in conformity to God's universal law is an assault on humanity itself.

Consider:

- The superior golfer becomes free to execute beautiful shots only after hundreds of hours of practice applying the proven methods of a good golf swing.
- The award-winning novelist is free to write another book because she has learned, and lives by, the rules of language.
- Human beings are truly free when they act on the truth that God has revealed in our hearts—to do not what we like but to do what we ought. The eminent American Catholic theologian Cardinal Avery Dulles, S.J., said it well: "True freedom is not the same as license. It is not the power to do whatever we like but to choose what is good. Morality is not a barrier to our freedom but a condition of authentic self-realization."[9]

Read Genesis 3:1–7. What sin did our first parents commit? How did they abuse their freedom?

"The more one does what is good, the freer one becomes. There is no true freedom except in the service of what is good and just. The choice to disobey and do evil is an abuse of freedom and leads to 'the slavery of sin.'" (CCC, 1733)

REVIEW AND REFLECTION

1. What is human dignity? In what way do all people have this dignity? Does it have to be earned? Why or why not?

2. List and describe some of the abilities that God gives to human beings as spiritual creatures.

3. What is the relationship between human reason and truth?

4. What is free will?

5. Explain how true freedom is not doing whatever we want to do.

FOR YOUR JOURNAL

Write a short reflective essay explaining why and how you are worthy of respect.

Principle of Subsidiarity

According to the *Catechism of the Catholic Church* (1883), the principle of **subsidiarity** is explained this way: "a community of a higher order should not interfere in the internal life of a community of a lower order, depriving the latter of its functions, but rather should support it in case of need and help to coordinate its activity with the activities of the rest of society, always with a view to the **common good**."

Because humans are relational (social) by nature, the *Catechism of the Catholic Church* underscores the following truths about people and society:

- The human person is and should be "the principle, subject, and object" of every society (cf. *CCC*, 1891).
- According to their gifts and talents, their positions and roles, all people have the right and duty to participate in the life of the various societies to which they belong. For example, citizens have the right and duty to take an active role in public life.
- To endure and develop, every society needs authority. Authentic authority comes from God. Authority figures must be devoted to the common good and use morally acceptable ways of exercising power. Political authority must be used morally and guarantee the conditions that promote true human freedom.
- Larger societies should support the participation of individuals and lower-level communities without taking over functions these smaller units can do for themselves. For example, the state must not subvert the authority of parents to raise their children in a particular religious faith. This is known as the principle of subsidiarity.
- Societies should promote virtue and challenge individuals to turn from sin, serve others justly, and contribute their gifts and talents to the common good. The common good is the sum total of social conditions that allow people, either as groups or as individuals, to reach their fulfillment more fully and more easily (*Pastoral Constitution on the Church in the Modern World*, 26).
- The common good requires that individuals and societies (1) respect the basic, inalienable rights of each human being; and (2) promote the social well-being and development of various social groups. For either of these to happen, authority figures must promote peace which results in stability and security so justice can take place.
- Living in community requires that we treat each person with utmost respect. Everyone is our neighbor, even our enemies whom Jesus told us to forgive. Everyone is another self. We share so much in common with others: the same human nature, the same rational soul, the same origin, the same salvation won by our Lord Jesus Christ, the same destiny of union with God. In addition, we all possess a God-given dignity that entitles us to fundamental rights which everyone must respect and promote.
- Because God made us to be with and for others, we must use our gifts and talents to help other people. In God's plan, some of us have been given wonderful gifts like health, education, financial wealth, and so forth. Those who are gifted are obliged to share their good fortune with others, and in a special way, with those who are most needy. In addition, we must work to eradicate sinful inequalities of wealth and social status that destroy justice, peace, equity, and human dignity.
- We are in **solidarity** with others. Solidarity is the Christian virtue of social charity or friendship. Solidarity gives us the courage and spirit of generosity to share both our material and our spiritual gifts with others, especially society's forgotten ones. The gift of solidarity recognizes that we are all members of the human family and that we must go out of our way to help one another.

subsidiarity

The principle of Catholic social teaching that holds that a higher unit of society should not do what a lower unit can do as well (or better).

common good

"Sum total of social conditions that allow people, either as groups or as individuals, to reach their fulfillment more fully and more easily" (*Pastoral Constitution of the Church in the Modern World*, 26).

solidarity

The Christian virtue of social charity and friendship.

The Social Nature of Humans *(CCC, 1877–1948)*

In creating humans in the divine image, God made us social beings. It is part of our human nature to live in various societies, that is, groups bound by a principle of unity that goes beyond each individual. In these communities (e.g., families, neighborhoods, schools) we relate to others by loving and sharing our gifts.

Recall that God is a perfect community of love—Father, Son, and Holy Spirit. God is a Trinity of relationships, three divine persons who relate perfectly to each other in giving, receiving, and loving. The Blessed Trinity created human and angelic beings out of self-giving love to share divine life. Our vocation is to express the love of this diverse community in our own relationships. Our vocation is to treat each other as sisters and brothers under a common heavenly Father, and to establish communities that benefit each person, the various societies in which we live, and the whole earth, as well.

The novelist and preacher Frederick Buechner compared humanity to an enormous spider web. This image suggests that if we touch the web anywhere, the whole thing trembles. Thus, if we are kind, our loving touch affects the whole human web of relationships for good. On the other hand, if we are indifferent or hostile,

The Icon of the Trinity by Andrei Rublev

our negative attitudes and behaviors will impinge on everyone in a harmful way. Buechner wrote:

> *The life that I touch for good or ill will touch another life, and that in turn another, until who knows where the trembling stops or in what far place and time my touch will be felt. Our lives are linked. No man is an island.*[10]

 REVIEW AND REFLECTION

1. How do we reflect the image of God in our role as social beings?

2. Discuss three truths that flow from our social nature.

3. Give an example of a violation of the principle of subsidiarity.

4. What is the common good?

5. What is the virtue of solidarity? Why is it necessary for Christians?

FOR YOUR JOURNAL

Read Matthew 25:14–30, the parable of the talents. What is the point of this parable? What might God be telling you through it? What is your greatest God-given gift or talent?

Humans Are Wounded by Sin

(CCC, 1707–1709; 1714–1715)

God's revelation reports how humanity is wounded by sin and inclined to evil and error. Genesis 2:15–3:24 tells how Adam and Eve chose themselves over God through an act of disobedience. Their pride led to their downfall and expulsion from the garden of Eden and subjected them to suffering and, ultimately, death. Moreover, their sin of disobedience infected the human race. All humans through history have suffered the consequences of the **Original Sin**.

Individually and collectively, humans have fallen victim to weakness, cowardice, avarice, and various other forms of evil. We often have the best of intentions to do good, but we are weak and inclined to commit sin. In short, we humans, though beautiful creatures of a loving God, are also sinners. And sin—choosing self by ignoring God's law—harms us as individuals. It also contaminates our communities, often polluting the way societies work, especially harming the weak and defenseless in our midst. What human history proves is that we cannot deliver ourselves from this condition of sin. We need a Savior, someone to rescue us from this hopeless situation.

A Savior

The Good News of salvation is the redeeming person and message of Jesus Christ. God, our loving Father, so loves us that he gave to us his only Son, Jesus Christ, "so that everyone who believes in him may not perish but might have eternal life" (Jn 3:16). Jesus Christ is God Incarnate (made flesh). He is Love—made flesh. "His death on the Cross is the culmination of that turning to God against himself in which he gives himself in order to raise man up and save him. This is love in its most radical form."[11]

As Pope Benedict XVI has observed, it is by contemplating the crucified Christ that we come to understand that God is love. God's Son shows us how to live moral, upright, loving lives. His example and his words are life-giving. (Jesus, and his example for our lives, is the focus of Chapter 4.)

But more important, the **Paschal Mystery** of Jesus' passion, death, resurrection, and glorification has delivered us from the clutches of sin and the Evil One, saving us from death and winning for us eternal life with the Triune God. In short, Jesus gave up his life so that we might live. Jesus showed us how to love by making the ultimate sacrifice. The Father accepted Jesus' self-surrendering gift and rescued him from death, raising him to superabundant life at his right side. Together, the Father and the Son have sent us the Holy Spirit who unleashes his power and his graces on us so that we might live wholesome, holy, and moral lives.

At Baptism we gain new life in the Holy Spirit. The graces of this sacrament adopt us into the divine family. We are no longer mere creatures, insignificant "nothings" in the cosmic scheme. By virtue of God's free gift of adoption, we become children of God and brothers and sisters to our Lord Jesus.

The consequences of God's graciousness toward us are absolutely amazing. Through the gift of the Holy Spirit, we now

Christ has no body now on earth but yours, no hands but yours, no feet but yours; yours are the eyes through which Christ's compassion looks out at the world, yours are the feet with which he is to go about doing good, and yours are the hands with which he is to bless us now.

—St. Teresa of Avila

Original Sin

The consequence of the sin of our first parents; the hereditary stain with which human beings are born because of our origins or descent from Adam and Eve.

Paschal Mystery

God's love and salvation revealed through the life, passion, death, resurrection, and glorification (ascension) of Jesus Christ. The sacraments, especially the Eucharist, celebrate this great mystery of God's love.

Write Jesus a personal letter telling him what his friendship means to you.

have God's own grace to live moral, loving lives. If we keep in touch with the God-power within, strengthening it especially by receiving the Lord himself in Holy Communion, we can begin to live as God intends us to live. We are not loners on our quest to reach our eternal destiny. God himself is with us on our journey.

Friends of Jesus

What does it mean to say God is with us? The Lord Jesus has befriended us. In so doing, he assures us of his presence, guidance, and help to live as his sister or brother, a child of his incredibly loving Father whom he invites us to call *Abba*, Papa. Jesus said,

As the Father loves me, so I also love you. Remain in my love. . . . I no longer call you slaves, because a slave does not know what his master is doing. I have called you friends, because I have told you everything I have heard from my Father. It was not you who chose me, but I who chose you and appointed you to go and bear fruit. . . . This I command you: love one another. (Jn 15:9, 15–17)

6 STEPS of LIVING A MORAL LIFE

1. *Be who you are.* Act like a good child of Abba, a loving parent who has given you everything. Be a loyal and faithful friend. Be a brother or sister to every other person.
2. *Respect everyone.* You and each person have incomparable worth. Respect yourself. Respect others.
3. *Develop and share your gifts.* God has given you many talents. Discover what they are. Develop them. And use them to make the world a better place.
4. *Love.* The heart of Christian morality is love. We must love God as the source and final goal of our lives, the source of all goodness. It is right to worship and to love and to thank God for all that God has given to us. In all our actions, Jesus wants us to love God above all.
5. *Love ourselves.* Each of us is precious in God's sight, uniquely talented, and possessing the gifts of life and salvation. We should only engage in acts that manifest genuine love of self.
6. *Love each other.* Every person is made in God's image. With us, they are here to use and develop responsibly God's good earth. Jesus challenges his friends to love in a special way the neglected ones in our midst, the poor and the weak, the "undesirables," even our enemies.

God is like a mother who carries her child in her arms by the edge of a precipice. While she is seeking all the time to keep him from danger, he is doing his best to get into it.

—St. John Vianney

St. Maximilian Kolbe

No one has greater love than this, to lay down one's life for one's friends. —**John 15:13**

Down through the ages, Jesus' self-giving sacrifice has motivated many of his followers to imitate him. A powerful twentieth-century example was that of St. Maximilian Kolbe, a hero who was killed in the Auschwitz death camp. His story has become an inspiration for all people. Pope John Paul II, who canonized St. Maximilian in 1982, called him "a martyr of charity." And the Polish bishops have said of him, "The life and death of this one man alone is proof and witness of the fact that God can overcome the greatest hatred, the greatest injustice, even death itself." When speaking of St. Maximilian's last days in the horrific Auschwitz, even his Nazi executioners testified about his calm, peaceful, and forgiving manner, "We have never seen anything like it."

Born Raymond Kolbe in Poland in 1894, he entered the Conventional Franciscan Order and took the name Maximilian. He studied in Rome and was ordained in 1918. While in the seminary, he developed a tremendous devotion to our Blessed Mother and established the "Immaculata Movement." This Movement encouraged people to consecrate themselves to the Immaculate Virgin Mary to help them grow in personal holiness, convert the opponents of religion and the Church, and help establish the universal reign of the Sacred Heart of Jesus. His lifelong motto was "Through Mary Immaculate to Jesus."

After receiving a doctorate in theology, Fr. Maximilian spread the Movement through a magazine titled *The Knights of the Immaculata*. In 1927, he founded an evangelization center near Warsaw, Poland, with the name "City of the Immaculata." Many friars joined him in his efforts to publish catechetical and devotional literature there. In 1930, Fr. Maximilian established a comparable community in Nagasaki, Japan. Miraculously, when the atomic bomb fell on this Japanese foundation, it was spared.

Fr. Maximilian was always in poor health. He suffered the debilitating effects of tuberculosis. This forced him to return home in 1936. When the Nazis invaded Poland in 1939, Fr. Maximilian was imprisoned for a time, then released. But he was arrested again in 1941 for his condemnation both in the press and over the radio of both Nazism and Communism. He correctly predicted that these "isms" would result in great suffering for humanity. When his tuberculosis returned, Fr. Maximilian was sent to the infamous concentration camp at Auschwitz. The guards assigned him hard labor, hoping to break his spirit. But Fr. Maximilian performed it with gentleness and kindness, never returning the hatred of his captors.

On July 31, 1941, a prisoner escaped from the camp. To thwart others from doing the same, the Nazis selected ten prisoners to die of starvation. One of the men selected, Sergeant Francis Gajowniczek, cried out in tears, "My poor wife and children! I will never see them again."

Fr. Maximilian spoke up softly, but with firm conviction, "I would like to take the place of Sergeant Gajowniczek." The commanding officer had never seen anything like this before. When he asked Fr. Maximilian who he was, Maximilian answered, "I am a Catholic priest." The officer allowed the substitution.

Prisoners who died slowly of starvation typically screamed, cursed, and uttered despairing groans. But not Fr. Maximilian. Rather, he calmed his nine fellow torture-chamber victims. He urged them to pray and to seek the help of the Blessed Mother so they might all die with dignity, not like the degraded animals their tormentors wished them to be.

The calm and peace that filled Fr. Maximilian shamed his Nazi guards who refused to look him in the eye.

The torture lasted into a third week. Fr. Maximilian and three others barely clung to life. Finally, the impatient Nazis ordered the camp executioner to inject the four survivors with carbolic acid. This took place on August 14, the day before the Feast of the Assumption.[12]

- Contrast Maximilian Kolbe's sacrifice with the case of a twenty-four-year-old man who poured gasoline over himself and lit a match in front of the United Nations Building. He did so to protest the lack of social justice for the poor nations of the world. His death was swift, but excruciatingly painful. How was this case different than Kolbe's? List some reasons why an action like this can never be justified.

FOR YOUR JOURNAL

Viktor Frankl, a survivor of the Nazi death camps, said, "Everything can be taken from man except the last of the human freedoms, his ability to choose his own attitude in any given set of circumstances—to choose his own way." What do you think Frankl's statement means? How did Saint Maximilian exemplify Frankl's statement? In your journal, write about a time when you—or someone you knew well—exemplified this attribute.

REVIEW AND REFLECTION

1. What does it mean to say that humanity has inherited the effects of Original Sin?

2. What is the Good News for sinful humanity in relationship to Jesus Christ?

3. Discuss four rules for living an upright, moral, and Christian life in light of God's revelation of the human person.

4. Who was St. Maximilian Kolbe? How did he exemplify Christ in a heroic way?

Catholic Life in Action

As stewards of God's beautiful creation, human beings must care for God's many material gifts, which are meant for future generations as well. Yet over-consumption of the goods of God's creation is a serious problem in today's world. Visit the following website to take an "Ecological Footprint Quiz" to discover how much productive land and water you need to support what you use and what you discard. Then compare what you use to what is available on our planet: www.earthday.net/footprint/info.asp.

After you see your results, investigate what individuals, communities, and schools can do to act as better stewards of God's good earth. Map out a strategy for action for the coming semester.

Investigate these helpful websites to learn ways to combat waste. Both are linked to the PBS broadcasts of the same names. Plan and then act on a strategy to reduce waste in your own life.

Affluenza: www.pbs.org/kcts/affluenza

Escape from Affluenza: www.pbs.org/kcts/affluenza/escape/index.html

Visit the Pollution Information site and discover who the polluters in your community are: www.scorecard.org. Then visit the Environmental Defense site and its Action Center page to learn some ways you can take action now to help protect the environment: www.environmentaldefense.org/home.cfm.

God's creation inspired many of the Psalms. After reading and praying the following—Psalms 8, 19, 29, 33, 65, and 104—compose your own hymn of praise to God the Creator in the style of a psalm. Include several photos to help illustrate the text version of your psalm.

Gifts to Serve. Someone once said that it is a grave mistake to bury one's talent. Blessed Mother Teresa of Calcutta reminds us, "Yesterday is gone. Tomorrow has not yet come. We have only today. Let us begin." With these thoughts in mind, list your five most precious talents or gifts. And then write of a time when you used each of these gifts/talents to benefit another person. For example, you might have the gift of a good sense of humor, which you used to cheer a younger sister after her team lost a game. Then, for two of your talents, write a specific resolution of how you can use them in the coming week to help a classmate, coworker, teammate, or family member. Here is a suggested format: "I resolve to use my gift of _____ for the benefit of _____ by doing the following: _____."

Check back to see how you followed through on your resolutions.

Summary Points

◆ Being true to yourself helps you to live morally.

◆ Our philosophy of life influences how we view humans. Our view of humanity affects what we consider to be moral or immoral.

◆ The book of Genesis reveals many important truths about the human person. For example, it tells us that God created us out of his goodness and love in his own image. He created us to be complementary beings, male and female.

◆ Humans have a privileged role in the created universe. God commissioned us to be stewards of the good earth, which we must responsibly develop as we cooperate with God's creative power.

◆ Made in God's image as male and female, men and women have a complementary and interdependent relationship that is realized most fully in marriage and in their roles as cocreators of children.

◆ Human existence is fundamentally good.

◆ All humans have incomparable dignity. We have value and worth because God created us in his image and wants eternal union with us. Our dignity is inherent, inviolable, and inalienable. We do not have to earn it. Human dignity exists independently of our roles, possessions, productivity, accomplishments, or talents.

◆ Humans are material-spiritual beings. We possess both a body and a soul.

◆ Being made in the divine image endows humans with tremendous abilities including the powers to think, to choose, and to love.

◆ Love is choosing the good of another.

◆ Because humans are intelligent, free, and capable of love, they are responsible for their acts. They are also capable of growth.

◆ Humans are social beings created with and for others. Societies exist for the benefit of human persons who have the right and duty to contribute their talents to the common good.

◆ Though fundamentally good, humans are flawed by the effects of Original Sin. We are prone to choose evil.

◆ The gospel proclaims that humans are saved sinners. Jesus is our Savior who forgives our sins and has won for us eternal life. With God the Father, Jesus sends us the Holy Spirit who endows us with gifts and graces to live a moral life.

◆ The Spirit adopts us into God's family, and Jesus invites us to be his friend. These truths give us tremendous value and personal responsibility to continue the Lord's work.

◆ All the truths revealed about the reality of the human person teach us how to live moral, upright, wholesome lives, including:

  • We should be ourselves.
  • We must respect everyone as worthwhile.
  • We must share our gifts and talents with others, especially the needy.
  • We must be like God, who is a Trinity of love.

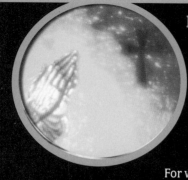

PRAYER REFLECTION

Lord God, we thank you
for the gift of life,
for the gift of faith,
for the gift of each other,
and for the promise of eternal life with you.
We pray these words in the name of Jesus,
our Lord, Savior, and friend. Amen.

For what are you most grateful?
Identify a gift or talent that you suspect you have but which you have done little to develop.
Do something to investigate this gift.

NOTES

1. Adapted from *Chicken Soup for the Teenage Soul*, compiled by Jack Canfield, Mark Victor Hansen, and Kimberly Kirberger (Deerfield, FL: Health Communications, Inc., 1997), 166–169.

2. Found at the Quotations Page <www.quotationspage.com/quote/1382.html> (9 August 2006).

3. You can read more great quotes from this inspiring man at About.com's "African-American History: Colin Powell Quotes," http://afroamhistory.about.com/od/colinpowell/a/quotes_powell_c.htm. (9 August 2006).

4. Pope Benedict XVI, General Audience, 9 November 2005 <www.vatican.va/holy_father/benedict_xvi/audiences/2005/documents/hf_ben-xvi_aud_20051109_en.html> (9 August 2006).

5. Source: PBS Online, *Affluenza*, "Test Your Consumption Quota," <www.pbs.org/kcts/affluenza/diag/what.html>. (9 August 2006).

6. Encyclical Letter *Deus Caritas Est* of the Supreme Pontiff Benedict XVI to the Bishops, Priests, and Deacons, Men and Women Religious, and All the Lay Faithful on Christian Love (*Liberia Editrice Vaticana*, 2005), No. 11 <www.vatican.va/holy_father/benedict_xvi/encyclicals/documents/hf_ben-xvi_enc_20051225_deus-caritas-est_en.html> (9 August 2006).

7. Original source attributed to an essay John Paul II wrote for the *Times of London*, May 18, 1988. See DallasNews.com, "In His Own Words" <www.wfaa.com/sharedcontent/dws/img/04-05/pope3.pdf> (9 August 2006).

8. Quoted at Dr. Marcellino D'Ambrosio's *Crossroads Initiative* website <www.crossroadsinitiative.com/library_article/524/Quotes_from_Pope_John_Paul_II.html> (9 August 2006).

9. Rev. Avery Cardinal Dulles, S.J., "God's Gift of Freedom Must Be Used to Choose the Good," Acton Institute for the Study of Freedom & Religion <www.acton.org/publicat/randl/interview.php?id=307> (9 August 2006).

10. From his *The Hungering Dark* (1969), quoted at www.appleseeds.org/April_98.htm (9 August 2006).

11. Pope Benedict XVI, Encyclical Letter *Deus Caritas Est*, No. 12.

12. You can read more about Saint Maximilian Kolbe in Fr. Boniface Hanley, O.F.M., *Ten Christians* (Notre Dame, IN: Ave Maria Press, 1979). Check these websites for additional information:
    - www.catholic-forum.com/saints/saintm01.htm
    - www.kolbenet.com/kolbe
    - www.catholic-pages.com/saints/st_maximilian.asp
    - www.catholicism.org/maximilian-kolbe.html

CHAPTER OVERVIEW

Right Reason in Action

The virtue of prudence, according to St. Thomas Aquinas, is "right reason in action." Prudence helps us to discover goodness and choose the right means of achieving it.

Search Out the Facts

Making good decisions requires finding the facts. Catholic morality is grounded in reality—on the ways things are—and on how God intends them to be.

Think About the Alternatives and Consequences

Doing the right thing requires considering various alternatives and their likely consequences. We also need to take responsibility for our actions.

Others

Christian morality asks us to be truly sensitive to the impact of our actions on others. We must be considerate and seek the advice of people who have made wise choices.

Pray

Christian moral living needs to be fed and strengthened by prayer. Simply put, prayer is the living, ongoing relationship we have with God.

CHAPTER TWO

Making Moral Decisions

Trust in the Lord with all your heart, on your own intelligence rely not.
Proverbs 3:5

Thomas Edison in his laboratory

Right Reason in Action

It is reported that the brilliant inventor Thomas Edison used two thousand different materials in his effort to discover the right filament for the light bulb. They all failed. This caused his assistant to complain that all their effort was wasted, that nothing was learned. The great inventor disagreed, "Oh, we have come a long way and we have learned a lot. We know that there are two thousand elements which we cannot use to make a good light bulb."

Edison is known for the famous quote, "Genius is one percent inspiration and ninety-nine percent perspiration." In his own way, Edison was telling the world that the search for scientific truth takes work. It is similar in the area of morality. We have to work hard to search for truth, and then we should act on it.

Perhaps one of the reasons we live in a world that has difficulty discerning right from wrong is that people do not take the time to think. It is like a wealthy businessman who enrolled his son at an Ivy League school. When the father examined the college's catalog of courses and the requirements for a business degree, he quizzed the Dean of Studies, "Does my kid have to take all these courses? Can't you put him on the fast-track program so he can get out and join me in the business?"

The dean replied, "Of course, he can speed up his course of studies. But a lot of his college experience depends on what he wants to make of himself. God takes twenty years to grow a solid oak, but only two months to produce a squash."

Have you seen a squash lately? Let it ripen a bit and it gets awfully mushy inside.

How does one guard against "intellectual mushiness" in learning to do the moral thing? We do so by exercising the virtue of prudence (see *CCC* 1806; 1835) the virtue that helps us discover goodness and choose the right means of achieving it.

Following the ancient philosopher Aristotle, St. Thomas Aquinas described **prudence** as "right reason in action." This moral virtue governs other virtues because it guides them by setting rule and measure. Prudence inclines us to lead good, ethical, moral lives of action. This cardinal virtue helps our conscience make correct judgments about right and wrong, about the good and evil in each situation we encounter. Prudence shows us how to act based on clear-headed foresight.

In short, prudence is necessary for correct judgment. We can grow in this virtue by cooperating with God's grace, through personal experience, and by making an honest evaluation of our mistakes. Prudence, like all virtues, forms our character and helps us to more easily make good choices and then act on them.

Consider the tragic story of the young nature photographer who, in May of 1981,

prudence

The moral virtue that inclines us to lead good, ethical, and moral lives of action; "right reason in action," as St. Thomas Aquinas put it.

had himself flown into northern Alaska to photograph the natural beauty and mysteries of the tundra found there. For his task, he took with him five hundred rolls of film, firearms, and provisions.

Months passed. As his diary later revealed, his entries changed from those of awe into a living nightmare. In August he wrote, "I think I should have used more foresight about arranging my departure. I'll soon find out."

In November, he died of exposure in a desolate valley near an unnamed lake, 225 miles northeast of Fairbanks. When his death was investigated, it was discovered that although he made careful plans for most of his trip, he imprudently failed to arrange for a pilot to come pick him up.[1]

As St. Basil the Great taught:
Prudence must precede every action that we undertake; for, if prudence be wanting, there is nothing, however good it may seem, which is not turned into evil.

The English martyr Robert Southwell said, "Foresight is to be sought, for hindsight is dearly bought." And the popular saying, "Fools rush in where angels fear to tread" also reminds us to stop and consider what we are doing before making moral decisions. A method of moral decision-making heeds well this sage advice. It includes four major steps:

Search out the facts

Think about alternatives and consequences

Others—consult them and consider how your actions will affect them

Pray to the Lord for guidance

This chapter will examine each of the steps in the "**STOP** Sign" approach in more detail.

discernment
A decision-making process that attends to the implications and consequences of an action or choice.

DISCERNMENT

Some decisions are relatively easy to make; for example, what kind of soda to drink at lunch. Others are more difficult; for example, choosing which set of friends to go out with on a Friday night. Still others are potentially life-changing, such as what career to choose, whether to marry or not and if so, whom. You will also need to decide whether Jesus Christ and his values will or will not make a difference in your life.

For good decisions on big and important issues, a decision-making process known as **discernment** is needed. Discernment for a believer is a keen and insightful judgment about some important choice. It is done in a prayerful atmosphere, taking into consideration Christian values.

Here are some widely-recognized elements that go into the discernment and the decision-making process. For each factor, evaluate how you typically use this particular element in important decisions you make, especially on issues involving right and wrong. Use the following scale:

A—very present in my decision-making process
B—usually present
C—present about half the time

D—rarely there
E—never present

_____ 1. **Gather information.** Before acting, I research issues well.
_____ 2. **Monitor feelings.** I check to see if my emotions are clouding my judgment or speaking to my heart about the right course of action.
_____ 3. **Open to growth.** I'm willing to learn new information, seek guidance from wise people, and correct my prejudices.
_____ 4. **Use my imagination.** When stuck in a rut, I trust my imagination to suggest alternative courses of action.
_____ 5. **Flexible.** I'm willing to look at the issue from another perspective, shifting from one part of the problem to another.

_____ 6. **Hard work.** Some decisions take effort. I avoid oversimplification. I try to clear up prejudgments. I anticipate the consequences of various actions.

_____ 7. **Courage to be myself.** I don't always follow the crowd, pushed along by the way the wind is blowing. I can stand on my own two feet. I take responsibility for my actions because they are mine.

_____ 8. **Learn from past experiences, mistakes, and personal weaknesses.** I know my strengths and weaknesses. I know what can slow me down, and I am willing to take steps to overcome or compensate for my limitations. When faced with a decision similar to ones I've made, I've learned from past setbacks as well as former triumphs.

_____ 9. **Prayer.** When faced with tough decisions, I turn to the Lord for his help and to the Holy Spirit for inspiration and encouragement. I recognize that I am not essentially alone and know that with God on my side, I will be able to make good decisions.

FOR YOUR JOURNAL

Write of a difficult decision you recently had to make. Reflect on which factor was the key for you to arrive at a decision. Judge whether you were prudent or not in the decision-making process.

Search Out the Facts

(CCC, 1757—1761)

Any good decision requires using your God-given intellect to dig out the facts. In that way your decision can be both informed and real. Catholic morality is based on reality, on the way things are, on how God made them and intends them to be. It is not based on wishful thinking or on the whims of current fancy. As Rudyard Kipling put it in "The Elephant Child,"

I keep six honest serving-men
(They taught me all I knew):
Their names are What and Why and When
And How and Where and Who.

Kipling had it about right. The foundation of all knowledge we acquire comes from answering questions beginning with who, what, when, where, why, and how. These reality-revealing questions unearth the three major aspects of every moral action: the moral object (what), the intention or motive (why), and the circumstances (who, where, when, and how). The *Catechism of the Catholic Church* teaches, "The object, the intention, and the circumstances make up the 'sources,' or constitutive elements, of the morality of human acts" (1750).

MORAL OBJECT *(CCC, 1751)*

We cannot begin to decide whether something is moral or not until we know the nature of our proposed action. The simple question that begins with *what* helps tell us what is the content or "matter" of our moral decision. A *what* question helps reveal to us whether the matter of our action is good or bad, that is, if it is directed to our true good or is harmful and destructive of what it means to be a person made in God's image.

Take the example of a high school junior who goes out of her way to drive a freshman to school. This act of driving a car is a good matter because it is directed toward the good of another person; it is helping the freshman achieve the desirable human goal of acquiring an education. On the other hand, take the example of a high school senior who creates a fake ID so he can buy beer illegally. This action is basically dishonest, a form of lying. It distorts the integrity of a person made in God's image and likeness.

In most cases it is relatively easy to discover if what we propose to do conforms or does not conform to our true good. Human reason—using our intellects—helps us recognize and judge which actions correspond to our true good, which ones make us the kind of people God intends us to be. And objective norms of morality, like the Ten Commandments, "express the rational order of good and evil, attested to by conscience" (CCC, 1751).

Some actions are intrinsically always evil and, therefore, wrong because they go against God's will and destroy human good. These actions can never be justified. According to Jesus, these prohibitions allow no exceptions:

If you wish to enter into life, keep the commandments . . . You shall not kill, You shall not commit adultery, You shall not steal, You shall not bear false witness. (Mt 19:17–18)

Other examples of actions that are always wrong are perjury, rape, and blasphemy (uttering hateful or defiant words against God). Murder, the killing of an innocent person, is always seriously wrong. It is a great assault on human dignity, contrary to the good of humans and God's will. A particularly condemnable form of murder is abortion, the unjustified killing of unborn human life.

An answer to the *what* question reveals that geneticists today have concluded that at conception a unique human being comes into existence. An unborn fetus is a human being with dignity and worth precious in the eyes of God:

We need now more than ever to have the courage to look the truth in the eye and to call things by their proper name, without yielding to convenient compromises or to the temptation of self-deception. . . . Especially in the case of abortion there is widespread use of ambiguous terminology, such as interruption of pregnancy, which tends to hide abortion's true nature and to attenuate its seriousness in public opinion. Perhaps this linguistic phenomenon is itself a symptom of an uneasiness of conscience. But no

word has the power to change the reality of things: Procured abortion is . . . deliberate and direct killing. . . . (Gospel of Life, 58)

Without determining the matter of our action—what we are doing—we cannot determine whether an action promotes or destroys the good of humans. We must ask this question to make informed, conscientious decisions on moral issues.

Therefore, *what* we do is incredibly important. God calls us to become fully human by loving him above all and loving our neighbor as ourselves. Our actions give flesh to our love; through them we become the precious child of God that we truly are. Actions—what we do—make up the content of the moral object. They are the pivotal element in judging if something is moral or immoral, in determining if something is for our good or is harmful, if something is according to God's plan or contrary to it. Actions consist of some of the following elements:

- Actions *express* who we are; for example, a teen who regularly visits her grandmother reveals herself to be a sensitive, loving person.
- Actions also *make* or *form* us into the persons we are growing to be; for example, a person who cheats regularly is transforming himself or herself into a cheater.
- Finally, actions *impact* the world around us, doing good or bringing about harm. Thus, a boyfriend who encourages his girlfriend to abort their unborn child is

moral object

The moral content of an action that suggests whether the action is directed toward the true good.

participating in murder. An abortion kills an innocent, precious child of God.

The **moral object** is the decisive element in morality. As Pope John Paul II wrote in *The Splendor of Truth*, "The morality of the human act depends primarily and fundamentally on the 'object' rationally chosen by the deliberate will" (78).

Two Rules of Morality

- *Your acts must promote the true good of humans or they are wrong.* If your reason is clouded as to what truly promotes the dignity of humans made in God's image, then,
- *Make sure your actions always conform to objective norms of morality like the Ten Commandments.* These norms indicate what actions to do (like worshiping God and honoring your parents) because they conform to our true good or what actions we should avoid (like killing, adultery, stealing, lying, and lusting) because they weaken or destroy what it means to be made in God's image.

An added bad intention (such as vainglory) makes an act evil that, in and of itself, can be good (such as almsgiving). (CCC, 1753)

Give your reasons for whether the following actions are moral or immoral. Judge them to be moral if they promote the true good of human beings and are in accord with God's will; judge them to be immoral if they are contrary to human good.

- hastening the death of an aged, terminally ill cancer patient

- refusing to pay taxes

- telling people what you think they want to hear rather than what you truly believe

- posing for a pornographic magazine

- passing a law that imposes penalties on couples who have more than the number of children dictated by the government

- poking fun at a classmate who exhibits effeminate behavior

INTENTION (*CCC*, 1752-1753)

intention

The aim or objective of a course of action.

The answer to the *why* question gets to the motive or **intention** for performing an action. It helps us discover the end, purpose, or reason for doing something. Why you did something (your intention) is an essential element for judging the morality of an action. Because intention resides in the will of the person (subject) acting, it is often referred to as the *subjective dimension* in morality.

Our legal system recognizes the importance of intention when it distinguishes between first- and second-degree murder and manslaughter. First-degree murder involves the free, premeditated, and willful killing of a person. Second-degree murder involves intent to kill, but without premeditation and deliberation. Manslaughter, on the other hand, involves the unlawful killing of someone but without premeditation or malicious intent. An example would be inattention while driving that results in an accident that kills a pedestrian.

Intention is targeted to the goal of an action, what good (or evil) I want to happen. *Why am I doing this?* For example, say you missed Mass last Sunday. Why? Was it because of laziness, to spite your parents, or because you were suffering the ill effects of partying the night before? Or did you fail to make the 12:30 Mass because you stopped to help an elderly lady fix her car, or you were called into work at the last minute, or you came down with the flu? Your motive or intention is a significant factor in judging the morality of the objective act—in this case, missing Mass.

Intention can include a series of actions that are geared to the same purpose. For example, the bank robber drives his vehicle to the scene of the crime, gets out of his car, walks into the bank, fills out a fake deposit slip, joins the teller line, walks to the teller's station, and then draws a gun to demand money. All these actions are motivated by one overriding purpose: the theft of money. The burglar's motivation directs all the previous seemingly harmless actions, like driving a car or walking into the bank building.

One action can also be motivated by several intentions, some of them mixed. For example, suppose I give you a ride to school. I do so for two reasons. First, you are a friend who deserves my help, and I want to give it. Second, you are a very capable math student, and I want you to help me study for the final exam. There are two rules for governing intentions: (1) keep the intention good, and (2) remember that the end does not justify the means. More information on each of these rules follows:

1. *Keep the intention good.* For something to be morally good, both your action (what you do) and your intention (why you do it) must be good. Note how a bad intention can contaminate even a seemingly good act, thereby making it wrong. For example, a person gives money to a worthy

cause, but the motive is to buy political favors. Although the act may benefit a particular politician's favorite charity, the donor's intention here is morally wrong (buying votes and political patronage). The bad intention contaminates the good act, making it wrong for the person doing it.

Jesus insisted on good intentions for all of our actions, even our religious duties. For example, Jesus taught that we should give money to the poor anonymously, not for the motive of getting the praise of others. He said we should fast and pray out of sincere hearts, not to draw attention to ourselves. In other words, Jesus would have us ask ourselves: "What's your motive? Do you genuinely love God and others? Or are you doing these good religious practices to show off?"

2. *The end does not justify the means.* Simply put, for an action to be moral, the **means** must be moral. My good intentions do not make an act good if the means I use are evil; that is, if they are contrary to the good of humans. What I do, the means,

means

A method, course of action, or instrument by which something can be accomplished.

must be good; they must fit the end or purpose for which I am doing something.

Therefore, I may not cheat (the means) to get good grades (the end). I may not lie (the means) to help someone get a good job (the end). Doctors may not perform dangerous medical experiments on nonconsenting patients (the means) to develop a vaccine for the AIDS virus. No matter how good the intention, we may not perform evil acts to achieve a good result. Violating this traditional, Christ-approved principle leads to the breakdown of morality.

Take the case of abortion. People have many good reasons they hope will justify this attack on innocent human life. They want to solve an unwanted pregnancy. They want to spare the child a life of pain or suffering if it has some genetic deformity. They fear they cannot support another child without making older children suffer. They want to protect their reputations or their partner's reputation. The list of good intentions is endless. But none of these reasons outweighs the right to life of a precious child made in God's image and likeness.

It is true that the decision to have an abortion is often tragic and painful for the mother, insofar as the decision to rid herself of the fruit of conception is not made for purely selfish reasons or out of convenience, but out of a desire to protect certain important values such as her own health or a decent standard of living for the other members of the family. Sometimes it is feared that the child to be born would live in such conditions that it would be better if the birth did not take place. Nevertheless, these reasons and others like them, however serious and tragic, can never justify the deliberate killing of an innocent human being. (The Gospel of Life, 58)

Why? Once again, it is worth stating—a good intention cannot justify morally evil acts. And abortion is always morally evil:

The deliberate decision to deprive an innocent human being of his life is always morally evil and can never be licit either as an end in itself or as a means to a good end. (The Gospel of Life, 57)

Take another case, that of dishonesty. People cheat on tests to get higher grades. A high grade certainly seems like a good end, but it cannot justify evil means. Intentions are critically important. It is always important to have a good reason for doing something. But good intentions can never transform an essentially evil act into something good. If the act is contrary to human good, then the intention cannot change that fact.

CIRCUMSTANCES *(CCC, 1754)*

The answers to questions that begin with *who*, *where*, *when*, and *how* help reveal the **circumstances** of a particular moral act. The consequences of a particular action are also related to the circumstances.

The circumstances of an action are also secondary. Circumstances can increase or decrease the moral goodness or evil of an act. For example, stealing is wrong. Stealing the last dollar from a poor person, however, is much more serious that stealing $10 from a millionaire. In the first case, you might be

circumstances

The conditions or facts attending an event and having some bearing on it. Circumstances can increase or decrease the moral goodness or evil of an action.

What Is the Motive?

Here are some issues. Decide if the case is moral or not. Use this procedure:

1. **Decide if the moral object is good.**
2. **Determine if the intention is good.**
3. **Finally, judge if the issue is moral (M) or immoral (I). Write the appropriate letter on the lines. Share your reasons.**

_____ 1. To protect property values, a neighborhood association conspires with local financial lenders to keep Hispanics out.

_____ 2. To control costs, a company lays off a certain percentage of older workers.

_____ 3. To boost everyone's grades, a math teacher curves a tough test.

_____ 4. To open the state medical school to members of historically excluded minorities, the admissions office looks beyond just undergraduate grade point averages and medical school admissions scores.

_____ 5. To punish their teen for lying about his whereabouts, his parents take away driving privileges for two months.

_____ 6. To deter drug use and the possession of weapons, the school administration randomly searches student lockers without permission.

_____ 7. To bolster farm prices, the government pays farmers hefty subsidies not to grow crops, despite the world hunger problem.

_____ 8. To save for a car, a student takes a twenty-hour-per-week job knowing that her grades will really suffer because of it.

_____ 9. To relax from a tough week at school, a student smokes a few joints on Friday night.

_____ 10. To beef up a résumé for college applications, a student agrees to volunteer at a hospital once a week.

guilty of placing the poor person in serious jeopardy, especially if that dollar represents food and, therefore, life. In the second case, the millionaire might not even miss the $10. Theft is wrong in both cases, but more seriously wrong in the first case.

Circumstances can also diminish or increase a person's responsibility or blameworthiness for a particular action. Let's say you came to a scene of an accident and failed to help because you panicked and simply forgot the first-aid training you learned in health class. Your act of omission may well result in a life-threatening situation for the accident victim. However, the circumstances, in this case your overwhelming fear and panic, undoubtedly lessen your blameworthiness for this particular action.

Take this same case and put a trained doctor at the scene of the accident. His knowledge and past experience minimize, if not extinguish, all fear in cases like this. He slows his car down enough to assess the situation, deciding that it would take too much time to help. He judges that he will be late for his golf round. The *who* involved in this case really makes the failure to act much more serious. This particular selfish doctor may be morally (if not

legally) responsible for a death should the unfortunate accident victim die.

Circumstances sometimes make no difference in judging the morality of a case. For example, if someone steals your iPod at school or at work, *where* it is done does not affect the moral evil of the case at all, nor does it diminish or increase the responsibility of the thief. A theft has taken place, and the act of stealing is wrong. However, at other times, *where* I do something can make all the difference in the world. Yelling the word "Fire!" might appear to be morally neutral. But screaming it in a crowded movie theater as a prank might result in panic that injures many people. Here the circumstance of place makes all the difference.

The same is true of the *when* question. Time may not affect the goodness or evil of a case at all. For example, there is little difference in the evil of the theft of your wallet whether it took place at 10 a.m. or at 2 p.m. In both cases, you are without your wallet. In other situations, time can make all the difference. Criticizing a good friend's miserable performance right after her soccer game, and within an hour of when she found out her boyfriend broke up with her, is insensitive at best and cruel at worst. The timing of negative feedback can be very important in such circumstances.

The *how* question usually gets at the means a person uses in doing the action. At times this does not add or subtract anything to the goodness or evil of a particular act. For example, suppose you cheated on a test. Doing it by means of a cheat sheet or by glancing at the answer sheet of a fellow student makes little difference in the morality of the case. In both cases, you cheated.

But in other situations, how we do something makes all the difference. Remember a previous moral principle: "A good end does not justify evil means." Thus, parents must never physically abuse or psychologically torment their children to discipline them. Discipline is a good thing; abuse and torture—the means—are not. Similarly, taking illegal drugs to relax, lying to get a job, engaging in terrorism to release political prisoners, killing an old person to relieve his or her suffering—these are all evil means that are contrary to the good of humans and against God's will. A key teaching involved with circumstances is expressed well by the *Catechism of the Catholic Church* (1754):

Circumstances of themselves cannot change the moral quality of acts themselves; they can make neither good nor right an action that is in itself evil.

Let's recap what it means to search out the facts in making a moral decision: If an action is to be morally good, the act itself must be for the good of humans and according to God's law, our intention must be good, and the circumstances should be fitting. If any of these conditions is missing, the act is no longer good in every respect; it is therefore morally wrong. And remember that the moral object (what we do) is the decisive factor. The moral object must always be good. Good intentions cannot justify evil means. And circumstances cannot make something objectively evil into a good act.

CASE: Courageous Sacrifice or an Old Fool?

An uncle and his nephew were sailing their boat in the ocean to set a time and distance record. At sea a number of days, the boat capsized. They spent hours trying to right it, finally succeeding, but only saving a little water from their provisions. The uncle decided it was not enough water for both of them to make it to land. He scrawled a message to his family on a tin can telling them he was sorry and that he loved them. He jumped into the sea against the advice of his teenage nephew. The uncle said it was better that one of them have a chance to live since both of them could not make it. A couple of days later the teen was rescued. He related to the world the story of his uncle.

- What are the critical circumstances of this case?
- Were the uncle's intentions good?
- Is the moral object wrong? In other words, did the uncle commit suicide?
- What were some alternatives that the shipwrecked duo could have pursued?

1. What six questions help us to discover the facts of moral cases?

2. What are the three sources, the constitutive elements, of moral acts? Define each.

3. Of the three sources of morality, name and explain the most important element.

4. "The end does not justify the means." What does this statement mean?

FOR YOUR JOURNAL

Oscar Wilde, the celebrated Irish novelist, poet, dramatist, and death-bed convert to Catholicism, wrote in his famous novel, *The Picture of Dorian Gray* (1891), "Whenever a man does a thoroughly stupid thing, it is always from the noblest motives."[2] Reflect on your own life or the lives of people you know well. Write about a "thoroughly stupid thing"—a mistake or foolish decision made with good motives.

Think About the Alternatives and Consequences

Doing right involves examining various possibilities before acting. It also involves examining the consequences of each action. Rarely is there just one possible way out of moral dilemmas. Often, with a little thought and the exercise of imagination, we can discover moral and upright courses of action. Also, regarding consequences: we do not live in a vacuum. We must take responsibility for our actions. Let's take a fuller look at how thinking about alternatives and consequences can help us in making correct moral choices.

ALTERNATIVES

The medical community certainly knows the value of looking at alternatives before prescribing treatment. Suppose you suffer from an infection caused by an abrasion. Your hand is red and swollen and hurts badly. The doctor would be a fool, and highly unprincipled, if his first course of action were to amputate the infected hand, especially before putting you through various courses of antibiotics. Amputation would be a last resort, perhaps if gangrene set in, and only if your very life were threatened.

Recall the ancient proverb of several blind men trying to describe an elephant. One grabs the tail and thinks it is a rope; another embraces the leg and thinks he has hold of a tree; yet another touches the trunk and believes he has grasped a snake; and the final one touches the elephant's side and is convinced he is leaning up against a wall. This proverb tries to teach that we have only a partial grasp of the truth and that we need to look at various vantage points to arrive at the whole truth. Looking at moral problems is a lot like this.

Until alternatives are considered, moral decisions should not be made. Good hard thinking—using your intellect—can search out the facts necessary to make conscientious decisions. But there is also a time, especially when stymied, when we should exercise our imagination. Sometimes thinking out alternatives involves creativity and dreaming.

Consider again the question of cheating, a moral issue many consider an epidemic in our society.

Do students have to cheat? Is this the only way to pass the course? What about asking for an extension for work due, or asking for extra-credit assignments? What about going for tutoring or forming study groups? How about good, old-fashioned study? Honesty is the touchstone of character, the foundation of all human relationships. God's law, the seventh and eighth commandments,

forbid theft (cheating is a form of theft) and bearing false witness. Honest people actually follow what their consciences dictate—to be truthful and authentic. They know all too well that dishonesty breeds dishonesty; cheating turns people into cheaters.

CONSEQUENCES

We should never act without considering the consequences of our actions. While consequences or outcomes are important to consider, they are neither the *only* nor the *decisive* factor in the morality of actions. The moral object is the decisive factor—that is, *what* we do as well as how it does or does not contribute to our ultimate good. Nevertheless, we should look at the possible effects of our proposed actions. They can help us determine if something is morally good or evil. Take the issue of whether to smoke cigarettes or not. By now almost everyone knows that nicotine is a highly addictive and poisonous drug. Cigarette smoking contains almost four thousand chemicals, at least forty-three of which cause cancer. The American Cancer Society reports some frightening statistics about smoking and its effects:

In a recent summary of studies involving 18,000 students at 61 high schools, over 70 percent of the respondents admitted to one or more instances of serious test cheating. Sixty percent admitted to plagiarizing, while 50 percent said they use the Internet to lift materials without citation.[3] A Rutgers survey that found that about half the students did not consider that they were cheating when they copied questions and answers from a test.[4]

What Should Grace Smith Do?

Grace is a hard-working, honest, and efficient secretary for her school's principal. She has learned that this principal, who seems to be generally a person of good character, has recently changed the grade of a star athlete—a high school senior. He fixed the grade so the team standout would not be benched for the upcoming championship game because of academic ineligibility.

- Has the principal done anything wrong?
- What should Grace do?
- What alternatives does she have? Think creatively.
- What would result if Grace does nothing?

- In a recent year, more than 22 percent of high school students and 8 percent of middle school students smoked cigarettes. White and Hispanic students smoked cigarettes the most.
- Almost half of Americans who continue to smoke will die as a result of the habit. Currently, about 438,000 people die in the United States each year from tobacco use.
- One out of five deaths is related to smoking, killing more Americans than alcohol, car accidents, suicide, AIDS, homicide, and illegal drugs combined.
- Cigarette smoking is involved in 30 percent of all deaths from cancer.[5]

Facts like these should be enough for us to conclude that cigarette smoking does not contribute to the true good of humans.

Consider the consequences of shoplifting. It is the number one reason why small stores go out of business. Around 10 percent of people who come to stores shoplift.

Market analysts estimate that shops boost their prices by the same 10 percent to cover shoplifting losses.

Take another issue that is common in today's society that is often encouraged by popular culture. That issue is premarital sex, which is often promiscuous. Sexual indulgence outside of God's plan for humanity brings much human misery such as the spread of sexually transmitted diseases, unwanted pregnancies that often lead to abortions, emotional pain, and the erosion of the family. Further, the lack of self-control before marriage contributes to infidelity after marriage. There are many negatives that result from violating God's will for human sexuality, that is, an exclusive male-female union of love and the sharing of life within the context of a committed marriage.

When considering consequences, an excellent question to ask is: "Would I be willing to allow everyone in a similar situation to act this way?" If you answer no, then what you propose to do is most certainly wrong. Consider:

- What if everyone cheated on tests?
- What if everyone cheated on his or her taxes?
- What if everybody disobeyed traffic laws?
- What if everyone lied?

Visit the American Cancer Society web page at: www.cancer.org. Research the site and learn about the bad effects of smoking. Find out ways you can get involved in the fight against cigarette smoking. Write a letter, send an e-mail, make a phone call, or meet your representative face-to-face. Alternatively, write a letter to the editor of your local newspaper on some issue before Congress that deals with the health and welfare of young people.

Obnoxious Boss

Rarely are we faced with just one alternative in our decisions. By using our minds and imaginations, by examining our values and the consequences of our proposed actions, we can choose the most loving, Christian, and moral course of action. What if you found yourself in the following situation? What would you do? What should you do?

Your boss at the local fast-food restaurant is always on your case. He consistently gives you the rotten clean-up jobs, criticizes your performance in front of the other employees, and even questions your integrity. It has gotten to the point where you hate to go to work. Even your coworkers have commented on how unfair the boss has been toward you.

You have tried talking to him, but he never looks you directly in the eye and ignores most of what you say.

One of your best friends works with you. He suggests that you get even with the unfair employer. He said he will help you in a ploy to slash his tires.

Briefly describe three moral alternatives to the tire-slashing plan and the consequences for each.

REVIEW AND REFLECTION

Why is it important to consider alternatives and consequences in thinking about the actions you may take?

FOR YOUR JOURNAL

Write about a decision you are currently trying to make. List several alternative courses of action. Then, describe the various consequences that you think may result for each course of action.

There are two good rules to apply when considering the consequences of proposed actions. (1) Do only those things that you think would be morally acceptable for all people at all times. (2) Always respect others as persons of incomparable worth who are made in God's image.

Others

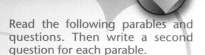

Read the following parables and questions. Then write a second question for each parable.

Good Samaritan (Lk 10:29–37)

- Do I ever go out of my way to help someone in need?

Lazarus and the Rich Man (Lk 16:19–30)

- Who is the Lazarus in my life?

Sheep and the Goats (Mt 25: 31–46)

- Who is someone I know who hungers and thirsts for love?

You are walking to your car in the mall lot. Suddenly you see a man knocked to the ground by a car backing out of its parking space. He appears to be severely injured. You and half a dozen other people rush to the scene. You are standing next to the driver of the car who is looking down on the injured person. He turns to you and says, "It's been a terrible day for Bob Smith!"

You ask, "Is that the name of the poor guy who has been hurt?"

"No," the perpetrator says. "I'm Bob Smith."

"Poor" Bob Smith! This guy is so self-absorbed in his own problems that he is totally oblivious to the injured pedestrian. In contrast, Christian morality is very sensitive to the impact that our actions have on others. Christianity recognizes that as human beings we live *with* others, and as Christians we live *for* others. Martin Luther King, Jr., put it, "Life's most persistent and urgent question is, 'What are you doing for others?'"

BE CONSIDERATE OF OTHERS

We must always ask how our proposed actions will affect others. And we must look to, and heed the advice of, those who are wiser than us.

For example, consider the buying habits in our consumer society. It may seem harmless to buy the latest CD or purchase the most desirable pair of sports shoes or attend the coolest concert. But all of these actions affect others. Consider these possible results of unchecked shopping:

- If we never deny our whims for consumer products, we may become selfish, materialistic people who lack compassion for others, especially the poor. A wise person once observed that we do not really grow up until we take some responsibility to help others and contribute to their welfare from our own resources.
- Are we aware that the shoes we buy may have been created in a sweatshop where workers toiled in oppressive conditions for subhuman wages?
- What about the concerts we attend? Our money enriches these media stars.

Are they worthy of it? Do we share their values? Do they share ours? Do we agree with their lifestyles?

None of these examples is meant to make you feel guilty. They merely point out that our actions affect others in many ways. When people are involved, we need to take extra care to guarantee that our actions mean what we want them to mean and that they do not hurt others . . . or ourselves.

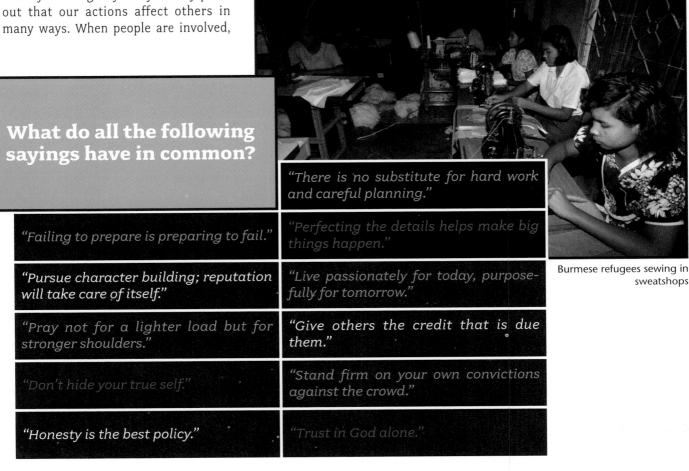

What do all the following sayings have in common?

"There is no substitute for hard work and careful planning."

"Failing to prepare is preparing to fail."

"Perfecting the details helps make big things happen."

"Pursue character building; reputation will take care of itself."

"Live passionately for today, purposefully for tomorrow."

"Pray not for a lighter load but for stronger shoulders."

"Give others the credit that is due them."

"Don't hide your true self."

"Stand firm on your own convictions against the crowd."

"Honesty is the best policy."

"Trust in God alone."

Burmese refugees sewing in sweatshops

BE CONSULTIVE OF OTHERS

One common thread in several of these sayings is that "no one goes it alone." It's worthwhile to consult with people who have made tough decisions before and to take their advice. Aphorisms or sayings like these are a result of this wisdom. Brilliant doctors seek second or even third opinions in tough cases. Golf pros seek the guidance of brilliant teachers to hone their skills. Talented singers go to voice coaches to improve their range. Seeking advice in the moral life is also the wise thing to do. The Church has several such guideposts that are of help when making moral decisions.

The Church and its Magisterium
(CCC, 2032–2040; 2049–2051)

Christ gave the Church the right and duty to teach moral principles, including those concerning society. He also entrusted the Church to make judgments concerning human affairs that deal with the fundamental rights of persons and the salvation of people. The Magisterium of the Church, that is, the Holy Father and the bishops, are the authentic teachers who have Christ's authority to "teach . . . the truth to believe, the charity to practice, [and] the beatitude to hope for" (*CCC*, 2034).

Jesus gave them the gift of infallibility, ensuring that the Holy Spirit would preserve them from error in matters of faith and morals without which the truths of the faith cannot be preserved, explained, or observed (*CCC*, 2035). This authority of the Magisterium to teach also extends to the precepts of the natural law and reason because observing them is necessary for our salvation (*CCC*, 2036).

For our part, we have the right to be instructed in God's saving precepts because they "purify our judgment and, with grace, heal wounded human reason." But we also "have the duty of observing the constitutions and decrees conveyed by the legitimate authority of the Church" (*CCC*, 2037).

Forming our consciences only after considering the good of all, and paying attention to the moral law as taught by the Church's Magisterium, is a proven way to discern and do God's will. Drawing on the *Catechism of the Catholic Church,* this text will present the Church's moral teachings, especially as they relate to the Ten Commandments.

The moral teachings of Jesus Christ are found in the New Testament, especially in the Sermon on the Mount. The pope and the bishops help us understand the meaning of these teachings and how they apply to the choices we face today.

The Sacrament of Reconciliation is also a priceless resource in helping us to consult with wise and holy mentors. Many Catholics through the centuries have found regular recourse to the Sacrament of Reconciliation an invaluable help in living the moral life and growing in holiness. A sensitive confessor can give you helpful and practical advice on how to make wise choices.

Fellow Christians. Elders—parents, grandparents, teachers, and counselors—are great sources of wisdom in the moral life. Their experience can be a great source of guidance in doing right. They can help you sort out your values; for example, in the areas of sexual morality, substance abuse, and career choices. Remember an old Chinese proverb, "To know the road ahead, ask those coming back." A close friend can also be a good source of advice as you struggle with your decisions. A friend can be a sounding board. A good friend can also preserve you from self-deception and level with you when you need to hear the truth.

It is always good to talk over decisions with a person who won't criticize you needlessly, one who is willing and able to help, one who believes in you and only wants the best for you.

 THREE QUESTIONS TO ASK WHEN CONSIDERING HOW OUR ACTIONS AFFECT OTHERS

1. Would I want what I am doing done to me?
   Jesus offers the Golden Rule: "Do to others as you would have them do to you" (Lk 6:31). If your answer is no, then don't do it!

2. Would I be proud to do this in front of my mom (or dad, or younger sibling)?
   If not, then don't do it.

3. Would I want my decision and action broadcast on the evening news?
   Would you be proud to do this proposed action in public? Would you be willing to share it on TV for the world to see? If you are ashamed of your decision, then don't do it.

Apply these three questions to several moral cases or dilemmas. What would be the right thing to do in each instance?

REVIEW AND REFLECTION

1. Describe the qualities of a person who is a good source of moral wisdom.

2. Define *Magisterium*. Why must Catholics heed its teaching in the areas of faith and morals?

3. State *The Golden Rule* in your own words.

FOR YOUR JOURNAL

After completing the *My Adviser* exercise below, write a short paragraph describing the good qualities of someone who would be a good adviser for you.

My Adviser

Write the initials of someone who:

_____ is a positive person, one who believes most problems can be solved.

_____ genuinely loves you, cares about your growth and well-being, and has your best interests at heart.

_____ is a prudent person who will tell you the truth.

_____ is a Christ-like person, kind and compassionate, and desires to be close to Jesus.

_____ gives you freedom to make your own decisions, but only after encouraging you to look over all sides of an issue.

The person who embodies most of these qualities for me is:

_____

Pray

Christian moral living is sustained by prayer. The *Catechism of the Catholic Church* defines prayer as "the living relationship of the children of God with their Father who is good beyond measure, with his Son Jesus Christ and with the Holy Spirit" (*CCC*, 2565). This is a definition of prayer that focuses on the "living relationship" we must have with a God who greatly loves us. This living relationship empowers us to live a moral life.

Jesus himself prayed often. For example, he retreated to the desert after his baptism, he prayed before choosing his apostles, and he withdrew to the hills or seashores after he performed miracles. A notable example of Jesus praying was during his dark hours in the garden of Gethsemane, where he asked his Father to give him the strength to follow his will. Finally, Jesus prayed from the cross, forgiving his enemies.

Further, Jesus taught us the importance of prayer. He instructed us to pray often—both alone and with others, to be persistent in our prayers, to pray with forgiveness and trust in our hearts, and to pray with childlike simplicity. He told us that God would answer our prayers, "For everyone who asks, receives; and the one who seeks, finds; and to the one who knocks, the door will be opened" (Lk 11:10).

Most important, Jesus taught us the perfect prayer, the Our Father, or the Lord's Prayer, which is known as "the summary of the Gospel." Two notable features of this prayer are that Jesus invites us to call God "Father" and that he asks us to petition that God's will be done. If God is our Father, then we are brothers and sisters to each other. So we should be who we are and act toward others as siblings worthy of respect and love. Second, we should really seek to do God's will which is our eternal happiness. We achieve happiness by doing what is good for us. Our own personal wills may be more attracted to the pleasurable, to the immediately satisfying, to that which is not really good for us. Praying the Our Father can teach us morality by strengthening our resolve to do God's will, for which we pray.

Another important and traditional definition of prayer is "conversation with God." Conversation has two parts: talking and listening. In the talking part of prayer, we praise God for his goodness; we thank God for his wondrous gifts; we express our sorrow over our sins; we pray for other people; and we ask God for various favors and graces. In the asking part of prayer, we can be certain that God will

always hear any prayer for divine assistance to live a moral life. He will send us the Holy Spirit to empower us to live as God's children:

If you, then, who are wicked, know how to give good gifts to your children, how much more will the Father in heaven give the holy Spirit to those who ask him? (Lk 11:13)

We must follow up the talking part of prayer with the listening part. Traditionally, Catholics believe that God can guide us through our minds, feelings, imaginations, emotions, and memories. But we need to slow down, "to let go and let God." When we quiet down, we may discover God sending us new ideas, possible solutions to our problems that we have not considered before. Or we might find our hearts strengthened by the Holy Spirit to do what our instinct tells us is the right thing to do. Often we know the moral response to a given situation, but we lack the firm resolve to do it or are tempted by peer pressure to go against what we know is right. Prayer can strengthen our hearts and wills to do right, for example, by being honest when "everyone" else is cheating.

Prayer teaches us to turn to the Lord for help. Prayer can teach us that God's love is present all around us: in our religious leaders, who stand ready to teach and guide us; in parents and teachers, who want only the best for us; in the sacraments, especially the Eucharist and Penance; in the Bible, which speaks to us of God's truth; in our friends, who call out the best in us. Prayer can remind us that all of these are wonderful signs and sources of God's continuing love and concern for us.

Responding to Challenges

QUESTION: What is the value of prayer? It seems like a waste of time. For something to be worthwhile, we should be able to see and measure the results.

ANSWER: In the famous novel *The Little Prince,* by Antoine de Saint-Exupéry, the Fox lets the Little Prince in on a simple secret, the key to really understanding human existence: "*It is only with the heart that one can see rightly; what is essential is invisible to the eye.*"[6]

Think of the essentials that cannot be perceived by the eye: the air we breathe sustains physical life; hidden computer code drives the programs we use on our PCs, which in turn are powered by electricity (also invisible to the naked eye). Our mind produces thoughts and ideas, both of which are non-material and cannot be seen. And then there is love—that mysterious and powerful quality that is rooted in the human heart.

In his first encyclical *Deus Caritas Est* (*God Is Love*), Pope Benedict XVI meditated on the truth that God is Love. God, too, is invisible, but he created everything that exists (including the material world) from nothing. He created human beings—composite creatures made up of spirit (soul) and body—who are capable of sharing God's own life, that is, capable of loving.

Prayer and love are inseparably linked. Prayer is not a useless activity because it is through prayer that we encounter God, who is Love. Prayer is a God-connection.

The Christian who prays . . .

> seeks an encounter with the Father of Jesus Christ, asking God to be present with the consolation of the Spirit to him and his work. A personal relationship with God and an abandonment to his will can prevent a Christian from being demeaned and save him from falling prey to the teaching of fanaticism and terrorism.[7]

> Prayer enables us to love our neighbor. Because we meet God in prayer, God can unite our wills to his, affecting even our feelings, helping us to learn to look on this other person not simply with my eyes and my feelings, but from the perspective of Jesus Christ. His friend is my friend. . . . If I have no contact whatsoever with God in my life, then I cannot see in the other anything more than the other, and I am incapable of seeing in him the image of God. . . . Only if I serve my neighbor can my eyes be opened to what God does for me and how much he loves me. [8]

Prayer is very practical because it enables us to meet Jesus Christ, who tells us of his great love and empowers us to see our neighbor as someone worthy of our love. What greater help could there be to living a Christian life or a life rooted in morality?

REVIEW AND REFLECTION

What is prayer? How can it help us to make moral decisions?

FOR YOUR JOURNAL

Compose three one-sentence prayers that ask help for living a moral life or making the right decisions. Address one prayer to Jesus, a second prayer to the Holy Spirit, and write the third asking the Blessed Mother to add her prayers to yours.

DISCERNMENT

In his *Spiritual Exercises*, St. Ignatius of Loyola taught an effective way to discern God's will. The following ways to choose right are based on his *Exercises*. Prior to using each way, put yourself in the Lord's presence. Describe how you would respond to either of these meditations based on a current moral decision with which you are struggling.

- Imagine a friend your age, with similar talents and interests, coming to ask you for your advice on this very problem. You really want to help this person. What would you say to help him or her search out the facts and reflect on the alternatives, consequences, and other people involved? Apply this same advice to yourself.
- Picture yourself on your deathbed or standing before Jesus right after your death. What do you wish you would have done concerning this decision? Now do the right thing.

CASE 1: THE SENATOR'S CONTRIBUTION

A famous Catholic senator wants to donate a considerable amount of money to the Catholic elementary school he attended as a child. However, though he claims to be personally against abortion, the senator is a vocal and strong pro-abortion advocate (the so-called "pro-choice" position). His gift will significantly help poor children gain access to a good Catholic education.[9]

Debate: Should the pastor accept this money? Why or why not?

CASE 2: THE CRYING BABY

The classic television program *MASH* closed its highly successful run with this riveting moral problem: Hawkeye—one of the doctor-heroes of the show—was on a bus with some fellow surgeons and a few Koreans. He informed the driver of the bus that some enemy soldiers were approaching, and the bus should be hidden by the side of the road. As enemy soldiers began to walk past the bus, an infant on the bus began to cry.

Debate: What should the mother do in this situation?

Catholic Life in Action

1. Review these ten rules taught in this chapter. Which *three* are the most helpful to you personally? Explain why.
   a. Your acts must promote the true good of humans or they are wrong.
   b. Make sure your actions always conform to objective norms of morality like the Ten Commandments.
   c. Make sure you have good intentions.
   d. Good intentions do not justify evil means.
   e. Circumstances themselves cannot change the moral quality of acts; they can make neither good nor right an action that is in itself evil.
   f. Act only in those ways that you think would be morally acceptable for all people at all times.
   g. Always respect others as persons of incomparable worth made in God's image. Never do anything that would treat a person as a thing, as a means to your end, for your own gain or profit.
   h. Do unto others as you would have them do to you.
   i. Ask yourself, "Would I be proud to do this in front of my mom?" If not, don't do it.
   j. Ask yourself, "Would I want everyone to know how I arrived at my decision and how I acted on it?" If not, don't do it.

2. After considering the STOP Sign method and the ten rules stated above, how would you solve the two cases on page 66? Jot down some notes to suggest your approach. Discuss your solution with your classmates.
   • What is an important decision you are facing right now?
   • Review your daily schedule. Find a good time and place to talk to the Lord for ten minutes each day for the next three weeks, especially over this decision.

3. This chapter discussed some of the consequences of shoplifting. Discover the price of shoplifting in your area of the country by interviewing the security managers of department stores or malls to find out how much shoplifting costs them. Ask about what they do to prevent it.

4. St. Francis of Assisi once said, "Remember that when you leave this earth, you can take with you nothing that you have received—only what you have given: a full heart, enriched by honest service, love, sacrifice, and courage." This quote challenges us to put the Golden Rule of love of neighbor into action. In the coming month, individually or in small groups, do one of the following:
   • Have a clothing collection drive. Donate the clothing to a local shelter.
   • Organize a community clean-up day in your school's neighborhood.
   • Volunteer to tutor younger students at your school or a nearby grade school.
   • Offer to do yard work or shopping for an elderly neighbor.
   • Collect toys for kids in the hospital. Distribute them in person.
   • Help prepare or serve a meal at a homeless shelter.

Summary Points

◆ Prudence, the cardinal virtue of right reason in action, is essential for discerning how to live a moral Christian life.

◆ The STOP Sign method of moral decision-making requires that we **S**earch out the facts (what, why, who, when, where, and how); **T**hink about the various alternatives and their consequences; consider the impact of our acts on **O**thers and consult wise advisers; and **P**ray.

◆ The object, intention, and circumstances comprise the sources of the morality of human acts. They must all be good for the action to be moral.

◆ Some actions are always intrinsically evil (like rape, murder, and blasphemy) because they are contrary to God's will and the good of humans.

◆ *What* we do corresponds to the moral object, the "matter" of our action. The morality of human acts depends primarily and fundamentally on the object rationally chosen by the deliberate will. Therefore, our acts must promote true human good and conform to objective norms of morality like the Ten Commandments.

◆ The *why* question gets at the intention or motive of our acts. It is the subjective dimension of morality. Our intentions must always be good. But good intentions do not justify evil means. A good end does not justify evil means to attain it.

◆ The *who, where, when,* and *how* questions reveal the circumstances of our actions. Circumstances of an act (including the consequences) are secondary. They can increase or decrease the moral goodness or evil of an act. They can diminish or increase a person's responsibility or blameworthiness for particular acts. But they *cannot* change the moral quality of acts. Circumstances cannot make an action good or right if it is evil in itself.

◆ Good, moral decision making requires the consideration of various alternatives and the examination of their respective consequences.

◆ When considering the consequences of our actions, it is a good idea to judge whether we would be willing to allow everyone to act the same way. If not, then what we plan to do is probably wrong.

◆ Catholics look to and heed the moral teachings of the Magisterium of the Church (the pope and bishops) as a sure guide in living the moral life.

◆ Jesus and his moral teachings, recourse to the Sacrament of Reconciliation, trusted and wise adults, and ethical and good friends are essential helps to consult in finding direction for living morally.

◆ The Golden Rule of doing to others as you would have them do to you, and the "mother" and "publicity" tests, are good guidelines for deciding what is moral and what is not.

◆ Prayer, a conversation with God, strengthens our relationship with him. It is of great help in discerning God's will and can assist us as we decide what is moral and what is not.

◆ In the listening part of prayer, God can affect our minds, hearts, imaginations, emotions, and memories. The Lord assures us that our prayers will be answered.

PRAYER REFLECTION

I wait for you, O Lord;
I lift up my soul to my God.
In you I trust; do not let me be disgraced;
do not let my enemies gloat over me.
No one is disgraced who waits for you, but only those who lightly break faith.
Make known to me your ways, Lord; teach me your paths.
Guide me in your truth and teach me, for you are my God my savior.
For you I wait all the long day because of your goodness, Lord.
Remember your compassion and love, O Lord; for they are ages old.
Remember no more the sins of my youth;
remember me only in light of your love.

—Psalm 25:1–7

NOTES

1. This story appeared in the March—May, 1998, issue of *Our Daily Bread* (page for March 24) and was reported on the Bible.org website: www.bible.org/illus.asp?topic_id=1107 (9 August 2006).
2. Found at The Quotations Page <www.quotationspage.com/quote/27154.html> (9 August 2006).
3. The Center for Academic Integrity citing research of Don McCabe released in June of 2005 <www.academicintegrity.org/cai_research.asp> (9 August 2006).
4. Kathy Slobogin, "Survey: Many Students Say Cheating's OK," CNN.com/Education <http://archives.cnn.com/2002/fyi/teachers.ednews/04/05/highschool.cheating/> (9 August 2006).
5. American Cancer Society, "Prevention & Early Detection: Cigarette Smoking" <www.cancer.org/docroot/PED/content/PED_10_2X_Cigarette_Smoking.asp?sitearea=PED> (9 August 2006).
6. Found at BrainyQuote, "Antoine de Saint-Exupery Quotes" <www.brainyquote.com/quotes/authors/a/antoine_de_saintexupery.html> (9 August 2006).
7. Encyclical Letter *Deus Caritas Est* of the Supreme Pontiff Benedict XVI to the Bishops, Priests, and Deacons, Men and Women Religious, and All the Lay Faithful on Christian Love (*Liberia Editrice Vaticana*, 2005), No. 37 <www.vatican.va/holy_father/benedict_xvi/encyclicals/documents/hf_ben-xvi_enc_20051225_deus-caritas-est_en.html> (9 August 2006).
8. Ibid, No. 18.
9. This is based on an actual case. The pastor refused to accept the money.

CHAPTER OVERVIEW

Look to the Law

Good law points out the boundaries to freedom. Knowing and respecting the law is essential to living a moral life.

Freedom and Responsibility

God gave human beings the freedom to think and choose. Freedom makes us responsible for our choices and helps us to grow in truth and goodness.

Responsibility

To the degree that our choices and actions are voluntary, we are responsible for them. We should accept responsibility for our mistakes and sinful behavior, committing ourselves to repairing harm done and resolving not to repeat them.

Law and Morality

Good law protects us from many actions that would hurt us or others. Rooted in the common good, law guides our thoughts and actions and provides the foundation for moral behavior.

CHAPTER THREE

Law as a Guide to Freedom

"Amen, I say to you, until heaven and earth pass away, not the smallest letter or the smallest part of a letter will pass from the law."

Matthew 5:18

Look to the Law

There is a true story about a high school senior who chose to ignore a sign . . . and it cost him. He talked his girlfriend into going for a midnight swim. His neighbors had recently installed a pool in their backyard. He and his girlfriend decided to try it out. They snuck into the yard and scaled the fence, ignoring the prominently displayed "No Trespassing" and "Do Not Enter" signs. Just as the senior hit the diving board, the girl yelled out a warning. But it was too late. The teen dove into the pool, which, tragically, had only a foot of water in it.

The result was a broken neck and a lifetime of paralysis. Had he paid attention to the signs, he would have avoided the unfortunate accident.[1]

This story suggests another. Suppose you are driving down a country road. You come to a large sign that reads, "Dangerous Curve Ahead." Suddenly, you have before you three choices: You can heed the warning and slow down. Or, you can ignore the sign and keep driving at the same speed. Finally, you can defy the warning and step on the accelerator. Whatever choice you make, the sign remains true: there is a curve in the road. It remains dangerous whether you acknowledge that reality or not.

Responsible use of freedom helps us live as God's children. Good law points out the boundaries to freedom and keeps us on the right path to our eternal destiny. Freedom, responsibility, and law go hand-in-hand in the moral life and are the main focus in this chapter.

NO TRESPASSING

Making Excuses

Gabriel Meurier (d. 1601) wrote, "He who excuses himself accuses himself." Morality involves accepting responsibility for our own actions and attitudes. Yet people often try to disown their behavior, pretending that they didn't really do it or are not responsible for it. Rationalization means devising self-serving excuses for one's behavior.

Write a "V" for those statements that seem to be valid reasons for certain behavior. Write an "R" for those that are clearly rationalizations. Be prepared to explain your answers.

_____ 1. "I didn't know you could not make a left-hand turn there."
_____ 2. "I flunked the test because the teacher doesn't like me."
_____ 3. "I came in late because the car had a flat tire."
_____ 4. "I didn't give the homeless man a dollar because I thought he'd spend it on alcohol or drugs."
_____ 5. Eve to God: "The serpent tricked me into it, so I ate [the forbidden fruit]" (Gn 3:13).
_____ 6. "Everybody else was drinking, so I did, too."
_____ 7. "I simply forgot about your birthday."
_____ 8. War criminal: "I was only following orders."
_____ 9. "When he started poking fun at my sister, I just got violent. I have a short fuse."
_____ 10. "So I littered! Big deal! There were no trash containers around."
_____ 11. "I don't see how you can blame me for hating them. It's how I was raised."

• What other facts would you like to know about each comment to judge it more fairly?
• Name a popular rationalization you or your friends use.
• "Be an owner, not a blamer." What does this quotation mean?

Freedom and Responsibility

(CCC, 1730—1749)

Because humans are made in God's image, we have the capacity to think and choose. We have the powers of reason and free will. Both of these capacities separate us from other creatures on earth. Human reason enables us to search for truth. Free will gives us the power to be a master of our own actions. And, because we are free, we have the greatest of all powers: the ability to love. This freedom to love ultimately enables us to seek the Triune God of love and unite with him for eternal happiness.

Freedom makes us responsible for our choices and actions, either good or evil. Freedom lets us shape our own lives. It can help us grow and mature in both truth and goodness. It gives us the power to choose between good and evil, to grow in holiness or to fail to grow and to commit sin. Freedom is the basis of truly human acts. A fuller description of freedom follows.

CHARACTERISTICS OF FREEDOM
(CCC, 1731; 1743—1745)

The *Catechism of the Catholic Church* offers the following definition of freedom:

Freedom is the power, rooted in reason and will, to act or not to act, to do this or that, and so to perform deliberate actions on one's own responsibility. (1731)

The Second Vatican Council taught that:

*only in freedom can man direct himself toward goodness. . . . [A]uthentic freedom is an exceptional sign of the divine image in man. . . . [M]an's dignity demands that he act according to a knowing and free choice. (*The Church in the Modern World, *17)*

But not everyone believes that human beings are truly free. For example, those

who believe in **determinism** deny that humans have the power to choose. They hold that every event, action, and decision inevitably results from something independent of the human will. Thus, some religions teach that fate, the stars, or some other named or unnamed spiritual force preordains and controls our choices. Similarly, some psychologists and sociologists say that we lack freedom because our personalities are fixed by our environment, upbringing, and education. Some biologists hold that our brain cells, genes, and emotional drives are so fixed that humans are not really free to do anything that is not caused by heredity.

Christians reject such strict deterministic views, and common sense backs up the Christian point of view. For example, if you wanted to, you could put down this book. You do not *have* to read it. If you are reading this at home, you could *freely* choose to go get a snack right now or watch television or call your friend on the phone. You have freedom. Another proof of your essential freedom is your pride or embarrassment or guilt after certain actions. If you were not free, you could not take credit or blame for *anything* you do.

freedom

"The power, rooted in reason and will, . . . to perform deliberate actions on one's own responsibility" (CCC, 1731).

determinism

The philosophy that holds that every event, action, and decision results from something independent of the human will.

Say not: "It was God's doing that I fell away";
for what he hates he does not do.
Say not: "It was he who set me astray";
for he has no need of wicked man.
Abominable wickedness the Lord hates;
he does not let it befall those who fear him.
When God, in the beginning, created man,
he made him subject to his own free choice.
If you choose you can keep the commandments;
it is loyalty to do his will.
There are set before you fire and water;
to whichever you choose, stretch forth your hand.
Before man are life and death,
whichever he chooses shall be given him.

—Sirach 15:11–17

THE BIBLE ON FREEDOM

Read John 8:31–32. According to Jesus, what will make us free?

Read 2 Corinthians 3:17. Who gives us freedom?

Read Galatians 5:13. According to St. Paul, how should freedom not be used? How should it be used?

Read Galatians 5:19–23. What does St. Paul tell us will result if we abuse freedom? On the other hand, if we live according to the Spirit, what results?

Because humans do have freedom, we are *self-determining*. We can select our goals and then perform certain acts to accomplish them. For example, you can decide to master the German language (your goal). You can then do what has to be done to achieve your goal; that is, study, practice, speak, practice, write, and practice some more. We freely make choices all the time: the music we listen to, the friends we hang out with, the people we vote for, the sports we participate in, and so forth.

Our freedom means that we are self-making. Our choices help form who we are. They build character. They give us identity. For example, if I decide to learn how to play the piano, and I stick with a regimen of practice, I may well become a good or great pianist.

Freedom essentially means selecting our own goals in life and then moving toward them. Our basic human pursuit is to go after what is good, what fulfills our needs, what satisfies our restless hearts. At its core, freedom is the God-given power to do good. And doing what is good gives us more freedom. The *Catechism of the Catholic Church* puts it this way:

> *The more one does what is good, the freer one becomes. There is no true freedom except in the service of what is good and just. The choice to disobey and do evil is an abuse of freedom and leads to "the slavery of sin." (1733)*

KINDS OF FREEDOM

Freedom is a positive quality that helps us to both express and develop our humanity. Freedom enables us to love. A good distinction to make here concerning freedom is between external and internal freedom.

External freedom includes freedom from factors outside ourselves that threaten or destroy our power to exercise choice; for example, the freedom from poverty or the freedom from tyranny. If a person is always on the brink of starvation, she is not free to pursue an education that can provide her with even more choices. If a person is under the rule of a tyrant, he is not free to vote or assemble or worship God with others—all freedoms that make us more human and contribute to our happiness.

Internal freedom includes freedom from interior factors that limit choice. Two examples are freedom from fear and freedom from addiction. Note how slavery to either fear or a substance can limit one's freedom. For example, the fear of flying may keep you from visiting Europe and expanding your human and cultural horizons. An addiction to alcohol can keep you from holding a responsible job or engaging in deep human relationships.

Freedom *from* both external and internal forces that limit choice provides the fertile ground for freedom's real purpose: freedom *for*. True freedom liberates us to develop our God-given talents in a responsible way so we can live our lives for others and for our loving God. Freedom serves what is good, just, and true.

LIMITS OF FREEDOM
(CCC, 1735; 1740; 1742; 1746)

Our modern world often sees freedom as creating as many choices as possible, for example, in the availability of consumer products. But how often are these choices really just opportunities for enslaving people?

Consider the true story of how some clever trappers in Africa capture monkeys. They hollow out a gourd or pumpkin, cutting a hole just big enough for a monkey's hand to squeeze through. Then they put some peanuts inside the pumpkin and tie it to a tree. The monkey eventually approaches the pumpkin, smells the peanuts, and reaches in to grab the food. To extract its hand from the small opening, the monkey has to open its hand because its fist will not fit through the opening. But in its greed, the monkey is unwilling to let go of the food. It becomes easy prey for its trappers who come by later and ship the monkey off to a zoo on the other side of the globe. Grasping after material things that we think will make us

happy often has the reverse effect. Our failure to let go enslaves us.

Much of modern society also views freedom as "doing whatever I want to do." This concept of freedom promotes absolute reliance on self, without being responsible to God, the human community, or the natural world in which we live. This mentality has created such an emphasis on the "freedom of choice" that the fundamental right to life itself of innocent human beings has been assaulted and denied (abortion). It is a gross distortion of the exercise of freedom to attack other human beings and the values God's law seeks to protect. True freedom elevates humans; it never demeans.

Human freedom is not absolute. Human freedom is, in fact, limited. I may not say or do everything I want to say or do. Another name for unlimited freedom is *license*. True freedom is not license. License is unbridled, excessive, undisciplined freedom that abuses true liberty. When people do whatever they want by disregarding God's law, their own good, or the rights of others, evil results. In the name of unbridled freedom, too often the economic, social, political, and cultural conditions that true freedom requires are trampled upon. Historian Will Durant noted that, "When liberty becomes license, dictatorship is near."

FREEDOM TO CHOOSE

Responsible decision making involves both external and internal freedom. *External* freedom enables you to act without undue restraint or control from another. *Internal* freedom is the state of mind and spirit that enables you to achieve your full human potential.

The following three situations involve both external and internal freedom. The conditions are present where you can choose responsibly, that is, in a way that will enable you to grow as a child of God endowed with dignity. How would you exercise your freedom?

Situation 1: Your folks are out of town on a business trip. Your aunt is watching your two younger siblings. You are at home alone, holding down the fort. But, for safety reasons, your parents have instructed you not to have any friends over.

> Would it be an abuse of freedom for you to have a couple of friends over to watch a movie? Explain.

> Would it be wrong to throw a party? Why or why not?

> *Reflection*: What would you most likely do and why?

Situation 2: You work at an ice cream shop spooning sundaes. Store policy allows you to eat one sundae or its equivalent per work shift. It does not allow you to give "freebies" to visiting friends. However, the policy is almost impossible to enforce since the boss is rarely around.

> Would it be theft if you gave out one sundae per shift and did not eat any yourself? Why or why not?

> Would it be wrong to give your friends sundaes if all the other high school workers are doing so for their friends? Why or why not?

> *Reflection*: What would you most likely do and why?

Situation 3: You have access to the Internet from your home computer. Your dad has installed a program to block access to pornography and other objectionable materials on the Internet. However, you know how to dismantle the software he has installed.

> Would it be an abuse of your freedom to visit pornographic websites? Why or why not?

> *Reflection*: What would you most likely do and why?

Discussion

Are the authority figures in the above situations within their rights to make the rules they made? Why or why not?

Are the rules reasonable? Why or why not?

Review the principles of morality you learned in the last chapter, for example, "The end does not justify the means." Apply them to the three situations described above.

ABUSES AGAINST FREEDOM

(CCC, 1739—1740; 1748)

Abuse of freedom results in sin. "By deviating from the moral law man violates his own freedom, becomes imprisoned within himself, disrupts neighborly fellowship, and rebels against divine truth" (*CCC*, 1740). In fact, humanity became a slave to sin through the Original Sin of Adam and Eve, which has spawned innumerable others, leading to human wretchedness and oppression.

Christians, of course, rejoice in the cross of Jesus Christ, which has redeemed us from the sin that enslaves humanity. "For freedom Christ set us free" (Gal 5:1). Jesus, our resurrected Lord, leads us to the truth and gives us the Holy Spirit who teaches us the true meaning of freedom.

There are other limits to human freedom. Physically, we are limited beings. Some of us are not free to be star gymnasts; we simply are not physically coordinated. Others of us are slow runners; we will never win track races. We are limited beings, and our freedom is limited as well.

Similarly, intellectual makeup can limit our freedom. For example, not many people are intellectually qualified to be rocket scientists or theologians. But you are still free to make the most of your intellectual ability or to learn only what you have to know to "pass the test."

Your emotional makeup may make you more prone to fly off the handle. Your temper may be an obstacle you have to deal with your whole life, and thus it may limit your freedom. But you can work to control your temper or use it as an excuse every time you blow up at a friend.

Your family, the school you attend, the friends you grew up with, bad memories from your childhood, and a host of other factors can limit your outlook on life and your freedom. But again, you can choose to make the best of the gifts you have or hide behind the things you lack.

Besides some of these psychological and social factors, the Catholic moral

tradition has recognized a number of *impediments* to freedom. These obstacles to freedom can limit our blameworthiness or responsibility for actions, depending on certain factors. Among the major impediments to the exercise of true freedom are:

Ignorance, or simply not knowing what we should do or not do. Sometimes the ignorance is not our fault; for example, you may not have ever been taught certain rules. At others times, we should have known better but were too lazy to find out. We always have the duty to overcome ignorance to the best of our ability.

Inadvertence, that is, not paying attention or being distracted while we are acting. For example, we might cause a car accident because we were distracted by talking on a cell phone.

Duress. Our freedom is certainly impeded when someone tries to force us to do something. For example, if a person has a gun to your head and threatens you with death if you do not do a certain action, your freedom (and resulting responsibility) are greatly reduced or destroyed.

Now the Lord is the Spirit, and where the Spirit of the Lord is, there is freedom.

—2 CORINTHIANS 3:17

AN EXERCISE IN HOW TO GROW IN VIRTUE

A traditional method Catholics have used to grow in virtue is to examine their consciences each day. Here is one method. Each evening, put yourself in the presence of our Lord Jesus Christ. Ask for his help and that of the Holy Spirit to assist you in reviewing how you lived the past day. Reflect on the questions listed below. Jot notes to yourself in a spiritual journal to mark your progress. At the end of the three weeks, consider celebrating the Sacrament of Penance to experience Christ's forgiving love for you.

◆ Lord, help me to see what I have done right today. What good have I done for other people and for myself?

◆ Holy Spirit, help me review what I have done wrong this past day. How have I hurt others or neglected them? What have I done to be less than the wonderful child of God I am called to be?

◆ Dear Lord, please show me what I could have done better today—all for your greater honor and glory.

Inordinate attachments. Sometimes money and other possessions enslave us to such a degree that we do not act with full freedom.

Fear. The worst case of fear is panic, what has been described as "sudden and overwhelming fear in the face of real or fancied danger."

Habit. Repeated behavior can lead to habits. Good habits are virtues. Bad habits are vices. A vice like gluttony, immoderate or excessive eating or drinking, is a vice that ensnares people and limits their freedom to live wholesome lives.

Although all of these obstacles to freedom limit us, they do not have to enslave us. We are free to change. We can overcome ignorance by learning. We can develop good habits and uproot bad ones. We can fight irrational fears. We can pay more attention to what is going on around us and what we are doing in particular settings.

Above all, we can cooperate with Christ's grace, his friendship, and the many gifts the Holy Spirit gives to help us live freely as children of God. God's grace supports and enriches our freedom, which is always at its best when we choose to do good. God's grace never destroys our freedom because God's grace is his love for us. And love always lets us be free.

Spiritual practices like prayer and acts of self-denial help us gain freedom over our inner selves so we can cooperate with God's grace and live more lovingly toward God, neighbor, and self.

FOR YOUR JOURNAL

Write of a time when you used your freedom for the benefit of a member of your family.

REVIEW AND REFLECTION

1. "Freedom is not license." Explain this phrase and what freedom is.
2. How can the claims of determinists be disproved?
3. What does it mean when we say freedom makes us self-determining and self-making?
4. Distinguish between *external* and *internal* freedom and freedom *from* and freedom *for*.
5. How are human beings truly freed from sin and death?
6. List and briefly discuss five obstacles to freedom.

Responsibility

(CCC, 1734, 1736—1737)

We are free, intelligent beings made in God's image. Thus, we have the ability to choose and to make intelligent decisions about how to act. But with this marvelous power of free will comes responsibility. A key teaching flows from this reality: To the degree that our choices are voluntary, we are responsible for our actions. "Every act directly willed is imputable to its author" (CCC, 1736).

The word **imputable** refers to actions that can be ascribed, attributed, or definitely linked to a specific person or entity. If a deed is imputable, someone can clearly be held "accountable" for it. This is another way of saying that our actions belong to us. They are attributable to us; we "own" them. Therefore, we must "own up" to them. Responsibility and freedom go hand-in-hand because our free choices, and the actions that result from them, help form us into the kinds of people we end up becoming. Our actions also have consequences. They affect us and everyone around us.

Certainly, when we do something well—like acing a test, serving the winning points in a volleyball game, writing a brilliant book report, or doing a kind deed for a friend—we want to take credit for our deeds. And we do deserve credit. On the other hand, we are also responsible for our mistakes. For example, it's our responsibility when we back into a car in the parking lot, miss some math problems on a test, or fail to show up for a job because we forget to set the alarm clock. Mature and honest people will own up to these actions and accept full responsibility for their consequences. And, one hopes, they will learn from these mistakes, recalling the proverb, "The only real failure is the one from which we learn nothing."

Finally, we must also accept full responsibility for sinful behavior that we freely and willfully commit (see Chapter 6).

Christ Jesus requires that we own up to our sins, repent of them, express our sorrow, try to repair any harm we have caused, and firmly resolve not to engage in such behavior again.

Though we must accept responsibility for every directly willed (voluntary) action we do, it must be noted that some actions are not *totally* voluntary because they result from negligence or ignorance. For example, you may have caused an accident because you made a left turn where you should not have done so. You did not *directly* intend the accident, but you should have known the law. You are still responsible for the accident, but you may be less blameworthy than if you caused the accident deliberately or recklessly.

Mature, Christ-like people use their freedom wisely. Before acting, they search out the facts, examine alternatives and foreseeable effects (including the impact on others), consult Jesus and prudent people (including the Magisterium), and prayerfully ask for the help of the Holy Spirit. In addition, they practice self-discipline and commit themselves to a life of growth in virtue and a rigorous pursuit of truth that reveals what is good for human beings. Christians dedicate themselves to Christ, who said:

"Everyone thinks of changing the world, but no one thinks of changing himself."[2]

–Leo Tolstoy

imputable

Ascribed, attributed, or definitely linked to a specific accountable person or entity.

"I am the way and the truth and the life." (Jn 14:6)
"If you remain in my word, you will truly be my disciples, and you will know the truth, and the truth will set you free." (Jn 8:31-32)

EMOTIONS AND MORALITY

(CCC, 1762—1775)

Catholic morality traditionally has discussed emotions under the term *passions*, that is, our "feelings." These passions are movements of the senses that predispose us to act or not act in relation to something we feel or imagine to be good or evil. Experiencing emotions is an important part of being human. Their function is to connect the five senses to the mind.

We have many emotions. The most basic emotion or passion is love, which is aroused by attraction to the good. St. Thomas Aquinas defined love this way: "To love is to will the good of another." Love's opposite is hate. Other important emotions are desire, fear, joy, sadness, and anger.

Emotions are morally neutral. However, to the degree that they engage our reason and will, we can find moral good or evil in them. For example, the passions are morally good when they lead us to do something good; they are morally evil when they contribute to our doing something bad.

Consider the example of anger. Suppose you hear someone tell a lie about a friend. The lie greatly angers you because false rumors are being spread about someone you love. Say your anger helps you get up the courage to firmly but without animosity remind the detractor not to spread lies about your friend. In this case, your anger was "righteous" because it moved you to intervene to protect the reputation of an innocent party. However, what if your anger came out in a different, retaliatory manner? Suppose you physically assaulted the liar or spread false rumors about him or her. In this case your anger contributed to something evil, a bad action that hurt another. Recall the old saying "two wrongs do not make a right."

Having strong feelings does not mean we are either holy or unholy, moral or immoral. It is what we do with our emotions that counts. Christians will train their wills in the virtues so emotions can be channeled toward what is good. If we cooperate with God's grace, the Holy Spirit can help our minds and hearts control the passions so we can use them lovingly. However, if we ignore God's help, there is always the danger that vices like lust or gluttony or pride will control our emotions for destructive and evil purposes.

- Give an example that shows how fear could lead to a good action. Give another example that shows how fear could lead to a bad action.
- Give the same type of examples for sadness.

REVIEW AND REFLECTION

1. For what actions are we responsible?

2. Define *imputable*.

3. What are the principal passions?

4. Give an example of when an emotion might be moral or immoral.

FOR YOUR JOURNAL
Write of a time in your life when either the emotion of joy or sadness moved you to do a good thing for another person.

IN UNION WITH CHRIST

Christians strive to make sure their actions are in harmony with the life, teaching, and person of Jesus Christ as a way to live responsibly. Jesus is the *fundamental norm* of Christian morality. This means that Jesus is the standard or model on whom we should pattern our lives. As St. Paul explained:

> I have been crucified with Christ; yet I live, no longer I, but Christ lives in me; insofar as I now live in the flesh, I live by faith in the Son of God who has loved me and given himself up for me. (Gal 2:19–20)

One of the major responsibilities of the Magisterium is to teach guidelines, norms, and laws to help Christians live as Christ lived. The sources for these norms include the *Scriptures*, God's revealed word, and *Tradition*, the history and teaching of the Christian community guided by the Holy Spirit. The Christian community has also applied the insights of *human reason* to reflect on human experience through the ages to discover what is truly good and what is truly evil.

The process of formulating norms works something like this. First, the Christian community states in its creeds and doctrines certain beliefs or expressions of our faith in Jesus. Beliefs lead to *values*, that is, certain standards or qualities that we deem worthwhile or valuable. For example, our belief in Jesus' core teaching on compassion makes us value qualities like mercy, forgiveness, kindness, empathy, and a host of others. Unfortunately, because we are weak and sinful, we do not always act on the values that flow from our beliefs. For example, we might try to get revenge on a person who did us harm. Or, out of selfishness, we may be reluctant to share our wealth with needy people. Neither revenge nor selfishness is compatible with Christian beliefs.

Therefore, we move on to articulate our values in *principles*, which are general and usually positive guidelines for living out our values. For example, if we value compassion, then we would support the principle of not being vengeful. Or a value of compassion might lead us to the principle of looking out in a special way for the poor to make sure that their basic human rights (food, shelter, clothing, education, a job, etc.) are being recognized.

Finally, principles are formulated more concretely into *norms* (which are often stated as particular laws). These norms translate our beliefs, values, and principles into concrete policies or courses of action to meet specific situations in human life. For example, our belief in Jesus and his teaching on compassion, the value of mercy, and the principle of special concern for the poor have prompted the United States Bishops to instruct Catholics to support laws that guarantee basic human services for the less fortunate in our country.

In short statements that tell us what to do or what not to do, moral norms convey the moral wisdom and the experience of the human community. They embody the values and principles of our Christian faith, teaching us what is for our ultimate good. Norms can be as general as "tell the truth," "use your God-given talents," and "be patient." Or moral norms can be very specific as in "Thou shalt not commit adultery." However, the purpose of both general and specific norms is to direct both individuals and societies toward responsible behavior and right action.

How to Treat Others

Below are some Scripture passages on how we should treat others. Read each passage carefully. Then complete the assignments that follow.

Exodus 3:7–10
Based on this passage, whom should God's people value in a special way?
Formulate a *principle* for the Christian community based on this biblical passage.

Deuteronomy 24:10–21
Write down a *general norm* given in this passage.
Note a norm that is more specific.

Matthew 19:13–15
Whom does Jesus value in this passage?
Write a *specific norm* that would follow from Jesus' example.

John 13:12–17
What does Jesus value here?
Write a *general norm* that could be used in a school setting that would reflect the values and principles of this passage.

James 2:14–18
Write a *specific norm* based on the teaching of this passage.
"If you are going to talk the talk, then you must walk the walk." How is this saying related to this passage?

Law and Morality

(CCC, 1950—1986)

Good law guides human freedom. Good law is like the rules of a game. It tells us how it should be played. Good law is like a train's railway tracks, which allow the train to do what it is made to do. If the tracks are missing or broken, the train is destined for a wreck. In life, good law protects us from license, that is, doing our own thing regardless of the consequences. License leads to wrecked lives. **Law** also serves as an objective standard outside of ourselves against which we can measure what we want to do. It warns us of pitfalls and harmful, dehumanizing actions.

The moral law has its source in the Blessed Trinity. We can view moral law as the work of God's providence, that is, God's wisdom, power, and goodness. From a biblical point of view, the moral law is God's fatherly instruction for us, prescribing the rules of conduct that lead to eternal happiness and banning evil that leads us away from God and his love.

St. Thomas Aquinas gave a classic definition of law as "an ordinance of reason for the common good, promulgated by the one who is in charge of the community" (quoted in *CCC*, 1976). This definition has several important elements:

Reasonable. First of all, law is reasonable. It is a participation in God's providence. Of all living beings, humans alone are endowed with reason and are able to conduct themselves with freedom and understanding, obeying God who entrusted everything to them. An example of a reasonable law is a gun ordinance that forbids the indiscriminate shooting of firearms in a crowd.

For the common good. Second, laws are for the common good. God wants us to take care of each other and to build up the human community. Therefore, good laws—an income tax law that is fair is good because it helps provide basic human services like police protection and the education of children—enhance society and respect the dignity of each person in that society. Laws also help provide for the poor in our midst who have a hard time taking care of their own basic human needs.

From competent authority. Competent authority makes law. Ultimately, all law derives from the moral law, God's loving plan for his creatures. The four interrelated expressions of the moral law are the *eternal law*, which has its source in God; the **natural law**, which is the light of understanding God has placed in us; *revealed law*, made up of the old Law and the Law of the Gospel; and *civil law* and *Church law*. Duly appointed civil and Church leaders derive their authority to make and enforce laws from God, the source of all authority.

Law must be promulgated. Law should be announced in such a way that people can be expected to know it. Reasonable, thinking, and discerning humans should be able to discover the natural law using their intellects. But God has helped us in this process by providing the moral instruction found in both the Old and New

15 Simple Rules to Live By

Children are often taught simple little rules or norms to live by. Here are some you might have learned when you were younger.

1. If you open it, close it.
2. Look both ways before crossing the street.
3. If you unlock it, lock it up.
4. Check to see how deep the water is before you dive in.
5. If you break it, admit it.
6. Never bother an eating dog.
7. If you borrow it, return it.
8. Never ride with strangers.
9. If you make a mess, clean it up.
10. Always check your work.
11. If it isn't yours, ask before you use it.
12. Always tell the truth.
13. Mind your own business.
14. If it ain't broke, don't fix it.
15. Always stick by your friends.

◆ Add at least five more simple rules.

◆ Identify the values that each of the rules is trying to enshrine.

law

"An ordinance of reason for the common good, promulgated by the one who is in charge of the community" (St. Thomas Aquinas, in *CCC*, 1976).

natural law

The reasoned participation of humans in God's eternal law that reveals what God intends us to do and to avoid according to his wise and loving plan.

A STORY

An unsavory businessman who tried to appear upright once told American author Mark Twain, "Before I die, I'm going to make a pilgrimage to the Holy Land. There I will climb to the top of Mount Sinai and read the Ten Commandments."

Mark Twain replied, "I have a better idea. Why don't you save yourself some trouble. Stay right at home here in Boston and keep the Ten Commandments."

Testaments. Civil and Church authorities have the duty to advertise rules and regulations (laws) in such a way that prudent people could be expected to know them. For example, school authorities could hardly penalize you for bringing a cell phone to school if the school rule banning them was never printed in the student handbook or announced in advance.

Jesus Christ is the fullness of the law. The moral law finds its unity in him. He shows us how to be perfect and is the one who teaches and bestows God's justice. As Romans 10:4 points out, Jesus is the end of the law; faith in him brings justification.

Let us briefly look at the various types of law.

NATURAL LAW
(CCC, 1954—1960; 1978—1979)

The Council Fathers at Vatican II taught that

> [the] highest norm of human life is the divine law—eternal, objective, and universal—whereby God orders, directs, and governs the entire universe and all the ways of the human community, by a plan conceived in wisdom and love. Man has been made by God to participate in this law, with the result that, under the gentle disposition of divine Providence, he can come to perceive ever increasingly the unchanging truth. (Declaration on Religious Freedom, 3)

Natural law is our participation in the divine law, the light of understanding that God placed in us at creation. Natural law refers to what human reason can discover about human nature and its moral duties independent of God's gift of revelation.

The natural law teaches us *what to do* and *what to avoid*. The eternal law is God's wise and loving plan for our good as humans. God so loves us that he allows us to discover his plan and gives us the freedom to choose and act according to his plan. Our moral sense of right and wrong, therefore, is a true sharing in God's wisdom and goodness.

Natural law corresponds to three basic human drives and needs:

1) preserving life;
2) developing as individuals and communities; and
3) sharing life with others.

The natural law is implanted in our hearts to discover the norms that help us achieve these goals according to God's plan. The norms expressed by the natural law can be positive or negative, general or specific, dealing with our actions (what to *do*) or governing our character (what to *be*). Classic examples of norms derived from the natural law include:

"Do good and avoid evil." (general—both positive and negative)
"Love your neighbor." (general, positive)
"Give everyone whatever is his or her due." (general, positive)
"Care for the precious life God gave you." (general, positive)
"Don't commit adultery." (specific, negative)
"Don't murder." (specific, negative)
"Don't steal." (specific, negative)

The natural law expresses human dignity and serves as the basis of all human rights. "The natural law, present in the heart of each man and established by reason, is universal in its precepts and its authority extends to all men" (*CCC*, 1956). The natural law is the foundation of both civil laws and moral rules. "The rules that express it remain substantially valid" throughout history, in many different societies and cultures (*CCC*, 1979).

In short, the natural law is universal, permanent, and unchanging throughout history. It applies to all people, in all places, for all time. For example, it always has been true and always will be true that killing innocent human beings is wrong and contrary to the true good of human beings. Rape was a violent, inhuman, ungodly act at the dawn of human history; it remains repugnant and immoral today. Flowery language, bad civil laws, Supreme Court decisions, popular opinion, and so forth cannot turn something that human reason and natural law deem evil and wrong into something good.

Because of human sin and our weakened intellects, we cannot always correctly discern the natural law. Therefore, what humans lack, God provides. God chose to reveal himself through human history and clearly spelled out his will for us. He graciously gave us the precepts of the moral law in the Old and New Testaments. The law of Moses, summarized in the Ten Commandments, contains the major precepts of the natural law. The Decalogue, however, is only the first stage of God's revelation, a preparation for the new law, the law of Christ Jesus.

What Is Civil Law?

Civil law is a *particular* application of the natural law for members of a given society. Societies apply the natural law differently according to custom and circumstances. For example, take the natural law that forbids the killing of innocent human life. A particular law regulating how we drive our cars (which can be lethal weapons) is a reasonable application of the natural law. It is for the common good and is promulgated by properly elected authorities. For their part, the British have passed a law to have all cars drive on the left side of the road. In America, the law requires drivers to drive on the right side of the road. The civil law in this case is different, but the natural law on which it is based—"Do not kill"—remains the same.

However, not all civil law is good law. Lawmakers have often passed laws that violate the dignity of humans. In the past, many societies legalized slavery. Today, some countries legislate an inferior position for women. And in the United States the law permits abortion on demand. Civil law is morally good only insofar as it conforms to God's eternal law, which we find written on our hearts and expressed in divine, revealed law. We are not required to obey evil civil laws and must do all in our power to change them.

GOOD OR BAD LAWS?

Judge whether the following are good or bad laws. Are they reasonable? Do they promote the common good? Are they pro-life? Mark with a *G* if the law is good; *B* if it bad; *?* if you are not sure.

G/B/?

____ 1. The state may not inflict the death penalty on anyone.

____ 2. No driver may use a handheld cell phone while driving the car.

____ 3. The government may not give any state aid to private (including Catholic) schools except for nonreligious textbooks.

____ 4. All passengers must be willing to submit to a personal search before boarding an airplane.

____ 5. No one may be permitted to smoke in a public building, including all restaurants.

____ 6. Any vendor selling pornography to a minor is subject to a year in prison.

____ 7. Desecration of the American flag is an exercise of free speech and not punishable as a felony or misdemeanor.

____ 8. Couples must be sterilized if they have more than one child. [Chinese law]

Discuss what makes a law good or bad? What other information for each item would you like to know?

REVIEW AND REFLECTION

1. List three general, positive norms.

2. What is St. Thomas Aquinas's definition of *law*?

3. Define *natural law*. List three precepts of the natural law.

4. What does it mean to say that the natural law is universal, permanent, and unchanging?

5. Discuss the relationship between civil law and natural law.

FOR YOUR JOURNAL

If you were a mother or father of a teenager, what three rules would you have for your teen? Explain why these rules would be good for a teen's growth.

THE OLD LAW
(CCC, 1961—1964; 1980—1982)

The old Law, also known as the Law of Moses, is the first stage of revealed law. The Ten Commandments (the Decalogue) summarize the moral prescriptions of the old Law, expressing the many truths concerning the natural law that human reason can discover on its own. The Ten Commandments prohibit what is contrary to the love of God and neighbor and prescribe what the demands of love require. The requirements of these commandments are covered in Chapters 7–10.

Christians believe that the old Law is holy, good, and spiritual. But Christians also believe that it is imperfect. The old Law does not give us the grace and strength of the Holy Spirit. According to St. Paul, the special function of the old Law is to reveal and condemn what is sinful. Therefore, it prepares both God's Chosen People and each Christian for conversion and faith in Jesus, our Lord and Savior. It is a preparation for the Gospel, for the coming of the New Covenant in Jesus Christ and his new law of love.

The Ten Commandments
(CCC, before 2052)

I. I am the Lord, your God. You shall not have strange gods before me.

II. You shall not take the name of the Lord your God in vain.

III. Remember to keep holy the Lord's day.

IV. Honor your father and your mother.

V. You shall not kill.

VI. You shall not commit adultery.

VII. You shall not steal.

VIII. You shall not bear false witness against your neighbor.

IX. You shall not covet your neighbor's wife.

X. You shall not covet your neighbor's goods.

THE NEW LAW
(CCC, 1965—1974; 1983—1986)

Recall that the highest norm of human life is divine law, which we find in both the old and new Law. According to St. Thomas Aquinas, divine law has four purposes:

1. It helps us stay on the right path on our journey to God.

2. It helps us discern what is right when there are conflicting ideas of right and wrong.

3. It speaks to our motivation.

4. It indicates what is sinful, that is, those actions and attitudes that kill or stifle our relationships with God and others.

The Gospel of Jesus Christ is the new Law, a law of love. The Gospel of Christ perfects the divine law, both the natural law and revealed law. The new Law is the work of Christ, who most perfectly reveals it in the Sermon on the Mount. The new Law is also the work and grace of the Holy Spirit. The Spirit works within our hearts by writing the law there, reforming us so that we imitate our heavenly Father more closely.

The new Law does not add new precepts for us to follow. Rather, it helps us understand the core attitudes that precede our actions. For example, it requires us to have pure intentions when we act. It requires that we pray for and forgive our enemies. And it teaches us to be sincere when we perform religious duties like fasting, praying, or giving money to the poor.

The new Law can be summarized in these two Gospel teachings:

> *"Do to others whatever you would have them do to you." (Mt 7:12)*
> *"Love one another as I love you." (Jn 15:12)*

The Sermon on the Mount and the apostolic teachings in the New Testament letters (e.g., Romans 12—15, 1 Corinthians 12—13, Ephesians 4—5, and Colossians 3—4) teach that the new Law is a *law of love*. This law empowers us to translate into deeds the gift of love the Holy Spirit gives us at baptism.

The new Law is also a *law of grace*. It gives us God's help to love obediently, through faith and the graces of the sacraments.

The new Law is also a *law of freedom*. It enables us to be the children of God we are called to be. It helps strengthen our friendship with Jesus so we can hear his voice that calls us to love. And through the Holy Spirit, it teaches us how to act lovingly toward others.

The so-called **evangelical counsels** of poverty, chastity, and obedience also flow from the new Law. These special Gospel virtues aim to remove any barrier to charity in those Christians who are striving to be closer to Christ.

CHURCH LAW *(CCC, 2041—2043; 2048)*

What civil law is to natural law, Church law is to divine law. "The precepts of the Church are set in context of a moral life bound to and nourished by the liturgical life" (*CCC*, 2041). The **precepts of the Church**, decreed by our Church leaders, are minimal obligations for Catholics to observe. They are obligations to both God and each other as members of Christ's body. The full body of officially established rules governing the Catholic Church is known as the **canon law**. It was revised in 1983.

The six precepts of the Church are listed below with a short explanation.

1. *You shall attend Mass on Sundays and holy days of obligation.* Christians worship the Lord on the day Christ rose from the dead. Christians refrain from activities that would hinder the renewal of their souls and bodies. We recognize our duty to worship our loving God who has given us everything.

2. *You shall confess your sins at least once a year.* The Sacrament of Reconciliation (Penance or Confession)

---

evangelical counsels

Vows taken to poverty, chastity, and obedience in order to live the Gospel more fully. The evangelical counsels were typically embraced by those in religious life.

precepts of the Church

The minimal obligations for members in good standing of the Catholic faith community.

canon law

The full body of officially established rules governing the Catholic Church, which was last revised in 1983.

For Catholics in the United States, there are six holy days of obligation. In some areas, celebration of Ascension Thursday is moved to the following Sunday. The holy days of obligation are:

◆ Solemnity of Mary (January 1)

◆ Ascension Thursday (40 days after Easter)

◆ Assumption of the Blessed Mother into Heaven (August 15)

◆ All Saints Day (November 1)

◆ Feast of the Immaculate Conception (December 8)

◆ Christmas (December 25)

celebrates the ongoing work of our baptism: conversion and forgiveness. This precept ensures the worthy reception of Holy Communion.

3. *You shall humbly receive your Creator in Holy Communion at least during the Easter season.* The minimum requirement for being a Catholic in good standing is to receive Holy Communion in connection with the Easter feasts, the origin and center of the Christian liturgy.

4. *You shall keep holy the holy days of obligation.* This precept "completes the Sunday observance by participation in the principal liturgical feasts which honor the mysteries of the Lord, the Virgin Mary, and the saints" (*CCC*, 2043).

5. *You shall observe the prescribed days of fasting and abstinence.* In the

Sermon on the Mount, Jesus expects his followers to perform works of self-denial, works like fasting and abstaining, almsgiving, and praying. These practices help prepare us to celebrate the liturgy. They also help discipline our wills and train our instincts so we can become more free to love God and others. Fasting and abstaining from certain foods is also a great reminder to care for the hungry in our midst.

6. *The faithful also have the duty of providing for the material needs of the Church, each according to his abilities.* As members of a community, we are responsible for each other. It takes money, energy, and effort to support the good works of the Church. Everyone is responsible for helping out.

SELF-EXAMINATION ON LIVING THE PRECEPTS OF THE CHURCH

Judge how well you are currently following the precepts of the Church. Use this scale: A=a strong point with me; B=needs some work; C=needs a lot of work.

_____ 1. Worshiping our God is a top priority. I go to Mass each Sunday.
_____ 2. I confess my sins on a regular basis.
_____ 3. I receive Holy Communion worthily and frequently.
_____ 4. I attend Mass on the holy days of obligation.
_____ 5. I engage in acts of self-denial to build up spiritual muscles.
_____ 6. I perform acts of sacrifice on behalf of others.
_____ 7. I contribute to the financial support of my local Catholic parish.
_____ 8. I give what I can to missions or other good causes sponsored by the Church.
_____ 9. I lend my talents when I can.

REVIEW AND REFLECTION

1. What is the old Law? How is it summarized?

2. What are the purposes of divine law?

3. List two New Testament quotes that summarize the Law of Christ.

4. What is the function of Church law?

5. List the precepts of the Church as found in the *Catechism of the Catholic Church*.

FOR YOUR JOURNAL

Write a paragraph reflecting on what Jesus' teaching—"Love one another as I love you"—means to *you* personally.

Catholic Life in Action:
A Civil Law May Not Always Be Moral

The legalization of abortion is an example of an immoral civil law that fails to respect the dignity of each human being. The following quotes from Pope John Paul II's important encyclical *The Gospel of Life* show why abortion is wrong and why we must resist it.[3] Study these quotes carefully.

Everyone has the right to life.

"The human being is to be respected and treated as a person from the moment of conception; and therefore from that same moment his rights as a person must be recognized, among which in the first place is the inviolable right of every innocent human being to life." (Gospel of Life, 60)[4]

Abortion is contrary to the natural law; it is always wrong.

I declare that direct abortion, that is, abortion willed as an end or as a means, always constitutes a grave moral disorder, since it is the deliberate killing of an innocent human being. This doctrine is based upon the natural law and upon the written Word of God, is transmitted by the Church's Tradition and taught by the ordinary and universal Magisterium. (*Gospel of Life,* 62)

No circumstance, no purpose, no law whatsoever can ever make licit an act which is intrinsically illicit, since it is contrary to the Law of God which is written in every human heart, knowable by reason itself, and proclaimed by the Church. (*Gospel of Life,* 62)

We must oppose an immoral law that attacks human life.

Abortion and euthanasia are thus crimes that no human law can claim to legitimize. There is no obligation in conscience to obey such laws; instead, there is a *grave and clear obligation to oppose them by conscientious objection.* From the very beginnings of the Church, the apostolic preaching reminded Christians of their duty to obey legitimately constituted public authorities (cf. Rom 13:1–7; 1 Pet 2:13–14), but at the same time it firmly warned that "we must obey God rather than men." (*Gospel of Life,* 73)

Christians may never cooperate in abortions.

Christians, like all people of good will, are called upon under grave obligation of conscience not to cooperate formally in practices which, even if permitted by civil legislation, are contrary to God's law. Indeed, from the moral standpoint, it is never licit to cooperate formally in evil. (*Gospel of Life,* 74)

You Can Save Someone's Life Today!

You *can* fight the immoral legalization of abortion. Here are some strategies on how you can make a real difference!
1. Pray daily for an end to abortion.
2. Read. A good starting point is *Abortion: Questions and Answers* by Dr. and Mrs. J.C. Willke (Hayes Publishing at 513-681-7559).
3. Wear pink and blue ribbons to show support for unborn children.

4. Wear the "precious Feet" pin.
5. Use pro-life pins, decals, envelopes, etc.
6. Attend the annual January 22 March for Life in Washington, DC.
7. Write letters to newspapers, elected officials, and other persons and institutions urging them to respect life.
8. Distribute pro-life literature wherever you can.
9. Establish a memorial stone to the unborn in a local cemetery or on Church grounds.
10. Support a local Crisis Pregnancy Center with donations of baby/maternity clothes and other items.
11. Work on the campaign of a pro-life politician.

- Many of these ideas come from the excellent Priests for Life website. Check this link to get more ideas: www.priestsforlife.org/brochures/youcan.html. Also provided on this website are some other excellent pro-life resources on the Internet.
- As a class, design a project using one or more of these ideas as a concrete way to be pro-life in a peaceful way.

Summary Points

◆ As beings with free wills, humans possess freedom, that is, the power rooted in reason and will to perform deliberate actions.

◆ Determinists deny that humans have true freedom. They claim that all events, actions, and decisions result from something independent of the will.

◆ Freedom enables humans to be *self-determining*; that is, it empowers us to select and work toward our own goals. Freedom enables us to be *self-making*, which means our choices help form our characters.

◆ *External* freedom liberates us from external factors (like tyranny) that limit or destroy the power to choose. *Internal* freedom liberates us from internal factors (like fear) that limit choice.

◆ True freedom enables us to live our lives *for* God and others. The more one does what is good, the freer one becomes.

◆ The opposite of freedom is *license*, that is, unbridled freedom to do whatever one wants without accountability.

◆ Human freedom is prone to abuse and sin.

◆ Freedom is not absolute. We are limited by our physical, psychological, intellectual, and social backgrounds. Impediments to the exercise of true freedom include ignorance, inadvertence, duress, inordinate attachments, fear, and habit.

◆ To the degree that we choose voluntarily (freely), we are responsible for our actions.

◆ The passions (emotions) connect the five senses to the mind. Passions are morally neutral. But to the degree they engage our reason and will, we can find moral good or evil in them.

◆ Principal passions include love and hate, desire and fear, joy and sadness, and anger.

◆ Norms are guidelines or laws that can help regulate human freedom. Norms result from beliefs, values, and principles.

- The fundamental norm of Christian morality is Jesus Christ.

- Law is an ordinance of reason for the common good promulgated by the proper authority.

- The moral law has its source in the Blessed Trinity. It is God's fatherly instruction, the work of God's providence, wisdom, power, and goodness.

- Natural law is our reasoned participation in God's eternal law. It expresses human dignity. It is the foundation of human rights. Natural law is universal, permanent, and unchanging throughout history.

- Civil laws are particular applications of the natural law for members of a given society.

- Human sin and a weakened intellect sometimes have misled humans in discerning the natural law. God reveals the precepts of the moral law to make up for this weakened condition.

- The law of Moses (old Law), summarized in the Ten Commandments, is the first stage of revealed law. Its special function is to reveal and then condemn sin, thus preparing people for conversion and faith in Jesus.

- The Gospel of Jesus Christ is the new Law, a law of love. It is the work of Christ who teaches it in the Sermon on the Mount. It is also the work and grace of the Holy Spirit, who writes the law of love in our hearts.

- Church law, or canon law, is the official list of laws by which the Church governs itself. The *precepts* of the Church are minimal obligations for Catholics in good standing.

PRAYER REFLECTION

Lord of My Heart[5]

> *Lord of my heart, give me vision to inspire me, that working or resting,*
> *I may always think of you.*
> *Lord of my heart, give me light to guide me, that, at home or abroad,*
> *I may always walk in your way.*
> *Lord of my heart, give me wisdom to direct me, that, thinking or acting,*
> *I may always discern right from wrong.*
> *Lord of my heart, give me courage to strengthen me, that, amongst friends or enemies,*
> *I may always proclaim your justice. . . .*
> *Heart of my own heart, whatever may befall me,*
> *rule over my thoughts and feelings, my words and actions.*
> *Amen.*

Find or create a symbol that you can carry with you to help remind you of the Lord's presence (for example, a small cross, a rosary, a slip of paper with a line from this prayer written on it, a heart drawn with the Lord's name inscribed on it). Carry this object with you and be sure to look at it often during the day to remind you of the Lord and his love for you.

NOTES

1. Story adapted from John McDowell's *New Man*, March/April 1995, p. 55, and found on Bible.org website <www.bible.org/illus.asp?topic_id=870> (10 August 2006).
2. Found at Wisdomquotes.com <www.wisdomquotes.com/cat_changegrowth.html> (7 December 2005).
3. You can find the entire text of *Gospel of Life* online at: www.vatican.va/holy_father/john_paul_ii/encyclicals/documents/hf_jp-ii_enc_25031995_evangelium-vitae_en.html.
4. The original source of this quote is: Congregation for the Doctrine of the Faith, *Instruction on Respect for Human Life in its Origin and on the Dignity of Procreation, Donum Vitae* (22 February 1987), I, No. 1: AAS 80 (1988), 79.
5. Found originally at: www.diakonia.clara.net.

CHAPTER OVERVIEW

Called to Beatitude
God made us to know, love, and serve him so that we could be eternally happy with him. We are called to live the Beatitudes; we are called to happiness.

Jesus Is Our Moral Norm
Jesus, God's only Son and our Redeemer, is the perfect example of God's love, and the perfect norm for moral living.

The Sermon on the Mount: Jesus, the New Moses
Just as Moses gave the people God's law on Mount Sinai, Jesus, the New Moses, delivered his instructions for moral living in the Sermon on the Mount.

Justification, Grace, Merit, and Holiness
Justified and cleansed of our sins through Christ's redemption and through grace, we are now empowered to live morally, as Jesus asks us to do.

Discipleship
As baptized Christians, we are followers—disciples—of Christ and share in his ministry as priest, prophet, and king.

CHAPTER FOUR

Jesus as Moral Guide

"I give you a new commandment: love one another. As I have loved you, so you also should love one another. This is how all will know that you are my disciples, if you have love for one another."

John 13:34–35

Called to Beatitude

An anonymous storyteller reports how one day Jesus took his apostles up a mountain and began to teach them as follows:

"Blessed are the poor in spirit for theirs is the kingdom of heaven.
Blessed are the meek.
Blessed are they who mourn.
Blessed are the merciful.
Blessed are they who thirst for justice.
Blessed are you when you are
*   persecuted.*
Blessed are you when you suffer.
Be glad and rejoice for your reward will be great in heaven."

Simon Peter spoke up and asked, "Do we have to write this stuff down?" Andrew queried, "Are we supposed to remember this?" James added, "Will we be tested on this?" Philip asked, "What if we don't understand it?" Bartholomew chimed in, "Is this an assignment we have to turn in?" John commented, "The other disciples didn't have to learn all this." Matthew said,

"When do we get off this mountain?" Judas questioned, "What does this have to do with real life, anyway?"

Then one of the Pharisees who had come with the apostles demanded to see Jesus' lesson plans. Another wanted to know what his course objectives were. Still another. . . .

And Jesus went away from them and wept.

Of course, most of this story never happened. However, perhaps many of us are like the apostles depicted here. We want to second guess the teaching of Jesus. We want to wiggle out of dealing with Jesus' life-giving words. But all Christians—not just priests, those in religious life, or others typically understood to be "holy" people—must heed the Beatitudes. The Beatitudes are at the very heart of Jesus' preaching, taking up the promises made to Abraham and fulfilling them by leading us to God's kingdom.

God made us to know, love, and serve him so we might attain our heavenly reward. God implanted in us a desire to be eternally happy. The very word **beatitude** means "happy." In the Beatitudes, which begin Jesus' great Sermon on the Mount (Mt 5–7), we learn the *how* of our Christian vocation. We learn what attitudes we should have and what actions we must do to live like Jesus and attain true happiness. The Beatitudes depict Christ; they reveal his love. They teach us, both as individuals and as a Church community, the goal of our very existence—to become partakers of God's own divine nature and sharers in eternal life. They lead us to God's kingdom, which results in the vision of God, adoption into the divine family, and eternal rest in God.

The happiness God calls us to, and which Jesus teaches in the Beatitudes, goes beyond human power. The beatitude is a free gift from God, above our human nature (thus "supernatural"). This tremendous grace (gift) from God enables us to enter into Christ's glory and into the joy of the Blessed Trinity's own life.

Values of Jesus: A Self-Check

Jesus is our guide and role model on how to live morally. Below are four important values of Jesus with a scriptural quote to highlight each. Evaluate how your life reflects them now by checking (√) the statements that apply to you.

1. Each individual has worth.

"Are not two sparrows sold for a small coin? Yet not one of them falls to the ground without your Father's knowledge. Even all the hairs of your head are counted. So do not be afraid; you are worth more than many sparrows." (Mt 10:29–31)

When I meet others,

	I try to see Our Lord in them.
	I see a brother or sister, a person of worth.
	I see a stranger.
	I don't notice others.

2. Doing God's will is high priority.

"But you, go and proclaim the kingdom of God." And another said, "I will follow you, Lord, but first let me say farewell to my family at home." (To him) Jesus said, "No one who sets a hand to the plow and looks to what was left behind is fit for the kingdom of God." (Lk 9:60–62)

	Helping others ranks nearly at the top of my list of personal goals.
	The pursuit of money or possessions is my top priority.
	Popularity is more important to me than anything else.

3. We should deny ourselves as we sacrifice for others.

"Whoever loves his life loses it, and whoever hates his life in this world will preserve it for eternal life. Whoever serves me must follow me, and where I am, there also will my servant be. The Father will honor whoever serves me." (Jn 12:24-26)

	I sometimes deny myself some pleasure to help develop self-discipline.
	I try to think of fulfilling the needs of others rather than always immediately taking care of my own.
	I often defer to others, believing Jesus when he says the first will be last, and the last will be first.
	I think it is important to look after myself. If I don't make sure I get what I need, who will?

4. Love everyone, even your enemies.

"But to you who hear I say, love your enemies, do good to those who hate you, bless those who curse you, pray for those who mistreat you." (Lk 6:27–28)

	I am able and willing to forgive those who hurt me.
	I usually offer my help if I can get something out of it.
	I make a special effort to help those who are tough for me to love.
	I pray for those who have hurt me.
	I love my friends and family, but if people don't like me, I don't waste my time on them.

Which of these teachings of Jesus do you find the toughest to put into action? Why?

The beatitude that God calls us to requires that we live moral lives so we can attain our true happiness. It means being "poor in spirit," that is, dependent on God for all our needs. To learn the course of true happiness also requires that we purify our hearts, that we root out bad habits that hold us back from loving God above everything and loving our neighbor as ourselves. We draw from the Ten Commandments, Jesus' Sermon on the Mount, and various apostolic teachings. Our tutors on how to live the Christian life in today's world are the Magisterium, our Christ-appointed teachers who share and apply God's teaching for us. And our teacher *par excellence* for learning morality and the way to true happiness is Jesus himself. He is the "way, the truth, and the life" (Jn 14:6).

This chapter will focus on Jesus' role as our moral guide. We will be studying his specific teachings concerning moral living, especially as they appear in the Sermon on the Mount. We will also review some important concepts taught by the *Catechism of the Catholic Church*. Along the way, you will have a chance to examine your own personal values in light of the challenge of Jesus' ethical teachings.

Jesus Is Our Moral Norm

Jesus is the perfect norm for upright living, the fullest expression of God's self-emptying love. Saint Paul teaches, "Put on the Lord Jesus Christ" (Rom 13:14). We live morally when Christ's life is incorporated into ours.

We look to Jesus as our moral norm because he is God incarnate and he has won for us eternal salvation. Because of Jesus, we are able to be called children of God and we are adopted members of God's own family. More explanation of Jesus' titles and mission follows.

GOD INCARNATE

Jesus was a historical person who walked the earth. But Christians also believe in Christ's divinity, that he is the Son of God, the Word-of-God-made-flesh, who dwelt among us. As God's own Son, showing forth God's love with a human face, Jesus redeemed, sanctified, and justified humankind. His passion, death, resurrection, and glorification, to which we are united in baptism, has won for us eternal life and made us partakers of God's own nature.

Yet, it is important to keep in mind that as a historical person Jesus was truly *man*, a human being "born of a woman" (Gal 4:4). He was like us in every respect, even being tempted as we are, yet he never sinned (see Heb 2:17, 4:15). As a human, Jesus was perfectly in tune with his Abba, God the Father, and he used his freedom most responsibly.

Jesus lived a humble life. He showed compassion, for example, through his healing ministry and his forgiveness of sinners, even his enemies on the cross. He was outspoken in proclaiming the truth, an outspokenness that agitated his enemies and led eventually to his death. He was accepting of all people: the rich, the poor, those on the margins of society. He was prayerful, always staying close to his Father so he would remain steadfast in his mission. He was patient with his followers, one of whom betrayed him while most of the others abandoned him in his hour of need. He treated women equally, including them among his followers, and teaching men to treat them with respect and dignity. He was sensitive to children, to the lonely, to the hurting, to the rejects of society, and often spoke of them as examples of those who are most open to God's goodness. He was a perfect teacher, one whose deeds backed up his words, and one whose message reveals God's will for us. Jesus was many things. As the Gospel of John concludes,

> There are also many other things that Jesus did, but if these were to be described individually, I do not think the whole world would contain the books that would be written. (Jn 21:25)

One Solitary Life

Here is a young man who was born in an obscure village, the child of a peasant woman. He grew up in another village. He worked in a carpenter shop until he was thirty, and then for three years he was an itinerant preacher. He never wrote a book. He never held an office. He never owned a home. He never had a family. He never went to college. . . . He never did one of the things that usually accompany greatness. He had no credentials but himself.

While he was still a young man, the tide of public opinion turned against him. His friends ran away. He was turned over to his enemies. . . . He was nailed to a cross between two thieves. While he was dying, his executioners gambled for the only piece of property he had on earth, and that was his coat. When he was dead, he was laid in a borrowed grave through the pity of a friend.

Twenty centuries wide have come and gone, and today he is the central figure of the human race, and the leader of the column of progress.

I am far within the mark when I say that all the armies that ever marched, and all the navies that ever sailed, and all the parliaments that ever sat, and all the kings that ever reigned, put together, have not affected the life of man upon this earth as has that One Solitary Life.

—Attributed to James Allen Francis (1864–1928)

Write your own version of who Jesus is. Adapt the style of James Allen Francis, the author of "One Solitary Life."

Kingdom of God (or reign of God)

God's peace, justice, and love that was proclaimed by Jesus and inaugurated in his life, death, and resurrection. It refers to the process of God reconciling and renewing all things through his Son, to the fact of his will being done on earth as it is in heaven. The process has begun with Jesus and will be perfectly completed at the end of time.

Jesus' Teaching

Mark's Gospel summarizes the central focus of Jesus' teaching:

"This is the time of fulfillment. The kingdom of God is at hand. Repent, and believe in the gospel." (Mk 1:15)

The **Kingdom of God** refers to God's love, a reign of peace and justice breaking into our world. The Kingdom is God's rule over us, God's vision for the human race, a plan that God's word and the Holy Spirit are bringing about right now. This vision of peace and love and justice, of following God's will for humanity, is fully present in Jesus who has inaugurated it among us. Yet the Kingdom is not fully accomplished. As the Lord's disciples, it is our task to help further God's loving plan for

For Your Journal

Transcribe into your journal several Gospel passages that help capture who Jesus is for you. Explain how these passages are particularly meaningful for you. Note any similarities or differences among the passages you selected.

Review and Reflection

1. For what purpose did God create us?

2. What is the connection between Jesus' Beatitudes and our happiness?

3. Why is Jesus the perfect norm for moral living?

4. Give several examples of how Jesus lived an exemplary life.

metanoia

Greek term for repentance, a turning away from sin with the intention of living a Christian life.

humanity by cooperating with Jesus in his work. For this to happen, we must repent.

Repentance means we must reform our hearts, minds, and wills. We must avoid sin. Jesus calls for repentance (**metanoia** in the Greek) for his Father's vision to take root in our hearts. We must give up whatever is enslaving us, that is, whatever captures our loyalties and leads us away from God. We must accept God's gift of conversion, and the graces of the Holy Spirit, because these will detach us from sin and enable us to look at the world through God's eyes.

Our willingness to repent is tied to our faith in Christ. Faith is an acceptance of God's total, unconditional love for each of us. Faith means saying "yes" to God's forgiveness. Faith is also our positive response to Jesus and to his gospel. Faith is the first step in accepting our need to convert and repent of sin. People of faith accept Jesus into their lives, allow Jesus to live in them by the power of the Holy Spirit, and make a serious effort to translate Jesus' teachings about how to live into concrete action.

Jesus' essential message for living the good and the moral life is love:

> *"I give you a new commandment: love one another. As I have loved you, so you should also love one another." (Jn 13:34)*

How does Jesus love? Jesus loves with a self-giving, self-emptying love, a love that serves. Jesus' command to love centers on the Great Commandment:

> *"You shall love the Lord, your God, with all your heart, with all your being, with all your strength, and with all your mind, and your neighbor as yourself." (Lk 10:27)*

APPLYING THE PARABLE OF THE GOOD SAMARITAN

Read Luke 10:29–37, the parable of the Good Samaritan.
- With whose actions and motives do you most closely identify—the priest? the Levite? the Samaritan? Why?
- Could you think of some circumstances that would serve as a good reason for the priest or Levite not to help?
- Rewrite this parable in a modern-day idiom.

Tell how you should respond to these situations:
- You notice a classmate eating alone at lunch almost every day.
- A casual friend shoplifts an item worth $30 while you are both walking through a department store at the local mall.
- A classmate mimics a friend with a speech disability.
- You read in the newspaper that a family living in your town lost all its possessions in a house fire. Unfortunately, they have no insurance.
- Your school cafeteria is usually a mess because of a litter problem.
- You have paid for your seat on a city bus, but an old woman boards the bus and has no seat since they are all taken. She looks directly at you.
- Your close friend has a drinking problem.
- Your parish youth minister makes a passionate appeal to the youth group to help raise money for a local drop-in center for runaway kids.

Would it be wrong not to do something to get involved in some of these situations? Explain why or why not.

Love for Jesus is not a warm, fuzzy feeling. Love is difficult sometimes and includes Jesus' charge to love our enemies (see parable of the Good Samaritan, Lk 10:29–37). And in the parable of the last judgment (Mt 25:31–46), Jesus teaches that God will judge us based on the corporal works of mercy: feeding the hungry, giving drink to the thirsty, welcoming the stranger, clothing the naked, and visiting the sick and imprisoned (Mt 25:35–36). These actions involve love, too.

Loving as Jesus loves requires remaining close to him. We are not necessarily called to slavishly imitate him by living the life of a wandering preacher, giving away all our possessions, gathering disciples, and surrendering our lives via crucifixion. We are, however, called to be conformed to him, allowing him to live in us and teach us by power of the Holy Spirit.

In the Eucharist, Jesus has given us a way to grow in holiness and stay connected to him. The Eucharist—the sacrament of love—celebrates Jesus' Paschal mystery (his passion, death, resurrection, and glorification). Our celebration of it with other Catholic believers enables us to enter into the mystery it represents for us.

In the Liturgy of the Word, we hear Christ's Gospel proclaimed anew. It challenges us to take the good news to heart and live it in the present on our journey to the Triune God.

In the Liturgy of the Eucharist, the Holy Spirit prays through us as we thank and praise God the Father for all he has accomplished for us in Christ Jesus. We unite ourselves to Jesus, offer our lives to him, and re-enact and recall his sacrifice of love. In Holy Communion, our risen Lord comes to us under the forms of bread and wine. Jesus gives himself to us and dwells in us, as unworthy as we are. The divine life we received in Baptism is nurtured and strengthened in the Eucharist. Our Lord comes to us and unites us as children of his Father and brings us in union with himself as members of his body, the Church. Most remarkably, our union with the Lord in Holy Communion enables Christ to act in us, to affect our thinking and our behavior, and to help transform our lives into acts of love.

At the end of the Mass we are sent—fortified with the gifts of the Spirit and Christ's own life in us—in peace "to love and serve the Lord."

> *"Union with Christ [in the Eucharist] is also* union with all those to whom he gives himself. I cannot possess Christ just for myself; I can belong to him only in union with all those who have become, or who will become, his own. Communion draws me out of myself towards him and thus also towards unity with all Christians. We become 'one body,' completely joined in a single existence. Love of God and love of neighbor are now truly united: God incarnate draws us all to himself."
>
> —POPE BENEDICT XVI, *DEUS CARITAS EST* (*GOD IS LOVE*), NO. 14

DO WHAT JESUS DID

In everything ask yourself only what the Master would have done, and do that.
—BLESSED CHARLES DE FOUCAULD

Anticipate how Jesus would solve the following problems. Check the Gospel passage given to see what he actually did for each situation.

- What to feel and do when confronted with an obvious injustice. (See Mk 3:3–5)
- What to do with a needy person. (See Mt 10:42)
- What to do after a busy day working for others. (See Mt 14:22–23)
- What to do when someone is being harshly criticized for a wrongdoing. (See Jn 8:3, 6–7, 9–11)
- What to do when someone repeatedly wrongs you. (See Mt 18:21–22)

Create five scenarios that you confront in your daily life that pose a moral issue. Search the Gospels to find out how Jesus might have responded. Put into practice Jesus' teaching for one of the scenarios you will most likely experience in the coming week.

REVIEW AND REFLECTION

1. What is the core message proclaimed by the historical Jesus?

2. To what does the term *Kingdom of God* refer?

3. What is the meaning of *metanoia*? What is its connection to Jesus' essential message?

4. How are we to love? List five attributes of Christian love.

5. How can the Eucharist help Catholics to love?

FOR YOUR JOURNAL

Read what St. Paul says about love in 1 Corinthians 13:3–13. Write about one quality of love that you seem to practice well. Mention several examples of how you put this quality into practice. Then, note one quality of love you need to work on. Write a resolution to practice that quality in regards to a specific person during the coming week.

The Sermon on the Mount: Jesus, the New Moses

When he saw the crowds, he went up the mountain, and after he had sat down, his disciples came to him. He began to teach them, saying.... (Mt 5:1–2)

The opening passage begins Jesus' Sermon on the Mount, a proclamation of the requirements for Christian discipleship recorded in Matthew 5–7. The evangelist Matthew, writing for a Jewish-Christian audience, compares Jesus, the new lawgiver, to Moses. Just as Moses handed down God's law on Mount Sinai, so the New Moses, Jesus, delivers his instructions from a mountain. The Law Jesus teaches to his disciples brings the old Law to its fullness and completion.

Because Jesus is with us, and God's Kingdom has taken root, we are in a new age. The values the world regards highly are being toppled. The secret to happiness for Jesus' followers is to live the Beatitudes, imitate and trust an incredibly loving and compassionate Abba-Father, and translate the Lord's law of love into concrete actions. Faith without works is not enough. Christian morality translates beliefs into actions for God and others:

"Not everyone who says to me, 'Lord, Lord,' will enter the kingdom of heaven, but only the one who does the will of my Father in heaven." (Mt 7:21)

We begin our study of the Sermon on the Mount with the Beatitudes, that is, those "attitudes" of being Christian that lead to happiness for the followers of Christ.

THE BEATITUDES (MT 5:3—12)

God implanted in us a desire for happiness, both in this life and in the next. In truth, the things of this world—money, athletic or scholarly achievement, fame, possessions—can never satisfy the hungry heart we all possess. Only through God's goodness and love can our thirst for happiness be quenched.

Jesus teaches us what we have to do *right now* to develop the kind of attitudes that lead to happiness, even in this life. The Beatitudes, the core lesson of Jesus' Sermon on the Mount, are the attitudes and actions Jesus teaches for our happiness.

Blessed are the poor in spirit, for theirs is the kingdom of heaven (v. 3)

Spiritual poverty recognizes that all we have and all we are is a total gift from God. We are totally dependent on God who is in charge of the universe and of our lives. We should not hoard what we have been given as gifts. Rather, we should use our talents, intelligence, possessions, and the like to help others.

Blessed are they who mourn, for they will be comforted (v. 4)

In their sorrow, those who mourn are with God. Those who mourn are also clearly able to recognize those who are much worse off—the poor, the abused, the hungry, the discriminated against, the victims of crime and prejudice. Their sorrow can move them to lend a helping hand to those who suffer and be Jesus' instrument of comfort to them.

Blessed are the meek, for they will inherit the land (v. 5)

"Meek" describes people who are *not* self-centered or controlling. In humility, they treat others with utmost respect, understanding, and compassion. They do not gripe when hurting or when they are ridiculed for their beliefs. Rather, they identify with the Lord who suffered wrongs patiently and with forgiveness in his heart.

Blessed are they who hunger and thirst for righteousness, for they will be satisfied (v. 6)

A Christian is not satisfied with mediocrity. This beatitude refers to a Christian's desire for high ideals and goals. The highest plateau of all is to desire above all else to put God's righteous will into action and then work unceasingly with his help to grow in holiness, justice, and truth. Part of striving to do God's will is to realize that God teaches that we prove our love for him by taking care of each other, as Blessed Mother Teresa of Calcutta put it, "by doing something beautiful for God."

Blessed are the merciful, for they will be shown mercy (v.7)

God has shown us profound compassion by loving us into existence, by forgiving our sins, and by giving us his Son so that we might live. As disciples of Jesus we

◆ Which is the toughest beatitude for you to put into action? Why?

◆ Discuss ways you have suffered for your Christian beliefs.

◆ Read Luke 6:20–23. Note two differences in Luke's version compared to Matthew's version of the Sermon on the Mount.

must forgive others, even our enemies, without strings attached. We must stop holding grudges. We must stop harping on the faults of those who have hurt us. We must genuinely care for others by showing true compassion, as Jesus did when he died on the cross for everyone. If we show mercy, God will be sure to be merciful to us as well.

Blessed are the clean of heart, for they will see God (v. 8)

Those who are clean of heart are single-hearted, undivided in their loyalties, without fakery or pretense. They put on the mind and heart of God, looking on others with the eyes of Jesus, accepting them as brothers and sisters, persons of incomparable inner beauty and worth. The clean of heart know what is really important—closeness to the Lord who alone can satisfy their inner longings for love and understanding.

Blessed are the peacemakers, for they will be called children of God (v. 9)

Since we are all God's children, it is wrong to fight, quarrel, and cause dissension. This only tears down the human family. Rather, we are called to work to settle disputes, to root out violence, to forgive and show compassion. We are to be those who unite, not those who divide; those who cooperate, not those who compete; those who build bridges, not those who erect walls. The risen Lord says, "Peace be with you" (Jn 20:19). His followers carry the same message.

Blessed are they who are persecuted for the sake of righteousness, for theirs is the kingdom of heaven (v. 10)

The Quaker founder of Pennsylvania, William Penn, once said, "No cross, no crown." To stand up for what is right, especially in the face of mockery, rejection, and verbal and even physical abuse, is to stand with Jesus Christ and help him carry his cross. Jesus never promised us a rose garden; he did promise us eternal happiness united to the Blessed Trinity. At times we might have to pay the price of our convictions, even to the point of paying with our lives. But for Christians, the cross is not a sign of defeat. It is the ultimate sign of victory, of life with our Lord and Savior Jesus. To be willing to stand with him guarantees that he will never abandon us.

> "Blessed are you when they insult you and persecute you and utter every kind of evil against you (falsely) because of me. Rejoice and be glad, for your reward will be great in heaven. Thus they persecuted the prophets who were before you." (Mt 5:11–12)

Salt and Light

Read Matthew 5:13–16. Here Jesus tells us that those who adopt his attitudes will be salt of the earth and light of the world. These two rich images stress that living by Jesus' moral code makes us a sign of God's active presence in the world.

Salt has two ancient functions: it flavors food, and it preserves it. Similarly, Christians who live the Beatitudes (through their forgiveness, love, compassion, etc.) help Jesus in his work of salvation. They also bring a certain flavoring to ordinary life—spicing it up, pointing the way to God's Kingdom, showing that there is more to human happiness than the ordinary fare that is offered to us.

In your journal, note a time when you brought the light of Christ to someone.

OLD LAW	NEW LAW
You shall not kill; and whoever kills will be liable to judgment.	Whoever is angry with his brother will be liable to judgment.
You shall not commit adultery.	Everyone who looks at a woman with lust has already committed adultery with her in his heart.
Whoever divorces his wife must give her a bill of divorce.	Whoever divorces his wife (unless his marriage is unlawful) causes her to commit adultery, and whoever marries a divorced woman commits adultery.
Do not take a false oath, but make good on all that you vow.	Do not swear at all. . . . Let your "Yes" mean "Yes," and your "No" mean "No."
"An eye for an eye and a tooth for a tooth."	Offer no resistance to one who is evil. When someone strikes you on your right cheek, turn the other one to him as well.
You shall love your neighbor and hate your enemies.	Love your enemies, and pray for those who persecute you.

JESUS IS THE FULFILLMENT OF THE LAW (MT 5:17–48)

Writing for a Jewish-Christian audience, the author of Matthew's Gospel compares Jesus to Moses, the one to whom God gave the Ten Commandments. Jesus proclaims that he has "come not to abolish but to fulfill" the Mosaic Law.

Jesus fulfills the Mosaic Law by emphasizing its spirit and intent rather than stressing a strict interpretation of the "letter" of the Law. Jesus perfects the Old Testament Law by intensifying it and by setting a higher standard—the law of love. We discover how Jesus does this by his transformation of six Mosaic laws recorded in Matthew 5:20–48. These are known as the "six antitheses" of Jesus.

Note how Jesus is teaching here that *external* observance of the Law is not enough. For example, he assumes we will not murder. However, Jesus wishes that his followers will not even be angry with one another because anger and resentment often fester until they explode in violence. If we have an enemy, we must make things right with him or her before worshiping. His message is that we cannot claim to love God unless we love the neighbor (and enemy) right before us.

Similarly, Jesus upholds the sixth commandment against adultery. But he also condemns *lust*, the inordinate sexual desire that leads to sinful misuse of one's sexuality. Jesus restores God's original intent that marriage should be a life-long covenant relationship between a man and a woman. In this way, Jesus emphasizes the virtue of fidelity in marriage. Furthermore, he is telling men to treat women as equals, persons to be respected and cherished, not property to be cast aside at the mere whim of husbands. Divorce and remarriage are contrary to God's plan.

Jesus also teaches that his disciples should steer clear of idle oaths and swearing on this or that to back up their word. By definition, Christians should be persons of integrity.

Finally, Jesus perfects the old Law by teaching his law of love which extends to loving even one's enemy. The old Law endorsed a code of strict justice, "an eye for an eye, a tooth for a tooth." This may seem barbaric to us today, but at the time of the Mosaic code, it was a major moral advance over the *vendetta*, the vengeful law of the jungle that was common in the ancient world. Jesus expects more of his followers than a strict tit-for-tat. We have heard and experienced his good news. We have tasted God's forgiveness. We know about

God's incredible love for everyone. Therefore, we, Jesus' disciples, should forgive even our enemies in order to break the chain of violence and root out vengeance. Our neighbor is not just a fellow citizen or co-religionist. Our neighbor is by definition a brother and sister to us in the Lord.

Jesus calls us to high standards of behavior, ones motivated by love. In fact, Jesus calls us to "be perfect, just as [our] heavenly Father is perfect" (Mt 5:48). He requires us not to set any boundaries to our love, just as our heavenly Father sets no limits to his love. For centuries, Christians have been struggling to take Jesus' message to heart and translate it into action.

From a human point of view, we might conclude that Jesus is making impossible demands on us. Yet, Jesus does not demand more of us than we can achieve with his help and that of the graces which the Holy Spirit showers on us. By cooperating with these graces, by trying our very best to live Jesus' standards of morality, we will indeed become light for the world and salt of the earth. We will help attract others to the Good News of the Gospel, to God's Kingdom.

JESUS ON GOOD WORKS, PRAYER, AND TRUST (MATTHEW 6)

Jesus challenged his followers to a higher level of moral response than that given by some so-called religious hypocrites of his day. Jesus assumes that his followers will perform certain religious works, namely, almsgiving (sharing wealth with the poor), praying, and fasting (limiting food intake to recognize our dependence on God and to identify with the hungry in our midst). But his disciples must do so humbly and with the purest of motives, not for show or for praise from others. For example, when we give to the poor, we should do it secretly and without

fanfare. When we pray, we should do it sincerely and without heaping up a lot of empty, useless words. (Jesus teaches the perfect prayer—the Lord's Prayer—as the prayer his followers should address to our Father. See accompanying feature, pages 110–111.) When we fast we should not act if we are in deep pain.

Note that in all his instructions Jesus gets at our motivation. We are to ask ourselves: "Why am I doing these things?" There is little merit if we are simply showing off or are trying to win earthly acclaim. In contrast, Christians should practice their religious duties out of a motivation of love for God and neighbor, trusting that

The school of Christ is the school of charity. In the last day, when the general examination takes place, there will be no question at all on the text of Aristotle, the aphorisms of Hippocrates, or the paragraphs of Justinian. Charity will be the whole syllabus.

—ST. ROBERT BELLARMINE

our heavenly Father will one day give us our just reward.

The double themes of pure motivation and trusting in God's goodness are stressed elsewhere in Matthew 6. For example, Jesus tells us not to put our trust in earthly treasures. They do not last and they distract us from our real goal in life: union with our loving God. Jesus wants us to examine ourselves:

"For where your treasure is, there also will be your heart." (Mt 6:21)
"No one can serve two masters. He will either hate one and love the other, or be devoted to one and despise the other. You cannot serve God and mammon." (Mt 6:24)

Positively, Jesus teaches us a lesson on trust in God (Mt 6:25–34). To worry is to waste energy. We should seek first God's Kingdom and his holiness, and all else will be given to us. Our loving Abba will take care of us.

Worrying results in anxiety and preoccupation with self and often leads to physical and psychological illness. Jesus has the best advice of all: Put your life in the hands of our loving God. Live each day as best you can, try your best to love, give your life to serving others, and God will watch out for you and take care of what you really need to be happy.

Trusting in God

Jesus tells us not to worry. Yet, many of us worry a good deal of the time. How about you? How many of the following do you worry about at least once a week?

your looks / do people like you? / something bad you did / money or lack thereof / your grades / getting into a good college / getting a date / your relationship with your parents / your relationship with God / safety issues / your job / world issues, like peace and poverty / your health

- How can Jesus' advice to "not worry, trust God" help you to stop worrying about one of the situations described in the feature?
- How do you define worry? Has it ever done you any good? Explain.

THE GOLDEN RULE AND OTHER TRUTHS TO LIVE BY (MATTHEW 7)

Some time ago, a missionary was coming home from Europe on an ocean liner. Because of overbooking, when he got on board he was told that he would have to share his room with another passenger. He examined the room and then went to the ship's information desk and requested that they lock up his wallet and a valuable religious object into the ship's safe. He said, "I don't ordinarily do this type of thing, but I've been to my cabin, and I don't like the looks of my roommate."

The desk clerk took the valuables and replied, "I'll be happy to take care of these. Your roommate has already been here, and he has left his valuables for the same reason."

The point of the story is this: We all make judgments. Sometimes our judgments are wrong. Jesus said: "Stop judging, that you may not be judged" (Mt 7:1). Jesus does not favor those who believe they are morally superior to others. He teaches that just as God will forgive us as we forgive others, so he will judge us as we judge others. It is a sign of pride and arrogance to think that we are morally superior to others. Jesus teaches the Golden Rule, a summation of the old Law and the teachings of the prophets: "Do to others whatever you would have them do to you. This is the law and the prophets" (Mt 7:12).

The Sermon on the Mount concludes with other important rules that Jesus wants us to heed. They are:

Enter through the narrow gate. In other words, do not live a risky or foolish life, pushing the law to its limits. Do not be enticed by the false voices beckoning you to go down the wrong path: the lure of power, prestige, possessions, pleasure, or putting self before others. Rather, love God above all. Love your neighbor. Love yourself. Follow Christ's will for you and you will not stray far from the path of righteousness.

Pray with trust in your heart. God loves us so much that he will give us what is good for us. But we have to ask him.

Build your life on Christ's words. Simply saying you believe in Jesus is not enough. You must listen to Jesus' words. You must learn from them. And then you must translate his words into action.

Responding to Challenges

Question: We hear so much today about tolerating differences. Doesn't it seem anti-Christian to judge anyone in a bad way? After all, didn't Jesus tell us not to judge anyone?

Answer: When Jesus says, "Stop judging, that you may not be judged" (Mt 7:1), is Jesus really saying to look the other way when we see sin and destructive behavior? This can hardly be the case. Even within the Sermon on the Mount, we see Jesus condemning such behavior as lust, hateful anger, selfishness, excessive worry, insincerity, and so forth. Later in Matthew's Gospel (Chapter 23), Jesus rather strongly condemns the hypocritical behavior of certain religious leaders. In fact, his criticism of their hypocrisy was one of the factors that led to their plotting his death.

There is an old saying about "hating the sin but loving the sinner." This is precisely what Jesus did when he forgave the woman caught in adultery (Jn 8:1–11). The people wanted to put her to death, but Jesus told her accusers that if someone was without sin, then he should throw the first stone. After Jesus wrote on the ground with his finger—perhaps pointing out the sins of the members of the crowd—no one stepped forward to kill the woman. They all recognized that they, too, were sinners. (Recall that in the Sermon on the Mount, Jesus doesn't want us to go looking for the splinter in someone else's eye and ignore the wooden beam in our own.) Jesus forgave the woman, but he also told her, "Go, (and) from now on do not sin any more" (Jn 8:11).

Jesus' teaching means that we can never judge the *motivation* of other people. Only God can look into the human heart. Only God knows the state of our souls, our true intentions. Why did the driver of the car that passed you cut in front of you? Is it because he is a selfish road hog who cares little for other people? Or was he distracted because he was rushing to the hospital to visit his dying mother? Or some other reason that you'll never know? But, can you judge the *behavior* of someone cutting you off as dangerous and against the law? Yes. Can you say that the person who did it is evil at his core and is worth condemnation in the afterlife? No, because you don't know his heart. Only God does.

Tolerating people by not judging their inner motivations does not mean we accept their values or lack of values. Sin exists. We must name it when we see it. Pedophilia is a moral outrage. It must be severely condemned, though we admit we don't know why the person committing the crime did it. Is he sick? Was he abused as a child? Is he a malicious deviant? We simply don't know. Only God does. But we do have every right to condemn and stop his deviant behavior.

REVIEW AND REFLECTION

1. Write the Beatitudes. Explain the meaning of any two of them.

2. "Jesus emphasizes the spirit, versus the letter of the law." Give several examples from the Sermon on the Mount to show the truth of this statement.

3. According to Matthew 6, what three religious practices does Jesus require of his followers? How should we perform them?

4. Why should Christians not be consumed by worry?

5. What is the Golden Rule? Give several examples of it in practice.

FOR YOUR JOURNAL
"Worrying is a lot like rocking in a rocking chair. It gives you something to do but you don't get anywhere." Write about a time when your worries turned out to be meaningless and a waste of your time and energy.

THE SERMON ON THE MOUNT APPLIED TO CASE STUDIES

Is Jesus' teaching relevant in today's world? In light of his law of love, decide what should be done in the following case studies. Write your ideas for handling each situation.

Terrorism and Immigration

Since the September 11, 2001, terrorist attack against America, the United States' government has declared a war against global terrorism. Many voices are clamoring that America needs to firm up its homeland defenses, including a more rigorous effort to secure the borders. One proposal is to erect a wall along the border between Mexico and the United States to stem illegal immigration and keep out potential foreign terrorists.

- Would building a wall at the border be opposed in any way to Catholic social teaching? Explain.
- Can a government—in time of war—be held to the standard of the Golden Rule? Why or why not?

Tailgater

A driver has been tailgating you in heavy traffic for the past three miles. You find his behavior extremely annoying, threatening, and dangerous. To say the least, you are quite agitated.

- How would you respond?

Abuse Victim

There is a classmate whom you know fairly well. Based on something she said after a health-class video, you have good reason to suspect that she may be subjected to sexual abuse by her stepfather.

- What course of action, if any, would you take?

A Wronged Friend

Recently, a friend went to a football game played against a rival school. Your friend has a disability that causes him to limp. At the concession stand during half time, some kids from the other school saw your friend and started to make fun of him. Some of the comments were cruel. One thing led to another until the security guards eventually had to disperse the gathering crowd.

The trouble had just begun, though. The kids from the rival school—there were four of them—followed your friend into the parking lot after the game. They continued to taunt him, and eventually tripped him. Unfortunately, your friend broke his ankle.

You and several of your friends are red-hot with "righteous" anger. You want to right this wrong.

- What do you think should be done and why?

Praying the Lord's Prayer (CCC, 2759–2865)

The Lord's Prayer is the Christian prayer. The Church Father Tertullian called it "the summary of the whole Gospel." Let's briefly analyze what we are praying for in the Lord's Prayer:

OUR FATHER

Jesus invites us to call God Abba (Daddy), to address the almighty God intimately, securely, and with childlike trust. Jesus teaches us that God is good, gracious, and absolutely loving. We learn that Jesus' Father is also our Father who has adopted us. We should imitate our Father and Jesus, our brother. And like little children, we should humbly trust our Abba to care for our needs.

In addition, God is our Father. We are God's people. We belong to him. Calling God our Father affirms that we are brothers and sisters to one another; every person is intimately related to us. Therefore, we must try to understand, love, and respond to everyone who comes into our lives.

WHO ART IN HEAVEN

"In heaven" refers not to a place but to God's way of being, God's majesty. Through Jesus, God lives in the hearts of the just. We profess that we are God's people who are in union with Christ in heaven. And we await the day when our heavenly reward will be fully ours.

HALLOWED BE THY NAME

When we "hallow" God's name, we enter into God's plan by praying that everyone on earth will regard God as holy (as he is in heaven). God alone is the source of all holiness, goodness, and love. We make God's name holy when we accept God's love and act on it by taking on the identity of our Savior, Jesus Christ. Living a moral life, living up to our Christian name, attracts others to come to know and praise God because they can see God's image in us.

THY KINGDOM COME; THY WILL BE DONE ON EARTH AS IT IS IN HEAVEN

Jesus' coming has brought into our world God's kingship (kingdom or reign), which is firmly established in heaven. This Kingdom is God's righteousness, peace, and joy in the Holy Spirit. God's justice, truth, community, and mutual love rules in heaven. Jesus' ministry inaugurated this reign on earth through his preaching the Gospel to the poor, bringing liberty to captives and wholeness to the broken, and healing and the gift of salvation to everyone.

God's Kingdom will be fully established only at the end of time, but we are to live, experience, and work for it right now. When we pray "thy kingdom come," we petition primarily for Christ's return, the final coming of God's Kingdom. Then there will be full righteousness, peace, and joy. But right now we are to imitate Jesus' obedience, suffering, and service. We must join him in his work by feeding the hungry, giving drink to the thirsty, welcoming the stranger, clothing the naked, visiting the sick and the imprisoned, and responding in a special way to "the least of these" in our midst.

GIVE US THIS DAY OUR DAILY BREAD

When we ask for bread, we are requesting what bread represents—life. Life in this sense refers to physical life (food, shelter, clothing); psychological life (friendship, love, companionship); and spiritual life (the Eucharistic Jesus, the Word of God accepted in faith, and the body of Christ received in Holy Communion).

When we pray for "our" bread, we ask for our needs and the needs of all people. The Lord's Prayer challenges us to share with others, especially the less fortunate. The parable of the last judgment (Mt 25:31–46) and the parable of Lazarus and the rich man (Lk 16:19–31) teach us that God's children must share their material goods with the poor. They also teach that God will punish those who are selfish in this life.

When we pray for our daily bread, we also pray for the fullness of God's material and spiritual blessings that will be ours in heaven.

AND FORGIVE US OUR TRESPASSES AS WE FORGIVE THOSE WHO TRESPASS AGAINST US

It is difficult both to forgive and to ask for forgiveness. When we ask God for forgiveness, we honestly admit that we are sinners who need God's saving love, the strength of the Holy Spirit to repent of our self-centeredness, and the humility to accept Jesus' help on our journey to the Father.

But we must also forgive others. We must become other Christs. Jesus connects God's forgiveness of us to our forgiveness of others, even our enemies. When we forgive, we give love and understanding and thus encourage others to respond to us in love.

AND LEAD US NOT INTO TEMPTATION

This petition is asking God to spare us the path that leads to sin. It asks God to let us persevere to the end of our days, when we struggle with our final test: death.

To follow Jesus means to pick up a cross, to endure some suffering in doing right. In this petition we pray that God will strengthen us to overcome any difficulties that might lead us away from a Christian life of service. This petition asks for the gifts of the Holy Spirit that help us fight the temptations that befall all of us: fortitude, watchfulness, perseverance, and a discerning heart that can distinguish between trials that strengthen us spiritually and temptations that lead to sin and death.

BUT DELIVER US FROM EVIL. AMEN.

One with the communion of saints, we pray to God to manifest the victory Christ has already won over this world's ruler, Satan, and his false deceptions opposed to God's plan of salvation. We ask the Father to free us from Satan's snares and the seductions of a sensuous, materialistic, violent, and godless society. We pray that God may spare us from the evil of accidents, illness, and natural disasters. We pray that God will strengthen us to confront the evil for which we too share some blame—using others, injustice, prejudice. And we pray that no situation arises that might tempt us to deny our loving Creator. This would be the worst evil of all. Finally, we pray with the Holy Spirit and all God's people for the second coming of the Lord, which will free all humanity forever from the snares of the Evil One.

Amen means "so be it." When we say it with conviction, we make the Lord's Prayer our prayer, too.

REVIEW AND REFLECTION

1. What is the significance of Jesus' invitation to us to call God "Our Father"?

2. Discuss the meaning of any three petitions of the Lord's Prayer.

FOR YOUR JOURNAL

Jesus teaches us to ask our Father for our daily bread. List three needs you have in each of these areas: physical, psychological, and spiritual. Write a prayer about these needs.

justification

The Holy Spirit's grace that cleanses us from our sins through faith in Jesus Christ and baptism. Justification makes us right with God.

grace

A free and unearned favor from God, infused into our souls at Baptism, that adopts us into God's family and helps us to live as his children.

Justification, Grace, Merit, and Holiness

(CCC, 1987—2029)

Jesus asks much of his followers. But he has given us the grace that "justifies" us before God and that empowers us to live morally as he requires of us. The topics of justification, grace, merit, and holiness as reflected in the *Catechism of the Catholic Church* are the subjects of this section.

JUSTIFICATION

The term **justification** refers to the gift of the Holy Spirit's grace that cleanses us from our sins through conversion, faith in Jesus Christ, and Baptism. Because God's grace justifies us, God's own righteousness is given to us, and we are united to the Lord's saving passion. By the power of the Holy Spirit, we take part in the Lord's resurrection by being born into a new life as members of the Church, the body of Christ. In the Church the Holy Spirit teaches us to repent of our sins and accept the saving Lord into our lives.

The grace of justification—the life of the Holy Spirit in us—forgives our sins and brings inner renewal to our hearts. Justification, won for us by Jesus' sacrifice

on the cross, bestows on us the gifts of faith, hope, and charity, the theological virtues that enable us to obey God's will. Without these spiritual gifts, we cannot grow in holiness. We only grow in holiness when we allow the Holy Spirit to live in us by cooperating with the gifts he has given to us in baptism.

GRACE

Grace is God's "favor, the free and undeserved help that God gives us to respond to his call to become children of God" (*CCC,* 1996). Grace is a total gift from God that we cannot earn in any way on our own. The Holy Spirit infuses grace into our souls at Baptism. It makes us·a new creation. This free gift from God brings many blessings. Grace:

- enables us to address God as "Abba"
- adopts us into God's family
- enables us to share in the life of our loving, Triune God
- makes us heirs of heaven
- gives us the ability to live as God's children, in the way Jesus instructed us
- unites us to our Lord and Savior, Jesus Christ
- allows the Holy Spirit to live in us

The Catholic tradition calls this type of grace *sanctifying,* from the Latin word *sanctus,* which means holy. Sanctifying grace makes us holy. It is a *habitual* grace, a "permanent disposition to live and act in keeping with God's call" (*CCC,* 2000). We distinguish it from *actual* graces, which are God's interventions "at the beginning of conversion or in the course of sanctification" (*CCC,* 2000). Other types of grace are *sacramental* graces, which are specific gifts that come from particular sacraments; **charisms**, which are special gifts of the Holy Spirit given to individual Christians to build up the Church; and "graces of state," which are the help God gives to particular ministries in the Church.

Since God never forces his love or his gifts on us, we must freely respond to the graces he bestows on us. God has made us with a hunger to do good and to search for truth. This hunger points us to God, the only One who can satisfy the deepest cravings of our hearts. Thus, he has already begun the work of grace in us by preparing for and calling forth our free response. If we say "yes" to God's inner call, and use the gifts and helps he gives us, then our human freedom is made perfect. Our inner longing for truth and goodness is satisfied.

MERIT AND HOLINESS *(CCC, 2006—2016; 2025—2029)*

As you know, the efforts you put into living a moral life and performing good deeds require self-denial and a lifelong commitment. However, these efforts are worthwhile because they lead to ultimate happiness. They "merit" for us an eternal reward of union with the Blessed Trinity in heaven.

Merit is a word that means "what is owed to us," either as a reward or punishment, because we did something that helps or harms our relationship with God, other people, or ourselves. Strictly speaking, God, the Supreme Being, owes us nothing. He has already given us all that we are and all that we have: the gift of life,

the gift of our talents and possessions, the gift of salvation, the gift of adoption into the divine family.

However, God has freely chosen us to join him in his work of grace. When God adopts us into the divine family, he bestows tremendous dignity on us. He makes us co-heirs with Christ and makes us worthy of obtaining eternal life. But there is one condition: We must *cooperate* with the many graces God gives to us to live upright, holy lives so we can merit the reward God has in store for us.

The concept of merit always begins with God's grace. He made the first move in extending his forgiveness and justification to us at the beginning of our conversion. The second part is our cooperation with God's acceptance of us and the grace of conversion he has granted to us. We must freely permit the Holy Spirit to work in us by allowing his gift of charity to take root in our lives.

We can then merit for ourselves and for others the graces needed for our sanctification, for the increase of grace and charity, and for the attainment of eternal life. Even temporal goods like health and friendship can be merited in accordance with God's wisdom. These graces and goods are the object of Christian prayer. (CCC, 2010)

charisms

Special gifts the Holy Spirit gives to individual Christians to build up the Church.

Holiness does not consist in being odd, but it does consist in being rare.

—St. Francis de Sales

The source of all merit before God the Father is the love of Christ Jesus, whose sacrifice has won us everything. God gives gifts, and we gain merit, *through* the Son, *in* the Holy Spirit. We must allow the sanctifying grace of the Holy Spirit to live in us so we can live holy, prayerful lives, and thus truly deserve (merit) the eternal life our loving God of mercy has in store for those who do his will.

Living a moral life means living a holy life. To be holy means to be godlike, Christ-like. It means striving to be perfect as the heavenly Father is perfect (Mt 5:48). To be holy is to allow Jesus to live in us by the power of the Holy Spirit. To be holy means to live his law of love.

Christ calls everyone to holiness. We are all children of God; our vocation is to act like the children of God that we are privileged to be. Living holy, loving lives is not a task for the faint-hearted, but for those who are fortified by the strength of the Lord. It requires self-denial, death to our own selfishness. To follow Jesus requires walking in his footsteps:

> Then Jesus said to his disciples, "Whoever wishes to come after me must deny himself, take up his cross, and follow me." (Mt 16:24)

Living a holy life also requires prayer, as prayer keeps us in touch with God and strengthens in us the virtue of hope. This virtue helps us trust that God will give us the graces to keep loving until our birthday to eternity (the day we die). Hope gives us the strength to carry on when the road gets rough, trusting that Christ Jesus will welcome us with open arms and find us worthy of joining him in his Father's kingdom.

The Biblical Way to Holiness

Ephesians 4–5 is one of the important New Testament passages on how to live a moral life. Read Ephesians 4–5:20. It is addressed to the worldwide Church, not just the local church at Ephesus.

◆ List five positive actions that help us live holy lives; then list five practices that lead us away from God and should not be part of our Christian life together.

◆ Of all the negative things that Paul mentions, which seems most evident in your school? Your neighborhood? Your friendship group? Give examples.

◆ Of all the positive actions Paul mentions, which seem most evident in your school? Your neighborhood? Your friendship group? Give examples.

REVIEW AND REFLECTION

1. What is meant by the term *justification*?

2. What is *grace*? What are five of its effects?

3. Distinguish between and among these terms: sanctifying grace, actual grace, sacramental grace, and charisms.

4. Strictly speaking, why does God *not* owe us anything?

Discipleship

(*CCC*, 787; 897—945)

The Sacrament of Baptism incorporates us into the Body of Christ. Both Baptism and Confirmation shower us with the graces of the Holy Spirit. These graces enable us to live morally, and they strengthen us to live Jesus' command to love others the way he loves us. The Eucharist is the spiritual food of the Risen Lord himself, uniting us even more closely to the Lord. He is the vine; we are the branches who are to be fruitful witnesses to God's love.

As baptized Christians, we share in Christ's life and are disciples—followers of Jesus Christ. As disciples, we have accepted the Gospel of God's love for us in Jesus Christ. The Holy Spirit enables Christ's disciples to participate in his priestly, prophetic, and kingly offices. We participate in the priestly ministry by offering up everything we do in our daily lives to God our Father, especially through Jesus Christ when we celebrate the Eucharist. We participate in the prophetic mission by proclaiming the Good News in both word and in deed. A loving Christian life directed by the Holy Spirit is a most powerful way to attract others to the Gospel. Finally, all Christians, including lay people, participate in the kingly or royal ministry of the Lord by mastering their own passions, working for justice in the world, and serving God's people according to their gifts.

Simply stated, **discipleship** is the vocation of every Christian. Christians are to be followers of Jesus Christ by living upright, moral lives of charity that will announce the good news of God's love and attract others to the gospel.

But throughout Church history, there have always been men and women in religious institutes, orders, congregations, or societies, living what is popularly called "Religious Life." Those in religious life include priests, non-ordained men known as brothers, and religious women known as sisters or nuns. These generous individuals strive to live the virtue of charity in the most perfect way by following Christ more nearly and by dedicating themselves totally to God to signify in the Church the glory of the world to come. This dedication and perfection of charity is accomplished by taking public vows to live the evangelical counsels. These include the vow of chastity in celibacy for the sake of the Kingdom of God, poverty, and obedience. This state of life is known as the consecrated life.

The various religious families of those in consecrated life bring different gifts and ways to witness to the Church and the world. For example, there are **contemplative orders**, that is, congregations that put primary emphasis on living a life centered on the celebration of prayer. Examples of contemplative orders of men include the Benedictines, Trappists, and Carmelites. Contemplative orders for women include the Benedictines, the Poor Clares, Carmelites, and Trappistines.

Other religious orders are **apostolic orders**, orders that emphasize active ministries like caring for the downtrodden and sick, teaching, or preaching. The Sisters of Charity, Franciscan Sisters, Sisters of Mercy, and Dominican Sisters are examples of religious congregations of women who emphasize apostolic action. The Society of Jesus (the Jesuits), Franciscans, Salesians, Christian Brothers, and Dominicans are examples of men's orders that stress apostolic works.

There are yet others in the Church who try to follow Christ more closely. For example, *hermits*, who may not always publicly profess the three evangelical counsels, withdraw from the world. They live a hidden life of constant prayer and penance. They do so to praise God and to work for the salvation of souls. Similarly, from the Church's earliest days, there have been *widows* and *consecrated virgins* whose lives of prayer, penance, service, and apostolic works show forth their love

discipleship

The mandate of all baptized Christians to follow Jesus and participate in his role as priest, prophet, and king.

contemplative orders

Religious orders that put a focus on living a life centered on the celebration of prayer, rather than on active ministry. Contemplative orders of men include the Benedictines, Trappists, and Carmelites. Contemplative orders for women include the Benedictines, the Poor Clares, Carmelites, and Trappistines.

apostolic orders

Religious orders that stress apostolic works like caring for the downtrodden and sick, teaching, or preaching. Apostolic congregations for women include the Sisters of Charity, Franciscan Sisters, Sisters of Mercy, and Dominican Sisters. Apostolic orders for men include the Society of Jesus (the Jesuits), Franciscans, Salesians, Holy Cross, Christian Brothers, and Dominicans.

of Christ. They are a sign of the Church's love for Christ and a sign to the world of the life of the world to come.

There are also *secular institutes* of lay men and women who, inspired by perfect charity, vow the evangelical counsels in order to serve Christ through a life of self-dedication to God. Persons in a secular institute live in the world and dedicate themselves to strive for personal holiness by bringing Gospel values to their world of work and everyday activities. Examples of secular institutes in the United States are the Company of St. Paul, Don Bosco Volunteers, Fr. Kolbe Missionaries of the Immaculata, and the Holy Family Institute.

Another Catholic group that tries to follow Christ more closely are the Third Orders and Associates. They include lay people, married or not, who promise to live the spirituality of specific religious communities. Two promi-nent examples are the Third Order Franciscans and Third Order Carmelites.

Two other ecclesial movements for the laity have also generated great participation in recent years. The Focolare movement began in Italy during World War II from the simple revelation of a young Italian woman, Chiara Lubich, that Jesus had died on the Cross to bring unity to the world. The word *focolare* means "hearth." An intention of this movement is to achieve unity through the practice of a broad spirituality of communion. Likewise, the Communion and Liberation movement was founded in Italy in 1954. Its intention is to help the laity live their personal and professional vocation in the service of Christ and the Gospel by proclaiming Christ as the only true response to the deepest needs of humanity.

Catholic Life in Action

1. Read the Sermon on the Mount, Matthew 5–7. Extract from it five important teachings. Use these teachings to develop an outline for a short one-minute talk to be delivered to high school freshmen on a Witness Retreat. The title of your talk is: "What Jesus has to say about living a good life."
2. Create a PowerPoint presentation or make a collage to illustrate the Beatitudes.
3. Watch the PBS documentary *Merchants of Cool*. The documentary shows how advertisers create and sell popular culture to teens. After viewing it, write a report that discusses several ways those selling popular culture to today's teens contradict the teachings of Jesus on what is the good life as presented in the Beatitudes and the Sermon on the Mount. You can view the documentary online at: www.pbs.org/wgbh/pages/front line/shows/cool.
4. Read more about the Beatitudes at one of these websites. Write your own reflection on any two of the Beatitudes after you do your research:
   Fr. John Hardon, S.J.: www.catholic.net/rcc/ Periodicals/Faith/2001-10/hardon.html
   Bishop Fulton J. Sheen: www.ewtn.com/library/PROLIFE/BO18.TXT
5. Read about and report on the life of Blessed Charles de Foucauld. You can begin your research at one of these websites: The Crossroads Initiative: www.crossroadsinitiative.com/library_author/72/Charlesde_Foucauld_Blessed.html; www.charlesdefoucauld.org/en/index_en.htm
6. Interview a member of a religious order. Find out answers to these questions:
   How did you know you had a vocation?
   What type of work does your congregation stress?
   What steps are involved in becoming a member of your order?
   What is the spirituality of your order?
   How should a young person like me discern his or her vocation?

REVIEW AND REFLECTION

1. What does it mean for the Christian to participate in the priestly, prophetic, and kingly offices of Christ?

2. What is consecrated life?

3. What are the evangelical counsels? Why do people vow to live them?

4. Identify secular institutes and Third Orders.

FOR YOUR JOURNAL

Describe a couple of ways you can bring Christ to the "workplace"—to your school or place of employment.

Summary Points

◆ God made us to know, love, and serve him and to be happy with him in eternity.

◆ For Christians, Jesus is the best guide and norm for living a moral life.

◆ Jesus is God-made-man. Truly the Word-of-God-made-flesh, Jesus redeemed, sanctified, and justified us. He shows us the nature of divine love.

◆ Truly human, Jesus never sinned. He was perfectly in tune with the Father and used his freedom most responsibly.

◆ Jesus shows the nature of God's love through his humility, compassion, forgiveness, acceptance of all people, prayerfulness, patience, sensitivity, and in many other ways.

◆ The central theme of Jesus' preaching ministry was the advent of God's kingdom and the need for repentance and faith.

◆ God's kingdom refers to his reign over us, his love, peace, and justice breaking into our world through Jesus, our Lord.

◆ The Kingdom of God is not fully accomplished. We must help further God's loving plan for humanity.

◆ Jesus calls for us to repent of our sins, to reform our hearts, minds, and wills by making God number one in our lives.

◆ Jesus requires faith, that is, acceptance of God's total and unconditional love for us in Jesus Christ. Our faith must be active by translating our beliefs into concrete acts of love.

- The essence of Jesus' moral teaching is that we should love one another as Christ has loved us. It requires us to love God above all and our neighbor as ourselves. Love is a self-emptying life of serving others in imitation of Jesus who gave his all for humanity.

- Catholics grow in love of Jesus through the Eucharist, which celebrates the Paschal Mystery of the Lord's passion, death, resurrection, and glorification.

- Matthew's Gospel summarizes the ethics for the disciples of Jesus in the famed Sermon on the Mount (Mt 5–7).

- The Beatitudes are the attitudes of being Christian that followers of the Lord are called to enact in this life. Their reward is happiness.

- Jesus fulfills the Mosaic law by emphasizing the spirit and the intent of the old Law. He sets the higher standard of love that looks for the interior attitudes that lead to the external act. For example, Jesus teaches us to avoid anger, lust, and swearing. He outlaws divorce and revenge. He teaches the need to love our enemies.

- Jesus assumes that his followers will fast, give money to the poor, and pray. But we should do these religious duties not to gain favor with others, but to please our heavenly Father. Pure intentions are paramount to our Lord.

- Jesus tells us to trust God and leave needless worrying aside. If we give our life to following God's will, our heavenly Abba will look out for us.

- Jesus teaches the Golden Rule: "Do to others whatever you would have them do to you."

- Jesus instructs us not to judge, to enter by the narrow gate, to pray with confidence, and to build our life on Christ's words. He tells us that we must forgive as we ourselves have been forgiven.

- Jesus teaches the perfect prayer, the Lord's Prayer. In it we praise our loving Abba and petition that his Kingdom may come and his will be done. We also ask him to give us what we need for life, to forgive our sins, and to save us from the path that leads to sin and the snares of the Evil One.

- Justification is the Holy Spirit's grace that cleanses us from our sins through conversion, faith in Christ, and Baptism.

- Grace is God's favor, the free and undeserved help God gives us to be the children of God he calls us to be. Sanctifying grace makes us holy; it is habitual grace that disposes us permanently to live and act in accord with God's call.

- Merit is something that is owed us. God really owes us nothing because he has given us all we have and all we are. But God adopts us into the divine family and enables us to cooperate with his plan of salvation. If we do so by living holy lives, God has promised to reward us with eternal life joined to the Triune God.

- The source of all merit is the love of Christ Jesus, whose death won all for us.

- Christ calls everyone to holiness, that is, to be Christ-like. Holiness requires self-denial, prayer, and cooperation with the graces of the Holy Spirit.

- Those in consecrated ("religious") life publicly vow to live the evangelical counsels of poverty, chastity, and obedience. Some religious orders, like the Poor Clares and Benedictines, stress a more contemplative life by centering their life on the practice and celebration of prayer. Other orders, like the Jesuits and Sisters of Charity, focus on apostolic action, for example, caring for the sick, teaching, and preaching.

- Inspired by perfect charity, hermits, consecrated virgins and widows, and secular institutes of lay men and women live the evangelical counsels in a life of self-dedication to God.

- Members of Third Orders are lay people, married or not, who try to live the spirituality of a specific religious order.

PRAYER REFLECTION

Devotion to the Sacred Heart of Jesus has been a favorite of Catholics since about 1672. The devotion has its roots in Jesus' multiple appearances to St. Margaret Mary Alacoque, a French Visitation nun, and his request that people honor him in the symbol of his heart of flesh. Jesus requested acts of reparation for sins, frequent reception of Holy Communion, Communion on the first Fridays of each month, and the keeping of a holy hour. A traditional prayer of Offering to God in union with Jesus' Sacred Heart follows.[2]

Offering

My God, I offer you all my prayers, works, joys, and sufferings
in union with the Sacred Heart of Jesus,
for the intentions for which He pleads and offers Himself
in the Holy Sacrifice of the Mass,
in thanksgiving for Your favors,
in reparation for my sins,
and in humble supplication for my temporal and eternal welfare,
for the needs of our holy Mother the Church,
for the conversion of sinners,
and for the relief of the poor souls in purgatory. Amen.

What special prayer intention do you have (e.g., health of a friend or relative, success at your studies, strength to resist temptation)?

Pray this offering to God each morning for the next two weeks. Be sure to pray for your special intention(s).

NOTES

1. Found at The Quotations Page <www.quotationspage.com/search.php3?homesearch= worry&startsearch=Search> (10 August 2006).
2. This prayer can be found on the EWTN website: www.ewtn.com/Devotionals/heart/meditation.htm

CHAPTER OVERVIEW

With and Without Conscience
A well-formed conscience is essential to living a moral life. Those with a good conscience live not only a moral life—but a happy one.

Definition of Conscience
Conscience is a reasoned judgment by which a person recognizes the moral quality of an action. Conscience is an awareness of God's call to do what is morally good.

How Conscience Works
Christians must search out the truth to keep forming and informing their consciences. Then, they must follow judgments they are led to.

FAQ on Conscience
Frequently asked questions about conscience include questions about whether we must *always* follow our consciences and whether a conscience could be wrong. Forming conscience in a Christian community helps us to hear Church teachings and make moral decisions.

Peer Pressure and Conscience
To do what is right and follow the voice of conscience—in spite of peer pressure—takes fortitude. Prayer, self-denial, helping others, and hard work strengthen us.

CHAPTER FIVE

Conscience Formation

May you fight a good fight by having faith and a good conscience. Some, by rejecting conscience, have made a shipwreck of their faith.

1 Timothy 1:18–19

With and Without Conscience

Did you ever hear about the lady who returned to her car after a busy day of Christmas shopping at the local mall? The parking lot was loaded with cars. When she opened the door on the driver's side of her car, she noticed a piece of paper stuck under the windshield wiper. She unfolded it and read, "I have just backed into the front of your car. The two women who witnessed the accident are watching me. They think I am writing down my name, address, and phone number. Guess what? They are wrong!"

The deceiver in this story is a person "without conscience." He thinks he is clever, but his deception reveals a person of weak character. The American journalist H. L. Mencken wryly observed, "Conscience is the inner voice which warns us that someone may be looking." But here is a fellow who knew someone was looking, and it made no difference.

A young Native American knew what a bad conscience can do. Pointing his finger toward his heart, he said, "My conscience is like a three-cornered thing in here that stands still when I am good. But when I'm bad, it turns around, and the corners hurt a lot. But if I keep on doing bad, eventually the corners wear off and it doesn't hurt much anymore."

This chapter examines more about conscience, not only what it is, but how and why we must form and inform our conscience in order to live moral lives. Thomas à Kempis said, "The testimony of a good conscience is the glory of a good man; have a good conscience and thou shall ever have gladness."[1] The payoff to a good conscience is not only living a moral life, but a happy one as well.

CONSCIENTIOUS DECISIONS

conscience

A practical judgment of reason that helps a person decide the goodness or sinfulness of an action or attitude. It is the subjective norm of morality that we must form properly and then follow.

A *conscientious* person is someone who possesses a properly informed **conscience** that is guided by good principles. Judge whether the following principles are valid views on what makes up a good, "conscientious" way to make moral decisions.

"If I have a good intention and am sincere, then anything I do is okay."

"No one can tell me what to do. I am the sole judge of what is right or wrong."

"There are objective standards of morality, for example, the divine law and Church teaching. I must try to conform my actions to these standards."

"Something is all right if it feels good. Something is wrong if it feels bad."

Based on what you have learned in previous chapters, judge which of these views are not compatible with Christian morality.

Definition of Conscience

A dictionary definition of conscience is "the awareness of a moral or ethical aspect to one's conduct together with the urge to prefer right over wrong." This definition, though serviceable, is not complete from a Christian understanding of conscience. This section helps to delve deeper into a definition of conscience, first by explaining what conscience is *not*.

WHAT CONSCIENCE IS NOT

Today there are many wrong ideas that have surfaced about the meaning of *conscience*. None agree with a Christian definition of conscience, which will be examined on pages 124–125. Yet, they must be mentioned if only to be dismissed. These incomplete or wrong ideas of conscience are as follows:

Conscience as majority opinion. There are those who claim conscience is simply a matter of doing what the crowd does. If everyone is doing it, then it must be okay. This view of conscience surrenders personal responsibility to the group or to the latest survey. Its idea of correct behavior is to conform to popular opinion and practice. Contrary to this view, Harper Lee, the author of the classic *To Kill a Mockingbird*, has the hero Atticus Finch observe, "The one thing that doesn't abide by majority rule is a person's conscience."

Conscience as a feeling. A soft-drink advertisement once proclaimed, "When you make a choice, what's right is what feels right." A popular saying from the 1960s went, "If it feels good, do it." This view of conscience holds that individuals are the creators of their own moral rules and are only answerable to themselves. This perspective holds sincerity as the prime value. "As long as I am sincere and have a good intention, then what I do is okay." The novelist Ernest Hemingway shared this opinion when he wrote, "Everyone has his own conscience, and there should be no rule about how a conscience should function." But notice here that Hemingway has made a rule about how we should not make rules. The trouble with feelings, whether they are good or bad, is that our feelings may be out of touch with reality, and with what is truly right or wrong.

Conscience as superego. The influential psychiatrist Sigmund Freud saw conscience as the *superego*, that is, the leftover rules of childhood that we carry around in our subconscious. The superego is like an attic in an old house. Instead of containing furniture, we carry around all the "shoulds" and "have-tos" that we absorbed from the authority figures in our lives—parents, teachers, employers, coaches, and so forth. We followed these rules because we wanted approval (love) from these authority figures, not because we personally saw or understood the value of the rules on our own. When we disobeyed the rules, we sometimes felt guilty. However, this guilt does not result from awareness that we have acted contrary to God's plan for us, but rather from psychological conditioning related to feelings of moral approval or disapproval. In contrast, Christian conscience is a personal, self-chosen response to God's invitation to love. Conscience is based on our *own* study, decision, acting, and evaluating.

Conscience as gut-instinct. With little thought or study, some people will make moral decisions based on gut-instinct— "This feels right. My hunch tells me I should act this way." Although a gut-reaction or hunch to moral situations can be a helpful start in a decision-making process involving morality, a Christian conscience is much more grown-up. It applies one's intellect and judgment to figure out how we are to love both God and others.

Conscience as "Jiminy Cricket." Some people think of conscience as an internal voice, a separate person who lives inside of us, dictating to us what we should do. Conscience is *not* what the wooden-boy

What Would You Do?

Here are four situations that require conscientious decision-making. Draw on what you have learned in this course to answer each situation.

The Wallet
You find a wallet containing $500. From the identification papers in the wallet, you conclude that its owner is very wealthy. What would you do?

The Big Party
A friend is having a big party at her house this coming Saturday night. Her parents won't be home. Your parents would not let you attend if they knew that there would be no adult supervision. You very much want to go to the party. The temptation to lie or stretch the truth is great. What would you do?

Sexist Remarks
At lunch, some people at your table are making some strong sexist comments about women in general. What would you do?

The Test
A friend is taking the same math course as you are. Today, she took a test third period. Your teacher typically uses the same test for your sixth-period class. At lunch, your friend asks if you want to know which problems your teacher asked on the test. The problems are all homework problems you worked the previous two weeks. They are easily found in the text. What would you do?

For each situation, decide which mistaken idea of conscience is represented. Give reasons for your choices.

- A mission collection is being taken up at school for some orphans in hurricane-stricken Guatemala. Louise decides she must contribute $10 so her teacher will think she is generous.

- Carl is at work in a fast-food restaurant when some mentally-challenged adults come in to place an order. His co-workers begin to laugh at them. Carl joins in.

- Joe smokes pot regularly. He tells his girlfriend that he does-n't see anything wrong with doing something that helps him relax.

Report on a historical example—or an item in the current news or promoted by any media forum like a sitcom or film—where conscience is seen as the majority opinion.

Pinocchio thought it was—a cricket whispering what to do or what not to do. Neither is conscience a guardian angel whispering in our ear. Nor is it a telephone from heaven issuing divine instructions as in the view of James J. Metcalf, who wrote, "Conscience is a walkie-talkie set by which God speaks to us." This, too, is an incorrect definition.

Conscience as a myth. Finally, some people deny the very existence of personal conscience. These skeptics believe conscience is a fake concept, the creation of organized religions to help control people through guilt. In the last analysis, the denial of conscience results in each person doing his or her own thing, with little regard for personal responsibility or any special consideration for the rights of others. The denial of conscience leads to the death of morality.

WHAT CONSCIENCE IS (CCC, 1776—1782; 1795—1797)

The *Catechism of the Catholic Church* provides an excellent definition of conscience:

Conscience is a judgment of reason whereby the human person recognizes the moral quality of a concrete act that he is going to perform, is in the process of performing, or has already completed. (*CCC*, 1778)

The documents of the Second Vatican Council reveal more about the meaning of conscience in this definition:

In the depths of his conscience, man detects a law which he does not impose upon himself, but which holds him to obedience. Always summoning him to love good and avoid evil, the voice of conscience when necessary speaks to his heart: do this, shun that. For man has in his heart a law written by God. To obey it is the very dignity of man; according to it he will be judged. Conscience is the most secret core and sanctuary of a man. There he is alone with God, whose voice echoes in his

depths. In a wonderful manner conscience reveals that law which is fulfilled by love of God and neighbor. (Church in the Modern World, *16*)

This definition reveals three interlocking aspects of conscience, all of which deal with our awareness of moral truth. They are:

1. Conscience is awareness of God's call to be. Vatican II teaches that our conscience is the secret place at the core of our beings where we are alone with the Triune God. There we can hear God's loving invitation to each of us to be the persons he calls us to be from all eternity: God's special child, made in his image and likeness. Thus, conscience is very *personal.*

2. Conscience is awareness of God's call to know and do the good, that is, to love. Our vocation as persons with profound dignity is to reflect our Triune God, who is love. We do this when we respond to the good. We do this when we love. We do this when we shun that which is evil. We do this when we obey the law written in our hearts: the law of love of God and neighbor as oneself. Thus, conscience is a *basic awareness of good and evil.*

3. Conscience is a practical judgment of the intellect. This judgment helps us in the here-and-now of a particular, concrete act to discover the loving path and to avoid the path that is evil. Helped by God's inner call to love and to respond as his special creation, this practical judgment of conscience judges the moral goodness or the moral evil of concrete actions that we are about to perform, we are in the process of performing, or we have already performed. Thus, conscience is *very practical.* It urges us to do good or keeps us from doing evil, or guides us in doing an action, or judges as good or evil acts done.

These three points stress the *personal* nature of conscience, that is, an individual call by God to be a loving person, to search for moral truth, to do good in the concrete, here-and-now situation. The document *Church in the Modern World* also states:

In fidelity to conscience, Christians are joined with the rest of men in the search for truth, and for the genuine solution to the numerous problems which arise in the life of individuals from social relationships. Hence the more right conscience holds sway, the more persons and groups turn aside from blind choice and strive to be guided by the objective norms of morality. (16)

This tells us that our individual conscience must join the human community in a search for truth, in discovering and applying the objective norms of morality to issues that affect the common good. The Christian vocation not only applies to the individual follower of Christ, but also to our lives together. Many issues of right and wrong involve community decisions, like how a nation should deal with the poor, immigrants, those who are discriminated against, and so forth. An important element of a Christian's responsibility is to help the community examine its conscience and to judge the morality of those policies and practices that affect our life together.

Consider the virtue of honesty and your practice of it. Review your past week. List five honest actions you performed without much deep thought because honesty is a good habit (virtue) for you. Example: You turned in your own homework each day without copying the work from someone else.

REVIEW AND REFLECTION

1. List and discuss four wrong ideas about conscience.

2. Note a definition of conscience as given in the *Catechism of the Catholic Church*.

3. Explain conscience as *awareness*.

4. Where in the decision-making process does conscience come into play?

FOR YOUR JOURNAL

Reflect on a time when your conscience prompted you to help a friend or a group of friends to make a good decision.

How Conscience Works

In our daily routine, most of our decisions of conscience are implicit. We make them from rote or habit and give them little thought. They result from our already-acquired values and attitudes. Recall that a good habit is a virtue that empowers us to do good with ease. On the other hand, a bad habit, or **vice**, inclines us to choose the evil rather than the good.

For example, suppose you have gained and cultivated the habit of *honesty* (the virtue of integrity). Then, without going through a lot of mental gymnastics, you will usually resist a temptation to cheat. Almost instinctively you will choose the good, proper, and moral course of action without being *explicitly* aware of it. Similarly, say you have acquired the habit of laziness (the vice of sloth). Because of this bad habit, you may be late on a school assignment or haphazard about a task at work.

Because most daily decisions tend to be semiautomatic like the ones described above, you can see why becoming virtuous is important. Virtues are like spiritual

vice

A bad habit, such as laziness, that inclines us to choose the evil rather than the good.

word, recognize its truth, and then announce it and put it into action.

Christians are called to be seers. They search out God's truth about the human person. And using their God-given intellects, they judge what God wants them to do right here, right now. In other words, Christians are called to live these two important principles regarding conscience: **(1) You must always form and keep informing your conscience, and (2) You must follow your conscience.**

Here is how the SEER method can help:

1. Study

In an important sense, conscience is a judgment of the *intellect*. Therefore, conscience is concerned with discovering objective truth so we do not simply act on our feelings or preferences. A key principle of Catholic morality is to form our consciences and work throughout our lives to keep them informed. This requires study accompanied by reflection and deliberation.

Concerning a particular decision we must make soon, we should gather information about the moral object (what is being done), the motives, and the circumstances involved in particular decisions. We will then consider the various options before them and the consequences that flow from each. Also, we will review the fundamental principles of morality and consider how best to apply essential moral rules, like the following, that hold in every case:

- Never do evil so good may result from it. (A good end does not justify evil means to attain it.)
- "Do to others whatever you would have them do to you" (The Golden Rule, Mt 7:12).
- Love your neighbor as yourself (cf., Rom 14:21; *CCC*, 1789).

To guard against prejudice and self-interest, persons of conscience will also seek the advice of trusted moral mentors. Catholics listen to and accept the moral

muscles. They help us act responsibly with ease of effort. Similarly, we need to identify our bad habits so we can work, with God's grace, to overcome them. Both spiritual disciplines—acquiring virtues and conquering vices—are essential practices for growing in holiness and training Christian consciences.

In contrast to most of our daily choices, when we have more important decisions to make, we will typically take the time to make an explicit, more deliberate reference to our conscience. These are the times when we have to employ the "STOP Sign" approach previously discussed—to search out the facts, to think about alternatives and consequences, to consult others, and to pray about how God wants us to respond in love to the concrete situation.

STUDY, ELECT, EXECUTE, REVIEW

Another method for making moral decisions is known by the acronym SEER—*study, elect, execute, review*. Note the meaning of the word seer. A "see-er" is a person in tune with truth. A seer is also called a prophet, that is, "someone gifted with profound moral insight and remarkable powers of expression." From a biblical point of view, prophets listen to God's teachings of the Church because Christ himself speaks to us through the Magisterium. As expressed in the Vatican II documents:

In the formation of their consciences, the Christian faithful ought carefully to attend to the sacred and certain doctrine of the Church. The Church is, by the will of Christ, the teacher of the truth. It is her duty to give utterance to, and authoritatively to teach, that Truth which is Christ Himself, and also to declare and confirm by her authority those principles of the moral order which have their origin in human nature itself. (Declaration on Religious Freedom, 14)

Stolen Sign

A classmate was bragging to you about his weekend activities. He told you in confidence that he and some neighborhood buddies stole a stop sign from an infrequently traveled road. Tragically, you discover that there was a fatal accident at this very crossroad two days after the sign was stolen. The police believe someone failed to stop because of the missing sign, thus causing the death of a passenger in the car crash. Through the media, they are requesting information on the identity of those responsible for taking the missing stop sign.

Discuss the relevant facts in this case.

Would a person be wrong not to do anything in this situation? Why or why not?

2. Elect

After studying the issues involved in a particular situation, it is time to elect, that is, to choose the right course of action. Your decision should ultimately be based on whether your proposed action is consistent with who you are as God's special creation made in his image.

An essential part of making this decision is to be in the presence of the Lord and to pray (see "STOP Sign" approach, prayer). Prayer enables us to go to the divine Teacher who will assure us of his love for us, who will remind us of our special vocation to be persons of dignity, and who will give his graces to help us follow through on what we know is the right thing to do. Seeking counsel in prayer is also a way to slow down and react against a culture that constantly seeks instant gratification.

The listening part of prayer means to pay close attention to how the Lord might be speaking to us through our intellects, imaginations, and memories. In addition, we should also pay attention to how the Lord might be touching our emotions, judging if a proposed action "feels right," whether it is consistent with who we *really* are. Finally, in prayer, we should ask the Holy Spirit to strengthen our wills with the gift of fortitude so we might have the courage to do what our consciences tell us is the right thing to do.

3. Execute

Execution is the next part of making a moral decision. This involves putting into action what you have decided in conscience is the right course of action for you right now. Execution involves responsibility. You must do what your conscience tells you is right. If you do not do so, you sin.

A good rule here: Be an *actor*, not a *reactor*. Take control of your own actions and own them. Be like the friend described in this story:

A friend of a *Chicago Daily News* columnist always greeted a newspaper vendor with courtesy and class when he stopped to buy a newspaper every day. The vendor, however, was usually nasty, rude, and sullen.

When the columnist asked his friend why he was so nice to this obnoxious fellow, the friend replied, "Because why should I let him decide how I'm going to act?"

Mature people of conscience, after studying and choosing, execute a right course of action. They take charge and do what their conscience tells them is the right thing to do. Execution—doing the right thing—is the hardest part of the moral-decision process.

4. Review

A proverb contains much wisdom when it says, "There is no pillow so soft as a clear conscience."

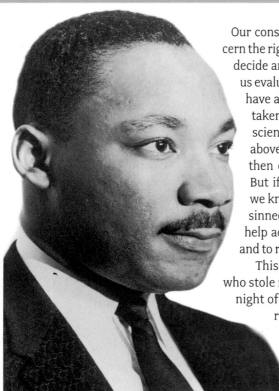

Cowardice asks the question, "Is it safe?"
Expedience asks the question, "Is it politic?"
Vanity asks the question, "Is it popular?"
But conscience asks the question, "Is it right?"

—MARTIN LUTHER KING, JR.

Our conscience not only helps us discern the right course of action before we decide and as we act, but it also helps us evaluate and reflect on actions we have already performed. If we have taken steps to develop a good conscience along the lines suggested above and have chosen the good, then our conscience will be clear. But if we have gone against what we know we should have done and sinned, then our consciences can help accuse us, calling us to repent and to reform.

This was the case of an employee who stole money from his boss. After a night of tossing and turning, he surrendered to the police, saying that he realized that theft could be addictive. He was worried about the effect his becoming a thief would have on his children. He did not want to set this kind of example for them. Because of his clean record, this particular criminal was paroled and subsequently became a model citizen, employee, and father.

Many saints through the ages have recommended a nightly "examination of conscience," that is, a review of our day to discover what we have done (or not done) to become (or not become) the kind of persons the Lord calls us to be. This regular examination of conscience is a great help for those who wish to grow in holiness and who want to do right according to God's plan for them.

CONSCIENCE IN ACTION

A recent news item told of how three men, one of them a police officer and another a teacher, turned in their father for his crimes of armed robbery. Law enforcement authorities asked the public if they recognized the thief whose image was captured on the surveillance cameras of the five banks he robbed. When the sons saw the pictures, they were shocked, sickened, and profoundly saddened. They met to decide the right thing to do and concluded that they must report their father, who had fallen into a life of crime, fed by his cocaine addiction. When the sons were questioned about why they would report their own father, they replied that they were only doing the right thing—what their ex-Marine father had taught them when they were young.

- Do you admire these brothers? Why or why not?
- Could you do the same thing?

REVIEW AND REFLECTION

1. Why is growth in virtue and overcoming vice important in moral decision-making?

2. What are the two key principles involving conscience?

3. What three moral rules must never be violated when making conscience decisions?

4. List several factors that we must study before deciding to act.

5. What role does prayer play in making moral decisions?

6. Why is it important to review our decisions?

FOR YOUR JOURNAL

Name a tough conscience decision you had to make recently. Were you proud of your decision? Why or why not?

FAQ on Conscience (CCC, 1783—1802)

This section contains answers to some frequently asked questions on conscience and how a person should apply his or her conscience.

Must I always follow my conscience?

Yes. Remember that through your conscience, God calls you to be the person he made you to be. Through your conscience God instructs you how to act in the concrete decisions you have before you. If you go against what your conscience tells you to do, then you are ignoring the voice of God. Not following what your conscience instructs you to do makes you guilty of sin. *The Catechism of the Catholic Church* explains it this way:

> In all he says and does, man is obliged to follow faithfully what he knows to be just and right. (CCC, 1778)

A human being must always obey the certain judgment of his conscience. Deliberately to act against conscience brings condemnation (*CCC*, 1790). The judgment of conscience requires us to do the good that we have recognized. A conscience judgment instructs us to follow the course of action that makes sense to us given all our study and reflection on the facts at hand. We must obey this verdict because it is God's call to us in this concrete situation.

Can my conscience ever be wrong?

Even a well-formed conscience can make mistakes. However, we must always follow the dictates of our conscience, even if it is erroneous (mistaken).

Recall, though, that we are assuming that you are *always* forming your conscience. This means you are doing the hard work of studying, consulting wise Christians, learning and heeding Church teaching, praying, reflecting, and so forth. The formation of conscience is a lifelong task. Conscience is never perfectly formed; it is always forming by staying informed.

If you follow your conscience in good faith, even if you later find out that it was objectively mistaken, you are not guilty of sin. On the other hand, if you violate your conscience—even if you later find out it was wrong—you are guilty. This is so because conscience is sacred, "the most secret core and sanctuary of a person . . . [where] we are alone with God" (*Church in the Modern World*, 16). If you go against what you believe to be right, you are ignoring what you believe to be true—God speaking to you about right and wrong:

> Conscience frequently errs from invincible ignorance without losing its dignity. The same cannot be said for a man who cares but little for truth and goodness, or for a conscience which by degrees grows practically sightless as a result of habitual sin. (Church in the Modern World, *16*)

What factors contribute to an erroneous conscience?

One major reason for an erroneous conscience is ignorance. Sometimes a person may have overlooked an important factor, or simply was never taught the truth about some issue in morality. For example, it could be possible that a young student never learned that drunkenness is a *serious* moral evil that results in diminished freedom and an inability to think clearly. Free choice and human intellect are two important qualities of being human. To compromise either causes a serious rift in our relationship with a loving God. In addition, drunkenness often leads to other harmful behavior that harms self and others, for example, sexual promiscuity, violence, and dangerous driving.

An immature student might drink without an awareness of its moral implications and thus be less blameworthy than a person who knows that "getting wasted" is mortally sinful and does so anyhow. However, drunkenness remains an evil whether the person is morally blameworthy or not for a particular incident. "One must therefore work to correct the errors of moral conscience" (*CCC*, 1793).

Another type of ignorance results from *insincerity*. In this case, a person makes little or no effort to discover what the truth is or where goodness lies. This type of person is lazy or closed-minded. For example, take a person who is trying to judge a moral course of action in regards

- ignorance of Christ and his Gospel
- the bad example of other people
- enslavement to one's passions
- holding a false idea of the autonomy of conscience (For example: "No one can tell me what to do. I am my own law.")
- rejecting Church authority and Church teaching in areas of morality
- lack of true repentance
- lack of love

How do I guard against a wrong conscience?

A special problem with some people is their misconception of the principle, "I must always follow my conscience." So often they interpret this to mean, "I can do whatever I want to do."

It is true that our decisions of conscience must be free. No one can be forced to act contrary to his or her conscience, nor be prevented from acting according to conscience, especially in matters dealing with religion (cf. *CCC*, 1782). Freedom is the essential ingredient that makes me responsible; therefore, I must be free to choose my own acts since they are what form me as a person. However, freedom of conscience does not mean *license* to do whatever I want, to make myself the law-giver, to ignore reality or God's will.

Sincere people will make a life commitment to forming and continually informing their consciences. They do so out of the virtue of humility, acknowledging that they do not know it all. They strive to have an upright and truthful conscience, one that is formed by reason and conforms to God's law. Moreover, they strive to form their consciences in light of God's word. Therefore, they will look to Christian mentors who are models of holiness and wisdom, which they have mastered from daily life, the Bible, and active living in Christian community.

Consider that the word *conscience* literally means "knowing with" or "being witness to oneself." It also means "a knowing together." Although your conscientious decisions are your own, Catholics form

You work at a restaurant as a food server. A significant part of your pay comes from tips. For tax purposes, your employer wants you to report all your tip income. You calculate that if you do so, you would be liable for at least $400 more in taxes per year.

◆ Read Romans 13:7 and Matthew 22:17–21.

◆ What do these verses suggest you should do?

to an issue of confidentiality. Instead of consulting wise and experienced individuals who are known for their tact, the person in question immediately starts blabbing about what he heard in confidence. This person is blameworthy for the harm he caused because he should have taken the trouble to find out the moral thing to do.

Another sign of an insincere conscience is the person who has fallen into a bad habit of sinfulness that makes choosing evil an easy thing to do. For example, consider a dishonest student who has rationalized cheating during her high school career. Her acts of cheating have transformed her into a cheater. She is blameworthy for her dishonesty because of her habit, a habit she makes little effort to overcome. She may even excuse herself by saying, "This is the way I am." On the contrary, this is not the way anyone is supposed to be. We can always repent of our sin and choose to do good.

The *Catechism of the Catholic Church* (1792) lists other factors that can lead us into making bad conscience decisions. These are:

their consciences in a Christian community that believes in Jesus, who continues to teach us through the Holy Father and the bishops. This is why, when making moral decisions, Catholics will give special consideration to the authentic teaching of the Church. No outside authority can replace one's conscience, but we cannot form a Christian conscience without the help, advice, and teaching of our Church leaders, who want and need to guide us on the path to holiness.

Finally, if we find that part of the reason we have an erroneous conscience is that we possess one of the factors described (e.g., being a slave to our passions or a victim of bad habits), we must then make a concerted effort, with God's grace, to overcome them. Faith in Jesus Christ, prayer, and seeking the guidance of our Christ-appointed teachers can help us form a good and pure conscience.

Peer Pressure and Conscience

The Watergate cover-up involved a major political scandal in the United States. It started with the burglary and wiretapping of the Democratic Party's campaign headquarters. Government higher-ups subsequently committed a number of illegal acts that eventually resulted in a constitutional crisis. It led to the first resignation of a president, Richard Nixon, in August 1974.

One of the Congressional investigators, Senator Howard Baker, asked the conspirators if they ever questioned the rightness of what they did. They said that they had, but they did not do anything because of group pressure.

This historical event points out that peer pressure is not just a problem with teens. At any age, conformity to the

As you surf the Internet for a class project, you accidentally pull up a pornographic website. You know the material in this site is offensive, especially to women. Besides, to enter this site you must affirm that you are 18 years old (you are under 18).

◆ Which of the "other sources of a faulty conscience judgment" mentioned in the *Catechism* might lead you astray here?

◆ What would you do? Why?

REVIEW AND REFLECTION

1. Must a person always follow his or her conscience? Why or why not?

2. List several factors that can lead to an erroneous conscience.

3. Discuss how we can guard against a wrong conscience.

FOR YOUR JOURNAL

Who would be the best source of guidance for you if you were trying to find out the correct way to act in a particular situation that is a matter of conscience? Why would you choose this person?

"Be who you are and say what you feel, because those who mind don't matter and those who matter don't mind."

—Dr. Seuss

standards and actions of members of our age group or social group greatly affects our way of looking at life, our values, and our way of behaving. Some conformity can be good, if, for example, we choose to associate with friends are hard-working and prod us on to higher achievement. Other conformity is neutral, if, for example, we are influenced by friends when we choose what baseball cap we wear. But caving in to some peer pressure can be very negative. President John F. Kennedy had this type in mind when he said, "Conformity is the jailer of freedom and the enemy of growth."[2] Negative peer pressure can turn people into proverbial lemmings, mouse-like arctic rodents who have been known to migrate in waves and drown while trying to cross the ocean in search of food.

Caving in to negative peer pressure can make us go against what our conscience tells is the right thing to do. We simply rationalize and say, "Everyone is doing it." "It" might refer to cheating, drinking, smoking pot, shoplifting, driving wildly, engaging in premarital sex, mocking an unpopular student, or whatever else. Going along with the crowd destroys our individuality and can even lead to personal tragedy.

FORTITUDE

To do what is right takes fortitude. The *Catechism of the Catholic Church* defines **fortitude** as:

the moral virtue that ensures firmness in difficulties and constancy in the pursuit of the good. It strengthens the resolve to resist temptations and to overcome obstacles in the moral life. The virtue of fortitude enables one to conquer fear, even fear of death, and to face trials and persecutions. It disposes one even to renounce and sacrifice his life in defense of a just cause. (CCC, 1808)

All virtues moderate between two extremes. For example, prudence prevents us from rushing into situations; at the same time, it helps us to make thoughtful decisions that lead to action. Similarly, the virtue of fortitude steers us between fearful inaction and foolish rashness caused by misdirected anger or a false sense of bravery.

Fortitude has an active dimension that prompts us to work for God's Kingdom, for example, by defending the right to life of unborn babies. It also has a passive side that involves patient suffering for God's Kingdom, for example, by settling for an honestly earned grade while classmates are cheating.

Prudence and justice help us exercise the virtue of fortitude. Prudence teaches us what is worth suffering for; justice points out situations contrary to the gospel and, hence, worth our efforts to correct.

The ultimate act of fortitude is martyrdom. Readiness to die for Jesus is one of the essential traits of being a Christian (see Archbishop Oscar Romero's profile, page 135). In a certain sense, we are a kind of **martyr** (a word that means *witness*) when we stand up to any evil and injustice.

With God's help, we can practice spiritual disciplines that help us grow in the virtue of fortitude. Regularly practice some form of self-denial for the Lord. Sacrifice builds character. Pray to be true to yourself. Ask the Lord to reassure you of his love so you don't have to surrender your principles simply to have others accept you. Help someone less fortunate than you. You will experience firsthand the joy of helping the Lord in his work. This will transform you into a sensitive person and help you courageously get involved in other justice issues.

You will also become a stronger, more virtuous person if you follow these student guidelines: play hard, study hard, work hard. In your studies, sports, extracurricular activities, employment . . . give 100 percent. Sticking to the task and

often turns us into cowards without moral backbone. Fortitude can also help you to resist negative peer pressure.

Here are some hints for how to do so:

Resolve to be your own person. If it doesn't feel like you, don't do it.

Know your own standards. You have the right to do right. Good friends won't force you to do something against your conscience. And if they do, it is time to find new friends. True friends bring out the best in us, not the worst.

Use humor and grace to say "no." You don't have to be preachy to be good. If possible, deflect peer pressure with humor.

Stay away from situations that might tempt you. The famous writer and wit Oscar Wilde said he could resist everything except temptation. Why put yourself in a situation that weakens your personal resolve to do right?

Remember the power of prayer. Ask the Lord to send you good and upright friends. Ask the Holy Spirit to strengthen you in the gifts of fortitude and prudence.

To build strength of character, try one of these exercises in self-discipline:

- Give up buying dessert, snacks, or soda for two weeks. Donate the money saved on these items to a hunger center.
- Pick up trash in the school hallways or cafeteria without being asked.
- Write short notes of gratitude to people who helped you.
- Greet fellow students whom you may not particularly like.
- Change the subject whenever conversations turn to gossip or trashing another's character.
- Refrain from the Internet or television for a week. Use this extra time to talk with your parents, spend time with younger siblings, visit grandparents, help an elderly neighbor, etc.
- Commit yourself to fifteen minutes of prayer every day. Pick a special time and place and be faithful to it.

giving your all will help you endure suffering when it comes your way. It will make a hero out of you.

People often fail to do the right thing out of fear of what others might think. Many of us do not want to stand out, so we go along. Unfortunately, "going along" too

---

REVIEW AND REFLECTION

1. What is peer pressure? Give examples of when it can be a positive factor in moral decisions.

2. Discuss several ways you can resist negative peer pressure.

3. What is fortitude? How can it help us make conscientious decisions?

4. How can you grow in the virtue of fortitude?

Suppose a friend told you he was gay. You are the first person in whom he has confided. He will soon tell his parents. Before long, you suspect word will get out.

You have decided to support your friend. However, you are positive that when others find out, they will make all kinds of insinuations about you, too.

- What would you do?

- How would your circle of friends react if something like this happened?

- What advice should you give your friend?

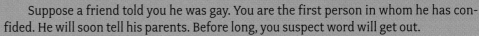

Sportswriter Dave Anderson once wrote about the game of golf as a sport that puts a premium on conscience. He reported how the great golfer Babe Didrikson Zaharias disqualified herself from a tournament because she hit the wrong ball out of the rough. A friend chided her on her act, observing that no one would have known. Babe replied, "I would've known." Honesty of any kind takes fortitude. It is a testing ground for the virtue of fortitude.

- What would you do in a similar situation on the golf course?

On a senior class trip to the state capitol, some boys broke into one of the girls' rooms and left on their beds some obscene notes, pornographic pictures, and other objectionable items. The occupants of the room rightfully expressed outrage, felt threatened by the highly inappropriate behavior, and obtained permission to get a chaperone to accompany them home.

In school the next week, the principal said he would cancel the senior prom unless the culprits come forward or are turned in by someone who knows who they are.

- If you knew the identity of the culprits, what would you do?

WHAT THE BIBLE SAYS ABOUT LIVING WITH FORTITUDE . . .

Therefore, put on the armor of God, that you may be able to resist on the evil day and, having done everything, to hold your ground. So stand fast with your loins girded in truth, clothed with righteousness as a breastplate, and your feet shod in readiness for the gospel of peace. In all circumstances, hold faith as a shield, to quench all (the) flaming arrows of the evil one. And take the helmet of salvation and the sword of the Spirit, which is the word of God. With all prayer and supplication, pray at every opportunity in the Spirit. To that end, be watchful with all perseverance and supplication for all the holy ones.

—Ephesians 6:13–18

ARCHBISHOP OSCAR ROMERO: A COURAGEOUS MARTYR FOR CONSCIENCE

Archbishop Oscar Romero is a great example of a man of fortitude who did the right thing, even though he knew it would likely lead to his death.

Oscar Romero was born in Ciudad Barrios, a mountainous town in El Salvador, on August 15, 1917. The second of seven children, Oscar entered the seminary at age thirteen. He eventually studied in Rome and was ordained a priest there in 1942.

In 1944, he went to the city of San Miguel in El Salvador and soon became secretary of the diocese, a post he held for twenty-three years. In his tenure there, he founded a number of organizations and became an inspired preacher whose sermons were broadcast on various radio stations.

Because of his talent, in 1970 Oscar was named an auxiliary bishop of the capital city in San Salvador, where he honed his skills as an administrator. This led to his being named bishop of a rural diocese in 1974. Finally, he was named archbishop of San Salvador in February of 1977.

At first, Oscar Romero was seen as a safe choice for archbishop of the leading city in a corrupt country controlled by a right-wing oligarchy that oppressed the poor and stamped out human rights. But in March of 1977, a Jesuit friend of Romero, Fr. Rutilio Grande, and two of his companions were summarily shot by the militia who were intent on stopping Grande's advocacy of the poor and land reform in El Salvador. There was no official inquiry into this massacre. This callous disregard for basic human rights led Romero to conclude that his beloved country was ruled by violent men who were supported in their positions of power by the rich who had made their fortunes on the backs of the poor. In short, the Salvadorian military was at war with the people, both in the city and the countryside.

Archbishop Romero was outraged, refusing to side with the wealthy landowners and their government puppets. When a rigged election upheld the status quo, Romero became a stronger spokesman for the poor and persecuted. He led Church efforts to document human rights abuses and spoke out in defense of the poor and the voiceless. He was mercilessly attacked in the press and labeled a revolutionary.

It took courage to speak out on behalf of those without a voice, especially in the face of extreme criticism, even from some of his own clergy. But the bishop remained undaunted. Living a simple life alone in a cottage, he regularly celebrated the Sunday Mass at 8 a.m. in the diocesan cathedral, which was attended by the poor. Week after week, he preached Christ's message of justice. In the face of persecution, he said,

To be a Christian now means to have the courage to preach the true teaching of Christ and not be afraid of it, not be silent out of fear and preach something easy that won't cause any problems.

On March 24, 1980, while celebrating Mass in the chapel of the hospital where he lived, a red car drove up. A hired marksman got out, approached the church, and took deadly aim at Oscar Romero, who had just concluded a homily that had justice as its theme. The assassin shot the archbishop, and Oscar Romero died near the altar.

Today, this courageous spokesman for the oppressed of the world is revered as a martyr, not only by the people of El Salvador, but by the poor and disenfranchised around the world.

FOR YOUR JOURNAL

Archbishop Oscar Romero wrote the following to Jose Calderon Salazar in March 1980, the month of his assassination:

> *I have often been threatened with death. Nevertheless, as a Christian, I do not believe in death without resurrection. If they kill me, I shall arise in the Salvadoran people. . . . As pastor, I am obliged by divine mandate to give my life for those I love—for all Salvadorans, even for those who may be going to kill me. If the threats come to be fulfilled, from this moment I offer my blood to God for the redemption and for the resurrection of El Salvador.*[3]

• Would there be people or causes for which you would be willing to sacrifice your life? Compose your own prayer asking God for the strength to live your Christian convictions . . . no matter what the price.

Catholic Life in Action

1. Read more about the life of Bishop Oscar Romero. You can find many links to his life and work at this website: www.silk.net/RelEd/romero.htm.
2. Report on the life of one of the four Catholic women who were killed for helping the poor in El Salvador: the laywoman Jean Donovan, Sister Ita Ford, M.M., Sister Maura Clark, M.M., and Sister Dorothy Kazel, O.S.U.
3. Report on the life of Franz Jäggerstatter, an icon of conscience, who refused to serve in Hitler's army.
4. View the film version of *To Kill a Mockingbird*, *Les Miserables*, or *A Man for All Seasons*. Report on the conscience decisions of Atticus Finch from *To Kill a Mockingbird*, Jean Valjean of *Les Miserables*, or Saint Thomas More, the hero of *A Man for All Seasons*. You can learn more about Saint Thomas More at: www.apostles.com/thomasmore.html.
5. With several others, compose a credible moral dilemma that might face your peer group in everyday life. Enact and discuss one of your dilemmas with the larger group. As part of your discussion, brainstorm ways to resist negative peer pressure.
6. Interview an adult whom you regard highly, for example, a respected professional like a teacher, doctor, attorney, accountant, business manager, etc. Ask this person to tell about a time when his or her conscience was challenged on the job and how he or she went about making the right, moral decision. Report on the results of your research.
7. Read more about conscience at one of these websites:
    • www.catholic.net/rcc/Periodicals/Faith/0708-96/article5.html
    • www.catholicherald.com/keating/ morality.htm
8. *Pray.* Check out this website produced by the Irish Jesuits. It is a fun way to make prayer a part of your life—every day as you work at the computer: www.sacredspace.ie.

Summary Points

◆ Conscience is not "following the crowd." Nor is conscience a feeling, the superego, gut-instinct, or some voice whispering in our ear.

◆ Those who deny the existence of personal conscience open the way to the death of morality.

◆ The Church defines conscience as a judgment of reason whereby humans recognize the moral quality of acts about to be performed, in the process of being performed, or already performed.

◆ Conscience involves awareness of the person God calls us to be, of knowing what to do and not do, and of how to make a particular judgment in a concrete setting.

◆ Many moral decisions happen almost automatically, born out of good habits (virtues) or bad habits (vices). As a result, we must ask God for help to grow in the virtues and overcome our vices.

◆ Two key principles of conscience are (1) always form and inform your conscience and (2) always follow your conscience.

◆ In ordinary decisions of conscience, we must study the facts, elect a course of action, execute the action, and review our decision.

◆ Since conscience is a judgment of the intellect, we must search for objective truth by studying the decision to be made, by consulting the advice of moral mentors, by incorporating the magisterial teaching of the Church, and by reflecting on our true motives.

◆ Before deciding to act, Christians should pray, asking for God's guidance and the strength of the Holy Spirit to choose morally and wisely.

◆ Eventually, as persons of conscience, we must act and then review our actions. If we went against the dictates of our conscience, we must accuse ourselves of sin, repent, and seek the Lord's forgiveness.

◆ We are always obligated to follow our consciences. By the same token, we must continually inform our consciences, paying particular attention to Church teaching concerning morality.

◆ A person's conscience can be wrong. At times, the person is not at fault for an erroneous conscience, for example, by making an honest mistake of judgment because of insufficient or inaccurate information. At other times, a person is blameworthy because he or she made little effort to discover the truth out of laziness or closed-mindedness, ignorance of Christ and his gospel, the bad example of one's companions, enslavement to passions, and so forth.

◆ We can guard against a wrong conscience by making a commitment to form and continually inform our consciences. Following one's conscience does not mean "doing my own thing." It means discovering the truth of what the Lord wants us to do right here, right now.

◆ People often fail to do what they know is the morally correct course of action out of negative peer pressure. To combat this, one must resolve to be one's own person, commit to upright personal standards of morality, say "no" to inappropriate behavior, avoid temptation, and pray for God's help to do right.

◆ A great help in following one's conscience is the virtue of fortitude, which "ensures firmness in difficulties and constancy in the pursuit of the good" (*CCC*, 1808).

◆ The cardinal virtue of fortitude helps us conquer fear and sacrifice in defense of a just cause, even to the point of giving up our lives.

◆ Archbishop Oscar Romero is an outstanding example of a person of conscience who spoke out for the poor and marginalized, even knowing that it might lead to his death.

PRAYER REFLECTION

Mary's humility and trusting stance toward God find great expression in her *Magnificat* (Luke 1:47–55), also known as Mary's Song.

> *My soul proclaims the greatness of the Lord;*
> *my spirit rejoices in God my savior.*
> *For he has looked upon his handmaid's lowliness;*
> *behold, from now on will all ages call me blessed.*
> *The Mighty One has done great things for me,*
> *and holy is his name.*
> *His mercy is from age to age to those who fear him.*
> *He has shown might with his arm,*
> *dispersed the arrogant of mind and heart.*
> *He has thrown down the rulers from their thrones*
> *but lifted up the lowly.*
> *The hungry he has filled with good things;*
> *the rich he has sent away empty.*
> *He has helped Israel his servant, remembering his mercy,*
> *according to his promise to our fathers,*
> *to Abraham and to his descendants forever.*
> —Luke 1:46–55

- Think of five gifts God has bestowed on you.
- Pray Mary's *Magnificat* as though it were your own song of praise to our loving, gracious God.

NOTES

1. Found in Anthony Castle, *A Treasury of Quips, Quotes, & Anecdotes for Preachers and Teachers* (Mystic, CT: Twenty-Third Publications, 1998), 274.
2. John F. Kennedy Quotes, *BrainyQuote* <www.brainyquote.com/quotes/authors/j/john_f_kennedy.html> (10 August 2006).
3. Quoted in Phyllis Zagano, *Twentieth-Century Apostles: Contemporary Spirituality in Action* (Collegeville, MN: The Liturgical Press, 1999), 119.

CHAPTER OVERVIEW

We Are Sinners

Sin is a part of our lives, and the major barrier to living a moral life. Nonetheless, conversion is the antidote to sin, and Christ truly is our Savior.

The Reality of Sin

Although some people deny the reality of sin, the evidence of it is all around us. Sin is an offense against reason, truth, and our mandate to love God and neighbor.

The Bible on Sin

From the Bible's Genesis account of "Original Sin," we see that sin is part of the human story. But God's loving and hope-filled promise of a Savior reminds us that God still calls us to live and be happy with him—forever.

Different Kinds of Sin

"Original Sin" is the condition of sin into which all people are born while "personal sin" is a person's failure to love God and neighbor in a specific act. Personal sins can be "mortal," which totally alienate us from God, or "venial," which weaken our relationship with God.

Conversion and the Sacrament of Reconciliation

Since we are sinners, repentance and conversion are needed. In the Sacrament of Reconciliation, sinners find God's reconciling love and forgiveness.

CHAPTER SIX

Sin and Forgiveness

What I do, I do not understand. For I do not do what I want, but do what I hate. . . . Sin . . . dwells in me.

Romans 7:15, 17b

We Are Sinners

A fable tells of twin brothers who lied so much that, as teenagers, their townsfolk branded on their foreheads the letters "CL," which represented *Chronic Liar*.

Totally ashamed, one twin fled to a foreign land, where he constantly had to answer questions about his forehead. He lived an embittered life, often lying about his brand, claiming it stood for "Cool Lad." Most people did not buy the story, which led to the twin's great depression and early death caused by bitterness and an unrepentant heart.

Meanwhile, the other brother "bit the bullet" and stayed in his own country. He totally turned from his sinful, lying ways, determined to win back the trust and respect of his neighbors. He always truthfully reported the meaning of the letters burned into his forehead. But as the years passed, people stopped inquiring about them. They saw the brother as a totally loving, trustworthy, honest citizen who was always doing his best to help others. Many years passed, and the brother grew into an old man, highly revered in the community.

One day a stranger came to town and saw the old man with the "CL" branded on his forehead. He asked a villager what the meaning of the letters was. She responded, "It happened a long time ago. Frankly, I have forgotten the details, but I think the letters stand for *Christ-Like*."

This story has much to teach us. We are also branded, but with the invisible letters "CS," which stands for "convicted sinner." In the face of this reality, we have a choice. We can deny the truth of our weakness and sin and refuse to face the facts. Or we can repent of our sins and turn back to God, allowing the Holy Spirit to transform us into loving people.

As Saint Paul observed, we are sinners. Sin does dwell in us. Sin is the major barrier to living a moral, Christ-like life. The antidote to sin is conversion, always remembering the good news that the "CS" invisibly branded on our foreheads also stands for "Christ Saves"!

Chapter 6 will address the topics of sin and conversion.

SEVEN CAPITAL SINS (*CCC*, 1866)

Among other things, the adjective *capital* means "grave," that is, having serious consequences. It also means "principal," that is, "comprising the highest category." The list of seven capital sins fits both of these definitions.

What follows is a brief description of each of the capital sins. To determine how well you are striving to fight these basic sinful attitudes and habits, rate yourself on the statements that reflect a virtuous counterpart to each sin. Use this scale:

A = This statement describes me quite well.
B = This reflects my basic approach most of the time.
C = I'm so-so on this.
D = I have a long way to go.

Pride: an unlimited appreciation for one's own worth; arrogance; excessively high opinion of oneself
____ I realize that God is the source of all gifts that I have. Without him, I would be and have nothing.
____ I am grateful for all my talents, gifts, and possessions and use them for the benefit of others.

Greed (Avarice): immoderate desire for earthly goods; love of money or possessions rather than loving God and others
____ I am content with what I have.
____ I exercise delayed gratification to strengthen my will against the temptations of consumerism.

Envy: sorrow over another's good fortune; covetousness; jealousy over another's possessions or characteristics
____ I refrain from comparing myself to others.
____ I make an effort to praise the accomplishments of others, especially siblings, classmates, co-workers, and teammates.

Anger (Wrath): intemperate desire for revenge; hostile and wrathful feelings toward others
____ I cultivate a forgiving heart toward those who have harmed me.
____ When I have negative feelings toward others, I try to find peaceful ways to deal with my feelings.

Lust: inordinate, unrestrained craving for pleasure, especially sexual pleasure
____ I treat others as people with dignity, not as objects for my own gratification.
____ Because the sexual appetite is so easily aroused, I avoid situations that will tempt me sexually.

Gluttony: unrestrained, immoderate consumption of food or drink
____ I stay away from drinking alcohol.
____ I eat healthy foods, exercise reasonably, and get sufficient rest.

Sloth: laziness in keeping the faith or practicing virtue; neglecting to do one's duties out of lethargy
____ I take the time to do what God expects of me, for example, I pray every day and make sure I get to Mass every Saturday night or Sunday.
____ I commit myself to complete essential tasks, for example, my studies or chores around the house, no matter how boring they can be at times.

capital sins

Moral vices that give rise to many other failures to love. They are pride, avarice, lust, anger, gluttony, envy, and sloth.

Gather a week's worth of daily newspapers. In small groups, find several examples of each capital sin that shows itself in contemporary life.

◆ As a class, list three creative and realistic spiritual practices that could effectively combat each of the "capital sins."

For each of the social sins in this list, judge which of the capital sins (pride, avarice, envy, anger [wrath], lust, gluttony, sloth) probably gave birth to it:

1. racism
2. homelessness
3. hunger
4. high-paying salaries for sports and entertainment personalities versus low wages for various service-oriented occupations
5. unemployment caused by companies downsizing simply to increase profits
6. the crushing debt of poor nations
7. sexism
8. inequities of the legal system that especially harm members of minorities
9. alcoholism and drug addiction

◆ Pride is often called the root of all sin. In small groups, discuss how pride gives rise or can lead to the other six capital sins.

The Reality of Sin

(CCC, 1846-1851; 1870—1872)

Sin is defined in various ways. According to the *Catechism of the Catholic Church* (1849), sin is:

- an offense against reason, truth, and right conscience;
- a failure in genuine love for God and neighbor caused by a perverse attachment to certain goods;
- an utterance, a deed, or a desire contrary to the eternal law.

Simply put, sin is an offense against God whereby sinners turn from God's love through a false love of self. Unlike Jesus, who was always obedient to our heavenly Father, sinners disobey God's eternal law. Through willfulness and pride, they make themselves "like gods." This proud disobedience has led to the wounding of human nature and the injuring of human solidarity.

Although evidence of sin is all around us, many people deny its reality. A famous *Peanuts* cartoon has Linus asking the question, "Charlie Brown, do you know what's the trouble with you?" With great self-assurance, Charlie answers, "No." The two stare at each other. Finally, Linus responds, "The trouble with you, Charlie Brown, is that you don't want to know what is the trouble with you."

In the 1970s, Dr. Karl Menninger wrote a book titled *Whatever Happened to Sin?* A major thesis of the book was that people do not like to talk about sin because they refuse to admit that they are capable of sinning. However, to deny that we are sinners is unhealthy. Refusal to accept the reality of sin leads to pathological conditions in individuals and to corrupt societies.

Not much has changed in the years since the publication of Menninger's landmark work.

We now live in an age that encourages self-indulgence and stresses the pursuit of individual whims with little regard for the consequences to self or others. Yet it is *really* sick not to admit that, in both individuals and societies, there is much evidence of sin. Consider, for example, the following:

- the daily occurrences of sin we experience in our own lives (the angry outbursts directed at a younger sibling, a refusal to help with family chores, disobeying a reasonable request of one's parents, refusing to stand up for a classmate who is being unfairly verbally attacked, viewing pornographic material, etc.);
- widespread dishonesty, including the lying by those holding the highest political offices, the rampant cheating in schools, the shoplifting that drives up consumer prices, the overall cutting of corners and thereby falling far short of performing an "honest day's work for an honest day's pay";
- gossiping (e.g., the spreading of false rumors about a person that trashes her reputation);
- hate and prejudice, beginning with the harboring of hateful feelings toward people who are different and resulting in

Dr. Karl Menninger

prejudice that seriously discriminates against women, racial, ethnic, and religious groups, people with a homosexual orientation, and many others;

- alienated students who bring guns to schools and kill classmates at random;
- drivers who are under the influence of alcohol or high on drugs who injure or kill thousands of innocent motorists per year;
- the slaughter of countless thousands of innocent unborn human beings on a daily basis through abortion;
- the greed of multinational corporations that impoverishes developing nations and contributes to the daily starvation of thousands of children;
- a consumer society that exploits the natural resources of God's good earth and threatens the quality of the air we breathe and the water we drink;

- a world plagued by terrorists, who often act in the name of religion, instigating conflicts that lead to the death of countless innocent people.

The First Letter of John addresses the pervasiveness and deception of sin:

If we say, "We are without sin," we deceive ourselves, and the truth is not in us. If we acknowledge our sins, he is faithful and just and will forgive our sins and cleanse us from every wrongdoing. If we say, "We have not sinned," we make him a liar, and his word is not in us. (1 Jn 1:8–10)

It is both healthy and realistic to admit the existence of sin. However, to acknowledge the existence of sin does not lead us to despair. The Good News that Christians have to offer the world is that Jesus Christ has come to save people from their sins.

Jesus, a name that means "God saves," is God's mercy to sinners. Christ's own passion and death most clearly prove the existence of sin in its many forms: unbelief, hate, mockery, cowardice, cruelty, betrayal, and abandonment. But from the depths of this darkest hour, the sacrifice of Jesus Christ on the cross became the source of the forgiveness of sins. Jesus' bottomless love for us, his death and his resurrection, which we celebrate in the Eucharist, the sacrament of our redemption, is why we have tremendous hope in the midst of a world of sin.

However, for Christ's forgiving grace to touch our hearts and for us to receive his mercy, we must own up to our sins. To do so requires conversion, an interior judgment of conscience that acknowledges that we are sinners. For God's mercy to reach us, we must allow the Holy Spirit, a Spirit of truth, to lead us to God the Father through Christ as we reach for the healing forgiveness for our spiritual illness.

- In your judgment, are any of these examples not sinful? Why or why not? If you said "no," what would make them sinful?

- What makes something a sin?

- For you, what one action (or failure to act) is the strongest evidence that there is sin in the world?

REVIEW AND REFLECTION

1. Define and give an example of each of the capital sins.

2. Give and explain the meaning of any two definitions of sin.

3. Why do people sometimes deny the reality of sin?

FOR YOUR JOURNAL

"Jesus is a friend who knows all your sins but loves you anyway." Write a couple of paragraphs explaining what this sentence means to you personally.

The Bible on Sin

As you know, the Bible is filled with the Good News about God and his love for humanity. However, we also learn in the Scriptures the sad story of human willfulness, of humanity's decision to choose self over the good and loving God.

From the opening pages of the Bible and the story of the "Original Sin," the disobedience and pride of our first parents, we learn of human weakness, selfishness, stubbornness, and vanity. The fall of Adam and Eve graphically portrays the essential elements of sin. Adam and Eve deliberately violated a command God gave to them (see Gn 3:3–6). Their outward act of disobedience flowed from their interior rebellion against God. Adam and Eve thought they knew better. They wanted more freedom and desired something they thought would be good for them ("knowledge of good and evil"). They did not fully trust their loving God.

The effect of this original sin was tragic for Adam and Eve and for us. Their disobedience alienated them from God, from each other, from themselves, and from God's good creation. When confronted with their sin, Adam and Eve resorted to lies and rationalizations to cover up their behavior. However, the harm was done and the sad effects of their sin touched them and all their descendants through the ages.

The story of the original sin is recounted in the very first chapters of the Bible. But sin does not have the last word. The Old Testament proceeds with a story of God's love for humanity, especially viewed with the establishment of a gracious covenant with his Chosen People. This covenant reveals God's absolute fidelity to humanity, despite a continual pattern of human sin: choosing self over God, pursuing false goods, rebelling against God's commands, failing to take care of each other, submitting to the wiles of Satan. Saint Paul, in reviewing the condition of humanity concluded, "All have sinned and are deprived of the glory of God" (Rom 3:23).

The essential message of the Bible remains one of tremendous Good News about the promise and coming of the Son of God, Jesus Christ. Jesus was the Savior who came in our midst to forgive sin, to extend God's mercy, and to give us the Holy Spirit who enables us to live worthily as God's special children. Sin and death entered the world through Adam's transgression. But Jesus Christ has overcome them. His grace is more powerful than sin:

Read in Genesis 2:16–17; 3:1–24 the accounts of the Original Sin. Locate answers to the following questions:

- What command did God give Adam?

- What was to happen if Adam disobeyed God's command?

- How did Adam and Eve react when they met God after disobeying him? Why?

- What rationalization (excuse) did Eve offer for her sin? What excuse did Adam offer?

- List three consequences of Adam and Eve's sin for them.

For if, by the transgression of one person, death came to reign through that one, how much more will those who receive the abundance of grace and of the gift of justification come to reign in life through the one person Jesus Christ. In conclusion, just as through one transgression condemnation came upon all, so through one righteous act acquittal and life came to all. For just as through the disobedience of one person the many were made sinners, so through the obedience of one the many will be made righteous. . . . [W]here sin increased, grace overflowed all the more, so that, as sin reigned in death, grace also might reign through justification for eternal life through Jesus Christ our Lord. (Rom 5:17–21)

OLD TESTAMENT IMAGES OF SIN

There are over fifty different words to describe sin in the Old Testament. The three most common Hebrew words for sin are *hattah*, *pesha*, and *awon*. Each sheds some light on the true nature of sin.

Hattah ("hamartia" in the Greek) means "missing the mark." Related to the sport of archery, this concept of sin makes lots of sense. Our target in life should be union with God, that is, doing God's will here and now so we can be with our loving Triune God in eternity. When we sin, however, we miss our ultimate target. We willfully reject what God has made known to us for our own benefit.

Usually what happens when we "miss the mark" is that we take something intended to be good and make it into our god. We deliberately choose to be less than we can be—to be less thoughtful, less honest, less loving. We make choices that are unworthy of our dignity as God's children.

Here are some examples of sin that fit under the definition of "missing the mark":

- A politician accepts illegal donations in an election campaign. He feels he can do a lot of good once elected, but he has compromised his integrity by violating the laws he will one day promise to uphold.
- A student has a stuttering problem that results in occasional mocking by her classmates. Stephanie joins in the routine teasing to be accepted by her "friends." Stephanie is surrendering her individuality and participating in unkindness toward someone who needs sympathetic understanding. She is being less than she can be.
- Jason refuses to give blood to help a fellow classmate who is going in for surgery. His excuse is that his time is precious, and he can't afford to waste to an hour to give blood. In his selfishness, Jason is blinded to the needs of a neighbor. He is choosing self over the welfare of

another, unable to see the needs of a neighbor over his own short-term needs.

Pesha means "rebellion." To the Jews of the Old Testament era, this word for sin meant "a willful violation of God's law" or "deliberately rebelling against God's reign." Adjectives like "stubborn," "stiff-necked," or "hard-hearted" were often used to illustrate the nature of willful rebellion. The prophet Jeremiah wrote: "But this people's heart is stubborn and rebellious; they turn and go away" (Jer 5:23).

And Moses said of the Israelites:

"For I already know how rebellious and stiff-necked you will be. Why, even now, while I am alive among you, you have been rebels against the Lord! How much more, then, after I am dead!" (Dt 31:27)

Sin in the context of rebellion referred to the violation of the rights of others or Israel's infidelity to God's loving covenant with his people. The Old Testament prophets clearly saw sin as a deliberate choice made with full knowledge, a contempt for Yahweh. The prophets Amos and Isaiah imaged this rebellion as *pride*; Hosea, Jeremiah, and Ezekiel likened it to *adultery* because it violated the covenant relationship God established with his people; and Isaiah and Jeremiah called it childish *disobedience* and *ingratitude*.

In the New Testament, Jesus taught that the rebelliousness of sin is rooted in deep-seated attitudes in the human heart:

"For from the heart come evil thoughts, murder, adultery, unchastity, theft, false witness, blasphemy."(Mt 15:19)

Examples of stiff-necked, hard-hearted rebellion against God would include attitudes and actions like the following:

- Apathy, that is, lack of interest in anything, for example, the plight of the poor. "Poor people are not my problem. I can't do anything about their needs . . ."
- Refusal to take correction based on the attitude that "no one can tell *me* what to do."
- Hostility toward people who are different, directly contradicting Jesus' command to love everyone as we love ourselves.

Awon means "guilt" or "iniquity." It refers to the consequences of sin, how sin causes permanent damage to the sinner. The *Catechism of the Catholic Church* teaches some of the many consequences of sin that has distorted humanity from what God intended us to be. Sin:

◆ **alienates us from God.** Sin deprives us of the glory of God (*CCC,* 705) and if serious, kills charity in us and results in the loss of sanctifying grace (1861). Alienation from God's love and his grace lead to sickness and death.

Originally, God did not intend for us to die, but death entered the world as a consequence of sin (*CCC,* 1008).

◆ **alienates us from ourselves**. Sin crushes the lives of sinners, hardens our hearts, weakens our intellects, and enslaves our wills. By sinning, we get into the habit of sin, creating vice through repetition of the same acts. This results in perverse inclinations that cloud conscience and corrupt the concrete judgment of good and evil. Thus sin tends to reproduce and reinforce itself, but it cannot destroy the moral sense at its root (1865).

◆ **alienates us from others.** Sin is relational. When we sin, we hurt others. It leads to our separation and harms our communion with others and injures church unity (*CCC,* 817, 845, 953).

IMAGES OF SIN

Drawing on Old Testament insights into the nature of sin, judge which image would best match the descriptions given.

A. stiff-necked hard-heartedness
B. missing the mark
C. iniquity
D. rebellion (failure in covenant love)

_____ 1. Attitude: "Sin is an old-fashioned, outdated concept used by the Church to control people."
_____ 2. Attitude: "No one has the right to tell me that I might be sinning."
_____ 3. Attitude: "If I don't think I have sinned, then I haven't sinned."
_____ 4. Action: a telephone solicitor calls an elderly woman with a scheme to defraud her of her retirement income
_____ 5. Action: a classmate makes a vicious slur against Jews
_____ 6. Action: a terrorist threatens to unleash a biological weapon in a city subway
_____ 7. Action: Internet sites gather information about you and sell it to vendors
_____ 8. Action: an American company moves its business to Mexico so it can pay its workers $3 an hour versus the $26 it has to pay its American workers
_____ 9. Omission: knowing he is infected with the AIDS virus, a man keeps it a secret from his sexual partner
_____ 10. Omission: not using one's God-given talents (for example, laziness in studies)

Discuss:
Would you consider any of the above *not* to be sinful? Why or why not? If not, what would make them sinful?

REVIEW AND REFLECTION

1. What was the nature of the Original Sin of Adam and Eve? What were some of the consequences of original sin for Adam and Eve? for us?

2. What is the Old Testament's essential message about sin?

3. Explain the meaning of sin as: (1) missing the mark; (2) rebellion; and (3) iniquity.

4. List the three major consequences of sin.

FOR YOUR JOURNAL

In your journal, write about whether you think it is healthy (psychologically) to recognize the existence of sin in the world. Would it be overwhelmingly depressing? Could it make us feel helpless, hopeless, unable to answer "the darkness" with our own good deeds and virtues? Give several reasons for your opinion.

THE NEW TESTAMENT ON SIN, JESUS, AND FORGIVENESS

Those who have sinned must not despair. Let that never be. For we are condemned not for the multitude of evils but because we do not want to repent and learn the miracles of Christ.

—St. Mark the Ascetic[1]

Like the Old Testament, the New Testament emphasizes the description "missing the mark" when defining sin. Other descriptions are *lawlessness*, or contempt for God and his law; *injustice*, that is, refusal to accept God and his reign revealed in Christ; *falsehood*; and *darkness*. These last two descriptions point out that sin opposes God's truth, which we find in Jesus.

The most profound explanation of sin as found in the New Testament is "a refusal to love, to accept God's offer of friendship and grace in our Lord Jesus Christ."[2]

Jesus is the key to understanding sin and forgiveness. He is God's mercy. His essential message is related to sin:

"This is the time of fulfillment. The kingdom of God is at hand. Repent, and believe in the gospel." (Mk 1:15)

Jesus preached the advent of God's Kingdom of justice and peace, a kingdom he helped usher in and of which he was a principal sign. Accepting and living God's Kingdom demands a new attitude on our part. We must make a wholehearted commitment to Jesus and to the Kingdom. We must turn from our sinful ways and love others with his love.

Sin is, ultimately, a failure to respond to God's love, a failure to love God above all and our neighbor as ourselves. Jesus abhorred sin because it drew people away from his Father's love for them, and he had some harsh warnings about sin, even saying that some sins lead to eternal damnation. Examples of sins he strongly condemned included *actions,* like being a bad example, which causes others to sin (Mt 18:6); *failures to act,* like not responding to the needy in our midst (Mt 25:41–46); and *attitudes,* like the anger that leads to violence (Mt 5:22).

But, Jesus forgave sin. The heart of the Christian message is that Jesus Christ—his passion, death, and resurrection—has overcome sin and death. Jesus Christ has taken on all the sins of the world—those committed before he became incarnate; those committed during his lifetime, including the horrendous crimes that led to his execution; and all sins ever to be committed. He took these sins, and as the Lamb of God, bore them on our behalf, and has forgiven them.

Time and again during his earthly ministry, he showed that his essential mission was on behalf of sinners. His association with sinners, outcasts, and those outside the law brought much grumbling from the religious leaders of his day. But Jesus retorted,

"Those who are well do not need a physician, but the sick do. Go and learn the meaning of the words, 'I desire mercy, not sacrifice.' I did not come to call the righteous but sinners."(Mt 9:12–13)

Jesus is the *Divine Physician* of sinners (and *all* of us are sinners). In his earthly ministry, he actively sought out lawbreakers, prostitutes, and the hated tax collectors. He often announced God's forgiveness of sinners by mercifully attaching it to a miracle he performed for a needy person, for example, for a man born lame:

> *And there people brought to him a paralytic lying on a stretcher. When Jesus saw their faith, he said to the paralytic, "Courage, child, your sins are forgiven." (Mt 9:2)*

Jesus used these occasions to prove his power to forgive sins, a power only God possesses. Thus, Jesus, God's only Son, revealed himself to be God's mercy, God-made-man for our salvation.

One of the most dramatic examples of Jesus in action was his forgiveness of a woman caught in adultery (Jn 8:3–11). Confronting an irate crowd ready to stone the woman to death, Jesus pointed out that everyone was a sinner, "Let the one among you who is without sin be the first to throw a stone at her" (Jn 8:7). When the woman's accusers crept away shortly after, he turned to the woman and forgave her sins. His instruction to her after his forgiveness is the same instruction he gives us today, "Go, (and) from now on do not sin anymore" (Jn 8:11).

This dramatic example not only shows how Jesus forgave sin, but underscores an important part of his preaching about sin:

> *"Stop judging and you will not be judged. Stop condemning and you will not be condemned. Forgive and you will be forgiven." (Lk 6:37)*

With his dying breath Jesus forgave sinners. Looking down on those who were taunting him at the site of his crucifixion, Jesus prayed to his Father, a prayer he also says today for sinners of all ages: "Father, forgive them, they know not what they do" (Lk 23:34).

Jesus simply asks us to heed his message of conversion. He asks three things of us. He asks us to repent for our sins. He asks us to believe in the Gospel message that God loves us. And he asks us to live the Good News of love he has given to us—with the help of the Holy Spirit.

> *"(And) be kind to one another, compassionate, forgiving one another as God has forgiven you in Christ."*
>
> —Ephesians 4:32

JESUS AND FORGIVENESS: A SCRIPTURAL SEARCH

Sample Jesus' powerful message of forgiveness by reading the following passages from the Gospel of Luke, often called the Gospel for sinners. Answer each corresponding question.

1. Penitent Woman (Luke 7:36–50)
- What negative judgment did Simon the Pharisee have about Jesus?
- What is the point of the parable Jesus told to Simon?

2. Lost Sheep, Lost Coin (Luke 15:1–10)
- Why was Jesus being criticized?
- Why will there be rejoicing in heaven?

3. The "Good" Thief (Luke 23:39–43)
- What promise did Jesus give to a condemned sinner?
- What did the criminal ask of Jesus?

4. Seven Times (Lk 17:3–4)
- What are Christians obligated to do?

5. Prodigal Son (Lk 15:11–32)
- What sins were committed by the younger son?
- What sins were committed by the older son?
- Why could the father forgive the younger son?
- What does this parable reveal about God?

REVIEW AND REFLECTION

1. List three New Testament words that describe sin. According to the New Testament, what is the most profound meaning of sin?

2. Tell why Jesus hates sin.

3. Discuss two examples of how Jesus dealt with sin in his earthly ministry.

FOR YOUR JOURNAL

Rewrite the parable of the Prodigal Son in a modern setting. Make yourself one of the characters in the parable.

Different Kinds of Sin
(CCC, 1852—1864; 1866—1867; 1873)

Through the centuries, Christian tradition has considered sin from many different perspectives. For example, as mentioned in this chapter's opening exercise, certain vices can be linked to the so-called seven capital sins.

Tradition also lists five sins described in the Bible as acts so terrible that they are "sins that cry to heaven" for God's justice. These five sins are the Blood of Abel (fratricide, cf. Gn 4:10), the sin of the Sodomites (perverted sexual relations, Gn 18:20, 19:13), the cry of God's people oppressed in Egypt (Ex 3:7–10), the cry of foreigners, widows, and orphans (Ex 22:20–22), and injustice to the wage earner (Dt 24:14–15; Jas 5:4).

The letter to the Galatians mentions "works of the flesh" in contrast to the fruit of the Holy Spirit. The *New American Bible* translates these sins of the flesh as immorality, impurity, licentiousness, idolatry, sorcery, hatreds, rivalry, jealousy, outbursts of fury, acts of selfishness, dissensions, factions, incidents of envy, drinking bouts, orgies, and other things similar (Gal 5:19–21). Incidentally, the exact opposite of these ungodly acts are the following virtues, which flow from allowing God's Spirit to live in us: love, joy, peace, patience, kindness, generosity, faithfulness, gentleness, self-control (Gal 5:22–23).

The *Catechism of the Catholic Church* (1853) also distinguishes between kinds of sins according to:

- their objects;
- the virtues they oppose;
- the commandments they violate;
- whether they concern God, neighbor, or oneself;
- whether they deal with the spirit or with the body; and
- whether they are sins in thought, word, deed, or a failure to act (omission).

A distinction is also made between Original Sin and personal sin. Personal sin is divided into two categories according to their gravity—*mortal sin* and *venial sin*. The gravity of sin is usually determined by the moral object (what is done). Regardless of how various sins are classified, please note that the root of all sin is the human heart, that is, the exercise of free human will.

Original Sin Versus Personal Sin *(CCC, 386—410)*

To Adam and Eve, the Original Sin was also their personal sin. From their time onward, individual humans do not commit Original Sin. They are not blameworthy for the Original Sin. The Original Sin does not come from their free acts. It only comes from the free acts of Adam and Eve.

However, all humans are born into the *condition* of Original Sin, that is, the disharmonious situation of our world to which all of us are subject. Genesis 3 uses figurative language to point to a primeval event at the beginning of human history to teach the truth that our first parents committed an original fault. As a result, all of human history has been marked by this Original Sin (*CCC*, 390).

Adam and Eve misused their freedom. Tempted by the devil, they failed to trust God and they disobeyed his command. They chose self over God, thus scorning God by not recognizing that they were creatures, not the Creator. All subsequent human sins resemble the original sin of our first parents because they are in disobedience and a lack of trust in God.

The consequences of Original Sin meant that Adam and Eve lost the grace of original holiness. The harmony they had at the beginning of creation was now gone. This meant several things: the control of the soul over the body was lost, the relations between man and woman would be marked by lust and domination, harmony with creation was broken, and death entered human history.

With this Original Sin came a human race infected by sin. Scripture attests to this from the beginning, for example, in Cain's killing of his brother Abel (Gn 4:1—16). Our own viewing or reading of the daily news shows the massive prevalence of sin in the world today.

Though Adam and Eve each committed a personal sin, their Original Sin affected us all. Transmitted to us through propagation, it deprives all humans of the original justice and holiness. It means we have a weakened human nature,

> wounded in the natural powers proper to it; subject to ignorance, suffering, and the dominion of death, and inclined to sin—an inclination to evil that is called "concupiscence." Baptism, by imparting the life of Christ's grace, erases Original Sin and turns a man back toward God, but the consequences for nature, weakened and inclined to evil, persist in man and summon him to spiritual battle. (*CCC, 405*)

Because we are subject to the effects of the Original Sin, we must constantly battle the temptations of the world, the flesh, and the devil. As human beings, we are powerless to combat the effects of our weakened nature. However, as Jesus Christ has conquered Original Sin and won for us our salvation and eternal life with a loving, Triune God, he has also given us the Holy Spirit and his many graces to combat **concupiscence** (our inclination to evil) and the temptation to commit personal sin in our own life.

---

concupiscence

An inclination toward evil caused by Original Sin. More specifically, in Christian theology, it means "the rebellion of the 'flesh' against the spirit" (*CCC*, 2515).

"Sin is present in human history; any attempt to ignore it or to give this dark reality other names would be futile" (*CCC*, 386). Brainstorm examples of sinful human behavior that has been called something else in our day and age in order to justify it. (E.g., lying about a political opponent is sometimes called "negative campaign advertising" or abortion has been called "removal of fetal matter.")

"Getting Over" Temptations

A young priest beginning his ministry went to an older and wiser priest, age seventy-four. He told him that the beautiful figure of one of his young female parishioners was a constant source of temptation to him. The younger priest told his priestly brother that he thought these temptations were sinful. But the older priest assured him that temptation is not the same as actually consenting to the sin. He simply reminded his younger colleague of Jesus' wise injunction, "Watch and pray that you may not undergo the test. The spirit is willing but the flesh is weak" (Mk 14:38).

The younger priest was relieved. But he asked, "Father, at what age does one get over such temptations?"

The older priest replied, "Three days after you're dead."

In contrast to Original Sin is **personal sin**, which you and I personally and freely commit. Personal sin is any free and deliberate act, word, thought, or desire that turns us away from God's law of love. Personal sin either weakens (**venial sin**) or kills (**mortal sin**) our relationship with God.

MORTAL SIN

(CCC, 1855—1861; 1874)

Mortal sin is deadly sin, a grave violation of God's law that destroys charity in the human heart. We sin mortally when we freely choose a grave disorder, something that contradicts the love of God in a serious way—for example, blasphemy or perjury—or destroys the love for neighbor—for example, murder or adultery. Because mortal sin destroys God's love in us, we need God's help, mercy, and grace to turn from our mortal sins and seek his forgiveness. For Catholics, this is normally done in the Sacrament of **Reconciliation**.

To sin mortally, three conditions must be present:

1. *Grave matter.* What we do (the object of the act) must be serious enough to destroy God's love in us, turning us away from him. The Ten Commandments point to what constitutes grave matter. Examples of a serious matter are murder, adultery, apostasy, abortion, blasphemy, sexually perverted acts, and defrauding the poor.

2. *Full knowledge.* To commit mortal sin, we must know that what we are doing is seriously wrong, that is, gravely contrary to God's law. If we are ignorant of a particular wrong through no fault of our own, then our blameworthiness for a particular action may be diminished or removed. However, pretending to be ignorant does not excuse us from sin. Rather, phoniness and insincerity increase our guilt. Also, recall that the basic principles of God's law are written on the human heart. We can hardly claim to be ignorant of the gravity of actions that cause serious harm to ourselves or others, for example, driving recklessly.

3. *Complete consent.* For an action that involves serious matter to be mortally sinful, the person must give full consent of the will. Supposing I kill someone in a car accident on an icy road. The person I hit dashed out into the road, and when I tried to stop the car, it slid into the pedestrian. Did my car kill the person? Yes. Am I guilty of mortal sin? No, because I did not intend to do so. The death resulted from an accident I did not intend to cause.

Full consent makes our choices personal and deliberate. Factors that can limit full consent, and thus limit the voluntary nature of our actions, include strong emotions and passion, physical or psychological force inflicted from the outside, or emotional illness. Maliciously choosing to commit evil is the worst sin of all.

Make no mistake about it. It *is* possible to sin mortally. Because we have freedom, we can love or not love. Because we have freedom, we can choose God or not

personal sin

A failure to love God above everything and our neighbor as ourselves.

venial sin

Personal sin that weakens but does not kill our relationship with God.

mortal sin

Personal sin that involves a serious matter, sufficient reflection, and full consent of the will. It results in total rejection of God and alienation from him.

Reconciliation

A sacrament of healing, also known as Penance or Confession, through which Christ extends his forgiveness to sinners.

choose God. Because we have freedom, we can do good to others or harm them. In other words, freedom makes it possible for human beings to sin mortally.

Mortal sin is something we should avoid at all costs. Its effects are serious. For example, in the  state of mortal sin, we suffer the loss of charity, sanctifying grace, and friendship with the Lord. If we do not repent of any mortal sin we have committed, mortal sin will keep us out of heaven and merit for us eternal separation from God, the state of being known as hell. Thankfully, Christ has left us with the Sacrament of Reconciliation, which is the normal way for Catholics to approach the Lord and ask for his forgiveness of any mortal sins we may have committed.

Christ, the Church, and our own well-formed consciences teach us what acts constitute grave offenses against God. But we must be very careful in judging whether specific persons who commit a particular act are guilty of mortal sin. Jesus taught us to leave judgment of souls to God himself, a God of justice and mercy.

REVIEW AND REFLECTION

1. What is the root of all sin?

2. Define *Original Sin*. How does all personal sin resemble the "Original Sin" of our first parents?

3. What is *concupiscence*? Give several realistic examples of concupiscence at work in the life of a teen.

4. Define *personal sin*.

5. What is the distinction between mortal and venial sin?

6. What must be present for a person to be guilty of mortal sin?

7. Discuss three examples of sinful actions that involve "grave" matter. Explain why each involves a serious matter.

8. What can limit full consent of the will?

9. What are the effects of mortal sin?

FOR YOUR JOURNAL

Write out your own definition of sin. Briefly explain each element in your definition.

VENIAL SIN
(CCC, 1862—1863; 1875)

The word *venial* means "easily forgivable." We commit "venial" sin when we fail to follow the moral law in less serious matters or when we disobey God's law in something grave, but without full knowledge or without complete consent.

Venial sin is a partial rejection of God whereby charity is weakened, but not destroyed. It represents an attachment to some created good, but is not so serious that it deprives us of sanctifying grace, friendship with God, love, or the loss of eternal happiness.

Typical examples of venial sin include disobeying your parents' rule about a curfew, being resentful about helping a sibling with homework, copying homework from a classmate and passing it off as your own, and telling a fib to avoid giving an acquaintance a ride home from school. Though these sins do not directly oppose God's will, or break the friendship relationship we have with Christ, they do keep us from growing in holiness. Furthermore, "deliberate and unreported venial sin disposes us little by little to commit mortal sin" (*CCC*, 1863).

For our spiritual growth, the Church recommends that we confess our venial sins in the Sacrament of Reconciliation. Asking for God's forgiveness in the penitential rite at Mass or in our daily prayer (for example, in the Lord's Prayer—"forgive us our trespasses") are two other ways these sins can be forgiven. A good spiritual practice to counteract venial and other sins and vices is to engage in some act of self-denial. For example, a good way to counteract the tendency to pride is to practice its opposite virtue—humility. Instead of boasting about one's own achievements, a person tempted to pride could pay a sincere compliment to a classmate. Or an avaricious person can combat greed by giving something of personal value away to a needy person. A slothful (lazy) person could volunteer to help out on a particular project without being asked.

SOCIAL SIN

Sin is a personal action. Yet we are also responsible when we cooperate in another person's sin. This cooperation can take place in the following situations:

- When we directly and voluntarily participate in the sins of another. (*Example:* joining classmates in the mockery of another person.)
- When we order, advise, praise, or approve the sins of another person. (*Example:* excusing an unjustified violent act committed by a friend by saying, "He had it coming to him.")
- When we do not disclose or stop the commission of a sin when we are duty-bound to do so. (*Example*: by looking the other way when a friend shoplifts from a store where one is employed.)
- When we protect evil-doers. (*Example*: by lying about their sinful behavior.)

There are major problems when people band together and sin. The personal sins of individuals, especially when they blind individuals and groups to the condition of their sinfulness, often lead to "structures of sin" in society. These structures of sin result from and express personal sin. They create unjust policies, practices, and laws that victimize people and tempt these victims to lash out at the "system," often using sinful means. Thus is created **social sin**, that is, a cycle of sin, violence, and injustice caused by individual sins.

Here are some examples of social sin caused by personal sins.
- Greed, fueled by consumerism, often leads to the neglect of the poor in our midst. Personal greed along with the gluttonous behavior of the well-off are major causes for the evil of hunger.
- Selfish actions on the part of individuals and groups lead to the rape of the environment.

social sin

A cycle of sin, violence, and injustice caused by individual sins.

- Pride and prejudice lead to policies and laws that deny people fundamental rights, for example, to housing, jobs, and education.

- Pride, envy, greed, and other sinful attitudes have created a "culture of death" that denies unborn babies the right to life and encourages euthanasia and assisted suicide.

- Unbridled lust in some individuals has led to the acceptance of pornography and violence in various media, the cheapening of human life, and the degradation of women.
- Avarice of individuals, groups, and nations has led to violent competition among nations, thus contributing to the exploitation of poor nations, the depletion of natural resources, and war.

Unfortunately, sin holds great power in our world. Personal sin leads to sinful structures that beget more sinful acts that lead to more social sin. A vicious cycle takes place that requires the repentance of individuals, the conversion of groups, and an active battle against the forces that divide people and cause alienation. Christians look to Jesus and the help of the Holy Spirit to renew our hearts, to bring inner conversion and divine mercy, and to strengthen us to fight our inclination to sin.

Mortal or Venial Sin?

For one to sin mortally, "grave matter" must be present. "Grave matter" involves something that produces significant harm, that is, causes real damage. Or the sinner *intends* to cause grave harm. The serious harm caused by mortal sin is often directed against other people. But grave matter also involves hurting God's good creation or oneself, including one's relationship with our loving God. Factors to consider in judging what is grave matter would be to ask how the act, attitude, thought, word, or failure to act

- hurts human dignity;
- abuses another's physical well-being;
- harms a person's freedom, good name, or property;
- damages the ecology;
- injures our life together—the common good.

- What other information would you need to know about any of the items to make a decision about the gravity of the moral object?
- Give examples to show how a person's blameworthiness for a particular act might be lessened for something you judged to be grave matter.

MORE OR LESS SINFUL?

fym Yas.

Judge which of the following probably constitutes "grave matter," thus constituting mortal sin (**M**), or "less serious matter," which would ordinarily constitute venial sin (**V**), or no sin at all (**N**).

M   1.   lying under oath
M   2.   not stopping at the scene of an accident you caused
M   3.   verbally abusing a person with a disability
M   4.   cheating on income taxes
M   5.   torturing political prisoners
N   6.   playing favorites among two parents
M   7.   suicide
V   8.   refusing to forgive someone who asks for forgiveness
M   9.   child pornography
V   10.   refusing to go to Mass
M   11.   carrying a concealed weapon
V   12.   intoxication
M   13.   performing medical experiments without patient consent
M   14.   refusing to help a stranger who needs life-preserving first aid
N   15.   having sexual feelings toward a member of the same sex
M   16.   saying you love someone in order to gain sexual favors
M   17.   selling drugs to support an addiction
M   18.   wanton killing of animals for the fun of it
V/M   19.   routinely disobeying traffic laws
M   20.   committing adultery

REVIEW AND REFLECTION

1. Why should Christians be concerned about committing even venial sins?

2. Explain the term *social sin*. Give an example of a sinful social structure caused by personal sins of individuals.

FOR YOUR JOURNAL

Note personal venial sins that seem to crop up in your life. For each sin, think of a practical act of self-denial you can engage in to help counteract that particular shortcoming.

Baby As Trash

A notorious case made big news a few years ago. At her high school prom, a student gave birth to a baby in the restroom. She deposited the baby's body in the trash receptacle where it was discovered some time later. To the girl, who had tried her best to hide her pregnancy, disposing of the baby was the same as taking care of a routine bodily function.

- *List all the possible sins committed by individuals and tolerated by society that led up to this outrageous act.*

Conversion and the Sacrament of Reconciliation

To live a moral life requires that we admit sin, admit that we are weak and sinful, and admit that we suffer from the effects of Original Sin, including concupiscence. The first step to holiness is admitting that we are not perfect, and that we need God's help to grow in holiness.

The next step is to pay close attention to Jesus' message of repentance. **Repentance**, or conversion (*metanoia* in the Greek), is at the heart of the Gospel message. With God's help, it is possible for us to change our hearts, minds, and attitudes in order to reorient our priorities. Because of God's help and graces, it is possible for us to convert, that is, turn away from our sins and the alienation they cause, and turn anew to God. And, because God is good, he can and will forgive anyone who repents of his or her sins.

A central theme of Jesus' preaching is the unlimited mercy of our loving God. This is the very point of the parable of the Prodigal Son. Recall how the younger brother hit rock bottom in licentious living, but finally he came to his senses (Lk 15:17). He repented and came back to his father, a father who deeply loved his boy, waiting day and night for his return. Note in the parable how the father ran out to greet his son, accepted his confession of sinfulness by warmly embracing him, and threw him a big party to welcome him home.

When the self-righteous older brother complained of this magnanimous treatment, the loving father simply replied,

> *My son, you are here with me always; everything I have is yours. But now we must celebrate and rejoice, because your brother was dead and has come to life again; he was lost and has been found. (Lk 15:31–32)*

God is like the father in this story. God will forgive the sins of anyone who approaches him for forgiveness. The only "unforgivable sin" is the sin against the Holy Spirit. This is the *deliberate* refusal to accept God's mercy through repentance, a total rejection of the Lord's forgiveness and the salvation the Holy Spirit offers to each human being (*CCC*, 1864). God does not force his love on us. We must freely consent to it by turning away from our sins and to the warm embrace of God's forgiveness.

The Sacrament of Reconciliation is a powerful sign Christ left with his Church to celebrate and proclaim God's reconciling love. Through this sign of love and healing, Christ reaches out to repentant sinners. This sacrament of healing love has traditionally been known as *Penance*, *Confession*, and *Reconciliation*. Each title reveals something about the special graces of and Jesus' intentions for this sacrament.

Penance is the English equivalent of *metanoia*, or "conversion." By means of this sacrament, sinners acknowledge that they are indeed sinners and that they want to turn from their sins. Proof that they are willing to convert includes feeling and expressing genuine sorrow (**contrition**) for sins, owning up to their sins, approaching the Lord for his forgiveness, and making a firm commitment to sin no more. Conversion is the heart of Jesus' message and the heart of being his disciple. But conversion is not just a one-time thing. Conversion is a lifelong process. It

---

repentance

From the Greek word *metanoia,* it means change of mind or change of heart. A key aspect of following Jesus is to turn from our sins and embrace the way of the cross.

contrition

Heartfelt sorrow and aversion for sins committed along with the intention to sin no more.

If you were a priest assigning penances, what would you suggest for the following sins?

◆ lying to one's parents

◆ cheating

◆ intoxication

◆ making fun of minority groups

◆ missing Mass

◆ using another person for sexual gratification

◆ failing to share one's resources with the poor

demands a daily struggle with temptation and the tendency to sin.

Following the steps of Jesus, who recommended frequent acts of penance—including traditional works like praying, fasting, and almsgiving—the Church commends the frequent celebration of the Sacrament of Penance as a tremendous aid in the conversion process. Our obligation as Catholics, however, is minimally to confess any mortal sins of which we are aware at least once a year (*CCC*, 2042).

Calling this sacrament *Confession* emphasizes one aspect of the sacrament—the "telling," or confession, of our sins. Owning up to our sins is a true sign that we are sorry for them. By confessing our sinfulness, we are also "confessing" our faith in God's mercy. Confession is good for the soul. In turn, the priest, as Christ's and the Church's official representative, assures repentant sinners that our merciful Father does indeed forgive us and welcomes us back into the community, especially if our sins have separated us ·from God and fellow believers.

Naming this sacrament *Reconciliation* shows that sin alienates us from God, from others, and from self. All sin harms relationships. Turning from sin, and being truly sorry for one's sins, leads to the reconciliation that helps to mend relationships. Through this sacrament, and the words of **absolution** recited by the priest, sinners are assured of God's mercy and forgiveness. God and sinner are reconciled, brought together again because of God's love. So, too, are the sinner and the Church reconciled. Sin harms not just the individual, but the whole community. Through reconciliation, the community is healed.

When British author G. K. Chesterton was asked why he became Catholic, he responded, "To have my sins forgiven." Catholics are privileged to have this sacrament of healing as a special means to experience the Lord's forgiveness. Through this sacrament, the priest, who represents Christ and the Christian community, reassures us of God's saving love.

Through the centuries, Christian seekers have found this sacrament and regular reception of Holy Communion to be two powerful ways to grow in holiness. The sacramental graces of Reconciliation help us face ourselves honestly, peacefully, and joyfully. They help us root sin out of our lives and strengthen us for a life of conversion . . . and *moral* living.

absolution

The statement by which a priest, speaking as the official minister of Christ's Church, declares forgiveness of sins to a repentant sinner in the Sacrament of Reconciliation. The formula of absolution reads: "I absolve you from your sins; in the name of the Father, and of the Son, and of the Holy Spirit. Amen."

Elements of the Sacrament

The five steps of the Sacrament of Reconciliation (Penance, Confession) are as follows:

1. **Examine your conscience.** Ask the Holy Spirit to help you examine sin in your life. Reflect on Christ's law of love of God, neighbor, and self, the Ten Commandments, your practice of (or failure to practice) the virtues, and your following of Jesus.

2. **Have contrition for your sins**. "Contrition" is another word for "sorrow." Sorrow is not simply grief over making a wrong choice, but genuine sadness for not loving, for causing harm in your relationships with God, others, or self.

3. **Confess your sins.** Being able to own up to one's sins takes maturity and sincerity. The naming of our sins helps us pinpoint those actions and attitudes that need the healing touch of God. Confession helps us be true to ourselves and to God and is an external sign of true sorrow.

4. **Absolution.** After confessing our sins and making an act of contrition, the priest pronounces the words of absolution, announcing God's forgiveness.

5. **Do the penance assigned**. Before the words of absolution, the priest assigns a "penance," some action or prayers you should do or say to help you in the conversion process or help you heal some of the hurt your sin may have caused others. Ideally, the penance relates to the sins committed, for example, sins of selfishness may be given a penance of an act of kindness toward others. Truly, the Sacrament of Reconciliation is not finished until the penitent does his or her penance.

EXAMINATION OF CONSCIENCE

In preparation for celebrating the Sacrament of Reconciliation, examine your conscience by using one of the following online formats:

1. Saint Charles Borremeo Catholic Church's "Guide for Examination of Conscience for Confession of Sins": www.scborromeo.org/confess.htm

2. California Youth Grateful to the Pope at EWTN website: www.ewtn.com/library/YOUTH/CONFESS.TXT

3. Fr. Thomas M. Casey's Youth Update, "Preparing for Confession": www.americancatholic.org/Newsletters/YU/ay0491.asp

FOR YOUR JOURNAL

Write of a time when you truly had contrition for something that you did that was wrong. What was at the root of your sorrow for this wrongdoing?

REVIEW AND REFLECTION

1. Explain the three different names for the sacrament of healing known as Reconciliation, Confession, and Penance.
2. What is the "sin against the Holy Spirit"? Why is it known as the "unforgivable sin"?
3. List and briefly discuss the five elements in the Sacrament of Reconciliation.

Catholic Life in Action

1. A Fable: In a certain town, there was a notorious horse thief who stole a horse a week from a wealthy rancher. His wife finally convinced him that he was a great sinner. He promised to mend his ways. He told her, "You are quite correct. I will stop stealing a horse a week. From now on, I will steal a horse only every other week."
   a. What does this horse thief lack in the conversion process?
   b. Create a list of examples of how people are like this horse thief, giving mere lip service to repentance.
   c. Compose your own fable of an insincere penitent.

2. Compose a list of five good reasons to go to confession. You may be helped by checking out this website: www.catholicyouth.org/whyconfession.htm.

3. Read and report on the Youth Update "Reconciliation: An Experience of Forgiveness," written by Ellen Fanizzi: www.americancatholic.org/Newsletters/YU/ay0199. asp.

4. After defining the term and presenting some statistics about it, prepare a brief report on the *causes* of one of these social sins:
   a. racism
   b. homelessness
   c. hunger
   d. sexism

5. Read Luke 23:39–43, which reports Jesus' forgiveness of the "Good Thief" as they both hung on the cross. Write an imaginary reflection on what the Good Thief must have thought about Jesus after he heard these words and before he died.

6. Practical Applications: Thus far, you have learned various moral principles. Now is a good time to review them because failing to follow them leads to sin.
   As a class, list several sins that would violate each principle. Then, for each of the brief cases listed, decide what is the right thing to do by applying the correct moral principle. Decide if sin would be involved if you followed one course of action rather than another.

   The Principles
   A. Do good; avoid evil.
   B. One may never do evil that good may result from it. ("A good end does not justify using evil means to attain it.")
   C. Do unto others what you would have them do unto you.
   D. Give a good example. Never do anything to make others sin.
   E. Be the human being God intended you to be.
   a. You are filling out an application for a college that you really want to attend. Most of your classmates are inflating their extracurricular résumés to give them "the edge." Should you follow their example?
   Yes   No   Principle(s): _____

   Would it be sinful for you to exaggerate a little bit? _____

   b. You personally know a classmate who has developed a clever system of making fake IDs that some of your friends use to buy beer illegally. School authorities learn of the scheme and ask students who know the identity of the culprit to come forward. Should you reveal what you know?
   Yes   No   Principle(s): _____

   Would it be sinful for you to keep silent? _____

   c. Your youth ministry team asks you to participate in a project to help inner-city kids. You have never before joined in any kind of service project. Would it be wrong for you once again to refuse to pitch in?
   Yes   No   Principle(s): _____

   Would you be committing a sin if you did not help on the project? _____

   d. You are stuck watching your thirteen-year-old brother. Some friends want you to see an R-rated film (bad language, adult situations, some nudity). You could probably sneak your brother in. Should you go?
   Yes   No   Principle(s): _____

   Would you sin if you took your brother to the movie? _____

   Discuss: In the cases that involve sin, decide whether it would be mortal or venial sin.

Summary Points

◆ According to the *Catechism of the Catholic Church*, sin is an offense against reason, truth, and right conscience. It is also the failure to love God and neighbor because of a disordered attachment to some good. Sin can also be defined as a word, deed, or desire contrary to the eternal law.

◆ There is much evidence in the world, and in our personal lives, to prove the existence of sin. To deny its reality is unhealthy for societies and for individuals. St. John tells us if we say we are without sin, we lie and are victims of self-deception.

◆ The Gospel's story of sin is also the Good News of Jesus' conquering sin. He is God's mercy for us. However, for Christ to touch our hearts, we must first admit that we need the Divine Physician.

◆ The Old Testament reveals a loving God who is faithful to his covenant despite a constant pattern of human sin, of choosing self over God, of pursuing false gods, of rebelling against God's commandments, and the like.

◆ Old Testament images of sin include "missing the mark" (forgetting our ultimate goal of choosing God over other things), "rebellion" (that is, "stiff-necked" and stubborn violation of God's law or deliberately revolting against God's reign), and "iniquity."

◆ Sin alienates us from God, self, and others.

◆ New Testament concepts of sin include missing the mark, lawlessness, injustice, falsehood, and darkness. The most important New Testament teaching about sin, however, is that sin is a refusal to love or accept God's offer of friendship and grace in our Lord Jesus Christ.

◆ Ultimately, sin is a failure to respond to God's love—in act, word, attitude, or by omission.

◆ The heart of the Christian message is that Jesus Christ—his passion, death, and resurrection—has overcome sin and death, both of which alienate us from our loving God.

◆ Jesus' essential message is to repent of your sins because God's Kingdom has arrived. He also teaches us to believe in the Gospel and allow the Holy Spirit to help us live the Good News and his message of love.

◆ Christian tradition has categorized sin in many ways, including the seven capital sins, sins that cry to heaven, sins of the flesh, and original and personal sin. The root of all sin is the human heart, that is, the exercise of free human will.

◆ All humans are born into the condition of Original Sin, that is, the disharmonious situation of our world to which all people are subject. We inherit this condition. Though each individual human is not personally responsible for committing Original Sin, all human sins resemble the Original Sin of our first parents in their disobedience of God. These sins show a lack of trust in his goodness.

◆ Personal sin is any free and deliberate act, word, thought, or desire that turns us away from God's law of love.

◆ Mortal sin is a grave violation of God's law that destroys charity in the human heart. To commit mortal sin three conditions must be met: grave matter ("the object" of the act must be serious enough to kill relationships); full knowledge; and complete consent. Ignorance for which we are not to blame or strong emotions, passions, physical and psychological force, and emotional illness can reduce blameworthiness for the person who does something involving grave matter.

◆ Venial sin involves less serious matter, or grave matter but without full knowledge or complete consent. Venial sin partially rejects God, but does not kill charity in the soul.

◆ The personal sins of individuals can result in structures of sin that create unjust policies, practices, and laws that victimize people and create a cycle of violence and even more sin. Prejudice is a good example of personal sin that creates structures that deny people their fundamental rights and may cause them to retaliate to secure their rights.

- The Sacrament of Reconciliation, a sacrament of healing, is the ordinary way for Catholics to have mortal sins forgiven. The Church recommends frequent celebration of this sacrament of peace, variously known as Penance, Confession, and Reconciliation.

- Christ will forgive the sins of any repentant sinner. God's mercy for the sinner is a central theme of Jesus' ministry. There is great rejoicing in heaven over sinners who repent.

- The five elements of the Sacrament of Reconciliation comprise examining one's conscience, contrition (or sorrow) for one's sins, confession, absolution, and doing the penance assigned by the priest.

PRAYER REFLECTION

Pray the following traditional Act of Contrition:

O my God, I am sorry for my sins.
In choosing to sin, and failing to do good,
I have sinned against you and against your Church.
I firmly intend, with the help of your Son,
to do penance and to sin no more. Amen.

Who needs to hear you say "I am sorry"? What realistic steps can you take to repair harm you have done for a particular sin you have committed?

Express your sorrow to someone you have hurt. Try to find ways to make up for a sin you have committed against a certain person. Write your own act of contrition.

NOTES

1. Quoted in Ronda De Sola Chervin, *Quotable Saints* (Ann Arbor, MI: Servant Publications, 1992), 194.

2. William E. May, *An Introduction to Moral Theology,* Revised Edition (Huntington, IN: Our Sunday Visitor Press, Inc., 1994), 156–158.

CHAPTER OVERVIEW

Nothing More to Give

God gave his greatest gift—his only son, Jesus—to the world. To live a moral life, we must put God first, loving him above all else.

Keeping the Commandments

Keeping the commandments is essential for attaining eternal life. Jesus also said that he came to fulfill the law, not to abolish it.

The First Commandment and the Theological Virtues

Faith, hope and love, the theological virtues, enable us to accept and worship the one, true God.

The Second Commandment

Privileged to know and call on God's name, we are commanded to respect his name and the mystery of God himself.

The Third Commandment

On Sunday, the Lord's Day, with God's grace, we celebrate God's creative activities and his covenant with us as we renew our minds, bodies, and spirits.

CHAPTER SEVEN

Love for God

I, the Lord, am your God, who brought you out of the land of Egypt, that place of slavery. You shall not have other gods besides me. You shall not carve idols for yourselves in the shape of anything in the sky above or on the earth below or in the waters beneath the earth; you shall not bow down before them or worship them. For I, the Lord, your God, am a jealous God, inflicting punishment for their fathers' wickedness on the children of those who hate me, down to the third and fourth generation; but bestowing mercy down to the thousandth generation, on the children of those who love me and keep my commandments.

Exodus 20:2–6

Nothing More to Give

A few years ago, salvage divers found a four-hundred-year-old sunken ship off the Irish coast. The most emotionally moving treasure they found was a man's wedding ring. After cleaning away the sediment of centuries, they saw engraved on the wide band two hands holding a heart with the inscription, "I have nothing more to give you."[1]

These words could have come from our God, spoken to us in the oft-quoted verse John 3:16:

> *For God so loved the world that he gave his only Son, so that everyone who believes in him might not perish but might have eternal life.*

This verse tells us that God, who is Love, has given every creature the greatest gift of all, his Son, Jesus Christ. Jesus, in turn, has won for us victory over sin and death. Think of that wondrous truth. Everything you do—your hard work, your fun, your loves, your studies—has value and meaning because you will enjoy eternal life with a Triune God who loves you beyond what you can possibly imagine.

So what should we do in the face of this remarkable truth? First, we should believe it. Second, we should trust in God's word. And third, we should return our love to the Supreme Lover, who has brought us into existence and given us everything we have.

One safe bet is that living a moral life will be a reality if you make God the top priority in your life. It also stands to reason that if we do not put God first, we will eventually surrender control to some other ruler (money, greed, lust, power, etc.). This chapter deals with the most basic of moral principles: love God. As Jesus, the very source of a moral life, said: "You shall love the Lord, your God, with all your heart, with all your being, with all your strength, and with all your mind, and your neighbor as yourself" (Lk 10:27).

Theological Virtues: A Personal Check-up

Recall that the theological virtues—faith, hope, and charity—have the Triune God as their origin, motive, and object. The theological virtues relate us to God and help us participate in God's own life. Christian moral life builds on them (*CCC*, 1812–1813). We express our love for God when we put these three virtues into action.

Faith enables us to believe in God, what he has said and revealed to us, and what the Church proposes for our belief. The Christian moral life is rooted in faith in God. Our faith comes alive through charitable works. As Christians we must live by our faith, profess and proclaim it, and bear witness to it (*CCC*, 2087; 1814–1816).

Hope leads us to desire heaven and eternal life, not through our own strength, but through trust in Christ and the graces of the Holy Spirit. Hope not only helps us to confidently expect God's blessing and the beatific vision, but it also instills in us a healthy fear of offending God's love and meriting punishment. We express and nourish hope through prayer (*CCC*, 2090; 1817; 1820).

Charity, the greatest of all virtues, enables us to "love God above all things for his own sake, and our neighbor as ourselves for the love of God" (*CCC*, 1822; 2093). Jesus commands us to love as he loved, including our enemies and the poor, and to obey his commandments (*CCC*, 1823–1826).

Read the following scripture passages to answer the questions related to the theological virtues.

Faith
- Romans 10:17: Where does faith come from?
- Hebrews 11:1: What is faith?
- James 2:14–18: What proves that our faith is real?

Hope
- Sirach 2:6–9: What good advice is given?
- Jeremiah 17:7: Who is blessed?

Charity (Love): John 15:8–17
- How does Jesus love us?
- What does Jesus command?
- What is the greatest sign of love?
- What does Jesus call us if we do his will?

Grade yourself on the following beliefs and practices that flow from these three virtues.

A = try hard, do well; B = good effort, good achievement; C = pretty average;
D = need work; F= need lots of commitment and effort

Grade

_____ 1. I firmly believe in our Triune God: Father, Son, and Holy Spirit.

_____ 2. I am proud to call myself a Christian.

_____ 3. I share my beliefs with others, both in words and in actions.

_____ 4. I believe in the truths taught by the Catholic Church.

_____ 5. With God's help, I hope one day to be united with him and my loved ones in heaven.

_____ 6. I trust that God is in charge of my life, that he has a plan for me.

_____ 7. Prayer is an important part of my life to help me keep hope and faith alive.

_____ 8. I am grateful to God for all he has given and promised to me.

_____ 9. I want to live my life as Jesus did—loving and serving others—and I am taking steps toward that goal.

_____ 10. I love everyone, including those less fortunate than I am and those who have hurt me.

Laws, Days, Joints

The Ten Commandments are a summary of the Law. Scholars count 613 laws in the Old Testament. According to the Talmud, the Jewish body of civil and religious law, 613 laws are explained this way: the 365 negative laws correspond to the days of the year; the 248 positive laws correspond to the number of joints in the human body.

covenant

the strongest possible pledge and agreement between two parties.

Keeping the Commandments
(CCC, 2051—2082)

When a rich young man approached Jesus and asked him what he had to do to attain eternal life, the Lord replied, "If you wish to enter into life, keep the commandments" (Mt 19:17). Keeping the commandments is essential to following Jesus. As Jesus said in the Sermon on the Mount, he did not come to abolish the law, but to fulfill it. When asked what was the greatest commandment, Jesus taught love of God above all else and then love of one's neighbor as oneself. Love fulfills the law. It summarizes the demands both of the first three commandments, which deal primarily with our relationship to God, and of the last seven, which treat our relationships with our neighbors.

THE DECALOGUE

The Ten Commandments are often termed as the "Decalogue," which literally means "ten words." Revealed to Moses by Yahweh, the Decalogue is found in the books of Exodus (20:1–17) and Deuteronomy (5:6–22). The traditional catechetical formulation of the Ten Commandments follows.

THE TEN COMMANDMENTS

First Three Commandments: Loving God

1. I am the Lord your God: you shall not have strange Gods before me.
2. You shall not take the name of the Lord your God in vain.
3. Remember to keep holy the Lord's Day.

Last Seven Commandments: Loving Neighbor

4. Honor your father and your mother.
5. You shall not kill.
6. You shall not commit adultery.
7. You shall not steal.
8. You shall not bear false witness against your neighbor.
9. You shall not covet your neighbor's wife.
10. You shall not covet your neighbor's goods.

The Exodus experience, by which Yahweh delivered the Jews from slavery and led them to the Promised Land, helps us understand the scriptural meaning of the Ten Commandments. God established a covenant with his people, calling them by love for love. A **covenant** is the strongest possible pledge and agreement between two parties. By means of the Sinai covenant, Yahweh declared that the fleeing Israelites would be his special people and that he was their one, true God. He would give them peace, prosperity, protection, and their own land. The Ten Commandments outlined the way the Israelites (freed slaves) were to respond to God's gracious love. Today, the Commandments indicate how we who have been rescued from sin should act. They are our path to life. Thus, the Decalogue, which is really a summary of the Law, spells out how both individuals and communities must respond to a saving, loving God.

CHURCH TRADITION

The Church has always viewed the Ten Commandments as a loving response to God's special favor, not a list of burdensome obligations. Keeping the commandments is not optional, but a grave obligation because they teach us the specific requirements of love. Engraved on our hearts and discoverable by the natural law, the Ten Commandments express our fundamental duties in love to God (the first three) and the basic requirements of love to neighbor (the other seven). The Decalogue is a unity. Each commandment refers to each of the others and to all collectively. To break one of the commandments is to break the whole Law (*CCC*, 2079). Loving God means we must love our neighbor. By loving our neighbor, we show our love for God.

The Ten Commandments teach how we must reverence our loving, saving God and respect others and ourselves. Jesus taught the rich young man, and he teaches us today, that the commandments are the way to life. A disciple of Jesus who wants to be moral and holy will accept and believe in Jesus, receive the risen Lord by

power of the Holy Spirit in the sacraments, and obey his teaching about keeping the commandments. Doing so allows the Lord to live in us, where he reaches out in love to God his loving Father, to us, and to all people we meet. Christ asks much of his followers, but he gives us the graces necessary to follow him. He empowers us to be his presence in the world, showing through our words and deeds the way to love and the "way of Love."

Do the following mind logo activities on your own. Record your answers in a notebook or in your journal. Be prepared to discuss your answers later with the whole group.

Read Exodus 19–20.

◆ What message was Moses to deliver to the Israelites?

◆ Name two things the people were to do (or not do) to prepare for Yahweh's coming.

◆ What caused the Hebrew people to fear God after Moses received the Ten Commandments?

◆ Read of Abraham's staunch faith in Genesis 22.

◆ Read about Mary's reaction to the announcement from the angel in Luke 1:26–56.

Keeping the Commandments

A Christian and a Jew were discussing their respective faiths. After discussing their beliefs about Jesus, the Jew said, "You Christians like taking things from us Jews—for example, the Ten Commandments."

The Christian said, "You're right. But you know what? We're not very good at keeping them."

FOR YOUR JOURNAL

List and reflect on the three strongest proofs in your life that God really does love you.

REVIEW AND REFLECTION

1. What are the theological virtues? What does each do?

2. Repeat each one of the Ten Commandments.

3. What is the connection between the Ten Commandments and God's covenant?

4. How is Mary an exemplar of faith?

The First Commandment and the Theological Virtues

(CCC, 2084—2094; 2133—2134)

You shall worship the Lord your God and Him only shall you serve.

The first commandment teaches us to accept the one true God of love who has created us in his image out of love, rescued us from sin, won for us eternal life, and bestowed on us the gift of the Holy Spirit who empowers us to live Christ-like lives. To accept God means we must worship him. The theological virtues of faith, hope, and love enable us to relate to God and carry out this divine command.

FAITH

Faith is the theological virtue that empowers us to say "yes" to God. It enables us to believe everything God has revealed to us, simply because of his divine authority and trustworthiness.

An Old Testament exemplar of this virtue was Abraham, who responded to Yahweh by leaving his home and journeying to an unknown land. Though his faith was tested many times, especially when God asked him to sacrifice his only son, Isaac, Abraham steadfastly obeyed Yahweh and remained faithful. Because of his fidelity, Yahweh blessed the aged Abraham, making him the father of a people, the ancestor in faith of all Jews, Christians, and Muslims.

The perfect New Testament model of faith is Mary, the Mother of God. Not fully understanding what God was asking of her, Mary answered the angel Gabriel, "May it be done to me according to your word" (Lk 1:38). Mary's faith in God helped in the plan of salvation. Her faith-filled assent helped bring the Savior into our world. Mary's entire life was an obedient surrender to God's word, trusting in it, and committing herself to serve God as he asked.

We exercise our gift of faith when we believe in God's word revealed to us in Scripture and through his holy Church. Faith is a journey that involves sharing and living with other believers. Our faith is often tested. Therefore, we should strengthen the virtue of faith through various practices like the following:

Prayer. Pray to the Lord for your faith to be strengthened. A model of prayer is the father who asked Jesus to cure his epileptic son, "I do believe, help my unbelief!" (Mk 9:24).

Read the Bible. Scripture is God's word, an inspired record of God's revelation. Reading and meditating on it will strengthen your faith in God. Catholics should pay special attention to the readings at Mass and listen to the homily. These daily and weekly readings challenge us to take the Good News out into the world to others.

Celebrate the sacraments. The sacraments celebrate the mysteries of our faith: the incarnation, the love of Jesus, salvation, redemption, the message of

MARY AND FAITH

Describe what took place in the following two passages:

◆ Luke 2:8–19

◆ Luke 2:40–52

everlasting life, and so forth. Receiving the Lord Jesus in the Eucharist and speaking to him in your heart is a tremendous way to strengthen your faith in him. Hearing the priest absolve you of your sins in the Sacrament of Reconciliation is also an excellent means to experience the Good News of God's forgiveness.

Study your faith. With knowledge of truth often comes love for the truth. In your religion classes, on your retreats and days of recollection, you can gain greater knowledge about the truths of the faith. Study the Nicene and Apostles' Creeds, which profess the major truths of the faith. Learn what they mean. Ask questions of knowledgeable persons if you are not sure.

Associate with and listen to people of faith. Choose friends and companions who believe as you do—in Christian values and virtues and in the saving love of Jesus. Join them in youth group activities at your parish.

Put your faith into action. Faith is necessary for salvation. We cannot earn the gift of faith, because God himself gives it to us. However, our faith must translate into deeds. Volunteer for school and community service activities. Putting faith into action actually increases the gift of faith because it becomes alive in us.

Avoid temptations and sins that threaten or destroy the gift of faith. Among these are:

- ◆ **Voluntary doubt**, which ignores or refuses to believe what God has revealed or what the Church teaches us to believe.
- ◆ **Incredulity**, which either neglects revealed truth or willfully refuses to assent to it.
- ◆ **Heresy**, the outright denial by baptized persons of some essential truth of the Catholic faith we must believe.
- ◆ **Apostasy**, the total rejection of the Christian faith.
- ◆ **Schism**, the refusal to submit to the pope's authority or remain in union with members of the Catholic Church.

voluntary doubt

The decision to ignore or a refusal to believe what God has revealed or what the Church teaches.

incredulity

A mental disposition that either neglects revealed truth or willfully refuses to assent to it.

heresy

Outright denial by a baptized person of some essential truth about God and faith that we must believe.

apostasy

The total rejection of Jesus Christ (and the Christian faith) by a baptized Christian.

schism

Refusal to submit to the pope's authority or remain in union with members of the Catholic Church.

REVIEW AND REFLECTION

1. Discuss three practices that can increase the virtue of faith.

2. Distinguish between these terms: *heresy*, *schism*, and *apostasy*.

FOR YOUR JOURNAL

Name and then write about the qualities of the person you most admire for being a person of faith—one who trusts God in everything.

HOPE

The theological virtue of hope is intimately related to the virtue of faith. We believe God is all-good, all-loving, all-just, all-merciful. Therefore, we trust that the Lord controls the future and is watching out for us. Good will triumph over evil; eternal life will conquer death; every wrong will be righted.

Hope gives us confidence that God keeps all his promises, especially his promise to bless us with eternal happiness in heaven if we live a good life united to our Lord and Savior, Jesus Christ. This confidence in God's word, and the graces God has promised to us strengthens us to cope with the trials of everyday life. In addition, hope gives us the confidence to help work for the establishment of God's Kingdom by working for peace and justice right now.

St. Monica (fourth century) is a wonderful model of hope who prayed for years for the conversion of her brilliant son. Through steadfast determination, sacrifice, and works of piety, St. Monica never wavered in believing and hoping that her son would one day turn to Christ and embrace him. After many years of dissolute living, which included having a son out of wedlock and fascination with attractive pagan philosophies of the day, her son eventually repented of his sins and devoted his brilliant mind to the service of Christ and his Church. St. Monica's hope bore fruit with the conversion of her son, St. Augustine, who eventually became a priest, a bishop, and one of Christianity's greatest theologians.

Jesus Christ is, of course, the perfect model of hope and trust in God's goodness. While suffering and dying on the cross for us, Jesus confidently prayed to his Father, trusting that Abba would embrace him in his utmost loneliness and agony, "Father, into your hands I commend my spirit" (Lk 23:46).

God gives us hope because he gives us himself. God is our hope and our salvation. God gives us the vision to see the possible when things seem impossible. A good way to grow in this virtue is to ask God frequently in prayer for an increase in hope. We can also thank and praise God for what he has in store for us. We can participate at Eucharist. We can stop worrying about our futures and trust that our loving Abba will give us what we need to live good lives and put up with the setbacks that will come our way.

There are two ways to violate the virtue of hope. The first is through *despair*, that is, losing hope that God can save us, give us help to attain heaven, or forgive our sins. Despair insults God's goodness, justice, and mercy. Despair says that God is not faithful to his promises. Despair, for a Christian, is a grand deception and grave sin. A despairing person lacks trust in God and will do nothing to help Jesus in his work of salvation.

Presumption, on the other hand, comes in two forms. In one form, it takes for granted that we can save ourselves without God's help. It is a proud "going it alone" philosophy in which we believe we really don't need God. In the other form, one who is presumptuous expects that God will automatically be merciful even if one does not repent. Presumptuous people arrogantly want "forgiveness without conversion and glory without merit" (*CCC*, 2092).

CHARITY

St. Thomas Aquinas described charity—also called love—as the "mother of all virtues." However, we must be careful with the word "love" because of its various uses. For example, love is often used in place of "like" or "sexual desire" or "friendship." One type of love described in the New Testament is *agape*, that is, selfless, giving love. This is the type of love Jesus has for us and the kind of love he tells us to show to others.

Our ancestors in the faith translated *agape* into the Latin word *caritas* which we render "charity" in English. *Caritas* is rooted in the word for "heart" in the sense of "holding someone close to one's heart." This is the understanding of love that is the bedrock foundation of Christian life. God loves us this way because God's very nature is to love. We must be godlike. Few biblical passages stress the importance of this virtue of love as does this one from the first letter of John.

Beloved, let us love one another, because love is of God; everyone who loves is begotten by God and knows God. Whoever is without love does not know God, for God is love. In this way the love of God was revealed to us: God sent his only Son into the world so that we might have life through him. In this is love: not that we have loved God, but that he loved us and sent his Son as expiation for our sins.

Beloved, if God so loved us, we also must love one another. No one has ever seen God. Yet, if we love one another, God remains in us, and his love is brought to perfection in us.

This is how we know that we remain in him and he in us, that he has given us of his Spirit. Moreover, we have seen and testify that the Father sent his Son as savior of the world. Whoever acknowledges that Jesus is the Son of God, God remains in him and he in God. We have come to know and to believe in the love God has for us. God is love, and whoever remains in love remains in God and God in him. (1 Jn 4:7–16)

Because God is love, we must also love: Love God above everything. Love ourselves. Love our neighbors. We love God when we root out sin in our lives and embrace him in worship. We love ourselves when we accept, develop, and use the gifts God has given to us. We love others when we seek their good, refuse to

HOPE IN PRACTICE

Read the following Scripture passages. Answer the accompanying questions.

Matthew 20:30–34

◆ Who are the two people who show trust in Jesus? How do they show it?

Matthew 9:27–30

◆ What did the blind men do to demonstrate faith and trust in Jesus?

Luke 12:22–31

◆ What things does Jesus tell us not to worry about?

An anonymous author once said,

People will forget what you said. People will forget what you did, but people will never forget how you made them feel.

"Charity begins at home." Exercise the virtue of charity by making someone you love feel better. Write a short note of appreciation to a special family member who means much to you. Thank this special individual for the gift he or she has been to you in your life.

harm them, and treat them as our brothers and sisters in Christ.

Love is steadfast because it is rooted in God. It is not a mushy feeling, but a decision and a commitment to imitate our Triune God: God the loving Father, the beloved Son who proved his love for us on the cross, and a Holy Spirit of love who binds the Lover and Beloved into a perfect community.

We learn *how* to love from the perfect exemplar of love, Jesus Christ. Jesus taught by word and example that the virtue of charity involves:

- *Obedience.* Jesus' will was perfectly attuned to that of his Father. To love, we must be willing to do what Jesus asks: obey his commandments.
- *Reverence.* To love means we must respect and value the absolute goodness of God and goodness in other people.
- *Sacrifice.* Love often is difficult because it involves long-term commitment. Love never gives up. Spiritual disciplines like fasting and doing acts of self-denial make us more able to love.

- *Beginning.* One philosopher was noted for saying he loved humanity. The problem with him, however, was that he could not stand to be in the same room with another flesh-and-blood human being. Loving means responding to God right now. One way to do it is to show kindness, compassion, and consideration for those who are closest to you. Love them because God loves them.
- *Rooting out sin.* Sinfulness that must be rooted out of our lives includes:
  - *indifference* which either neglects or refuses to appreciate and reflect on God's love, thus denying its power;
  - *ingratitude* which fails or refuses to recognize God's love and to return love to him;
  - *lukewarmness* or *spiritual laziness* that neglects to respond to God's love;
  - *hatred of God* which arises from pride. It is the exact opposite of charity since God is love.

REVIEW AND REFLECTION

1. How was Saint Monica a symbol of hope?

2. Define *despair* and *presumption*.

3. List and discuss five concrete ways to exercise the virtue of charity.

FOR YOUR JOURNAL

Read Galatians 5:22 to discover what Saint Paul tells us are the signs that the Holy Spirit is living in us. Name and discuss some evidence of how these "fruits of the Holy Spirit" are present in your life.

LIVING THE FIRST COMMANDMENT
(CCC, 2095—2109; 2135—2137)

The theological virtues inform and give life to the moral virtues. One outstanding moral virtue that pertains to the first commandment is the virtue of *religion,* which leads us to give to God what is due him as our loving Creator. This includes *adoration, prayer,* and *sacrifice.*

Adoration is the first act of religion. Adoration is acknowledging God as the loving Creator and merciful Savior whose infinite goodness is the source of everything. When we adore God we praise and exalt him, acknowledging that without God, we would not even exist. In true humility, we should worship the one true God, or else we will become slaves to sin and give our primary allegiance to some creature that is not God.

A key way of exercising our faith, hope, and love in relationship to a loving God is through prayer, "lifting one's mind and heart to God." We should frequently praise and thank God, express sorrow when we sin, and unceasingly offer prayers of intercession for others and petition God to meet our own needs. Communion with God in prayer is essential for following God's law, that is, for keeping the commandments that he gave us for life.

God also deserves our heartfelt sacrifice, that is, offering ourselves in adoration, thanksgiving, supplication, contrition, and communion. Our Lord Jesus made the perfect offering of himself on the cross in loving obedience to his Father and for our salvation. We celebrate this perfect sacrifice in the Eucharist. By uniting ourselves to the Lord's sacrifice in the Mass, the Holy Spirit transforms our lives as a sacrifice to God.

Another way to honor God and his love for us is to observe any promises or vows we make to God. Sacraments like Baptism, Confirmation, Matrimony, and Holy Orders involve making promises to God. At other times, out of special devotion, we might make promises to God. For example, during a youth retreat, you might promise God to pray fifteen minutes each day. Keeping your promises shows respect to a God who will always be faithful to you.

Out of personal devotion and special love for God, some Christians take vows. A *vow* is a "deliberate and free promise made to God concerning a possible and better good which must be fulfilled by reason of the virtue of religion" (*CCC,* 2102). You are probably familiar with the vows taken by priests, sisters, and brothers in religious orders—the "evangelical counsels" of poverty, chastity, and obedience. These dedicated Christians are trying to imitate more closely our Lord's own sacrificing love and become more free to serve God by dedicating themselves more wholeheartedly to serving God's people.

Freedom of Religion

The Church teaches that all people—both individuals and communities—have a basic right to worship and adore God as their conscience dictates. Government has a duty to guarantee this right by law. Although people have a duty to worship God, no one can be forced to act against personal religious convictions. Within proper limits, exercise of religion must be free because the nature of love is free.

Catholics are privileged to have received the Good News about God's Son. As members of Christ's body, we are charged with the responsibility of respecting and bringing to life in each person whom we meet the love of what is true and what is good. We are duty-bound to share with others "the worship of the one true religion which subsists in the Catholic and apostolic Church" (*CCC,* 2105). Therefore, Christ expects us to witness our faith to other people, all of whom are searching deep in their hearts for truth. But we should not do so out of pride or arrogance, but with love, prudence, and patience, and with respect for the aspects of truth we can find in their religions. Jesus calls us "light of the world" (Mt 5:14). By living our faith in deeds, and proclaiming it in word, we can help lead other people to Christ Jesus. He alone can satisfy the hidden hungers for truth, which all people are seeking.

AVOIDING OFFENSES AGAINST THE FIRST COMMANDMENT

(CCC, 2110—2132; 2138—2141)

idolatry

The worship of false gods.

Living the First Commandment also involves avoiding several offenses against this commandment. These include the following:

Idolatry. The first commandment insists that we honor and worship only the one true Lord who has revealed himself to his people. Therefore, the first commandment condemns **idolatry**, that is, the worship of false gods. Many people around the world have yet to hear the Good News about the one true God. Polytheism, the worship of many gods, is still present in some cultures and is as false today as it was when the Scriptures condemned the worship of golden idols thousands of years ago.

What is more widespread today is the all-too-human tendency to take a created good and turn it into a god. Humans are guilty of idolatry whenever they honor or revere a creature as a substitute for God. Some people worship Satan, a terrible offense against a loving God. But more people are guilty of making the pursuit of money, power, popularity, pleasure, or sex their gods. Still others elevate the state or racial purity as their god. Although these are only created "goods," when we make them our primary focus in life, we turn ourselves away from the loving God and become slaves. Jesus told us, "You cannot serve God and mammon" (Mt 6:24). An unholy pursuit of money can blind us to the needs of others; a craving for popularity may lead us to sacrifice our character to please others; an obsession with sex treats others as objects to be used instead of persons to be cherished.

Explaining Our Faith:

Are we guilty of idol worship when we have religious statues and crucifixes?

The Old Testament Law prohibited the Israelites from making "graven" images, that is, a "carving" of a god, because of the Chosen People's tendency to worship the statue or object like their pagan neighbors did. They invested the created object with divine powers, instead of worshiping the almighty, "totally other" God, who can never be contained in a mere statue.

But this Old Testament prohibition was not absolute. Yahweh permitted the making of objects like the bronze serpent and the Ark of the Covenant, images that symbolically pointed to the salvation won for us by Jesus Christ, God-made-man.

In Church history there were those who wanted to ban all sacred images, also known as icons. However, the Seventh Ecumenical Council at Nicea in 787 approved the veneration of icons of our Blessed Lord, the Mother of God, and the angels and saints. Catholics "venerate," they do not worship, sacred images. Veneration is giving honor to the holy person behind the icon. It is similar to the regard you have for a favorite picture of a girlfriend or boyfriend. You don't worship the picture. Rather, it is a reminder that points to the beloved person that the picture represents.

- *Superstition, divination, and magic.* Faith in the one true God acknowledges that he is in control. Superstition, on the other hand, is a false religious practice that claims certain external acts or practices (e.g., the presence of certain objects or the recitation of certain words) can automatically bring about the desired outcome independent of God's will or one's own interior disposition, like a faithful or loving heart.

    Divination seeks to unveil what God wants hidden (occult). It takes many forms: calling up the power of Satan and the demons, conjuring the dead, consulting horoscopes, reading the stars (astrology), palm reading, consulting mediums, playing with Ouija boards, and the like. All these practices dishonor and disrespect a loving God who is in control of our futures. They are also arrogant practices that surrender our freedom to some external power or force, failing to trust in a loving Father who knows what is best for us.

    Magic (not to be confused with the tricks of professional entertainers who seek to amuse us with their sleight of hand and other skills) seeks to control the future by trying to harness occult (hidden) powers to gain an advantage over others. *Sorcery* is "black magic" that tries to get results using demonic powers. It is extremely dangerous to religious faith and most condemnable when sought to harm others. *Spiritism,* summoning the ghosts of the dead, usually involves divination (seances and mediums) or the practices of sorcery. The Church strongly warns us against all these practices because they open the way to a fascination with evil spirits. These practices are in opposition to the one true God, who has our welfare at heart and guides us in his own way with the help of prayer. These practices also open us to grand deception from unscrupulous people who are trying to gain profit or power over us.
- *Irreligion.* This offense leads to the sins of tempting God, **sacrilege**, and **simony**. We tempt God, in word or deed, when we ask God to prove his almighty power or goodness. Asking God to prove himself to us, as Satan did when he asked Jesus to cast himself down from the Temple, profoundly disrespects our loving God and distrusts his providential care. Sacrilege profanes, or treats unworthily, the sacraments, other liturgical actions, and persons, places, or things consecrated to God. Sacrilege is seriously wrong especially when committed against our Lord in the holy Eucharist. Simony consists of buying or selling spiritual goods. God's gifts to us—like his forgiveness in the Sacrament of Reconciliation—are freely given graces. They cannot be bought and sold like a commodity. We should receive them with humble gratitude.
- *Atheism and agnosticism.* An atheist denies God's existence. An agnostic claims ignorance about God's existence (from the Greek *agnostikos* for "not knowing"), saying it cannot be proved. Therefore, an agnostic "decides not to decide," often out of indifference or laziness. In effect, most agnostics are "practical" atheists.

    Modern non-belief in God takes many forms: **humanism**, which makes humanity its god, the be-all and end-all of existence; *Marxist communism*, which makes the economic or social order the sole source of human freedom; *Freudianism*, which claims belief in God is mere wishful thinking; **materialism**, which affirms that the physical, material world is the only reality and denies any spiritual existence; plus a host of other ways that renounce God's existence.

    One problem with atheism is the false belief that faith in God thwarts human freedom and dignity. On the contrary, human dignity is grounded and perfected in God. To abandon belief in God opens us up to many false gods. G. K. Chesterton reputedly said, "A man who won't believe in God will believe in anything." How true this was in the twentieth century, when certain atheistic philosophies made

divination

Attempts to unveil what God wants hidden by calling up demonic powers; consulting horoscopes, the stars, or mediums; palm reading, etc.

sacrilege

Profane or unworthy treatment of the sacraments; other liturgical actions; and persons, places, and things consecrated to God.

simony

The buying or selling of spiritual goods.

humanism

A belief that deifies humanity and human potential to the exclusion of any belief in or reliance on God.

materialism

A belief that the physical, material world is the only reality, and that spiritual existence, values, and faith are illusions.

- What are some superstitions you have observed? Comment on them in light of the above.

- Is it okay to read the daily astrology charts in the newspaper? Would it be wrong to take them seriously? Explain.

- Why do you think interest in the occult is so keen in our day? Are people searching for some spiritual meaning? Explain.

the state their god. Citizens ended up being enslaved or destroyed, as happened in both fascist Germany and the Marxist Soviet Union.

Atheism contradicts the virtue of religion because it rejects or denies God. It is a serious offense. However, intention or circumstances can lessen a nonbeliever's blameworthiness for this sin. Christians especially must make sure they live worthy lives so they reveal the true and living God to a world that craves knowing him.

THE PRACTICE OF PRAYER

"To walk with God, we must make it a practice to talk with God."

Prayer is not optional for human beings. For Christians, prayer is essential because it is an outstanding tool to strengthen the virtues of faith, hope, and love. God deserves our worship and praise simply because he is God and we are not. If that is not enough reason to pray, we should also remember that God gave us the best friend we could ever have—Jesus Christ.

When we converse with God, we should thank him for all the good things he has given us. We should praise him often for his goodness and express sorrow for our sins. And we should ask him for our needs and the needs of others.

St. Teresa of Avila recommended that when you pray you might picture Jesus sitting next to you or taking a walk with you. You should turn to the Lord and talk to him as you would with a very close friend. Try this and see if you do not experience the warmth of the Lord, who loves you beyond compare.

Schedule a ten-minute prayer session with your loving God each day for the next month. Here are some suggestions to get you started:

- **Set aside ten minutes at the same time each day for your prayer conversation.** (Examples: after breakfast or dinner, before bed, during homeroom)
What time will you choose?

- **Pick a place with minimum distractions.** (Examples: your bedroom, the school chapel, outside taking a walk in a quiet area, etc.)
What will be your special prayer place?

- **Calm yourself by assuming a comfortable position.** Breathe slowly and deeply, allowing the tensions of the day to drain away. If it helps, gaze at a candle or close your eyes while you pray.
Which method of calming down helps you most?

- **Sense God's presence to you, in the very air you breathe, within your heart.** Perhaps you can recite a prayer word (or short phrase) over and over to help you be aware of God's presence. (Examples: Abba, Love, Come Holy Spirit, Jesus, Savior, Praise God, etc.)
What seems like a good prayer word or phrase for you?

- **Begin your conversation.** Praise God first for his goodness to you. Thank him for his many gifts: life, your faith, your family and friends, your intelligence, abilities, etc. Then enter into a conversation with him. Honestly share your concerns with the Lord. Listen. Feel the Lord's love for you.
For what do you especially want to thank God?

- **Thank the Lord for your special time together.**

Conclusion: In a prayer journal, jot a thought that emerges from each of your prayer sessions. Review these at the end of thirty days.

REVIEW AND REFLECTION

1. Name at least three things that the First Commandment requires.

2. Why do religious people make vows?

3. Are having religious paintings, pictures, and the like a violation of the First Commandment? Explain.

4. Describe and explain these violations of the First Commandment: *superstition, divination, magic, sorcery,* and *spiritism.* Why are these serious practices to be avoided at all costs?

5. Give an example of sacrilege. What is simony?

6. Distinguish between *atheism* and *agnosticism*.

7. How can prayer help us to live a moral life?

FOR YOUR JOURNAL

Write a letter to Jesus as your best friend. Mention some things to him for which you are particularly thankful.

The Second Commandment
(CCC, 2142—2167)

You shall not take the name of the Lord your God in vain.

The name God revealed to Moses— *Yahweh* ("I Am who I Am")—stresses God's mysterious nature and perfect holiness. Believers are privileged to know God's holy name and must always respect it through blessing, praise, and adoration. By respecting God's name, we show respect for the mystery of God himself. By taking care of how we invoke God's name, we recognize that some things are sacred and holy.

For Christians, the name Jesus Christ is also a holy name, one we proclaim to others with reverence, respect, adoration, and humility. We who are privileged to bear the name *Christian* will take great care never to abuse the names of God, Jesus, the Blessed Mother, or any of the saints.

The Second Commandment also underscores the holiness of our own personal names. We are baptized "in the name of the Father and of the Son and of the Holy Spirit." Each time we make the Sign of the Cross, we invoke God's name and call on his divine help to live a life worthy of the name Christian. In Baptism, each of us receives the name of a patron saint or a baptismal name that expresses a Christian virtue or mystery. Our patron saints serve as models of charity and give a good example on how to live like Christ. They also take us under their protection as they pray to our loving God for us.

God treats each of us uniquely, calling each one by his or her name. Our name is sacred, a name received for eternity. It is an "icon," or holy image of the person. We should cherish our own name and those of others.

- Find, discuss, and name examples of irreverence toward God and God's name depicted in recent films, television sitcoms, and music.

blasphemy

Hateful, defiant, reproachful thoughts, words, or acts against God, Jesus, his Church, the saints, or holy things.

AVOIDING OFFENSES AGAINST THE SECOND COMMANDMENT

The following are some key offenses against the precepts of the Second Commandment. Each of these offenses should be avoided:

- *Breaking promises made in God's name.* When we invoke God's name in a promise, we are calling on his honor, truth, fidelity, and authority. To break a promise misuses God's name, making him out to be a liar.
- *Blasphemy.* **Blasphemy** is speaking words of hate, defiance, or reproach against God. These words can be spoken or uttered inwardly. A blasphemer speaks ill of God, misuses his name, or fails to show proper respect for God in speech. Blasphemy is a grave sin that also includes language spoken against Christ's Church, the saints, and sacred things.
- *Taking the Lord's name in vain.* *Swearing* involves taking an oath in God's name. When we swear in God's name to tell the truth, for example, and then fail to do so, we are asking God to be witness to a lie. This is a serious offense against a loving, truthful God. Perjury takes place when one fails to keep a promise sworn under oath or when one takes an oath with no intention of keeping it. It, too, is a grave offense showing a total lack of respect to the Lord of all speech.

In the Sermon on the Mount, Jesus taught his followers to be people of integrity, not to swear, to make our "yes" mean "yes" and our "no" mean "no."

Integrity and plain-speaking are very important to Jesus. Christian tradition has interpreted that it is permissible to make oaths for grave and morally correct reasons (for example, sworn testimony in court). We never have to take an oath, however, when required by illegitimate civil rulers or when an oath contradicts human dignity or the unity of the church.

Distinction of Terms

Swearing is the misuse of God's name in making false promises, cursing other people, or using God's name frivolously.

Obscenity is indecent, lewd, or offensive language, behavior, appearance, or expressions. (Obscenity is designed to incite lustful feelings and cheapens the sacredness of sexuality.)

Cussing is an informal word that means the same as cursing, the calling down of evil on someone.

Vulgarity is tasteless or coarse behavior or language. Vulgar or "bathroom" language is ill-bred, boorish, crude, bawdy, and unrefined.

Swearing, obscenity, and cussing are sinful because they harm our relationship with God and others. Vulgar language is immature, unimaginative, and unrefined. However, it is not necessarily sinful of itself. In many cases, however, it is used with intent to offend another person or to make them uncomfortable, fearful, or embarrassed. Under those circumstances, it is a failure to love.

The Third Commandment

(CCC, 2168—2195)

Remember to keep holy the Lord's day.

The Third Commandment stresses the values of play (recreation) and prayer on the Sabbath day, which celebrates both God's creative activity and God's covenant with his people.

We learn from the Genesis creation stories that God rested on the seventh day. Yahweh's example teaches his creatures that we should stop our routine daily pursuits, turn from the idol of pursuing money, and spend some time to refresh and renew our minds, bodies, and spirits. Healthy exercise, quiet pursuits of enriching the mind, relaxing activities, quality time spent with our families, stepping out of our ordinary routine to help old folks or poor and needy people, enjoying outdoor activities in God's beautiful creation—all these and similar activities help sanctify (make holy) the Lord's day. This day of Sabbath rest (and play) is God's gift to us: "The Sabbath was made for man, not man for the Sabbath. This is why the Son of Man is lord even of the Sabbath" (Mk 2:27–28).

Equally important is the need to use the Sabbath day to praise, worship, and adore a God who covenanted with the Chosen People by freeing them from slavery in Egypt and who covenants with all people in his Son Jesus Christ. We owe God everything. Sabbath worship is our small gift to God in thanksgiving for all his gifts, including the gift of his Son.

For Jews, the Sabbath is *Saturday*, the seventh day which closes the week. For Christians, the Sabbath, Sunday, commemorates Easter and begins the week. Sunday is the day Christians gather to celebrate the Paschal Mystery of Christ's love. It is a day for thanksgiving (*Eucharist* means "thanksgiving") when Christians recall and praise God for the passion, death, and resurrection of our Lord Jesus

Christ. On this day, we thank God, who has given us a birth into eternal life through our hope in Jesus' resurrection from the dead.

Catholics consider it a grave obligation to worship God on Sunday (or Saturday night) because Christ himself commanded us to break bread in his name. In fact, except for sickness or some other serious reason, to fail deliberately to observe this duty is mortally sinful. Jesus invites us to Mass to praise and worship the Father for the gift of our Savior, his Son, and to thank the Triune God for the many gifts showered on us through the Holy Spirit, most especially the gift of our salvation and new life.

The Eucharistic liturgy celebrated in the parish church is vitally important because it is the preeminent way to meet our Lord and receive him in Holy Communion as spiritual food that strengthens us to live Christ-like lives. The Second Vatican Council explained how our Lord comes to us in this special celebration:

> [Christ] is present in the sacrifice of the Mass, not only in the person of His minister . . . but especially under the Eucharistic species. By His power He is present in the sacraments. . . . He is present in His word, since it is He Himself who speaks when the holy

Sanctifying Sundays and holy days requires a common effort. Every Christian should avoid making unnecessary demands on others that would hinder them from observing the Lord's Day. (CCC, 2187)

Scriptures are read in the church. He is present, finally, when the Church prays and sings, for He promised, "Where two or three are gathered together for my sake, there am I in the midst of them" (Mt 18:20). (Constitution on the Sacred Liturgy, 7)

WHY WE GO TO MASS

How do you answer those who give excuses for missing Mass? You've probably heard excuses like:

"Mass is boring."

"I don't get anything out of it."

"Only hypocrites go to Mass."

"I can worship God just as well in nature."

You have probably heard various other excuses for not going to Mass on Sunday. But be prepared to propose several counter-arguments.

Lots of things we do in life are boring, but essential to our welfare. Eating breakfast can be boring. Studying can be boring. Taking care of routine bodily needs like brushing teeth, showering, dressing, and so forth can be boring. Yet these are essential tasks for living wholesome lives not just for our own sake, but for the sake of others.

We go to Mass to give as well as receive. Our very presence supports and encourages our fellow believers. Paying attention can be difficult, but listening to the readings is hearing Christ proclaim his love for us. And every homily, no matter how dry or long, contains at least one nugget to help us live as Christians. Finally, we receive the Lord himself in Holy Communion. There is no more precious gift in life than receiving Jesus Christ. His presence in our lives empowers us to live moral, upright, and Christian lives.

True, hypocrites do go to Mass. But we are all hypocrites. There is always room for one more sinner at the table of the Lord. Christ is the Divine Physician, who came not for the healthy, but for the sick. We Christians profess high ideals, yet so often we fall short of them. The Eucharist is the major way the Lord helps us stay the course, to gain the strength and encouragement we need even to begin to live as he wants us to live. We need each other to signify God's love for us. In the liturgy we come together as needy pilgrims to hear Christ's message of forgiveness and to remember what he has done for us, sinners all. We add nothing by our absence. We add our very selves by our presence. We proclaim to the world, and to each other, "Here I am, Lord."

It is also true that we can worship in nature. And we should. In fact, we should pray daily in a variety of ways and in a host of different settings. But there is a time for group prayer, too. Jesus wants us to come together and to experience him in the Eucharist, in his scriptural word, and in each other. To be human is to be a social being. We need each other's love and understanding to make it through life. We need other people as signs of God's love for us. Our Lord told us to gather in his name. The principal way we do this as Catholics is through the holy Eucharist where, as a *community* of believers, we thank God together. A thanksgiving meal would be incredibly lonely and empty eaten alone. So, too, in the Eucharist we are meant to celebrate our belonging to the family of faith. We are missed when we are off doing our own thing. The Lord and the faithful community expect us to be there.

REVIEW AND REFLECTION

1. What does the Second Commandment require?

2. Define *blasphemy* and *perjury*.

3. Why is the Sabbath to be a day of rest? List some activities that could sanctify this day.

4. Why do Christians celebrate Sunday as the Lord's Day?

5. What is the meaning of the term *Eucharist*?

FOR YOUR JOURNAL

Write the most convincing arguments you can think of to rebut a Catholic who does not go to Sunday Mass because "Mass is boring."

Catholic Life in Action

1. Read the story of the Rich Young Man in Mt 19:16–30. Note how the young man affirmed that he kept the Commandments, but how he could not part with his wealth to follow Jesus more perfectly. Reflect on your own life. Check off any of the following that you believe is keeping you from giving your all to the Lord.

   _____ 1. possessions
   _____ 2. what others might think
   _____ 3. pleasure
   _____ 4. freedom
   _____ 5. popularity
   _____ 6. demands Jesus might ask of me
   _____ 7. money
   _____ 8. need to change my life
   _____ 9. need to pray more
   _____ 10. other [write your own]:

   _____

   Write a reflection in your journal about what you consider to be the biggest factor that keeps people from following Jesus "more nearly day by day."

2. When some youngsters were asked about the meaning of love, they responded with answers like the following:

   • "Love is like a little old woman and a little old man who are still friends even after they know each other so well."
   • "Love is when Mommy gives Daddy the best piece of chicken."
   • "Love is when someone hurts you. And you get so mad but you don't yell at them because you know it would hurt their feelings."[3]

   Using any medium you like, illustrate what for *you* is the meaning of love. Create a collage or PowerPoint presentation. Write a poem or short story. Take a picture and write a caption. Record live interviews of people you admire who would share their definitions of love.

3. Consult the Catholic Encyclopedia online (www.newadvent.org/cathen.) Prepare a report on spiritism, blasphemy, idolatry, superstition, sacrilege, or some other violation of the first three commandments. Define the term and explain how the practice contradicts God's law.

4. Consult the United States Conference of Catholic Bishops' website to discover the readings for the coming Sunday's liturgy: www.usccb.org/nab. After reading and prayerfully reflecting on the passages to be read at Mass, briefly outline a talk based on them to be given at a youth day of recollection.

5. Read about the life of your patron saint. Report on how he or she modeled in a heroic way one of the theological virtues of faith, hope, and charity. You can begin your research online at one of these websites:
   • Catholics Online: www.catholic.org/saints
   • Catholic Forum: www.catholic-forum.com/saints indexsnt.htm
   • Theology Library: www.shc.edu/theolibrary/saints2.htm

6. *Exercising the virtue of charity.* Practice one of the following in the coming weeks:
   • Write a letter to a teacher who contributed to your growth.
   • Collect clothes from family members and relatives to donate to the Saint Vincent de Paul Society. Read more about the good works of the Saint Vincent de Paul Society at: www.svdpusa.org.
   • Volunteer at an after-school program to help younger students learn how to read.
   • Write a letter of appreciation or support to a member of the armed forces or a veteran.
   • With friends, spend a Saturday afternoon cleaning up trash in a park or along a waterway.
   • Make "personal care" kits of toiletries for the homeless.
   • Volunteer to do some yard work or run an errand for an elderly neighbor.

Summary Points

◆ Faith enables us to believe in God, what he has said and revealed to us, and what the Church proposes for our belief.

◆ Hope helps us to desire heaven and eternal life, not through our own strength, but through trust in Christ and the graces of the Holy Spirit.

◆ Charity, the greatest of all virtues, enables us to "love God above all things for his own sake, and our neighbor as ourselves for the love of God" (*CCC*, 1822; 2093).

◆ The Ten Commandments are also known as the Decalogue, which literally means "ten words."

◆ A covenant is the strongest possible pledge or agreement between two parties.

◆ The commandments of the Decalogue are unified. To break one of the commandments is to break the whole Law (*CCC*, 2079).

◆ The First Commandment requires us to accept in faith the one true God of love. It requires us to put into practice the theological virtues of faith, hope, and charity.

◆ Ways to strengthen our faith include prayer, Scripture reading, celebrating the sacraments, studying the faith, associating with people of faith, putting our faith into action, and avoiding sins that threaten faith.

◆ Sins against faith include voluntary doubt, incredulity, heresy (denial of an essential truth of the faith), apostasy (rejecting the Christian faith), and schism (refusing to submit to the Holy Father's authority).

◆ We sin against the virtue of hope through despair or presumption, that is, taking for granted that we can save ourselves without God's help.

◆ Charity (love), *agape* in the Greek, or *caritas* in Latin, means holding someone close to our hearts. If we love, then God lives in us because God is love.

◆ A vow is a "deliberate and free promise made to God concerning a possible and better good which must be fulfilled by reason of the virtue of religion" (*CCC*, 2102).

◆ Idolatry is the worship of false gods. Polytheism means the worship of many gods. Humans are guilty of idolatry when they honor or revere a creature as a substitute for God.

◆ Superstition, divination, magic, sorcery, spiritism, and irreligion contradict the First Commandment.

◆ Irreligion breeds sins like tempting God, sacrilege, and simony.

◆ Atheists deny the existence of God. Agnostics claim that they cannot know for certain if God exists or not. In effect, they are also often atheists.

◆ Prayer is an essential practice for observing the First Commandment.

◆ The Second Commandment requires us to respect God's holy name through blessing, praise, and adoration.

◆ We violate the Second Commandment when we break promises made in God's name, blaspheme, swear, or perjure ourselves.

◆ We keep holy the Sabbath day through recreation and prayer.

◆ Christians observe Sunday as the Lord's Day, the day of his resurrection. Catholics, following Jesus' injunction, see it as a serious obligation to celebrate the Eucharistic liturgy to thank, praise, and worship God for the gifts he bestows on us, and to commemorate the Paschal Mystery of Christ's saving action on our behalf.

PRAYER REFLECTION

The Lord is my shepherd;
there is nothing I lack.
In green pastures you let me graze;
to safe waters you lead me;
you restore my strength.
You guide me along the right path
for the sake of your name.
Even when I walk through a dark valley,
I fear no harm for you are at my side;
your rod and staff give me courage.

You set a table before me
as my enemies watch;
You anoint my head with oil;
my cup overflows.
Only goodness and love will pursue me
all the days of my life;
I will dwell in the house of the Lord
for years to come.
—Psalm 23:1–6

- Think about the following: When has the Lord watched over you? What special gifts has he given you? What are your green pastures? What dark valleys have you been through lately? How has the Lord helped you get through the tough times?
- To strengthen your faith in the Good Shepherd, read Psalms 4, 16, 27, 40, 62, 103, 139.

NOTES

1. As told in Brian Cavanaugh, T.O.R., *Sower's Seeds of Virtue* (Mahwah, NJ: Paulist Press, 1997), 80.
2. Quoted by Fr. Tommy Lane in his Homily for the Fourth Sunday of Advent Year B. Found on his website <www.frtommylane.com/homilies/year_b/advent4-2.htm> (16 August 2006). Original source credited as *Monastic Spirituality: Citeaux,* Tape AA2083 by Thomas Merton; recorded and copyright by Credence Cassettes, Kansas City, MO.
3. Source Unknown, "What Does Love Mean?" Found on Fr. Brian Cavanaugh, TOR's Apple Seeds® website <www.appleseeds.org/love%2Dmean.htm> (16 August 2006).

CHAPTER OVERVIEW

Who Deserves Our Love

We must learn to love everyone as unique individuals with dignity and worth because that's how God loves us. Jesus even tells us to love our enemies.

Healthy Self-Love

Loving others begins with loving ourselves. Each of us has been made in God's image, and we have been redeemed by Jesus Christ.

The Fourth Commandment

To honor and obey parents and to respectfully abide by other lawful authorities, part of God's plan for order and happiness in our families and society.

The Fifth Commandment

Since human life comes from God, we must respect and protect it. Direct killing a human life or the failure to save a life through inaction are both gravely sinful.

Respecting Personal Health

Prudent protection and care of personal health is mandated by the Fifth Commandment. Indulging in unhealthy eating patterns as well as substance abuse are offenses against the Fifth Commandment.

CHAPTER EIGHT

Respect for Life

"Do to others whatever you would have them do to you. This is the law and prophets."

Matthew 7:12

Who Deserves Our Love

A disciple of a famous spiritual master complained, "Why is it that everyone is happy but me?"

The master replied, "Because they can see goodness and beauty everywhere."

"Why can't I?" asked the student.

"You want to know why?" responded the teacher. "I think it is because you can't see outside what you fail to see inside."[1]

Similar to the message of this story, American poet Edwin Markham wrote: "I sought my soul, but my soul I could not see; I sought my God, but my God eluded me; I sought my brother, and I found all three."

These short illustrations make two important points that help explain Jesus' summary of the Law: "Love the Lord, your God, with all your heart, with all your soul, and with all your mind. . . . Love your neighbor as yourself" (Mt 22:38–39).

The love we are to have for God, neighbor, and self is connected. Jesus pointed out a direct relationship between loving God and loving neighbor. In his famous judgment scene at the end of time, Jesus clearly stated, "Whatever you did for one of these least brothers of mine, you did for me" (Mt 25:40). The first letter of John also describes this intimate connection between love of God and love of neighbor:

If anyone says, "I love God," but hates his brother, he is a liar; for whoever does not love a brother whom he has seen cannot love God whom he has not seen. This is the commandment we have from him: whoever loves God must also love his brother. (1 Jn 4:20–21)

And recall Jesus never distinguished between brothers and sisters who are *deserving* of our love and those who are not. For Jesus, love is universal; we must love even our enemies. We must love each person as a unique individual, a person with dignity and worth. Why? Because this is how God loves us.

Similarly, if we do not love ourselves, then it will be nearly impossible to love God or other people. Psychology supports this religious truth when it reports that the higher our self-esteem (self-appreciation or self-love), the greater the probability that we will treat others with respect, kindness, generosity, and love.

Chapters 8–10 suggest ways for us to love others and ourselves based on the second tablet of the Decalogue (Commandments Four to Ten). The theme of this chapter is respect, focusing on the fourth commandment, relationships with family members, and the fifth commandment, which addresses respect for life in all forms.

Esteem for Yourself

The word *esteem* is Latin for "value." Our self-esteem is directly related to how we value ourselves. Those with low self-esteem are usually self-haters who think they are inferior and unlovable for who they are. Their image of God is often that of an unloving, vindictive judge who can never be pleased. Even those with average self-esteem are typically plagued by self-doubt and feel unworthy of love. Love is something they think they have to earn. Perhaps two-thirds of us suffer from low or average self-esteem.

Jesus already responded to any low self-esteem we might suffer by dying for each one of us. Just think about how worthwhile each of us must be if our loving Savior died for us. Low self-esteem comes from so-called "stinkin' thinkin'," ignoring the good news of our unique, precious worth in God's sight. It results from buying the lies of the evil one, which, tear us down, rather than build us up.

Here are some examples of "stinkin' thinkin'." Rate yourself according to this scale.

No one can make you feel inferior without your consent.

—ELEANOR ROOSEVELT

MOST OF THE TIME	SOME OF THE TIME	RARELY	NEVER	
				1. I have to be perfect in everything I do.
				2. I have to be right all of the time.
				3. I can't laugh too often (or share my hopes and dreams), or others will think I am foolish.
				4. I need everyone to love me.
				5. I expect other people to change to please me.
				6. I can't allow anyone to see me cry or they'll think I'm weak.
				7. I don't reveal my true feelings for fear someone will reject me.
				8. I don't like trying new things for fear of failure.
				9. I need to be first in everything, or I'll consider myself a loser.
				10. To be happy, I need to be free of conflict.

After you total your check marks in each of the columns, evaluate yourself by checking one of the following:

_____ I have healthy self-love and self-esteem.

_____ I am average on the self-esteem scale.

_____ I have lots of growing to do in the area of self-appreciation.

Healthy Self-Love

Bring to class examples from print advertising and other media—like TV sitcoms—that contribute to the false beliefs that are illustrated in the *Esteem for Yourself* exercise. Discuss as a class.

self-esteem

A sense of happiness and contentment about who you are as a human being. People with self-esteem consciously appreciate their own worth and importance as if viewed in the eyes of God.

Genuine self-love (another way to describe self-esteem) is necessary in order to love God and others. We should love ourselves because we are made in God's image, beings of incomparable value that God created out of nothing for himself. We should love ourselves because Jesus Christ loves us, forgives our sins, and stretched out his arms on the cross to embrace us and die for us. We should love ourselves because we have inherent dignity, and we are somebodys with unique talents to share with others. We deserve respect.

An oft-told story drives home the point of our inherent worth. A speaker began his talk by holding up a $20 bill and asked if anyone would like it. Audience members started to raise their hands. He promised he would give it to someone, but first he crumbled the bill up, then dropped it on the floor and stepped on it. He then asked, "Who would still like to have the $20?" Still, many hands remained in the air.

The speaker then made his point: "My friends, I take it that you still want the money because it did not decrease in value, despite what I did to it.

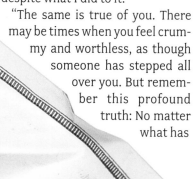

"The same is true of you. There may be times when you feel crummy and worthless, as though someone has stepped all over you. But remember this profound truth: No matter what has happened to you in the past or will happen to you in the future, God will always treasure and value you. You are priceless to him, the 'apple of God's eye'" (see Ps 17:8).[2]

God loves us all unconditionally. God's love is boundless. According to the book of Isaiah, God said:

I have called you by name: you are mine.
Because you are precious in my eyes and glorious, and because I love you.
Fear not for I am with you. (Is 43:1, 4–5)

If God loves us so much, how can we not love ourselves?

However, many of us have trouble accepting the Good News of God's unconditional love. We tend to listen to other voices, ones that say we are only lovable *if* we are successful, powerful, or popular. But these are false measures of acceptability that control and manipulate us. Love has no strings attached. We must accept ourselves as God accepts and loves us—unconditionally and totally. Only when we accept the awesome truth that we are already totally lovable and worthwhile for who we are as God's precious child can we, in turn, love others for who they are . . . without conditions.

GROWING IN THE VIRTUE OF SELF-ESTEEM

How can we grow in the virtue of **self-esteem**, the virtue that enables us to accept ourselves as God accepts us—as worthwhile persons apart from our achievements or talents or the opinion of others? These pointers can help:

- Pray for the gift of faith to know and believe that God loves you unconditionally.
- Look to the crucifix. Imagine that you are meeting the eyes of Jesus. In the stillness of your heart, can you hear him whisper, "I love you"?

- Repeat these words from the Gospel of John: "As the Father loves me, so also I love you. Remain in my love" (Jn 15:9).
- List all those people for whom you don't have to pretend to be someone else, that is, your friends and relatives who accept you for who you are.
- Ask God to forgive your sins. Go to confession and hear Christ's representative, the priest, proclaim the Lord's forgiveness (and love) for you.
- Apologize to the appropriate persons if you've done something stupid or thoughtless. Learn a lesson from each mistake that you made, and then let it go.
- Laugh at yourself. We are all less-than-perfect.
- Practice humility. Hopefully, you are not afraid to admit that you are gifted. True humility is to recognize your giftedness, that is, to accept what talents God has given you to be the unique person you are. Pride slips in only when we claim too much credit for our gifts or forget to thank God for them. Remember, all is grace. Existence, health, family and friends, and your many talents. They are all gifts from God.
- Praise and thank God. True humility leads to the virtue of gratitude. "Thanks, Lord, for making me all that I am and giving me all that I have" is the prayer of the truly humble person. Gratitude to God is basic for Christians who recognize the truth about themselves and their God.

It is a great thing to be humble when you are brought low; but to be humble when you are praised is a great and rare achievement.

—St. Bernard

REVIEW AND REFLECTION

1. What is the relationship between healthy self-love and love of God and neighbor?

2. What causes poor self-esteem? How can we overcome it?

3. Discuss how the virtues of humility and gratitude are related to authentic self-love.

FOR YOUR JOURNAL

Reflect on the special gifts the Holy Spirit has given to you. Answer the following questions:
- What are you good at?
- What good do others find in you?
- What brings you joy?
- How might you share some of these good things with others?

A Candle for Jesus

"You are the light of the world" (Mt 5:14).

Light represents life. It symbolizes the divine because Jesus is the light of the world. It signifies truth, as in the light of reason. Light stands for goodness, in contrast to the dark, which is evil.

By calling you light, Jesus wants you to bring life, God, truth, and goodness into the world. Judge your "candle power" by evaluating each of the following. Use this scale: *1—this is not me; 2—sometimes describes me; 3—really describes me.*

LIFE

____ You sense when others are depressed and know how to cheer them up.

____ You graciously recognize the accomplishments of others and praise them for their efforts.

____ You can say "thank you" and really mean it.

GOD

____ You recognize that some things are holy; for example, you are reverent when using God's name.

____ You imitate Jesus' mercy by forgiving those who hurt you.

____ You share your faith with others.

TRUTH

____ Instead of lying, you own up to it when you do something wrong.

____ You can gently remind friends when they are doing something harmful to others or themselves.

GOODNESS

____ When you see a need—whether at home, school, work, or play—you are the first to use your talents and pitch in to help.

____ You stand up for what you believe, even when faced with peer pressure.

Note in your journal a couple of examples of when "being light" by "doing right" enhanced your self-esteem.

Practical Exercise: Try one of these . . . and your life won't be the same.

• Imagine today is your last day on earth. Live it as though you were to be judged by God tonight.

• Today, treat everyone as though he or she was Jesus Christ in disguise.

The Fourth Commandment

(CCC, 2197—2257)

Honor your father and your mother.

Historically, the Fourth Commandment was intended to remind adult children of their responsibility to take care of their aging parents. In Old Testament times, nomadic contemporaries of the Jews often abandoned their old and sick to the elements as they moved on to new territories. The Israelites, in contrast, revered and took care of their aged ones. Today, we see examples in our own society of *ageism* (prejudice against old people), especially in the promotion of **euthanasia** and assisted suicide. The Fourth Commandment's original intent is still very much needed.

The Fourth Commandment also promotes family values. The family is society's foundational unit. The family supports the love of a husband and wife, the procreation of children, and the religious growth and education of children as responsible members of the human family. God's plan for the family calls for parents and children to experience worth and dignity and fundamental equality as people with rights, and to learn how to exercise those rights and relate to others responsibly.

The family is the basic unit of society, and it teaches us the values of respect, honor, obedience, gratitude, and affection. The family also schools us in how to live in relationship to others. And the family is fertile ground for helping us blossom into loving and caring persons, not only toward our own relatives, but to our fellow citizens and all of God's people.

Catholics also see the family as the "domestic Church," which mirrors the love and community of the Triune God—Father, Son, and Holy Spirit. In this basic Christian community, we practice the theological and other virtues, hear God's word, and learn how to pray (*CCC*, 2204).

The family is so fundamental that governments have a serious duty to protect and uphold families. Governments must guarantee basic rights to ensure that families prosper. Among these rights are a man and woman's right to marry, have children, and freely raise their children in their religious faith; the rights to private property, affordable housing, and a job with a wage high enough to support a family; the rights to health care and a safe environment free from violence; the rights to protection from the peddling of illegal drugs and destructive pornography and freedom from other injurious practices that undermine the family; and the right of families to join together to promote family values in the political arena (*CCC*, 2211).

HONOR

The Fourth Commandment helps regulate relationships within other social groups where authority is exercised, including the duties and responsibilities between students and teachers, bosses and their employees, and citizens and government officials (*CCC*, 2199). The key value at stake in all these relationships is

euthanasia

Direct or active euthanasia is any "action or omission which of itself and by intention causes death, with the purpose of eliminating all suffering" (*Gospel of Life*, 65). Direct euthanasia is always wrong despite one's good intentions.

honor. Honor involves respect, admiration, and recognition of another's dignity. When we honor others, we esteem them. Honor flows from the virtue of justice.

Some people are due honor because of who they are or what position they hold. God, of course, deserves to be honored above all. Next to our relationship with the Almighty, the parent-child bond is the most universal, important, and basic. Honor within this relationship is a two-way street. On the one hand, children must honor their parents and others who have lawful authority over them; on the other hand, parents and other authority figures must respect and esteem those entrusted to them.

Every human being is worthy of honor, but this is doubly so in the relationship between parents and children. In cooperation with God, biological mothers and fathers have given their children the gift of life. Adoptive parents have lovingly welcomed, nurtured, and protected their children. Parents are their children's first teachers. They derive their authority to guide their children from God.

Children honor their parents when they observe their parents' just wishes. In doing so, children are acknowledging God, the ultimate source of life and the "author" of all authority. (However, children must disobey any immoral command given by a parent or any other authority figure. God's law always takes priority over any human law.)

Adult children must continue to honor their parents by seeking their advice, by expressing their gratitude for all they have done, and by supporting them spiritually, psychologically, and financially if necessary in the tough and lonely times of aging.

We all belong to a spiritual family, too, with "mothers" and "fathers" of the faith who have witnessed the gospel to us and helped us learn to live. Special respect, gratitude, and honor is therefore owed our godparents, grandparents, other relatives, parish priests, religious, teachers, and friends who nourished our faith and who have supported us in our growth to spiritual maturity (*CCC*, 2220).

Without mutual respect, and the virtues of patience, tolerance, fairness, and a huge dose of love, sibling rivalry can destroy a family. Therefore, brothers and sisters must honor each other, as well.

The Fourth Commandment is not just a one-sided relationship requiring respect and obedience from children for their parents. Parents must also honor their children as precious images of God. They must educate their children intellectually and in the social skills. They must provide a safe, warm environment of care, love, forgiveness, tenderness, and service for their children. Moreover, they have the serious duty to educate their children religiously and morally, taking great care to protect them from the degrading influences of a violent, materialistic society and from the degrading and dehumanizing influence of the various media. And, because parents are their children's primary educators, the Church recognizes that they have the fundamental right to choose schools that reflect their religious and moral values.

Parental respect for children means honoring their children's basic right to choose their own vocations and careers. Faithful Catholic parents will make a special effort to encourage their children to consider service to God's people as priests, sisters, or brothers and support and nourish any religious vocation a child might choose (*CCC*, 2233).

Most of all, parents are expected to lead their children to Jesus Christ. Thus, parents must strive, through their own good example, to live the Christian virtues and to celebrate the sacraments, especially with weekly Mass attendance. More than ever, parents today need the help and

support of a believing community of faith to help nourish a Christian life in both themselves and their families.

In this regard, the Fourth Commandment requires us to honor all lawful officials, both in Church and civic communities, who hold their authority as a sacred trust from the originator of all authority—God. Jesus himself told us of this obligation when he taught, "Repay to Caesar what belongs to Caesar and to God what belongs to God" (Lk 20:25).

Authority figures are duty-bound to uphold basic human and political rights and to exercise their authority as a service to the human family. They must ensure that society's laws and policies never violate human dignity or go against the natural law. They must guarantee a just society that treats everyone as having equal dignity, while keeping in mind the special needs and contributions of each individual.

Citizens are responsible for obeying the legitimate regulations of those who justly hold positions of authority. We must do our part to help promote the common good, build up the virtues of solidarity and social justice, and promote the dignity of each human being. Paying taxes, voting, and coming to the aid of our fellow citizens in time of peril are necessary duties of responsible members of a just society. Citizens of countries blessed with abundant wealth are especially required to see that their officials pass laws to welcome immigrants seeking freedom to practice their religion and stake a claim in a safe nation that will allow them to work, live, and raise a family in peace.

Christians have the right and duty to share gospel values with their fellow citizens. We must bring Christ to the marketplace by working for social-justice principles like respect for human life, the virtue of solidarity, and the preferential love for the poor. Although citizens have the right to express their political, religious, and other views and work to establish policies based on them, Catholic teaching insists that responsible citizenship requires Christians to speak out on issues that threaten the sacredness of human life or against policies and laws that undermine people's salvation. As the *Catechism of the Catholic Church* points out:

> *The citizen is obliged in conscience not to follow the directives of civil authorities when they are contrary to the demands of the moral order, to the fundamental rights of persons or the teachings of the Gospel. (CCC, 2242)*

According to the Fourth Commandment

Judge whether the following situations are in violation of the fourth commandment. **Use "R" if a situation is right, "W" if it is wrong**.

_____ Joe, seventeen, never acknowledges his mother or father with a gift or card on Mother's Day or Father's Day.

_____ Steve wants to study English in college with a view to becoming a writer. His father, who is quite wealthy, says he won't pay a dime for Steve's education unless he majors in business administration.

_____ Susan and her friends aren't voting in the coming elections because they think all the candidates are alike and their vote won't make a bit of difference.

_____ Chris likes to play harmless little practical jokes on his little sister.

_____ The restaurant manager tells Amanda to ignore reporting all her tip income on her tax return since the IRS will never find out.

_____ A mother suggests that her nineteen-year-old son stop seeing his girlfriend because "she's a bad influence on you."

Explain your choices. And then discuss:

- Do parents have a duty to pay for your college education if they can afford to do so? Why or why not?
- Do parents have the right to tell their teenage children whom they can date or not?
- Is it immoral to deliberately choose not to vote?

FAITHFUL CITIZENSHIP

The Church teaches that responsible citizenship is a virtue. To participate in the political process is a moral obligation. As citizens in a democratic country, we have the *right* and *duty* to participate in the public arena. Public policies and laws have tremendous moral consequences for people. The Lord expects us to be the light of the world, to bring Gospel values to the marketplace.

In an election-year pastoral letter, the United States bishops wrote:

> *Believers are called to be a community of conscience within the larger society and to test public life by the values of Scripture and the principles of Catholic social teaching. Our responsibility is to measure all candidates, policies, parties, and platforms by how they protect or undermine the life, dignity, and rights of the human person; whether they protect the poor and vulnerable and advance the common good.[3]*

The bishops encourage American voters, both Catholic and concerned citizens alike, to ask of our leaders and candidates for political office questions like those listed below. Select a few public figures and research their stand on these questions. You might check to see if they have websites with answers to frequently asked questions. Or, write letters for answers to these questions. Compare and contrast the positions of your candidates and judge whether their views are compatible with gospel values.

- How will we protect the weakest in our midst—innocent unborn children?
- How will our nation resist what Pope John Paul II called a "culture of death"?
- How can we keep our nation from turning to violence to solve some of its most difficult problems—abortion to deal with difficult pregnancies; the death penalty to combat crime; euthanasia and assisted suicide to deal with the burdens of age, illness, and disability; and war to address international disputes?
- How will we address the tragic fact that more than thirty thousand children die every day as a result of hunger, international debt, and lack of development around the world, as well as the fact that the younger you are, the more likely you are to be poor here in the richest nation on Earth?
- How can our nation help parents raise their children with respect for life, sound moral values, a sense of hope, and an ethic of stewardship and responsibility?
- How will we address the growing number of families and individuals without affordable and accessible health care?
- How will our society combat continuing prejudice, overcome hostility toward immigrants and refugees, and heal the wounds of racism, religious bigotry, and other forms of discrimination?
- What are the responsibilities and limitations of families, community organizations, markets, and government? How can these elements of society work together to overcome poverty, pursue the common good, care for creation, and overcome injustice?
- When should our nation use, or avoid the use of, military force—for what purpose, under what authority, and at what human cost?[4]

The Family of Humanity

Hall of Fame shortstop Pee Wee Reese, born and raised in racially segregated Kentucky, was a teammate on the Brooklyn Dodgers of Jackie Robinson, the first African-American allowed to play major league baseball in the twentieth century. Reese rejected the idea posed by his teammates to go on strike to protest Robinson's breaking the color barrier. And in a heart-warming gesture, Reese helped Robinson be accepted into the big leagues. One day when Robinson was being jeered by a bigoted and mean crowd, Reese walked over and put his arm around Robinson's shoulders. This stunned and quieted the rowdy fans and helped pave the way for Robinson's acceptance.

Racism, ethnic bias, prejudgments about people who are different—sexually, religiously, socially, or whatever else—is a cancer in society and a blight on humanity. As God's children, we must combat stereotypes—overblown generalizations—whenever we hear them bandied about. We must refuse to make or laugh at ethnic or sexist or racial or homosexual jokes that insult and demean people.

As brothers and sisters to everyone, we must never take part in the many faces of prejudice: hateful language and slurs directed at people who are different; avoidance of them just because they are not like us; discriminatory behavior that denies them their basic human rights; or violent acts directed against them or their property.

- Which groups seem to be most victimized by prejudice in our society? in your school? Why do you think these groups are especially targeted?
- Have you ever been the victim of discrimination? If so, how did it make you feel?
- Can laws alone change prejudiced hearts and minds? If not, what else is needed?
- Give examples of insensitive, hurtful, and prejudicial remarks you have heard. How did you respond to them? Brainstorm ways you can respond to them in the future.

REVIEW AND REFLECTION

1. What is the Fourth Commandment? What are some values this commandment emphasizes?

2. What are some duties children owe parents? What are some rights of children?

3. What do parents owe their children? What do siblings owe each other?

4. What are some things government authorities owe citizens?

5. What are our some of our obligations as citizens?

6. How is prejudice a violation of the principles of the Fourth Commandment?

FOR YOUR JOURNAL

Write of a time when you were the victim of prejudice. How did you feel at the time? Did the experience of being unfairly judged make you more sympathetic toward the victims of prejudice? Explain.

The Fifth Commandment

(CCC, 2258—2269; 2302—2321; 2327—2330)

You shall not kill.

Human life comes from and returns to God. The Fifth Commandment teaches respect for human life and condemns as gravely sinful any direct, intentional killing. It also forbids any indirect act, or failure to act, that brings about a person's death. For example, refusing to help a person in mortal danger is seriously wrong. So, too, is greed that leads to the starvation of people in our own or other nations. This is a form of indirect homicide for which individuals and nations are blameworthy.

The Old Testament teaches that murder results from Original Sin and arises out of anger and envy (see Cain's murder of Abel, Gn 4). Murder destroys human dignity and violates God's holiness. According to Jesus' teaching in the New Testament, murder also contradicts Jesus' clear teaching to rid revenge and hatred from our hearts, love our neighbor as ourselves, and to love even our enemies. Hate contradicts Christ's law of love. Deliberately wishing anyone evil is sinful; desiring grave harm for another is seriously sinful.

SPECIAL EXAMPLES OF KILLING

The Bible does not condemn all killing. For example, killing in self-defense is morally permissible when people are protecting their own lives or are coming to the aid of someone else's life for whom they are responsible. Killing in self-defense is justifiable because one's intention is to save one's own life against an unjust aggressor. The taking of the life of the assailant is only permitted, not directly willed.

In an analogous way, the Church teaches that public authorities have the right and duty to defend citizens against unjust aggressors, even if this might lead to the death penalty or a defensive war.

Capital punishment. To defend against aggressors, we must always use

Infanticide, fratricide, parricide, and the murder of a spouse are especially grave crimes by reason of the natural bonds they break. *(CCC, 2268)*

• Define the terms used in this sentence. Give examples of each.

In a recent statement titled *A Culture of Life and the Penalty of Death*, the bishops have stepped up their opposition to the death penalty in the United States. They give the following reasons for their opposition to capital punishment:

• The sanction of death, when it is not necessary to protect society, violates respect for human life and dignity.
• State-sanctioned killing in our names diminishes all of us.
• Its application is deeply flawed and can be irreversibly wrong, is prone to errors, and is biased by factors such as race, the quality of legal representation, and where the crime was committed.
• We have other ways to punish criminals and protect society.[5]

The teaching of the *Catechism of the Catholic Church* is also clear:

> *If bloodless means are sufficient to defend human lives against an aggressor and to protect public order and the safety of persons, public authority should limit itself to such means, because they better correspond to the concrete conditions of the common good and are more in conformity to the dignity of the human person.* (CCC, *2267*)

War. The Catholic Church begins with a presumption *against* war, always promoting the peaceful settlement of disputes. However, in extreme cases (like unjust aggression), as a last resort, the Church recognizes that governments have the right and responsibility to pass laws to enlist citizens to help defend the nation. It is possible for Catholics to fight in a "just" war if *all* the following conditions are met (*CCC,* 2309):

• There must be a real, lasting, grave, and certain damage inflicted by an aggressor on a nation or a community of nations. Examples of these situations include the violation of basic human rights, killing of innocent people, or the urgency of a nation to defend itself.

bloodless means and avoid killing, if at all possible. This is true even with criminals. Criminals *do* merit punishment for their crimes. The purpose of punishment is threefold: to set right the disorder caused by criminal offenses; to preserve public order and personal safety; and to correct the offender.

As the United States bishops have taught, however, it is very difficult today to reconcile the death penalty with a consistent "respect-for-life ethic." We must always respect human life, valuing the dignity and sacredness of even the most heinous of criminals. For some supporters of capital punishment, revenge is their key motive for favoring capital punishment. But Jesus taught that revenge can never be a motive for our actions.

Furthermore, social science reveals that the poor and minorities have been most victimized by capital punishment, which can never reform the criminal. Also, deterrence has been the most common reason people have used to justify the death penalty, but sociologists have found that the death penalty does not, in fact, deter crime.

◆ Research and report on the laws of your state regarding the death penalty.

◆ "It is better to let 1,000 guilty persons go free than to condemn to death an innocent person." Agree or disagree?

◆ The *Catechism of the Catholic Church* holds that most modern nations now have so many ways to repress crime that the need for the death penalty is "practically non-existent." Explain how this is true.

- War must be a last resort. All peaceful alternatives must have been tried and failed.

- The rights and values in the conflict must be so important that they justify killing.
- A war cannot be just unless waged for the noblest of reasons and with a commitment to postwar reconciliation with the enemy. No just war can tolerate needless destruction, cruelty to prisoners, or other harsh measures like torture.
- Only proper representatives of the people, entrusted with the common good, have the right to declare a war of defense.
- The chances for success must be calculated against the human cost of the war to prevent hopeless use of force and resistance when either will prove futile, anyway.

- Armed conflict must not create even worse evil than that to be eliminated. Therefore, military damage and costs must be proportionate to the good expected.

Even in war, the moral law draws limits. Noncombatants, wounded soldiers, and prisoners deserve respect and humane treatment (*CCC*, 2313).

Torture is especially to be condemned as a totally evil means, even in a war. It is a serious violation of a person's basic dignity and fundamental goodness. It is an inhumane means that can *never* be justified.

The mass extermination of a people, nation, or ethnic minority is morally reprehensible and gravely sinful. Genocide is a terrible moral evil. Blindly following unjust orders can never excuse personal responsibility for participating in such heinous crimes.

Terrorism is a type of war waged on innocent people to gain some political or other advantage. It involves the threat to kill or the actual destruction of innocent lives, or the indiscriminate destruction of property, simply to spread all-pervasive fear. Terrorist acts can never be justified (*CCC,* 2297) and are the most hateful acts known to our contemporary society, ranking with the use of nuclear weapons.

Because the use of nuclear weapons is aimed at the indiscriminate destruction of regions and people, it merits total condemnation. The use of nuclear weapons is a crime against God and humanity and can never be justified. The same is true of chemical and biological weapons (like the use of anthrax).

The arms race is another sad cause of war—along with injustice, excessive economic and social inequalities, envy, distrust, and pride. The accumulation, production, and sale of arms all seriously threaten international order. The money involved in producing them seriously harms the poor and needy whose care is later diminished or withdrawn as too "expensive." An overabundance of arms intensifies the danger of conflict and squanders resources that should be spent on the starving in our midst (*CCC*, 2315). Christians are called to support the reduction, rendering useless, and elimination of all destructive chemical, biological, and nuclear weapons.

The Church respects citizens who serve in the military out of loyalty to their country. They are viewed as guardians of freedom and true peacekeepers. At the same time, the Church respects those Christians who refuse to meet violence with violence and supports laws that would make alternative provision for pacifists who refuse to bear arms, "provided they accept some other form of community service" (*Church in the Modern World*, 79).

Jesus is the Prince of Peace. His death reconciled us to God. He established his Church to be a true sign of peace, and he blessed peacemakers, calling them the children of God (Mt 5:9). True peace, defined as "the tranquillity of order," is the fruit of justice and the result of love and treating others as brothers and sisters endowed with dignity. To be a Christian means to be a peacemaker. We can engage in the work of peace by praying for it and by fighting the causes of war, that is, by committing ourselves to justice, respecting the dignity of others, and going the extra mile by loving all people everywhere.

◆ Under what circumstances would you consider it immoral to go to war?

◆ Drawing on historical examples, discuss any wars you definitely consider to be unjust.

Peace Begins with Me

◆ Discuss the different sources of aggression among teens that have led to several notorious cases of school shootings.

◆ Then brainstorm a list of practical strategies to reduce tension, conflict, and aggression in schools. Discuss ways to apply these principles to conflicts in your own school.

 REVIEW AND REFLECTION

1. What is the Fifth Commandment?

2. What are the root causes of murder?

3. What are the various purposes of punishment?

4. Should capital punishment be enforced today? Why or why not?

5. List the conditions necessary for a just war to take place.

6. Can a Catholic be a soldier in good conscience? Can a Catholic be a pacifist? If so, explain under what conditions.

7. Why can we never justify acts of terrorism, the use of nuclear weapons, and the use of chemical or biological weapons?

FOR YOUR JOURNAL
Given your own talents and personality, discuss several ways you can be a "person of peace" at home, at school, and on the job.

"Terrorism does not hesitate to strike defenseless people, without discrimination, or to impose inhuman blackmail, causing panic among entire populations, in order to force political leaders to support the designs of the terrorists. No situation can justify such criminal activity, which covers the perpetrators with infamy, and it is all the more deplorable when it hides behind religion, thereby bringing the pure truth of God down to the level of the terrorists' own blindness and moral perversion."[6]

abortion

The deliberate killing of unborn human life by means of medical or surgical procedures. Direct abortion is seriously wrong because it is an unjustified attack on human life.

ABORTION AND OTHER VIOLATIONS AGAINST THE FIFTH COMMANDMENT
(CCC, 2270—2275; 2276—2287; 2292—2301; 2322—2326)

Abortion is the deliberate killing of unborn human life by means of medical or surgical procedures. Willed either as a means or an end, **abortion** is a grave and unjustified attack on innocent human life. It seriously violates the Fifth Commandment, which seeks to protect life.

The Church has always unswervingly taught that human life must be respected and protected from the very first moment of conception. The Church's teaching of the grave moral evil of every procured abortion is unchangeable. So serious is this teaching that the Church has attached the canonical penalty of automatic excommunication of anyone who procures an abortion.

The Church teaches that society's laws must protect every human person's God-given right to life from the first moment of conception. This is a right that does not have to be earned:

> When the state does not place its power at the service of the rights of each citizen, and in particular of the more vulnerable, the very foundations of a state based on law are undermined. (CCC, 2273)

It is morally permitted to care for a human embryo medically since it is truly a human person. However, prenatal procedures engaged in for the purpose of abortion, medical experimentation that treats the embryo as disposable biological material, or genetic manipulation that is nontherapeutic are all seriously wrong.

Church teaching is clear:
> [F]rom the moment of its conception life must be guarded with the greatest care, while abortion and infanticide are unspeakable crimes. (Pastoral Constitution on the Church in the Modern World, 51)

All human life is sacred. Made in God's image, each human being has incalculable worth and dignity and is to be treated with utmost respect.

Abortion is also a violation of the natural law. Any society that allows the killing of unborn children has sowed the seeds of self-destruction. A society exists to protect life and communal living. When this protection is not extended to any one group in the society, then all groups are threatened. We are already seeing how some social engineers are judging other people to be unfit to live: old people suffering from dementia, the terminally ill, profoundly mentally challenged children and adults, and others who do not fit their definition of what it means to be "productive" members of society.

Abortion is a direct challenge to the ethics of Jesus. He instructed us in the strongest possible language to care for each other, especially those who are weakest and most defenseless. We will be judged based on how we follow his command.

What Can You Do About Abortion?

Abortion is one of the great moral issues of our day. There are many things you can do to work to eliminate abortions. Here are a few:

- *Respect all life.* Take care of your own precious gift of life. Eat properly, exercise regularly—both body and mind. Watch out for others; for example, drive carefully. Settle your disputes peacefully. Use, don't abuse, the environment (e.g., don't litter).

- *Don't judge others.* Prejudice sees others as less than human. Those who permit abortion have prejudged the unborn baby; they have concluded that unborn life is subhuman life. We do the same whenever we judge others negatively. Every person is a brother or sister and should be treated with respect.

- *Pray.* We believe in the power of prayer. Ask the Holy Spirit to enlighten others. Ask God's forgiveness for your own failures to respect life and for our society's callous disregard for human life. Ask for the courage to take unpopular stands and fight for justice. Pray for women tempted to abort their babies, for doctors and nurses, for lawmakers, for the clergy, and for those working in the pro-life movement.

- *Get involved.* Use the power of the pen. Write letters to newspapers, legislators, television stations. Express your concern for human life. Participate in pro-life rallies. Start a pro-life group at school. Financially support organizations like Birthright. Join the National Right to Life Society. Support a local Crisis Pregnancy Center. With friends, collect diapers, baby and maternity clothes, and other needed items.

- *Be informed.* Know pro-life responses to pro-abortion arguments (see following page). Learn more about abortion and other life issues. Study, understand, and commit to heart the following pro-life responses to typical pro-abortion arguments.

Other major violations of the "do not kill" prohibition of the Fifth Commandment include scandal—the of bad example that leads others to do evil; serious violations of fundamental human rights like kidnapping, hostage-taking, torture of prisoners, and terrorist acts; and bodily mutilations, amputations, and sterilizations that are performed for non-medical purposes.

The Fifth Commandment also governs medical ethics. By respecting life in cases of medical experimentation and organ transplants, we will ensure that such procedures conform to the natural law, respect the dignity of persons, promote public health and the common good, and always involve informed consent.

This "pro-life" commandment also calls on us to value and love dying persons, allowing them to die in dignity and peace, and treating human corpses with respect, in view of the Christian hope of the resurrection of the body.

In general, the Fifth Commandment enjoins us to defend human life whenever it is being assaulted. Christians must be ever-mindful to protect and defend the weak and helpless in our midst and guarantee that they have whatever is needed to live with the level of dignity and humanity that befits a child of God. This is why the Church has insisted that we put into practice the Corporal (bodily) Works of Mercy, works that Jesus taught serve as the basis of our judgment at the end of time. They are listed to the right.

Corporal Works of Mercy

1. Feed the hungry.
2. Give drink to the thirsty.
3. Clothe the naked.
4. Visit the imprisoned.
5. Shelter the homeless
6. Visit the sick
7. Bury the dead

THE ABORTION ARGUMENT	
Pro-Abortion Argument	***Pro-Life Response***
It's only an operation. No human being is present. Why not operate?	A person's genetic code begins at conception. The fertilized egg can only develop into a human life. Therefore, it is a human life worthy of protection.
The legal system supports abortion.	"Legal" does not make it right. Some laws are immoral or contradict higher laws.
A woman has an absolute right to do what she wants with her own body.	Suicide laws are based on the premise that we belong together and are responsible for each other. We are social beings. We do not have absolute rights over our bodies and lives.
It is an effective form of contraception.	Abortion is not contraceptive. Conception has already taken place.
It is better for the child to be dead than unwanted.	Isn't this presumptuous? Let the child grow up and decide on his or her own.
It's convenient and helps eliminate an unwanted pregnancy.	This fosters irresponsibility. People are accountable for their actions. There are other options, for example, offering this child for adoption.
It helps control overpopulation.	So does murder, euthanasia, and suicide. There are other, moral means to control population.
Abortion should be okay in cases of rape and incest.	This is a tough and emotional issue. Very few pregnancies result from rape or incest. When it does happen, an infant is not responsible for the original act. Though this life has begun in a tragic way, we must defend innocent life. Our faith says good can come from suffering. A good end does not justify evil means.
The baby may be born retarded or handicapped.	We can't say that such people have no value. This is a gross form of prejudice against a minority. Why not then eliminate anyone who is not fully conscious (e.g., a sleeping person)?
It is economical and keeps the cost of welfare down.	Is money of more value than life? There are other ways to control illegitimate births: sex education, the elimination of poverty, etc.
Pushing a pro-life amendment or law is forcing your religious beliefs on others.	Don't we have the right to defend innocent human life as we see fit in a democracy? Many civil rights laws were unpopular at first.

CORPORAL WORKS OF MERCY

Special mention must also be made of two topics that are a growing problem in today's world: **euthanasia** and **assisted suicide**.

By definition, *direct* or *active* euthanasia ("mercy killing") is any "action or omission which of itself and by intention causes death, with the purpose of eliminating all suffering" (*Gospel of Life*, 65).

Direct euthanasia is always wrong, despite one's good intentions, for example, relieving the pain of a seriously ill patient or a handicapped or dying person because, again, "a good end does not justify evil means."

However, the Church holds that one is not guilty of the sin of euthanasia when a decision is made with the patient's approval to withhold "aggressive medical treatment." Such medical procedures are often disproportionate to any expected results or impose excessive burdens on the patient and his or her family. "Extraordinary means," like heroic and costly operations on a dying patient, can be refused so nature can run its natural course. However, we must always use ordinary means (e.g., food, oxygen) to care for sick people. Additionally, a person may take painkillers to lessen suffering, even though one's life might be shortened. In this case, death is not willed as a means or an end; it is merely tolerated as an inevitable result.

Suicide, the taking of one's own life, is a serious evil that shows a total lack of self-love and a rejection of the God of life. Suicide also displays a serious lack of love of others, violating the virtue of solidarity with our families, neighbors, and the human community. When suicide is intended to give a bad example, especially to the young, it is an example of the worst possible kind of scandal (*CCC*, 2282).

Unfortunately, many people who commit suicide are suffering from grave psychological problems. Others are undergoing powerful fear in the face of anticipated suffering. In wartime, some who commit suicide might be the victims of torture. These and similar circumstances lessen one's blameworthiness for an act that is always *objectively* and gravely wrong. We should not judge the state of a suicide victim's soul before God. We should pray for such people and commend them to God's bounteous mercy.

Assisted suicide performed by rogue physicians or other misguided people is a grave sin, regardless of the intention. Pope John Paul II addressed this subject:

> To concur with the intention of another person to commit suicide and to help in carrying it out through so-called "assisted suicide" means to cooperate in, and at times to be the actual perpetrator of, an injustice which can never be excused, even if it is requested. (The Gospel of Life, 66)

assisted suicide

The intentional assistance of any dying or suffering person in taking his or her own life.

euthanasia

Direct or active euthanasia is any "action or omission which of itself and by intention causes death, with the purpose of eliminating all suffering" (*Gospel of Life*, 65). Direct euthanasia is always wrong despite one's good intentions.

Which Violate the Fifth Commandment?

Give reasons for each response to the following:
- A store owner shoots an armed robber in the back as he is leaving the store.
- Your father kills a late-night intruder in your house.
- The police use tear gas to disperse an unruly crowd at a rock concert.
- Two teens drag race on a deserted street.
- A boyfriend encourages his pregnant girlfriend to get an abortion.
- A big brother encourages his younger brother to jump off a garage roof into a pile of leaves.
- A computer hacker brings down the computers of an airline traffic control center.

REVIEW AND REFLECTION

1. What does the Church teach about the morality of abortion?

2. Briefly discuss five pro-life responses to typical arguments offered by those who support abortion.

3. What are the Corporal Works of Mercy?

4. Define *euthanasia*. Is it ever justifiable?

5. Why does the Church condemn suicide?

temperance

The virtue that regulates our attraction to pleasure and helps us use God's created goods in a balanced way.

Respecting Personal Health

(CCC, 1809; 2288—2291)

The Fifth Commandment requires us to exercise the virtue of prudence to take care of our health, one of God's precious gifts to us. Society also has an obligation to help its citizens secure basic living conditions to live healthy lives. These include food, clothing, housing, health care, education, employment, and help in time of need.

Although we must respect and care for our bodies, we should not make our bodies our god. Making a god out of physical perfection or athletic prowess encourages a mentality that the strong and fit are more precious than weaker and less healthy members of society. Worshiping the body easily perverts human relationships *(CCC, 2289)*.

Today, our well-being is assaulted by unhealthy eating patterns, misuse of medicines, and the abuse of alcohol, tobacco, and use of illegal drugs. These are all grave offenses.

Christians must regularly exercise the virtue of **temperance**, one of the cardinal virtues. Temperance regulates our attraction to pleasure and helps us use God's created goods in a balanced way. Specifically, the virtue of temperance helps us enjoy the pleasures of food, drink, and sex in a God-intended way. Temperance is the virtue of self-control, delayed gratification, and moderation. Because we humans are weak and subject to sin, we can allow the pursuit of pleasure to get out of hand, making it the number one goal in life. When this happens, we fall into the vices of greed, gluttony, or lust.

Saint Thomas Aquinas distinguished three parts to the virtue of temperance:

Abstinence tempers our desires for food and other pleasure-producing substances like tobacco and drugs. **Sobriety** moderates our desires for alcoholic drinks. **Chastity** (more information in

Chapter 9) helps us control our sex drive in a way compatible to our state in life.

Temperance frees us to become fully functioning persons. If we become slaves to our appetites, we tend to ignore the needs of other people. Pleasure becomes our god; we neglect those who need us. By controlling our desires, we gain self-mastery and grow in gentleness, compassion, and courtesy. Exercising the virtue of temperance also enhances self-esteem.

Morality of Teen Drinking

- The National Survey on Drug Use and Health (NSDUH) reported that in a recent year approximately 10.9 million underage youth, ages twelve to twenty, used alcohol in the month prior to the survey. Nearly 7.2 million underage youth also reported *binge drinking*, defined as drinking five or more drinks on a single occasion at least once in the past thirty days. Nearly one out of every five teenagers (16 percent) has experienced "black out" spells when they could not remember what happened the previous evening because of heavy binge drinking.
- According to the Substance Abuse and Mental Health Services Administration (SAMHSA), 2.6 million young people do not know that a person can die of an overdose of alcohol. Alcohol poisoning occurs when a person drinks a large quantity of alcohol in a short amount of time.
- People who begin drinking before the age of fifteen are four times more likely to develop alcohol dependence than those who wait until age twenty-one. Each additional year of delayed drinking onset reduces the probability of alcohol dependence by 14 percent.
- Adolescents who use alcohol are more likely to become sexually active at an earlier age, to have sex more often, and to engage in unprotected sex, which places them at greater risk of HIV infection and other sexually transmitted diseases.
- High school students who use alcohol or other substances are five times more likely than other students to drop out of school or to believe that earning good grades is not important.
- The average age when youth first try alcohol is eleven years for boys and thirteen years for girls. The average age at which Americans begin drinking regularly is 15.9 years old.
- It has been estimated that over three million teenagers are out-and-out alcoholics. Several million more have a serious drinking problem they cannot manage on their own.
- Long-term use of alcohol has the following effects: vitamin deficiencies, stomach ailments, loss of appetite, cirrhosis and cancer of the liver, heart and central nervous system damage, memory loss, loss of appetite, and sexual impotence.
- Dependence on alcohol and other drugs is associated with several psychiatric problems, including depression, anxiety, oppositional defiant disorder (ODD), and antisocial personality disorder.
- The three leading causes of death for fifteen- to twenty-four-year-olds are automobile crashes, homicides, and suicides—alcohol is a leading factor in all three.
- All states and the District of Columbia now have minimum drinking-age laws set at twenty-one years of age. The National Highway Traffic Safety Administration (NHTSA) estimates that these laws have reduced traffic fatalities involving drivers eighteen to twenty years old by 13 percent.[7]

abstinence

The moral virtue that tempers one's appetite or desire for food, drink, sex, or other pleasurable experiences, such as the use of tobacco and drugs.

sobriety

Moderation or abstinence from alcoholic beverages or the use of drugs.

chastity

The moral virtue that helps one control sexual drive and expression in a way compatible to his or her state in life.

◆ If junk food is basically not good for you, is it immoral to eat it? Why or why not?

◆ In light of all the evidence showing the high correlation between smoking and cancer, is it immoral to smoke? Why or why not? Should the government outlaw selling tobacco altogether? Explain your answers.

A Test

Alcoholics Anonymous reports that anyone who answers "yes" to even one of the following questions may have a drinking problem[8]:

- Do you drink because you have problems? To relax?
- Do you drink when you get mad at others, friends, or parents?
- Do you prefer to drink alone, rather than with others?
- Are your grades starting to slip? Are you goofing off at work?
- Did you ever try to stop drinking or to drink less—and fail?
- Have you begun to drink in the morning, before school or work?
- Do you gulp your drinks?

- Do you have loss of memory due to your drinking?
- Do you lie about your drinking?
- Do you ever get into trouble when you're drinking?
- Do you get drunk when you drink, even when you don't mean to?
- Do you think it's cool to be able to hold your liquor?

If you answered "yes" to these, or if you have a friend who would answer "yes" to any of these questions, seek help. You can help yourself by talking to a parent, a *trusted* teacher, counselor, or parish priest. Or look up the phone number of Alcoholics Anonymous and call them.

If you suspect your friend has a problem with drinking or drugs, don't ignore it. Talk to your friend when he or she is sober. Tell your friend that you are worried about what you've observed him or her doing. Be ready for denial and anger. Find out ahead of time where to get help, and be prepared to go with your friend for moral support. Your Christian concern and compassion might be a lifesaver.

The decision to drink has many implications. If you drink alcohol and have not yet reached the legal drinking age, you are breaking the law, a law designed to protect you and others. You can do what you know is right, or you can give in to pressure and compromise your conscience. The struggle to do right is tough.

But remember, you are not alone. You have the Lord Jesus, who is closer to you than you can possibly imagine. Talk to him regularly in prayer. Ask him to send his Holy Spirit to build up your spiritual strength. Remember, too, your Christian friends who believe as you do and who will bolster you on your journey.

Weak Excuses

Read and then discuss these common statements that teens (and others) use to justify their drinking. Circle the number of those excuses you have heard someone make. Then judge the validity of each statement, using this scale:

G—a good reason to justify drinking   W—a weak reason to justify drinking

____ 1. My parents drink. Why not me? I don't like their "do as I say, not as I do" morality.

____ 2. I drink because my friends do. It's hard to say no when you want others to accept you.

____ 3. It makes me feel good. It helps me relax in social gatherings. And it's a good way to escape the pressures of the week.

____ 4. There may be laws against it, but let's face it, you can find a way to get it if you really want it.

____ 5. A few drinks won't hurt anyone.

____ 6. Teen drinking is okay—as long as you don't drive.

REVIEW AND REFLECTION

1. Define the virtue of temperance. What three virtues are related to it?

2. Discuss at least two good reasons why teens should refrain from drinking alcohol or using illegal drugs.

FOR YOUR JOURNAL

What can or should you do for a friend who abuses alcohol? Write out a plan of action.

Catholic Life in Action

1. Read and report on the United States bishops' *Culture of Life and the Penalty of Death*. You can find it online at: www.usccb.org/sdwp/national/penaltyofdeath.pdf.

2. Check out JusticeNet, an excellent Internet site, to find out some current violations of human rights: www.justicenet.org.
   - Look at some links on children and youth, criminal justice, or war and peace. Report on a topic of interest.
   - Report on an archived article from the Catholic online Social Justice magazine *Salt of the Earth* at: http://salt.claretianpubs.org.

3. Conduct a class debate on the morality of the Iraq War begun in 2003.

4. Create a pro-life poster. Hang it in a prominent place around the school.

5. Read and report about a recent capital punishment in your state or nation. Then conduct a letter-writing campaign to convince legislators to abolish the death penalty.

6. Research the morality of embryonic stem-cell research. Prepare a report that presents the Church's position.

7. Create a PowerPoint presentation on the perils of drug or alcohol abuse. Be sure to present some of the moral arguments for the virtue of sobriety.

8. Check out the Mother's Against Drunk Driving (MADD) website: www.madd.org. Research and report on why the legal age for alcohol is set at twenty-one.

9. Read the following brochure online—"Tips for Teens: The Truth about Alcohol" at http://ncadi.samhsa.gov/govpubs/ph323. Using it as a guideline, prepare your own brochure on drug or alcohol abuse. Design it for high school freshmen. Include some moral arguments in the points you present.

Summary Points

◆ Christ tells us we must love ourselves so we can love God and others.

◆ Healthy self-love is known as self-esteem or self-appreciation. Each of us is fundamentally lovable as a child of God, made in his image, and redeemed by Christ Jesus.

◆ People suffer from poor self-esteem because of conditional love.

◆ Healthy self-love requires the practice of the virtues of humility and gratitude. Humility recognizes that God has given us gifts not to deny, but to use. Gratitude recognizes that God is the source of all one's gifts. We show our gratitude in a special way at the Eucharist ("thanksgiving"), where we receive the greatest gift of all, Jesus Christ, in Holy Communion.

◆ The Fourth Commandment promotes family values. It underscores the importance of the family as society's foundational unit. Christians recognize the family as the "domestic Church," the hearth wherein children learn about God's love and parents and children mirror the love of the Triune God.

◆ Children must honor their parents through respect, esteem, gratitude, and obedience of their just wishes. Adult children must continue to honor their parents by seeking their advice, expressing their gratitude, and supporting them in their declining years.

◆ Brothers and sisters must relate to each other with respect, patience, tolerance, fairness, and love.

◆ Parents must love, respect, and educate their children religiously, intellectually, and socially.

◆ Parents must honor their children's basic right to choose their vocations and careers.

◆ The Fourth Commandment requires us to honor lawful officials both in the Church and the civic community. Citizens must work for the common good, promote the virtue of solidarity, treat others as persons of dignity, and bring Christ to the marketplace. They must pay taxes, vote, and come to the aid of their fellow citizens in times of peril. Authorities must ensure basic human, social, and political rights and exercise their authority responsibly as a gift on loan from God for serving others.

◆ Neither children nor citizens should ever obey unjust, immoral orders made by parents or authorities. We must never violate God's law, no matter who tells us to.

◆ The Fifth Commandment forbids murder and the anger, envy, and hate that cause it. It calls on us to respect life from womb to tomb.

◆ People have the right to kill in self-defense only if it is absolutely necessary to defend their own life or if they are coming to the aid of someone for whom they are responsible.

◆ Strictly speaking the state has the right to inflict the death penalty as a means to protect society from heinous criminals. However, today, the situations in which it should be used are practically nonexistent because government authorities have other effective means to supress crime and render criminals inoffensive.

◆ Jesus calls all to be peacemakers. Catholic Church teaching begins with a presumption against all war, always advocating other peaceful means of settling disputes. But in extraordinary situations, as with unjust aggression, nations have the right to self-defense following very strict guidelines.

- The moral law holds in times of warfare. There must be no attacks on innocent noncombatants; genocide; terrorism; or use of nuclear, biological, or chemical weapons—all of which indiscriminately destroy persons and property.

- Abortion, the deliberate killing of unborn human life, is always seriously wrong. No one may procure an abortion or participate in one in any way.

- The Fifth Commandment forbids scandal, giving a bad example that leads others to commit evil deeds.

- Kidnapping, hostage-taking, torturing prisoners, terrorism, and non-medical amputations, mutilations, and sterilizations all violate the Fifth Commandment.

- Direct euthanasia is always seriously wrong. Withholding extraordinary means to sustain life is permissible for terminally ill patients. However, we must always give sick and dying people ordinary life-sustaining aid.

- Suicide, self-inflicted or assisted, is a grave violation that shows a disrespect for one's own life and a rejection of the God of life. One may never assist in a suicide, even if requested. This is gravely wrong.

- The Fifth Commandment requires us to exercise the virtues of prudence and temperance in caring for the precious gift of health.

- A major moral issue for today's teens is the issue of drinking and drugs.

PRAYER REFLECTION

A great Church teacher and saint, Saint Teresa of Avila, wrote the following litany of thanksgiving to God.[9]

May you be blessed forever, Lord, for not abandoning me when I abandoned You.

. . . for offering Your hand of love in my darkest, most lonely moment.

. . . for putting up with such a stubborn soul.

. . . for loving me more than I love myself.

. . . for drawing out the goodness in all people, even including me.

. . . for repaying our sin with Your love.

. . . for being constant and unchanging . . .

. . . for Your countless blessings on me and on all Your creatures.

- How do you know of the Lord's love for you?
- Make a list of things you have done that show that you have goodness in you. Make a similar list for at least five people who love you. Then thank God for these good people. Thank God for your own goodness.

NOTES

1. Adapted from Anthony de Mello, S.J., *One Minute Wisdom* (New York: Doubleday, 1986), 55.
2. Adapted from A.M.E. Today, "Inspiration: A Lesson in Values" <www.ame-today.com/inspiration/inspiration39.shtml> (7 March 2006).
3. United States Conference of Catholic Bishops (USCCB), "Faithful Citizenship: A Catholic Call to Political Responsibility," (Washington, D.C. United States Conference of Catholic Bishops, 2003). Found online at the USCCB website <www.usccb.org/faithfulcitizenship/bishopStatement.html> (23 January 2006).
4. For a full list of questions, please check the current version of "Faithful Citizenship: A Catholic Call to Political Responsibility," which can be found online at: www.usccb.org/faithfulcitizenship/bishopStatement.html.
5. United States Conference of Catholic Bishops, *A Culture of Life and the Penalty of Death* (Washington, D.C.: United States Conference of Catholic Bishops, 2005), p. 3. Accessed online at <www.usccb.org/sdwp/national/penaltyofdeath.pdf> (23 January 2005).
6. Pope Benedict XVI, "Address of His Holiness Benedict XVI to the Diplomatic Corps Accredited to the Holy See for the Traditional Exchange of New Year Greetings," January 9, 2006 <www.vatican.va/holy_father/benedict_xvi/speeches/2006/january/documents/hf_ben-xvi_spe_20060109_diplomatic-corps_en.html> (25 January 2006).
7. These facts were found at these Internet sites:
   - The Center on Alcohol Marketing and Youth, "Underage Drinking in the United States: A Status Report: 2004," http://camy.org/research/underage2004
   - Focus Adolescent Services, "Alcohol and Teen Drinking," www.focusas.com/Alcohol.html
   - National Institute on Drug Abuse, www.nida.nih.gov
   - U.S. Department of Health and Human Services and SAMHA's National Clearinghouse for Alcohol & Drug Prevention, "Consequences of Underage Alcohol Use," http://ncadi.samhsa.gov/govpubs/rpo992.
8. Alcoholics Anonymous, "A Message to Teenagers: How to Tell When Drinking Is Becoming a Problem," <www.alcoholicsanonymous.org/en_is_aa_for_you.cfm?PageID=15> (8 March 2006).
9. Found in *Three Minutes a Day: Reflections for Daily Life*, vol. 31 (New York: The Christophers, 1996), October 15.

CHAPTER OVERVIEW

The Goodness of Sex

God created human beings—males and females—in his divine image and saw that sexuality was good. As complementary beings, men and women can love and care for each other and share in God's creation of new human life.

The Sixth and Ninth Commandments

The Sixth and Ninth Commandments safeguard God's intended purpose for marriage. Sexual activity and union is for married couples.

Chastity, Purity, and Modesty

Chastity helps us to channel our sexual drives and activities in a way that is appropriate to our state in life. Purity and modesty help us guide sexual thoughts and desires and the way others see and react to us.

Offenses Against the Sixth and Ninth Commandments

Deliberate sexual stimulation or sexual intercourse outside of marriage against God's plan for sexuality and offends against the Sixth and Ninth Commandments

CHAPTER NINE

Respect for the Gift of Sexuality

Let us conduct ourselves properly as in the day, not in orgies and drunkenness, not in promiscuity and licentiousness, not in rivalry and jealousy. But put on the Lord Jesus Christ, and make no provisions for the desires of the flesh.

Romans 12:13–14

The Goodness of Sex

A father was dreading the mandatory father-son sex talk with his twelve-year-old son. But he figured it was time that he broached the subject.

So one day he called his son into the den, shut the door, and said, "Son, what do you know about sex?"

The son replied, "Plenty, Dad. Why? Is there something you want me to tell you?"

Another true story has it that when ninety-year-old Supreme Court Justice Oliver Wendell Holmes saw a beautiful young woman walk by he said, "Darn it. I'd give anything to be ten years younger."

The first story makes it pretty clear that kids today know a lot more about sex at an earlier age than most of their parents did. And the second story reveals that interest in sex is still alive, even into old age. According to gerontologists (scientists who study the aging process), if you are healthy, sex will play a role in your life well into your later years. For most people, this is good news.

Sex, in fact, is good. In the first creation account, the book of Genesis proclaims the goodness of sex:

God created man in his image; in the divine image he created him; male and female he created them. God blessed them, saying: "Be fertile and multiply; fill the earth and subdue it." . . . God looked at everything he had made, and he found it very good. (Gn 1:27–28, 31)

God created the first humans out of pure love for love. He created man and woman with the capacity for love and communion and empowered them to share with him in his creative activity of bringing new life into the world.

The second creation account in Genesis illustrates how God created Adam out of the mud of the earth and breathed a spirit or soul into him. But Adam was unhappy being alone and incomplete. So God created Eve to be Adam's companion. Created out of Adam's side, Eve completed Adam's yearning for love and companionship.

From the beginning, humans were sexual beings. The word *sex* is derived from the Latin *secare*, which means "to separate." God made us male and female, equal in dignity. This last point is absolutely essential for Christian teaching. One's gender—male or female—does not make one more important or better than the other. God created us beings of equal dignity and worth. And Jesus reinforced that message in the Sermon of the Mount when he restored God's original intent by condemning divorce.

Both created in God's image, men and women are complementary beings who display God's power and tenderness in different ways. God separated us, but he implanted in us a longing to unite with a beloved "other" for the purpose of tenderly celebrating their love and sharing the gift of life. The book of Genesis describes it this way:

That is why a man leaves his father and mother and clings to his wife, and the two of them become one body. (Gn 2:24)

The author of Genesis tells us that before Original Sin, our first parents were totally comfortable and unashamed in each other's presence:

The man and his wife were both naked, yet they felt no shame. (Gn 2:25)

Yes, according to Genesis, sex was intended to be very good.

However, in discussing sex it is important to note that the sex act is not all there is to being sexual beings. Being a sexual being means being in the world as either male or female, an identity we should acknowledge, accept, and embrace.

Our sexuality obviously is linked to our bodies because we relate to others through our bodies, either male or female. Thus, we

Therefore, what God has joined together, no human being must separate

—MATTHEW 19:6

Sex Attitudes

Here are some statements about sex, sexuality, love, children, and the like. Decide where you stand on each of these statements. Then discuss each statement and determine when you have heard it often expressed.

1—strongly agree; 2—agree; 3—don't know; 4—disagree; 5—strongly disagree

STATEMENTS	1	2	3	4	5
1. Guys are more interested in sex than girls.					
2. Reading or viewing pornographic material doesn't hurt anyone.					
3. Sex is meant for marriage.					
4. We live in a sex-obsessed society.					
5. Though difficult, it is possible to control the sex drive in a responsible way.					
6. It is immoral to treat someone as a sex object.					
7. Teen intimacy, even intercourse, is acceptable, but the couple has to be "in love."					
8. Even in this so-called sexual age of enlightenment, there exists in our society a different sexual standard for males and for females.					
9. Exercising the virtues of chastity, modesty, and abstinence is still the best way to avoid sexually transmitted diseases and prepare for marriage.					
10. Girls who dress provocatively are "asking for it."					
11. Sex education programs really don't help teens refrain from sexual relations.					
12. Sexual intercourse should reflect a total commitment made between a man and a woman. This total commitment can take place only in marriage.					
13. Homosexual couples should have the same right to marry as heterosexual couples.					

- Give evidence of a double standard—one standard for men and another standard for women—in sexual behavior today.
- Many people say the media portray women as "sex objects." Describe any examples of this that you have seen or heard. How does this stereotyping degrade women?
- The media offer a stereotype of men as "macho." How does this portrayal affect the way men treat women?

show affection and love with gestures like gifts, handshakes, smiles, or kisses—all of which are "body language."

But our sexuality also involves our emotional and spiritual makeup. Humans are a unity of body and soul. One's sexuality affects all aspects of the human person, especially our capacity to love and procreate new human life. More generally, though, our sexuality is our way of being in the world—emotionally, spiritually, as well as bodily. It is our way of reaching out to people both to receive and to give love.

If we have this fundamental understanding of sexuality in mind, then when we start talking about *sex* as sexual activity, we will return to the word *respect*. Respect involves looking at ourselves as precious creations of God. Respect also means looking on others as persons, not objects to be used.

REVIEW AND REFLECTION

1. What does the Bible teach about human sexuality?

2. What is the meaning of the word *sex*?

3. Discuss some biblical principles that flow from our sexual nature.

FOR YOUR JOURNAL
What does the word *respect* mean to you? Write about some of the ways you show respect to others: your friends, your parents, your siblings, your teachers and classmates, and members of the opposite sex.

The Sixth and Ninth Commandments

You shall not commit adultery.

You shall not covet your neighbor's wife.

The Sixth and Ninth Commandments serve as safeguards of God's intention for human sexuality. They warn against those disrespectful and harmful actions involving sex that are contrary to our own good. They encourage the practice of virtues that help us respect our sexuality and that of others. And they instruct us to uproot those sinful attitudes that distort the beauty of sex and lead to looking on ourselves and others in a disrespectful way, contrary to God's law.

SEXUAL INTERCOURSE IS FOR MARRIAGE
(CCC, 2360—2365; 2397)
The basic principle governing all sexual morality is that God intended sexual intercourse, and all actions leading up to it, to be shared exclusively by a man and a woman in the union of marriage.

Through the intimate acts of sexual activity, a husband and a wife give themselves totally and exclusively to each other. This act of total self-giving represents their relationship. In marriage, they have committed themselves to each other with no conditions in an exclusive covenant of love. They celebrate their commitment through this beautiful gift of sexual sharing in which two people—a man and a woman—become one. This celebration brings pleasure and joy, two gifts

God bestows on couples who use the sexual faculty according to God's plan.

Catholics believe that the marriage covenant is lifelong, faithful, and holy. Through it, the couple mirrors Christ's love for his people, which is also permanent, unconditional, and loyal. Thus, marriage is a sacrament, a powerful sign of love that brings the couple closer to Christ and to each other. A prime virtue that keeps couples together is **fidelity**, a faithfulness in which each spouse stands by the other through good times and bad. The model for couples in a Christian marriage is Jesus himself, who loves his Church as a bridegroom loves his bride.

In writing about the unity between sexual love (*eros* in the Greek) and biblical love grounded in and shaped by faith (*agape*, "to give and not to count the cost" kind of love), Pope Benedict XVI writes:

> Eros *is somehow rooted in man's very nature; Adam is a seeker, who "abandons his mother and father" in order to find woman; only together do the two represent complete humanity and become "one flesh." . . . From the standpoint of creation,* eros *directs man towards marriage, to a bond which is unique and definitive; thus, and only thus, does it fulfill its deepest purpose. Corresponding to the image of a monotheistic God is monogamous marriage. Marriage based on exclusive and definitive love becomes the icon of the relationship between God and his people and vice versa. God's way of loving becomes the measure of human love. This close connection between* eros *and marriage in the Bible has practically no equivalent in extra-biblical literature.*[1]

TWO PURPOSES OF SEX IN MARRIAGE
(CCC, 2366—2379; 2398—2399)

The sexual union in marriage has two purposes: the sharing of love between the

spouses and the transmission of life. A major gift of marriage is **fecundity**, that is, the ability to produce offspring. A married couple has the privilege, in other words, of sharing in God's creative power and parenthood: bringing forth and educating new human beings.

Church teaching holds that sexual intercourse can only be moral and according to God's plan if "each and every marriage act" remains open to the transmission of life:

> This particular doctrine, expounded on numerous occasions by the Magisterium, is based on the inseparable connection, established by God, which man on his own initiative may not break, between the unitive significance and procreative significance which are both inherent in the marriage act. (On Human Life, *quoted in* CCC, *2366*)

Married couples have both the duty and right to plan the size of their families. For moral and unselfish reasons—like the current size of the family, financial hardship, and psychological and physical health—the husband and the wife may decide to regulate the number and spacing of children in accord with God's plan

fidelity

Marital faithfulness between husbands and wives that requires reserving all sexual activity and affection for each other and also asks couples to be loyal to each other through good times and bad.

fecundity

The ability to produce offspring, a gift proper to marriage, which can allow a husband and wife to participate with God in the creation of new life.

Interview a couple who has a successful marriage. Ask this husband and wife: "What do you feel are necessary qualities for a successful marriage?" Ask the couple: "How has your love for each other grown or changed over the years?"

infertility

The physical incapacity of a female or male to cooperate with God's creative power in conceiving a child.

adultery

Sexual intercourse between a man and woman who are married to other people. (Or intercourse between an unmarried person and a married person.)

divorce

The dissolution of the marriage contract.

for family planning. Moral means of birth regulation must be in harmony with the two ends of marriage: openness to life and the sharing of love. Periodic abstinence from sexual relations and natural family planning methods (e.g., the sympto-thermal and ovulation methods) are two effective, natural means of regulating birth: "These methods respect the bodies of the spouses, encourage tenderness between them, and favor the education of an authentic freedom" (*CCC*, 2370).

It is always sinful to practice birth control out of selfish motives. An example would be materialistic couples who simply want to amass a quantity of possessions. Their pursuit of things turns them in on themselves. And their self-centeredness keeps them from passing on the gift of life that God has entrusted to them to share with children.

The Church also teaches that artificial contraceptive methods are morally contrary to God's plan for sexual sharing. Immoral means of birth control would include birth-control pills, condoms, and diaphragms, and surgeries like vasectomies or tubal ligations. These means are wrong because they deliberately and directly have as an outcome the closing off of one of the aims of sexual intercourse—the sharing of life. This is contrary to the natural law and God's will for sexual intimacy in a marriage.

Artificial means of birth control frustrate the nature of a Christian marriage which should signify both the mutual love of the couple and their openness to the transmission of life. To obstruct either of these ends is contrary to God's plan built into the very nature of marriage.

Unfortunately, not all couples can conceive a child. Some couples face the heartbreaking tragedy of **infertility**, the inability to cooperate with God's creative power in the normal way. The Church supports moral medical methods to help couples overcome infertility. However, no couple has an absolute right to have a child. A child is a gift from God, not a piece of

property to be possessed and manipulated. Today, the media gives much attention to the selling of human eggs, sperm donation, surrogate mothers, test-tube babies, and similar procedures. These means are all gravely wrong because they seriously intrude into the exclusive, permanent marriage bond of the husband and wife. Any procedure, including those that involve only husband and wife, that separates sexual lovemaking from the act of procreation (like artificial insemination) is disordered and contrary to God's plan.

Christian couples who cannot have children on their own often adopt children or dedicate their generous hearts to a life of service.

OFFENSES AGAINST MARRIAGE
(CCC, 2380—2391; 2400)

Marriage is a lifelong, faithful, exclusive commitment of love between a man and a woman. Because this relationship is where God intends us to use our sexual faculties, the following actions are contrary to God's law:

◆ **Adultery**, that is, sexual relations with someone other than one's spouse (or an unmarried person with a married person), is a grave injustice committed against one's marriage partner and the covenant of marriage. It undermines the marriage bond and threatens the stability of the family. Jesus condemns even the desire to commit adultery when he said, "Everyone who looks at a woman with lust has already committed adultery with her in his heart" (Mt 5:28).

◆ **Divorce** is the dissolution of the marriage contract. Jesus outlawed divorce by restoring God's original intent that marriage be indissoluble. Baptized persons who have entered into a valid and consummated marriage cannot have their marriage dissolved by anyone. Only the death of one of the spouses can end this lifelong covenant.

The Church cannot endorse divorce and remarriage because of Jesus' plain teaching against it. In some cases, though, Church law may allow couples to live apart, or even tolerate civil divorce to guarantee the legal rights of a wronged spouse or children. But if a couple freely has entered a true sacramental marriage, a spouse may not enter a new union while the other partner is still alive. To do so, Jesus taught, would make one guilty of adultery.

Divorce has tragic consequences for family unity and for stable societies. Children often suffer the most from fractured marriages that tear them apart from their mothers or fathers.

◆ **Polygamy**, having more than one spouse, is contrary to the moral law. Marital love, as intended by God, is between two people, equal in dignity, who share a total, unique, and exclusive love.

◆ **Incest** is sexual intimacy between relatives or in-laws within a degree that prohibits marriage. This sexual offense corrupts family values and often stoops to the level of mere animal behavior. Related to incest is sexual abuse of children, an outrageous and unjustifiable evil and criminal act that harms children physically, emotionally, and spiritually. It seriously violates the most helpless and innocent in our midst.

◆ **Free unions** are relationships where couples refuse to have their commitment sanctioned by law. These pseudomarriages reflect a serious failure in commitment and attack the very idea of family and faithfulness. Similarly, trial marriages are insincere attempts to play at marriage. They are subject to passing fancy. Research shows couples who engage in them and later marry have a significantly higher divorce rate than couples who live apart until married. True love requires the total, unconditional, and definitive giving of one person to another—with no strings attached. This can take place *only* in marriage.

polygamy

The practice of having more than one spouse.

incest

Sexual intimacy between relatives or in-laws.

free unions

Extended relationships where couples refuse to have their commitment formalized or sactioned by law.

CHECK ANY OF THE FOLLOWING STATEMENTS YOU AGREE WITH. EXPLAIN YOUR ANSWERS.

_____ 1. I feel a lot of pressure to have sex. But it is too important for me to cave in to this pressure.

_____ 2. I hear lots of people say they "do it." But I doubt it.

_____ 3. My sexuality is a precious gift.

_____ 4. To have sex with someone involves deep commitment, trust, and honesty. It should not be done lightly.

_____ 5. It's really tough to know what *love* means. Until I do, I should probably not be "making love."

_____ 6. Steady dating can be dangerous for high school students. It often leads to sexual involvement.

_____ 7. Self-control and love go hand-in-hand.

REVIEW AND REFLECTION

1. What are the Sixth and Ninth Commandments? What virtues do they commend to us?

2. Why does God intend for men and women to express full sexual commitment through intercourse only in marriage?

3. Define each of the following: *adultery, divorce, polygamy, incest, sexual abuse.*

4. Why are free unions and trial marriages wrong in the eyes of God?

5. What are the two purposes of sexual intercourse in marriage?

6. Why does the Church condemn contraceptive practices?

7. Do parents have the right to limit the size of their families? If yes, under what conditions?

8. List several unacceptable methods to treat infertility in a married couple who wish to conceive a child. Explain why these means are gravely disordered.

Inordinate love of the flesh is cruelty, because under the appearance of pleasing the body we kill the soul.

—ST. BERNARD OF CLAIRVAUX

A Case to Discuss: Changed Vows

Suppose a potential marriage partner, someone you deeply love, suggested that the two of you should marry. But in light of all the divorces in today's society, your beloved proposes that you change the marriage vows to read, "until our love for each other dies" instead of "until death do us part."

1. What do you think of this proposal? Is it a cop-out?

2. What does unconditional love mean to you? Give examples of where you have seen it in action in successful marriages.

3. Suppose you were dating someone seriously. You really like, and probably even love, this person. But your friend insists that he or she absolutely never wants to have children.
    a. What would you do?
    b. What would you say?

Chastity, Purity, and Modesty

(CCC, 2337—2351; 2394—2395; 2514—2533)

By the time you have moved through most of your teen years, you have experienced all the physical changes associated with puberty. Hormones seem to have control of your life. Sex may seem to be on your mind a majority of the time. Some people experience this physical maturing as confusing, others are a bit afraid of it, and some say, "What's the big deal?" Many others see it as a joyful transition to maturity as a male or a female.

What most teens, and healthy adults, learn, though, is that controlling their sex drive in God-intended ways is a lifelong task. Church teaching, reinforced by human reason, clearly leads us to conclude that the best way to express sexual activity is in the context of a mature, loving, committed, and faithful relationship—marriage. Yet this common-sense, God-inspired conclusion is often challenged in our society by what can be called the "playboy/playgirl" mentality.

The playboy/playgirl mentality is irresponsible because it totally ignores one of the aims of sexual activity: the sharing of life. It preaches a gospel of "do it if it feels good." It holds that seeking pleasure alone is the reason for sex. Self-indulgence is its creed. Its cautions are few: don't force sex, don't get pregnant, and don't spread AIDS or other sexually transmitted diseases. Commitment, fidelity, and love are antiquated ideas according to the playboy/playgirl mentality.

This mentality permeates our society. Think of movies you have seen, music you listen to, television sitcoms that promote this self-indulgent view of sex. A recent movie depicted how a bunch of high school friends vowed to lose their virginity before they graduated. Using humorous situations, the males involved looked on girls as simply objects of their passion. The guys considered themselves losers if they did not have sexual intercourse.

What was remarkable about this film is how little negative criticism it received from media critics. Maybe it was because the message of this film is what you are exposed to on a daily basis. Many in our society are selling you a message about sexual expression that is simply a lie. This message of "do it because it feels good" contradicts God's intent for sex and ultimately leads to unhappiness and feelings of being used.

With God's help, and effort on your part, you can use your sexual powers in the way God intends. You can put into practice several virtues to help you control your sexual urges and use them in responsible, loving ways.

BEING CHASTE

Recall from Chapter 8 that the virtue of *chastity* is *related to* the cardinal virtue of temperance. Chastity is the virtue that helps us control our sexual desires and use them appropriately according to our situation in life. Chastity enables us to respect our own sexuality and the sexuality of others. Here are some points to consider about chastity:

- To live a chaste life in marriage requires a husband and wife to be sensitive to how they relate to each other sexually and always to be faithful to their marriage vows.
- Couples engaged to be married are chaste when they exercise self-control and refrain from any sexual activity, like intercourse,

DESIRABLE QUALITIES

Which personal qualities do you value the most in a potential marriage partner? Which qualities do you possess? Check all the qualities that you think might be of value in a relationship with a member of the opposite sex.

_____ self-disciplined
_____ gentle
_____ compassionate
_____ kind
_____ intelligent
_____ good looks
_____ sense of humor
_____ gutsy (courageous)
_____ trustworthy
_____ good listener
_____ generous
_____ loyal
_____ affectionate
_____ understanding
_____ poised
_____ sensitive
_____ lover of music
_____ empathetic
_____ athletic
_____ self-starter
_____ self-reliant
_____ outgoing
_____ personable
_____ forgiving
_____ other: _____
_____ other: _____

modesty _____

The virtue of temperance applies to how a person speaks, dresses, and conducts himself or herself. Related to the virtue of purity, modesty protects the intimate center of a person by refusing to unveil what should remain hidden.

that God intends for married couples alone.

• Finally, single people and men and women who have taken religious vows must practice self-restraint by abstaining from sexual activity. *Abstinence* is the positive choice not to engage in sexual intercourse outside of marriage. To decide for abstinence is a mature and responsible decision and frees people to relate to others as persons of dignity, not objects for self-gratification.

In our sex-saturated society, chastity is a hard-won virtue that requires a life-long commitment to self-control. The battle to gain control over our sexual urges, though, is never fought alone since the virtue of chastity is also a gift of the Holy Spirit. The Holy Spirit will assist us, but we must also do our part to gain self-mastery. Great helps to strengthen the virtue of chastity include:

• avoiding temptations that might lead us to misuse our sexuality, for example, refusing to have anything to do with pornography;

• knowing ourselves well enough to know what might lead us to lose self-control in the area of sexuality;

• practicing works of self-denial to strengthen our wills;

• practicing the moral virtues, especially acts of charity for others;

• striving to live all of God's commandments;

• praying daily for God's graces;

• receiving the sacraments of Reconciliation and the Eucharist frequently.

BEING PURE AND MODEST

The virtues of purity and **modesty** help us combat the vice of lust, that is, the disordered craving for or enjoyment of sexual pleasure sought for itself, isolated from God's intention for sexual relationships: procreation of children and love-sharing between married couples.

One of the effects of Original Sin is *concupiscence*, that is, the desires of our sensual appetites (for food, drink, comfort, sexual pleasure, etc.) working contrary to human reason. Saint Paul called this the "flesh" warring against the "spirit." This internal warfare of our sensual appetites can lead to lusting after another sexually and turning other people into objects, something Jesus condemned as equivalent to the sin of adultery (Mt 5:28).

Lust is different from the ordinary sexual thoughts and desires we have as human beings. Lust enters the picture when we allow our thoughts to control us, when we look on others as objects for self-pleasure, when we obsess over our thoughts and take pleasure in them for their own sake.

The virtue of "purity of the heart" helps us control lust. Jesus praised the pure of heart who sought God's holiness, love, truth, and right faith. Purity of heart means wanting to do the right thing at all times, to please our heavenly Father, not just in the areas of sex, but in all areas of our life. We strengthen purity by making the efforts noted above to live chastely, seeking to do God's will in prayer, disciplining our feelings and imaginations, and turning from impure thoughts when they come our way.

We cannot be pure if we are not modest. Modesty is also a subset of the virtue of temperance. Modesty respects our own and others' sexuality by guarding intimacy and by refusing to unveil what common decency requires to remain hidden. To be modest means to be patient in our relationships, decent in the clothes we wear, and very careful in how we talk about sex. We live in an immodest society where sex is paraded before us. Followers of Christ must do their part to rid our society of an eroticism that turns people into objects and tempts us to sexual activity that ignores God's law for healthy, moral, sexual expression.

Modesty Protects the Intimate Center of the Person (*CCC*, 2533)

Judge whether the following situations are right or wrong. Note the relative seriousness of each case.

◆ Tony dates Melissa pretty steadily. Tony tells Melissa that when males are aroused, it is unhealthy not to have sex. Melissa wants to abstain from sex until marriage.

◆ Renee is very attractive. She likes to wear skimpy clothes and flirt shamelessly with guys. She tells her friends, "Hey, if God made me this way, I may as well show it off."

◆ Gary regularly rents X-rated DVDs and watches them alone. He tells himself it's his brand of sex ed.

Discuss:

1. What does our society define as immodest clothing for girls? for guys?

2. As a class, brainstorm some guidelines for dressing modestly for various social occasions.

Check the items that best describe how you view human sexuality. Add your own image. Human sexuality is . . .

_____ a. an unfolding flower

_____ b. a raging fire

_____ c. a beautiful melody

_____ d. a calm, deep, blue lake

_____ e. a tempestuous storm

_____ f. your own image:

_____

_____

REVIEW AND REFLECTION

1. What are some attitudes toward sex proposed by a "playboy/playgirl" mentality? Explain how these are un-Christian approaches to sexuality.

2. What is the virtue of chastity? Discuss several ways we can strengthen this virtue.

3. What is *lust*? How does purity of heart help control this vice?

4. Describe what it means to be a modest person in the area of sexuality.

FOR YOUR JOURNAL

List and discuss several ways you personally show *self-respect* in the area of sexuality.

Offenses Against the Sixth and Ninth Commandments
(CCC, 2352—2359; 2396)

Lust tends to make sexual pleasure its god. Lust deliberately inflames one's sex drive beyond the reasonable boundaries God has set for healthy and moral sexual attraction. As previously discussed, we have a weakened human nature and are often tempted to fail in this area. It is a sign of maturity to admit one's weakness and to take steps to strengthen our wills to combat the many temptations to sexual indulgence encouraged in our society.

Lust often engenders actions like those described in the following sections. All are contrary to the virtue of chastity.

MASTURBATION

Masturbation is the deliberate stimulation of the genitals to obtain solitary sexual pleasure. Masturbation seeks pleasure for its own sake, contrary to God's intent for sexual activity to be *relational*, that is, with a member of the opposite sex in a lifelong commitment that is open to life and the sharing of mutual love. Therefore, the Church has always taught that masturbation is "an intrinsically and gravely disordered action" (*CCC*, 2352). To knowingly and freely choose to engage in acts of masturbation is seriously wrong.

However, the Church shows compassion in this area and recognizes that as we mature, we often get caught up in actions that can become habits. For example, many teens (and even adults) masturbate to escape problems. But such activity does not cure the difficulties. In fact, masturbation leaves a person spiritually and psychologically empty, lowering one's self-esteem. Another downside to this habit is that one gets used to *immediate* self-gratification. When involved in a dating relationship, this habit can easily translate into wanting to use the other person simply for one's own personal pleasure. In contrast, true love requires discipline and control, patience, and the ability to deny oneself immediate gratification.

Sexual activity, like any good thing, becomes bad when used inappropriately, selfishly, or to harm others. Although masturbation is seriously wrong, a person's immaturity and psychological factors (e.g., compulsion) can lessen and even erase one's guilt or moral blameworthiness for this act. If you have unwittingly acquired this habit, never get discouraged. God still loves and accepts you. Some good questions to ask yourself as you try to master your sex drive:

- *Do you stay away from all forms of pornography?*
- *Are you careful about avoiding those situations that have led you to lose self-control in the past?*
- *Are you trying to live a loving, caring life for others?* By becoming a loving person, you are at least demonstrating to yourself, and to others, that you are making a sincere effort to master yourself and control those temptations that will always be with you.
- *Do you make an effort to ask for God's help in the sacraments of Reconciliation and Holy Eucharist?* The Lord will never deny the strength of the Holy Spirit to help us responsibly and lovingly use the gifts he gave to us.

FORNICATION

Fornication is sexual intercourse engaged in by unmarried people. It is clearly wrong because it is selfish and it exploits the other person. Selfishness and treating others as objects for self-gratification is cruel and irresponsible.

Premarital sex is also wrong even when a man and woman say, "But we love each other." As discussed previously, God intends sexual intercourse to express *total* love and commitment, which is open to the sharing of life. In marriage a lifelong

masturbation

The deliberate stimulation of the genitals to obtain solitary sexual pleasure. It is contrary to the virtue of chastity.

fornication

Sexual intercourse engaged in by an unmarried male and female.

Drawing the Line

Many times couples do not plan to have sex. It just happens once things get "hot and heavy." Sex, of its nature, is beautiful, exciting, passionate . . . and progressive.

Teens have asked, "Where are we supposed to draw the line so as not to lose control?" This is a good question to ask. Here are some rules that should help you stay in control.

- Avoid prolonged or open-mouthed kissing.
- Don't touch another person's private parts (petting). Don't let someone touch your private parts—clothed or unclothed.
- Keep your clothes on.
- Remember, contrary to the definitions of some, oral sex is sex and also an occasion of fornication.
- Immediately stop what you are doing when genital feelings are aroused.
- Before marriage, draw the line at hand-holding, hugs, and light kissing as acceptable ways to show affection.

- **Would your parents support these rules?**
- **Are they realistic for helping situations stay in control?**
- **Are rules in this area of your life necessary? Why or why not?**
- **What are some rules you could add?**

commitment to fidelity and exclusivity has taken place. Outside of marriage, there is no true commitment because a couple can always separate at any time. Therefore, sexual intercourse outside of marriage lacks the *unconditional love* that the Sacrament of Matrimony truly represents. Fornication seeks pleasure without responsibility. It is dishonest and a misuse of a profound symbol of love and openness to life.

PORNOGRAPHY

Pornography comes from a Greek word meaning "writing about prostitutes." Today, we understand pornography to mean movies, magazines, photos, and similar materials whose sole motivation is to depict human sex acts in a way that causes sexual arousal. Pornography removes sexual acts from the intimacy of a loving marriage and depersonalizes it for deliberate display to others. Pornography is seriously wrong and shows disrespect for, and damages the dignity of, those who create, sell, and use it to arouse sexual passions.

PROSTITUTION

Prostitution involves engaging in intercourse or other sexual activity for money or some other advantage. Prostitution seriously debases and dehumanizes those who sell their bodies, turning them into objects to be bought and sold, not persons to be loved. Prostitution is a serious sin for both parties involved, those who accept money and those who pay money. It is a sad commentary on the spiritual health of a society that some women and also some men feel they must sell themselves and their bodies in order to survive.

In fighting against prostitution, in holding out a saving hand to the prostitute, we are saving our mothers, our sisters, and our wives from this social leprosy. We are saving ourselves. We are saving the world.

—THOMAS SANKARA,
BURKINA FASOAN PRESIDENT,
MARCH 8, 1987

RAPE

Rape, forcing another to have sex, is *always* a serious, intrinsically evil act. In most societies, it is also felonious.

Through force, rape violates another's sexuality and assaults their dignity as a child of God. Everyone is owed basic human respect, in their person and in their sexuality. Rape violates both in a most serious way and does incomparable harm to its victims. Similar violent and deplorable acts that seriously offend against God's law are incest and sexual abuse of children, discussed previously.

Unfortunately, the rape of women (and men or young boys, too) in our society is sometimes one of the least reported crimes because the victim is often treated as the accused and must prove her innocence and virtue. (Perhaps as many as 40 percent of rapes or attempted rapes go unreported.) Over 75 percent of all rapes take place between people who know each other (*acquaintance rape*). *Date rape* is an especially serious problem today. One in four women report that a date has tried to rape her. Date rape is defined as someone forcing you to have intercourse or oral sex against your will while on a date. It is a serious crime and should be reported to the authorities. No one is "owed" sexual favors as a condition of going out on a date.

Guidelines for Preventing Date Rape

1. Avoid blind dates. Preferably, date a friend. Always begin dating in groups. Rapists want isolation.
2. Plan the specifics of your date beforehand. Communicate your standards of behavior ahead of time. Never cross the line. Never allow anyone to touch you inappropriately.
3. Stay out of each other's homes if no one else is there. Avoid any isolated places.
4. Dress modestly and avoid sexually suggestive movies and conversation.
5. Don't drink or do drugs. Don't ever drink a beverage that maybe "spiked" with a knock-out drug. It is fashionable today for some guys to use a date-rape drug like rohypnol ("roofies"), gamma-hydroxybutyrate (GHB), or ketamine to drug their dates and then force themselves on them sexually.
6. Avoid parking in make-out locales. These sometimes even attract a criminal element.
7. Say "no" strongly and firmly. If a date persists in pressuring you for sex, leave. You can even call someone to come and get you.
8. Recognize pressuring dialogue that can lead to forced sex.

Pressuring Dialogue	Response
"You'd do it if you loved me."	"I do care for you. If you really loved me, you wouldn't ask."
"Everyone's doing it."	"No, they're not. I'm not."
"Who are you saving it for?"	"My future spouse, the one I will love for a lifetime."

HOMOSEXUAL ACTIVITY

As sexual activity between a man and woman is wrong outside the context of marriage, similarly homosexual acts, that is, sexual activity between members of the same sex, are gravely contrary to God's intention for human sexuality. Church teaching, based on divine revelation, holds that homosexual genital activity is objectively sinful. Such activity frustrates the aims of God's gift of sexuality: unity between a husband and wife and the openness to the transmission of human life. Such acts cannot be justified. Saint Paul condemned homosexual activity as against nature (Rom 1:27).

Homosexual genital acts are wrong for the same reason that premarital or extramarital sexual activity is wrong: they all deny the life-giving and unitive nature of sexual love that Christ teaches should only take place in a *marriage* between a man and a woman. Persons who freely and knowingly engage in premarital, extramarital, or homosexual acts are guilty of serious sin.

Homosexual activity is not the same as homosexual orientation. The Church recognizes, and social science seems to agree, that persons with a homosexual orientation (predominant sexual attraction to members of the same sex) do not choose to be that way. Thus, those with a homosexual orientation are not morally guilty for who they are. In a similar way, a person is not "guilty" of being redheaded or black-haired or hot-tempered. However, persons with homosexual desires must resist acting on them in sinful ways.

Although homosexual acts themselves are sinful, we must always be careful about judging a person's subjective blameworthiness. Prejudice against someone who has a homosexual orientation is wrong. Our culture has difficulty distinguishing between persons with a homosexual orientation and homosexual activity. This is a tragic, often harmful mistake that has stigmatized homosexual persons as sex fiends or sexual predators. These stereotypes, and prejudice directed against persons with a homosexual orientation, are grossly anti-Christian, immature, unjust, unloving, and harmful.

Christians must be willing to accept persons with a homosexual orientation as brothers and sisters, beautiful people with dignity who deserve respect and love. We can do so without approving of sexual activity that God's law forbids.

Though the *Catechism of the Catholic Church* is very clear about the immorality of homosexual activity, it also teaches that people with homosexual tendencies "must be accepted with respect, compassion, and sensitivity" (*CCC*, 2358). Jesus loved everyone, and today he would surely have great love for a person struggling with his or her sexual identity.

REVIEW AND REFLECTION

1. Why is masturbation wrong?

2. Define *fornication*. Discuss several guidelines that would help a couple avoid this sin.

3. What is the intent of pornography? Why is it immoral?

4. Who is harmed by prostitution? Why?

5. Define *rape*. Why is it intrinsically evil?

6. Discuss several rules to help prevent date rape.

7. Why is homosexual orientation *not* sinful?

8. Why are homosexual acts sinful?

9. How should a Christian relate to homosexual persons?

In their pastoral letter titled *Always Our Children*, the American bishops make very clear that in teaching about the immorality of homosexual activity, we must never ever convey the idea of rejecting persons. For example, they strongly encourage parents always to love and accept any of their children who might display a homosexual orientation. Jesus loved everyone, and today he would surely have great love for anyone struggling with his or her sexual identity.

Read in John 8:2–11 how Jesus reacted to someone caught in a sexual sin. Then answer the questions that follow.

• What was the sin in question?

• What did the Mosaic law require?

• What specifically does Jesus condemn in the scene?

• What does Jesus tell the woman?

CASE STUDY: MEGAN AND JOSH

Megan and Josh have been dating steadily for seven months. They care deeply for each other and have even begun to talk about a future life together, perhaps marriage after college. They are increasingly withdrawing from group situations to spend more time alone "making out." They haven't had sex yet, but Josh, for one, thinks he'd like to.

Both are virgins. Both are highly principled. But both are very tempted right now.

As Catholics in a Catholic high school, they know the Church teaches that sexual intercourse is for marriage—that special relationship which is committed, lifelong, exclusive, and loyal. It is not that either disagrees with this teaching; it's just that they feel so deeply about each other that they wonder if they should not make an exception.

Megan's a little hesitant because she's worried about what would happen if they broke up in a few months. Would she feel used? She's overheard some of her classmates claiming they've had sex and liked it. However, a couple of them seemed very unhappy and bitter when they broke up with their boyfriends. She's not too sure what to believe.

Josh has heard some guys brag about having sex. He's sure some of this is a macho act, though he's certain some have had sexual intercourse. Some of his buddies tease him about "doing it" with Megan, saying he's not really a man until he's gone all the way. He feels their pressure, and he's certainly tempted, but Josh is a pretty moral guy. He loves Megan, and doesn't want to use her, but still. . . .

ANALYZE THIS CASE

How should Josh and Megan decide what to do? Begin by applying the "STOP Sign" method of moral decision-making (see Chapter 2).

Search Out the Facts—

1. *What is involved here? State the key issues at stake.*
- What decision will form them into good people?
- What decision will promote their true good?

2. *Why?* What is the true motivation or intention here?
- Is it moral?
- Are people being used?

3. *Who? Where? When? How?*
- Apply some principles (e.g., "A good end does not justify evil means." "The Golden Rule").
- Would they allow this exception for everyone? (If not, then they should abstain.)
- Are they treating each other with respect? Or as a means and not as a person?

Think About —

1. *Alternatives*
- Is this the only way to show love? Might abstinence be even more loving?

2. *Consequences*
- What might happen if they do have sex?
- If they abstain? (For example, will their respect and love grow even more?)
- What are some possible, immediate bad effects?
- What are some long-term effects?

Consider and Consult Others—

- How might having sex now affect their future relationships?
- How might having sex affect their relationship with a future marriage partner?
- How can the teaching of Jesus, the Church, and the Bible help direct them to do the right thing? What is this teaching? Does it make sense?
- Is there someone they can consult to help them do right here?

Are they willing to apply the Mother and Public Forum Tests: "Would they be proud to let others or their mothers know what they are doing?" (If not, then they should abstain.)

Pray—

How would talking this over with Jesus help?

What questions of love and respect would you want them to consider?

- The bottom line question: "What is the most loving thing for Josh and Megan to do?" Why?

From a Christian perspective, what should you say to someone who holds:

- "Sex is for pleasure only. If both persons want it, it's OK."
- "Couples should live together before they get married. You wouldn't buy a car without a test drive, would you?"

Catholic Life in Action

1. Check out some recent issues of magazines pitched toward teens. Point out some blatant symbols that are selling sex or appealing to lust.
2. Analyze a current song aimed at a teen audience that promotes sexual immorality. Critique the lyrics in light of Catholic moral principles.
3. Design a poster to promote the virtue of sexual abstinence.
4. Some biblical teachings on sex. Please read the following verses and note in your journal what they have to say about sexual behavior:

    1 Thessalonians 4:1–8
    > What behavior is condemned here?
    > In contrast, what does God call us to?

    1 Corinthians 6:18–20
    > What does sexual immorality sin against?
    > What is the human body?

Ephesians 5:3–7

    What should not even be mentioned?

Colossians 3:5

    What are the "earthly parts" of you?

Hebrews 13:4

    What is recommended here?

5. Read and report on an article dealing with the virtue of chastity found on one of these websites:

    www.catholic-pages.com/dir/sexuality.asp

    www.catholiceducation.org/directory/Current_Issues/Sexuality

    www.disciplesnow.com/catholic/yupdate.cfm (check under "Sexuality" in the Index)

6. Read and report on one of these articles by the excellent Catholic teacher on the virtue of chastity, Mary Beth Bonacci:

    "An Open Letter to a Wavering Virgin": www.ewtn.com/library/YOUTH/LETVIRG.TXT

    "An Open Letter to My Future Husband": www.ewtn.com/library/YOUTH/LETHUSB.TXT

    "The Burdens of Sexual Responsibility": www.ewtn.com/library/YOUTH/BURDSEX.TXT

    "The Dangers of Homosexuality": www.ewtn.com/library/YOUTH/DANGHOMO.TXT

    "How Do I Know I Am Ready for Sex?": www.ewtn.com/library/YOUTH/READYSEX.TXT

    "Banishing Unchaste Thoughts—the Healthy Way": http://catholiceducation.org/articles/sexuality/se0051.html

7. Read and summarize the teaching of Pope Paul VI's encyclical *On Human Life* (*Humane Vitae*). You can find it online at the Vatican website: www.vatican.va/holy_father/paul_vi/encyclicals/documents/hf_p-vi_enc_25071968_ humanae-vitae_en.html.

8. Read and report on one of the following through the lens of Church teaching on homosexuality found in the *Catechism of the Catholic Church*, 2357–2359:

- Fr. Richard Sparks, C.S.P., "What the Church Teaches about Homosexuality": www.americancatholic.org/Newsletters/CU/ac0799.asp

- Jim Auer, "Homosexuality: What's a Christian to Think": www.americancatholic.org/Newsletters/YU/ay1187.asp

9. Prepare a report on Natural Family Planning. Invite to class a speaker from the Diocesan Family Life Bureau on this or another topic of interest.

10. Invite to class a young Catholic married couple to talk about their courtship and tips on dating.

11. Construct a list of healthy dating ideas for teens. Share your list with classmates. Collate into one large resource with many healthy and good ideas for teen dating.

Summary Points

◆ We learn in the book of Genesis that God created us as sexual, complementary beings, equal in dignity, male and female. Our sexual nature is good.

◆ Our male or female sexuality affects how we relate to others. It involves both our emotional and spiritual makeup.

◆ The Sixth and Ninth commandments teach that the fundamental purpose of sexual activity is for sexual sharing between a husband and wife in the committed, exclusive, permanent, and faithful relationship we call marriage.

◆ The marriage covenant reflects Christ's love for his people—lifelong, faithful, and holy.

- Adultery, a sexual relationship with someone other than one's spouse (or an unmarried person with a married person), violates the fidelity and loyalty required of marriage. It is a serious offense.

- On the authority of Jesus, no couple may divorce, that is, dissolve a true marriage.

- Other offenses against marriage are polygamy (having more than one spouse), incest, sexual abuse, free unions, and trial marriages.

- Any judgment about birth control must be made in light of the unitive and procreative ends of marriage. Each act of intercourse must be open to these two ends or the action is seriously contrary to God's will for sexual relations. Thus, contraception is wrong.

- For moral and just reasons, it is morally acceptable for a couple to use natural methods of family planning.

- Because having a child is a gift and not a right, it is gravely wrong to use immoral means to conceive a child. Test-tube babies, surrogate mothers, egg or sperm donation, and the like are disordered because they separate sexual love-making from the act of procreation.

- The virtue of chastity enables us to control our sexual desires and use them appropriately according to our situation in life. Abstinence is the positive choice not to engage in sexual intercourse outside of marriage.

- The virtues of purity and modesty help us combat "carnal concupiscence." Purity of heart helps us look at things from God's point of view and control lust, that is, the disordered craving for sexual pleasure sought for itself.

- The virtue of modesty protects the intimate center of the person. It refuses to unveil what common decency requires to remain hidden.

- Masturbation, the deliberate stimulation of the genitals to obtain solitary sexual pleasure, goes against God's intent for sexual activity to be relational. Habit, compulsion, or immaturity can lessen blameworthiness for this act, but we must make an effort, with God's help, to control our sexual urges.

- Fornication is sexual intercourse engaged in by unmarried persons. It is a serious misuse of the gift of sexuality because unconditional love is missing; the couple has not entered a totally committed, exclusive, faithful relationship.

- Pornography aims solely to arouse sexual passion. It disrespects and damages the dignity of everyone associated with it.

- Prostitution, engaging in sex for money, seriously debases and dehumanizes persons who sell their bodies by turning themselves into objects to use, not persons to be loved. It is a serious violation against both chastity and charity for those who pay for prostitution.

- Rape, forcing someone to have sex, is an intrinsically evil act that violently assaults human dignity.

- Homosexual activity is a serious violation of God's intent for male-female bonding in a relationship open to life and love.

- No one chooses to have a homosexual orientation; therefore, someone is not a sinner for having such an orientation. It is sinful to display prejudice toward homosexual persons. They are our brothers and sisters, loved and redeemed by Christ.

- We grow in self-respect and respect for others in the area of sexuality by avoiding pornography, staying away from situations where our self-control is compromised, living lovingly for others, praying and acts of self-sacrifice, and celebrating Christ's forgiveness and love in the sacraments of Reconciliation and the Eucharist.

PRAYER REFLECTION

Dear Lord,
Thank you for the gift of my sexuality.
I am grateful to be a living, thinking,
feeling child of your loving Father.
Help me enjoy my friendships
with members of the opposite sex . . .
to cherish and respect and appreciate their uniqueness.
Help me accept my own sexual feelings,
to see them as good and wholesome and human.
Help me not to fear or be ashamed of this
mysterious, wonderful, yet confusing passion
that sometimes simmers inside me.
Finally, Lord, as God-made-man, you certainly
understand me and my feelings.
Send me the gift of your Holy Spirit
so I may respect myself and others
and always use my gift of sexuality in
responsible, caring, and loving ways. Amen.

What do you like best about yourself? List five qualities.
Devise a way to use some of these qualities as gifts to give to at least three people this coming week.

NOTES

1. Encyclical Letter, *Deus Caritas Est,* of the Supreme Pontiff Benedict XVI to the Bishops, Priests, and Deacons, Men and Women Religious, and All the Lay Faithful on Christian Love (*Liberia Editrice Vaticana*, 2005), No. 11 <www.vatican.va/holy_father/benedict_xvi/encyclicals/documents/hf_ben-x>

CHAPTER OVERVIEW

CHAPTER TEN

Respect for Justice and Truth

What good is it, my brothers, if someone says he has faith but does not have works? Can that faith save him? If a brother or sister has nothing to wear and has no food for the day, and one of you says to them, "Go in peace, keep warm, and eat well," but you do not give them the necessities of the body, what good is it? So also faith of itself, if it does not have works, is dead.

James 2:14–17

Right-On Justice

Four high school juniors missed their first-period chemistry class and quiz because they lined up extra early to purchase some tickets to a concert. The next day they told their teacher they were late because they stopped to help a stranded motorist change a flat tire. They asked permission to take the quiz.

The teacher was not buying the story. She put each culprit in a separate corner of the room and asked them in turn, "Which tire?"

The moral of the story: If you tell the truth, you don't have to remember anything.

A more serious large-scale issue is at the heart of another true story. New York City mayor Fiorello LaGuardia (1934–1945) was once sitting in for a judge when an elderly lady was brought before him. Her crime was stealing a loaf of bread, which she used to feed her family. LaGuardia fined the poor woman $10 for her act of theft. But out of his own pocket, he immediately paid her fine and then took up a collection of fifty cents from every person in his courtroom. He admonished his fellow citizens about the tragedy of living in a society where a poor person had to steal in order to eat.

LaGuardia's sense of justice was right on. He instinctively knew that God does not intend our world to be so cruel as to allow someone like an old woman and her family to go hungry. And he did something about this situation by showing compassion with his actions. But one person's singular effort is never enough. What needs to be done is to reform human hearts so we can build a society where people do not go hungry, where justice is done, and where the basic rights of people are secured.

Both stories are related to the theme of justice and the demands of the seventh, eighth, and tenth commandments, the subject of this chapter on justice and truth.

Fiorello LaGuardia

What Is Your Honesty Quotient?

One national survey revealed that 91 percent of Americans confess that they regularly don't tell the truth. It is, therefore, doubtful that today a person's word is his or her bond.

Honesty is the touchstone of a person's character. When we are honest, we do the right thing, even if it hurts. Honesty involves truth-telling to ourselves, to God, and to other people. Honesty is a virtue closely related to justice, fidelity, truthfulness, and courage.

Jesus taught, "Truth will set you free" (Jn 8:32). The poet Robert Burns wrote, "An honest man is the noblest work of God."

What's your HQ, Honesty Quotient? After all, this virtue is the antidote to concoctions, fabrications, prevarications, half-truths, spin-doctoring, misrepresentations, falsehoods, equivocations, "white" lies, exaggerations, truth shadings, and unadulterated, bare-faced lies.

Answer questions 1–10 using this scale: **5—always; 4—usually; 3—sometimes; 2—rarely; 1—never**

STATEMENTS	1	2	3	4	5
1. Do you refuse to cheat on tests and quizzes?					
2. Do you respond truthfully to your parents' questions when they ask you where you have been?					
3. Do you refrain from copying homework and passing it off as your own?					
4. Do you return the extra if you are given incorrect change when making a purchase?					
5. Do you refuse to lie for your friends?					
6. Do you pay parking fines?					
7. Do you tell people what you really believe rather than what they want to hear?					
8. Are you honest even when people aren't looking?					
9. If you find something of value, do you make a sincere effort to find its proper owner?					
10. If you broke a vase in a china shop, would you admit it?					

Answer questions 11–20 using this scale: **5—never; 4—rarely; 3—sometimes; 2—usually; 1—always**

	1	2	3	4	5
11. Do you look the other way when someone else is dishonest, for example, when a classmate cheats on a test?					
12. Concerning people who don't like you: Are you pleasant to their face, but attack them when they aren't around?					
13. If you have a job, do you take things that belong to your employer, saying to yourself, "They won't miss it."					
14. Do you exaggerate your achievements?					
15. Do you spread rumors about others, thus ruining their reputations?					
16. Would you do something unethical at work, especially if your job depended on it?					
17. Would you stretch the truth on a college application, for example, by inflating your extracurricular record?					
18. Do you say things you don't mean for the sake of politeness?					
19. Do you tell the truth, but not the "whole truth"?					
20. Do you lie on surveys like this?					

Total Your Points: 85–100: You're pretty honest, if not very honest. / 70–85: You're average on honesty. / 60–70: Your HQ is below average. / 60: You have some work to do in this area.

THINK ABOUT THIS

1. Which of the examples above seems to be a problem at your school? in society as a whole? What, if anything, can be done about this situation?
2. Would it be wrong for a parent to call school to say you are sick so you can stay home to finish a school project? Would this be lying?
3. A friend asks you to read her essay and to tell her if you think it is any good. It's terrible. But she is super-sensitive. She would be hurt if you told her it was bad. How could this sticky situation be handled without lying?
4. Is it easy for you to tell the truth? Why or why not?
5. Recall a time in your life when "Honesty was the best policy."

Understanding Justice

(CCC, 1807; 1928; 2401—2406; 2411—2412; 2464; 2534)

Justice is a pivotal virtue for being a moral person and following the commandments. The Seventh Commandment enjoins us to respect the property of our neighbors. It also requires us to support the "universal destination of goods," that is, that all people are due the sustenance of life. The Tenth Commandment calls us to refrain from coveting the goods of others, a fault which is at the root of theft, robbery, and fraud. Related to the Seventh and Tenth Commandments is the Eighth Commandment. It says that we must not bear false witness against our neighbor and requires us to be up front and truthful with others.

The cardinal and moral virtue of *justice* requires us to render to God and our neighbors what is due them by right. Therefore, we are just to the Creator God, the source of all, when we acknowledge his goodness, love him above all, thank him for his gifts, and worship him in humility. Toward our neighbor, justice requires us "to respect the rights of each and to establish in human relationships the harmony that promotes equity with regard to persons and to the common good" (*CCC*, 1807).

Catholic teaching distinguishes among the following types of justice: *commutative, distributive, legal,* and *social.*

social justice

The form of justice that applies the gospel message of Jesus Christ to the structures, systems, and laws of society in order to protect the dignity of persons and guarantee the rights of individuals.

COMMUTATIVE JUSTICE	DISTRIBUTIVE JUSTICE
individual ⇦ ⇨ individual	government authorities ⇨ individual

LEGAL JUSTICE	SOCIAL JUSTICE
individuals ⇨ social whole	Gospel of Jesus Christ ⇨ structures of society

Commutative justice regulates relationships of exchange. It calls for fairness in agreements and contracts between individuals and various social groups. This type of justice requires that we respect the equal human dignity of everyone involved in our exchanges.

With commutative justice, you get what you pay for. And you are required to pay for what you get. An example: You agree to cut the neighbor's lawn for $30. It is only just for him to pay you your wage if you actually cut the lawn satisfactorily. At the base of this type of justice is the principle of equality between what is given and what is received. We respect the dignity of others when we fulfill our obligations toward them. They respect our dignity when they follow through on their commitments. Without this give-and-take type of justice, society would be filled with fraud, theft, dishonesty, broken agreements, and a host of other problems that would lead to its ruination.

Distributive justice protects and guarantees the common welfare. Distributive justice seeks the fair distribution of the goods of creation that God intends for us all to use and share. Distributive justice strongly upholds the principle of "the universal destination of goods." This principle teaches that God gave the earth and its resources to the common stewardship of all of us. Everyone has the right to enjoy the fruits of God's creation. It is the function of distributive justice to see that the goods of creation are justly distributed to all people to use and share.

Distributive justice requires governmental authorities to guarantee the basic rights of citizens, especially the powerless in our midst. Fair tax laws are an example of distributive justice at work. For example, a graduated income tax from lower to higher economic levels helps redistribute wealth within a society to help pay for basic human needs. Such a tax looks to the common good, raising funds to allow society to hire safety forces, provide education for all children, provide social security programs for poor and unemployed people, maintain infrastructures, provide for national defense, help victims of disasters, and so forth.

Likewise, although people have the right to own private property, its ownership makes its holder a caretaker, God's steward. The held property must be used for the benefit of family and also for the common good of others.

Legal justice governs what individuals owe society as a whole. Because we are social beings who live with and for others, we must do our part to build up the common good. For example, as citizens we must obey the just laws of our government, like paying our taxes, serving on juries, and coming to the aid of our fellow citizens in times of peril.

Social justice applies the gospel message of Jesus Christ to the structures, systems, and laws of society in order to protect the dignity of persons and guarantee the rights of individuals. Social justice goes beyond distributive justice. It holds that each person has a right to a fair voice in the economic, political, and social institutions of the society in which he or she lives. According to his or her ability, everyone has a right to contribute to how society runs. Therefore, social justice sometimes goes by the name of *contributive* justice.

Which Type of Justice?

Place a check mark in the first column if you agree with a statement below. Then, in the second column, judge which type of justice should govern the statement according to the following code:

C = commutative justice; **D** = distributive justice; **L** = legal justice
SJ = social justice

STATEMENTS	AGREE?	JUSTICE TYPE
1. Welfare programs for the poor are a waste of good taxpayer money.		
2. Homeowners must be willing to sell their houses to anyone who can afford them.		
3. Every qualified student should be provided a college education.		
4. Auto companies must fix faulty engine components.		
5. Everyone has the right to health care.		
6. "Ask not what your country can do for you. Ask what you can do for your country."		
7. Medical and law schools and other professional programs should give preferential treatment to some persons from minority groups to level the playing field and open up opportunities for minorities who have historically been shut out of the system.		

◆ Share your answers and reasons for them.

◆ Create your own definition of justice.

True development of solidarity also requires sharing the Good News of Jesus Christ and his message of repentance, peace, and justice.

REVIEW AND REFLECTION

1. Distinguish between and among these types of justice: *commutative, distributive, legal,* and *social.*

2. What is meant by the "universal destination of goods"?

3. Why is social justice sometimes called "contributive" justice?

4. List or name ten things you owe others in justice and things others owe you. Do you have to earn these? Explain.

SOCIAL JUSTICE DOCTRINE OF THE CHURCH

(CCC, 2419—2449; 2458—2463)

The Church has the Christ-commissioned duty to take his Gospel and show people how his message of peace, justice, and love should make a difference in the lives of individuals and societies. This is particularly true regarding how we use the goods of the earth and in how we use our social and economic relationships. "By means of her social doctrine, the Church takes on the task of proclaiming what the Lord has entrusted to her. She makes the message of the freedom and redemption wrought by Christ, the Gospel of the Kingdom, present in human history" (*Compendium of the Social Doctrine of the Church*, No. 63).[1]

Especially since the Industrial Revolution of the nineteenth century, the Church has developed a body of social-justice doctrine. This teaching proposes principles for reflection, criteria for judgment, and guidelines for action in the area of social justice. Four key themes of that teaching, related to the values of the seventh and tenth commandments, follow:

1. Profit cannot be the only norm and sole goal of economic activity. Lust for money produces greed, leads to violence, and reduces people to the "collective organization of production," making individuals and groups mere cogs in the economic machine. Totalitarian and atheistic economic theories like communism are immoral. So, too, are economic theories of unbridled, or *laissez-faire,* capitalism. Both of these assault human dignity and freedom and fail to address real human needs.

2. The economy exists to serve people; people do not exist to serve the economy. Human work is a good thing because through it we share in God's creative activity. Work is a duty, but also an activity in which we use our God-given talents to honor God, provide for ourselves and families, fulfill our potential, and grow in holiness. Everyone—including the poor in our midst—has the right to economic initiative and the duty to contribute to the common good in a peaceful way. This requires that the state should guarantee individual freedom and the rights to private property, a stable currency, and efficient public services. It also requires responsible and ecologically sound practices on the part of entrepreneurs. Rights required by social justice include the right to a job without unjust discrimination, the right to a just wage for a decent day's work, and the right to strike peacefully as a last resort to achieve economic justice.

3. Richer nations must work hard for international solidarity. There is an ever-widening gap between rich and poor nations caused by various religious, political, economic, and financial factors. Out of a sense of solidarity, rich nations have a grave duty to help poorer nations develop. *Development* in this sense involves helping poorer nations rise to an acceptable level of economic independence through both direct aid to respond to immediate crises like famine and genuine reform in international economic and financial institutions to promote more equal relations among

"The universal right to use the goods of the earth is based on the principle of the universal destination of goods. Each person must have access to the level of well-being necessary for his full development."[2]

Read the following biblical references that deal with justice themes. Print or copy into your journal or notebook at least three of the readings that most impress you.

- Leviticus 19:9–10
- Matthew 14:15–21
- Acts 2:42–47
- Deuteronomy 10:14–19
- Luke 4:16–21 1
- Corinthians 11:17–33
- Psalm 146:5–8
- Luke 12:32–48
- 1 Timothy 6:6–19
- Proverbs 21:13
- Luke 16:19–31
- James 2:14–17, 26

nations. Rich nations must also make a strong effort to support poor nations that are working for economic growth and the liberation of their people. In a special way, help should be extended to farm workers, since much of the world's poor people are directly involved in farming.

4. *We must imitate Jesus by having a special love for the poor.* Inspired by the Beatitudes and the example of Jesus who lived in poverty, Christians must seek out and help poor people by putting into concrete action the *corporal* and *spiritual* works of mercy. Preeminent among these is almsgiving, that is, giving money or other material assistance to the less advantaged. Out-of-control love of riches and hoarding and selfishly using material possessions are absolutely contrary to the love of poor people. Christians are also required to work to reform society's economic, political, and social policies so they favor and benefit the poor in our midst, not just the rich, strong, and powerful.

QUESTIONS AND ANSWERS ABOUT CATHOLIC SOCIAL TEACHING

Question: What is the relationship between Catholic social teaching and the virtue of charity?

Answer: In his encyclical *Deus Caritas Est*, Pope Benedict XVI reminds us that the work of justice must be a fundamental norm of the state. This means that each person must be guaranteed, according to the principle of subsidiarity, his or her share of the community's goods. Recall from Chapter 1 that the principle of subsidiarity holds that a higher unit of society should not do what a lower unit can do as well or better.

Politics has the chief responsibility to order society and the state in a just way. Part of this just ordering is that the state must not impose religion. However, it must guarantee religious freedom between the followers of different faiths. Further, the state must recognize the Church and its proper independence as a faith community with its own unique contributions to make to the larger society. One of its contributions is the fruit of its faith in Christ, which brings a unique vision of humanity that is enlightened by its encounter with God.

Faith enables reason to do its work more effectively and to see its proper object more clearly. . . .
The Church's social teaching argues on the basis of reason and natural law, namely, on the basis of what is in accord with the nature of every human being. It recognizes that it is not the Church's responsibility to make this teaching prevail in political life. Rather, the Church wishes to help form consciences in political life and to stimulate greater insight into the authentic requirements of justice as well as greater readiness to act accordingly, even when this might involve conflict with situations of personal interest. . . .
The Church cannot and must not take upon herself the political battle to bring about the most just society possible. She cannot and must not replace the State. Yet at the same time she cannot and must not remain on the sidelines in the fight for justice. She has to play her part through rational

(continued)

REVIEW AND REFLECTION

1.   Discuss at least two important themes of Catholic social justice teaching.

2.   Define the virtue of solidarity.

3.   What does "development" have to do with justice and peace?

4.   Why should Christians have a special love for the poor?

5.   What is the relationship between doing justice and putting into practice the virtue of charity?

6.   What have you personally done for the poor? What would you like to do in the future? Given your talents, what can you realistically do?

QUESTIONS AND ANSWERS ABOUT CATHOLIC SOCIAL TEACHING *(continued)*

argument and she has to reawaken the spiritual energy without which justice, which always demands sacrifice, cannot prevail and prosper.[3]

The pope goes on to say what common sense can discover: There will always be a need for love—charity—no matter how just the society. Why? Because humans are always in need of love. There will always be those who suffer, who are alone, who need material help for their immediate needs. *Loving, personal concern is a basic human need that no state can ever satisfy.*

Not to enable the poor to share in our goods is to steal from them and deprive them of life. The goods we possess are not ours, but theirs.

—St. John Chrysostom

*   Give your opinion on St. John's statement. Are self-indulgent wealthy people responsible for the death of starving people? Why or why not?

Seventh Commandment
(CCC, 2407—2418; 2450—2457)

You shall not steal.

The Seventh Commandment outlaws theft, that is, taking someone else's property against his or her will. But there are many other ways to abuse a person's rights in this regard. Here are some examples of violations against the Seventh Commandment:

*   deliberately keeping objects that someone lends you;
*   keeping things you find without making an effort to locate the rightful owner;
*   business fraud;
*   paying unjust wages;
*   price-fixing;
*   participation in corrupt systems which often leads to some unfair financial, political, or professional gain or advantage;
*   the taking and personal use of supplies or common property that belongs to an employer or larger enterprise;
*   tax evasion;

◆   Calculate how much money a family of four would need to live a minimally satisfactory life in today's world. Factor in food, shelter, utilities, clothing, health care, education, transportation, and recreation costs. Then determine if a breadwinner earning the minimum wage (forty hours times fifty weeks) would have enough money to support his or her family.

◆   "Live simply that others may simply live." Brainstorm in small groups to make a list of twenty ways that those who are not poor can live more simply and share more generously with the needy in the world.

from providing for the needs of those who are dependent on them. Cheating at games and unfair wagers can easily be gravely wrong unless the stakes are very small.

The Seventh Commandment also requires us to respect the beautiful creation God gave us for the use of all humans—past, present, and future. This includes respecting animals, plants, natural resources, and the environment, all of which are for our use, enjoyment, and benefit. God made us stewards of creation. Thus, we must responsibly use and not abuse it. We must cultivate and care for the natural goods he gave to us.

Humans do not have an *absolute* right to dominate creation and other living beings. Animals, for example, are also God's creatures. Their existence blesses and glorifies a generous Creator God. Humans, made in God's image and likeness, have the right to use animals for food and clothing, as helpers in labor, and as companions for leisure. It is also morally acceptable to use animals for medical and scientific research if done so reasonably and for the purpose of caring for and saving human lives. However, it is cruel and unjust to cause animals to suffer or die needlessly. And it is wrong to spend excessive money on pets, for example, at the expense of relieving human misery. It is morally acceptable to show care for animals, but "one should not direct to them the affection due only to persons" (*CCC*, 2418).

Finally, the Seventh Commandment outlaws for any reason anything that leads to the enslavement of people, to their being bought, sold, or exchanged as mere merchandise. These are abominable practices that assault human dignity at its core. Humans are not commodities. This is why any economic theory or system that treats humans as mere cogs in some money-making machine is seriously wrong and dehumanizing. Humans are precious images of God. They deserve the utmost respect at all times and in all ways.

The Seventh Commandment forbids theft, that is, usurping another's property against the reasonable will of the owner. There is no theft if consent can be presumed or if refusal is contrary to reason and the universal destination of goods. This is the case in obvious and urgent necessity when the only way to provide for immediate, essential needs (food, shelter, clothing . . .) is to put at one's disposal and use the property of others.

—CCC, 2408

- doing shoddy or poor quality work, or failing to complete work that's been paid for;
- check or invoice forgery;
- expense-account padding in order to make unfair, personal financial profit;
- wasting time or materials;
- willfully damaging public or private property.

An important value underlying the Seventh Commandment is respect for the property rights of others. If people do not follow this common sense dictate, then it would be very difficult for a society to function. Imagine a society where contracts were routinely ignored and promises easily broken. The economy would disintegrate and social commerce would come to a halt. The moral law requires that we make reparation for violations of this commandment, for example, by returning stolen goods.

Although a Christian reading of the Seventh Commandment does not outlaw gambling or games of chance, it does judge these as morally evil practices when they enslave a person or keep breadwinners

Case Studies

Read and answer the follow-up questions for the case studies below.

Larry uses his own state-of-the-art computer to download music off the Internet and to make copies of compact discs. He sells them to friends and classmates for about half of retail.

- Is Larry stealing from the recording companies? Why or why not?

Jo Ann has written a brilliant term paper and received an "A" grade. However, the novel insight that is the centerpiece of her work was taken from a paper posted on the Internet. Jo Ann fails to footnote her reference or acknowledge that the idea belonged to another person.

- How is this plagiarizing?
- In what circumstances and to what degree must you credit the ideas of others?

A mechanical wizard, Michael, has dismantled the pollution-control device on his three-year-old car. In the face of rising gasoline prices, he figures he's saving $5 a week on gas.

- How has Michael violated the dictates of the Seventh Commandment?

Joe and his buddies like to hunt game for sport. Rarely do they consume the meat of the animals they kill.

- Is their hunting immoral? Does it show a disrespect to animals?

Seth works at a local convenience store. Whenever he can, he shortchanges his customers a dime or two. He rarely makes more than $3 a day from this scam. If a customer notices it, he laughs and says he's sorry for his stupidity.

- If you were Seth's boss, would you fire him if you found out about his practice?

Tim wastes about an hour each day visiting personal Internet websites when he is supposed to be working. He claims this "theft of time" makes him more relaxed and hence more productive when he does focus on the job.

- Do you buy his argument? Or is he really dishonest in claiming to do an "honest day's work for an honest day's pay"?

Therefore I tell you, do not worry about your life, what you will eat [or drink], or about your body, what you will wear. . . . But seek first the kingdom [of God] and his righteousness, and all these things will be given you besides.

—Matthew 6:25, 33

The Tenth Commandment
(CCC, 2534—2557)

You shall not covet your neighbor's goods.

Whereas the Seventh Commandment treats the external acts related to theft, the Tenth Commandment deals with inner desires, the "lust of the eyes," which is at the root of theft, robbery, fraud, and other acts forbidden by the Seventh Commandment.

The Tenth Commandment outlaws *greed,* that is, the desire to accumulate unlimited goods; *avarice,* which is the passionate desire for riches and the power that comes from them; and *envy,* sadness over another person's possessions and the inordinate desire to get them for oneself, even using unjust means.

In the Sermon on the Mount, Jesus taught, "For where your treasure is, there also will your heart be" (Mt 6:21). Disordered attachment to goods turns people away from God. Christians keep in check the strong desire to accumulate wealth and envy at the expense of others by practicing acts of love and humility and by being open to God, who is the only one who can fill up our craving hearts.

...teaches that we should desire him first, and his Father's Kingdom, and then he will give us all that we need. He requires "poverty of spirit" for us, that is, a certain detachment from earthly riches that eventually pass away. The pursuit of goods can enslave us. On the other hand, pursuing Our Lord as the source of our true fulfillment makes us both free and happy: "Blessed are the poor in spirit, for theirs is the kingdom of heaven" (Mt 5:3). The antidote to a false dependence on material things is to choose God's Kingdom and righteousness above all.

Your View of Money

Henry Fielding warned: "Make money your god and it will plague you like the devil." What is your reaction to the following statements? Mark **SA** for "strongly agree"; **A** for "agree"; **D** for "disagree"; and **SD** for "strongly disagree."

_____ 1. "The love of money is the root of all evil."

_____ 2. "Take the money and run." (American saying)

_____ 3. "Money can't buy happiness, love, or friends."

_____ 4. "Never esteem a man or thyself the more for money, nor condemn him for want of it." (English proverb)

_____ 5. "The rich get richer, and the poor get poorer."

_____ 6. "Money isn't everything; money is the only thing."

Share your responses and give reasons for your choices.

MONITORING MONEY

1. Examine your own spending habits by reflecting on how you spend your money over the course of a week or a month. List in your journal your patterns of spending. Then answer these two questions:

   a. How do you know if money is beginning to control your life?

   b. What can you do about it?

2. Give some examples of how having inordinate wealth can enslave someone.

3. Construct a list of five rules people should observe if they are wealthy.

What Did Jesus Say?

Here are several things Jesus taught about money. Read the quotations. Complete the exercises in the Monitoring Money feature.

"No servant can serve two masters. He will either hate one and love the other, or be devoted to one and despise the other. You cannot serve God and mammon." (Lk 16:13)

"Again I say to you, it is easier for a camel to pass through the eye of a needle than for one who is rich to enter the kingdom of God." (Mt 19:24)

"Take care to guard against all greed, for though one may be rich, one's life does not consist of possessions." (Lk 12:15)

"If you wish to be perfect, go, sell what you have and give to (the) poor, and you will have treasure in heaven. Then come, follow me." (Mt 19:21) [Said to the rich young man who asked Jesus what more he should do to possess eternal life.]

"Blessed are the poor in spirit, for theirs is the kingdom of heaven." (Mt 5:3)

1. What are some attitudes outlawed by the Tenth Commandment?

2. Define *envy.*

3. Define *theft.* List five different types of theft.

4. Examine today's newspaper. Find several examples of violations of the Seventh and Tenth Commandments.

Eighth Commandment

(CCC, 2464—2474; 2504—2506)

You shall not bear false witness against your neighbor.

On December 26, a pastor discovered that the Infant Jesus was missing from the nativity scene inside the church.

The parish staff gathered near the manger. As they discussed what happened, a little boy came in through the side door of the church pulling behind him a red wagon. The boy towed the wagon to the nativity area and gently lifted the figure of the Christ child that he had wrapped in an old blanket and tenderly placed Jesus back into his crib.

The pastor met the boy as he was leaving the side altar. "What do you think you are doing?" he asked. The little boy thought for a second, and then with pride in his voice replied, "Last week I visited the baby Jesus. I told him if I got a little red wagon for Christmas that I would take him for a ride. Today, I came back to keep my promise."[4]

A lesson we can learn from this touching story is simple: Keep any promises you make. Keeping promises is being faithful to the truth. It is one of the important values taught by the Eighth Commandment. By nature, all humans are inclined toward the truth. It is part of our human dignity to seek the truth, especially religious truth, and to follow it once it is discovered.

The Old Testament teaches that God is the source of truth. Both his word and his Law are true. Jesus is God-made-flesh. He is the Way, the Truth, and the Life (Jn 14:6). And Jesus and his Father send the Holy Spirit, who will help us abide in the truth.

Christians have a special vocation to witness to the truth, to obey the command of Jesus, who said, "Let your 'yes' mean 'yes,' and your 'no' mean 'no'" (Mt 5:37). Followers of Jesus must decide to live in the truth, that is, "in the simplicity of a life in conformity with the Lord's example, abiding in his truth" (*CCC,* 2470). An important way we do this is to proclaim, both in word and in deed, the gospel of Jesus Christ. Some may even be called to the supreme witness of *martyrdom,* that is, giving up one's life for the sake of the truth of Jesus, his gospel, or Christian teaching.

The virtue of truthfulness shows us to be true to ourselves in word and in deed. It rejects the triple vices of *duplicity* ("being deceptive or misleading"), *dissimulation* ("hiding something by pretense"), and *hypocrisy* ("the false claim or pretense of having admirable principles, beliefs, or feelings"). It involves both honesty in revealing what should be known and discretion in not expressing what justice requires us to keep secret.

When in doubt, tell the truth.

—MARK TWAIN

This above all: to thine own self be true, And it must follow, as the night the day, Thou canst not then be false to any man.

—POLONIUS IN WILLIAM SHAKESPEARE'S *HAMLET*

> *The false witness will not go unpunished, and he who utters lies will not escape.*
>
> —PROVERBS 19:5

Truthfulness is absolutely foundational for people to live together in mutual confidence. It is related to the cardinal virtue of justice by which we give others their just due, in this case, the truth.

VIOLATIONS AGAINST THE EIGHTH COMMANDMENT (*CCC*, 2475–2492; 2507–2511)

Offenses against the Eighth Commandment include the following:

False witness and perjury. False witness under oath is known as **perjury**. It seriously undermines justice by falsely accusing innocent people, by allowing guilty persons to go free, or by increasing the punishment of accused criminals.

Failing to respect the reputation of others. Rash judgment assumes without adequate evidence a moral fault in another person. To counteract the human tendency to prejudge others, we should always put the most positive interpretation on another's thoughts, words, and deeds. If we do not like or understand something a person said, we should ask him or her for clarification. If the person has made a mistake, we should correct him or her with love and gentleness.

Detraction reveals a person's faults and failings to someone who did not previously know about them and who has no right or need to know them. And **calumny** is lying about others so people will make false judgments about them. Both detraction and calumny seriously undermine the honor due someone's name and reputation. These twin evils violate both justice and love.

Encouraging others to do evil. Flattery (paying someone a compliment to gain a favor), *adulation* (giving excessive admiration to someone), and **complaisance** (pleasing others so they will carry out your wishes) are all wrong if they encourage another person to engage in immoral conduct. Adulation is seriously sinful if it makes the flatterer party to another person's vices or mortal sins. But it is venially sinful when it only seeks to be agreeable, avoid evil, meet a need, or get some ethical advantage.

Boasting and bragging. These are a form of lying and thus are wrong. As a proverb puts it, "Self-praise is no recommendation."

Irony. Speaking in an ironic or sarcastic way is also wrong if it mocks a person or maliciously pokes fun at some aspect of his or her behavior.

Lying. Saint Augustine defined a lie as "speaking a falsehood with the intention of deceiving" (quoted in *CCC*, 2482). The *Catechism of the Catholic Church* further clarifies the definition by saying it is "to speak or act against the truth in order to lead into error someone who has the right to know the truth" (*CCC,* 2483).

A lie is the most direct violation against the truth. Its seriousness depends on four factors:

perjury
False witness under oath.

detraction
Revealing a person's faults and failings to someone who did not previously know about them and who had no need or right to know about them.

calumny
Lying about others so people will make false judgments about them.

complaisance
Pleasing others so they can carry out your wishes.

1. the nature of the truth that is distorted,
2. the circumstances,
3. the intentions of the one who lies, and
4. the harm suffered by the victims of the lie.

A lie that might only constitute a venial sin becomes mortal when it does grave harm to the virtues of justice and charity, especially when it involves deadly consequences for those being deceived.

Lying should always be condemned. It distorts human speech, whose purpose is to communicate the truth to others. When we lie, we lead another into error by representing something contrary to the truth. This is a failure to be just and to love. Lying destroys our ability to live together, undermines trust, and sows discord into the fabric of society.

Any offense against the truth requires the duty to repair any harm that has resulted from the lie, even if forgiveness has been given. If a person's reputation has suffered as a result of the lie, we must especially try to correct the harm done and make others aware of the truth.

Although we must speak the truth, we are not always obligated to tell all we know. Sometimes we must use *discreet* ("circumspect, diplomatic, guarded, prudent, tactful") language for the good and safety of others, to respect privacy rights, or for the sake of the common good. Professionals like doctors and lawyers do not have to reveal everything they know about a patient or a client. "No one is bound to reveal the truth to someone who does not have the right to know it" (*CCC*, 2489).

Sins revealed in the Sacrament of Reconciliation must *never* be revealed. This "sacramental seal" is sacred and inviolable. It would be a most serious offense for a confessor to reveal anything he heard in the confessional in any way, shape, or form.

The media have a duty to carefully consider revealing the secrets of people's private lives. They should strike a fair and just balance between the public's right to know and the requirements of the common good. A good rule of thumb is always, "Do unto others as you would have them do unto you."

> If something uncharitable is said in your presence, either speak in favor of the absent, or withdraw, or, if possible, stop the conversation.
>
> —ST. JOHN VIANNEY

> Let anything you hear die within you; be assured it will not make you burst.
>
> —SIRACH 19:9

> He who betrays a secret cannot be trusted, he will never find an intimate friend.
>
> —SIRACH 27:16

WHAT YOU NEED TO KNOW ABOUT LYING . . .

1. People will stop trusting you if you lie.
2. People lie to avoid confrontation. But when the lie is found out, confrontation is worse. Lying increases the problem; it does not solve it.
3. Telling lies about yourself can be a major sign of low self-esteem. It doesn't get at the root of the problem.
4. Lies can have a chain reaction effect in your life, causing problems in the future that you can't anticipate now. They have a way of coming back to haunt you.
5. A pattern of lying can be a sign of a psychological or social disorder. Seek help. Begin with confession.[5]

Discuss: Add several more common sense observations to this list.

To Tell the Truth

Read the following cases involving honesty and the Eighth Commandment. Answer the corresponding questions.

Medical News. Would a doctor violate the Eighth Commandment by telling a cancer patient that the disease is in remission, knowing that there is a 90 percent possibility that the patient will die within the next two years?

- What if the doctor feels the truth will make the patient so anxious that his condition will significantly worsen?
- Do patients have the right to know the truth about the possibility of death so they can properly prepare for it?

Faulty Engine. You own a car with an engine that is on its last legs. You have found a buyer for your vehicle.

- Are you obligated to tell him about the faulty engine? Why or why not?

Insurance Scam. Your parents' insurance company covers your mother's wedding ring in cases of theft but not in cases of loss. Your mom loses her ring while on a business trip with your dad.

- Would your parents violate the Eighth Commandment if they report to the insurance company that someone stole the ring out of a hotel room when she was at the convention?

Classmate. A talented classmate is always badmouthing herself, tearing down her accomplishments, never acknowledging any good that she has done. You're not sure if she does it because she is insecure or because she wants to manipulate people to get them to praise her.

- In either case, is she violating the precepts of the Eighth Commandment? Why or why not?
- Do you know people like her?

Day Off From School. Your mother calls your school to report that you are sick so that you can finish a term paper. You both call it a "mental health" day.

- Is this lying? Why or why not?

FOR YOUR JOURNAL

Read and consider the five statements that deal with honesty in the feature *What You Need to Know about Lying* on page 251. Respond to one of these in your journal. Give examples and explain your response.

◆ Someone pressures you to reveal a secret. How would you handle this situation?

◆ Does the public have the right to know that a politician running for the office of United States Senate had an extramarital affair twenty years ago? Ten years ago? Last month? What if he were involved in a homosexual relationship? Would your answer change?

AN HONEST SOCIETY (*CCC,* 2493—2503; 2512—2513)

Any form of false witnessing or lying strikes at the fabric of society. The result of dishonesty is a person who is less than whole, one who lacks integrity. As Jesus put it when challenged by Pilate,

"Everyone who belongs to the truth listens to my voice" (Jn 18:37).

Individuals must listen to the truth, speak the truth, and live the truth. So must society as a whole, especially those in the communications media, whose vocation is to serve the common good.

Citizens have the right to information based on truth, freedom, and the virtues of justice and solidarity. Because the media have a powerful role in forming public opinion, they have a serious duty to communicate information honestly. Journalists, for example, must take care in gathering their facts and reporting them responsibly. When dealing with individuals, they must never defame a person as they follow the Golden Rule.

Government officials also have a serious obligation to defend and safeguard the just and free flow of information. Furthermore, they must enact laws that protect citizens' rights to a good name and to privacy. They should also see to it that public morality is not assaulted by pornography, propaganda, and other serious misuses of the media. Totalitarian governments that distort the truth, propagandize, control public opinion, and assault human rights are worthy of condemnation.

A society can do much to promote truth by encouraging people to express themselves in the fine arts. Humans are naturally tuned into truth and beauty because we are made in the image of God, who is Truth and the source of all beauty and goodness. Fine art, especially sacred art, can reflect and express some of the inexhaustible beauty of our loving Creator. It can be a source of drawing people to God.

The Epidemic of Cheating: "Everyone's Doing It"

Cheating is in the news. From stock manipulators, to CEOs of companies who misstate their profit statements, to politicians who dishonestly manipulate the system for their benefit, to workers in every field who take shortcuts, to taxpayers who inflate their deductions, and to students who regularly cheat—the epidemic of cheating touches everyone.

Cheating involves trickery, fraud, misleading, and dishonesty. Cheating involves both stealing and lying. It violates the Seventh Commandment by taking something that does not rightfully belong to you. It also violates the Eighth Commandment by bearing false witness—lying—about what you have done.

In the estimate of some moralists and sociologists, cheating in schools is at an all-time high. A recent poll revealed that 65 percent of students believe that there is "a great deal" or "a fair amount" of cheating done in their schools. Another survey of 18,000 public high school students showed that 70 percent admitted to cheating on exams and 60 percent admitted to some form of plagiarism.[6]

One knowledgeable commentator, Michael Josephson of the Josephson Institute of Ethics, said that in the past, cheaters were in the minority. They kept their cheating a secret, even from friends. Today, surveys seem to reveal that cheaters are in the majority and are quite up front about it.[7] Pressure to succeed regardless of the cost, pressure to get into desirable colleges, taking the easy way out—all of these contribute to the cheating culture in many of today's schools.

The digital age has also contributed to the cheating epidemic in academics. Graphing calculators store formulas, MP3 players store notes, camera phones send pictures of tests, the Internet makes it easy to buy term-papers or plagiarize material for papers.

Discuss:
1. How prevalent is cheating at your school? Among your friends?
2. What policies does your school have on cheating? Are they enforceable? Are they enforced?
3. Do parents and others value honesty? Or do they transmit the message that people have to do what they have to do in order to succeed?
4. Do teachers have a way to make students accountable for using materials downloaded from the Internet?
5. Would an honor code work at your school? Why or why not?

REVIEW AND REFLECTION

1. What is required by the Eighth Commandment?
2. Why should Christians be persons of truth?
3. Define these terms: *perjury, false witness, detraction,* and *calumny.* How do they violate the Eighth Commandment?
4. When are flattery or adulation or complaisance wrong? What does each of these terms mean?
5. Define the term *lying.* Give some examples.
6. Do you always have to tell everybody everything you know? Why or why not?
7. What is the "sacramental seal of the confessional"?
8. What are some duties of governmental officials when it comes to helping to create an honest society?
9. Write of a time when you told the truth and were proud of doing so.

Catholic Life in Action

1. Recall the corporal works of mercy studied in Chapter 8. Review them now and study the list of the spiritual works of mercy listed here. As a class, brainstorm a concrete and realistic way today's teens could put each of these into effect. For example, "feed the hungry" might suggest sponsoring a canned food drive for distribution to a hunger center. Or "comfort the afflicted" might suggest spending time with a classmate whose grandparent recently died. As a final class or individual project at the end of this course on morality, resolve to put one of your ideas into action.

   Spiritual Works of Mercy
   1. Counsel the doubtful.
   2. Instruct the ignorant.
   3. Admonish sinners.
   4. Comfort the afflicted.
   5. Forgive offenses.
   6. Bear wrongs patiently.
   7. Pray for the living and the dead.

2. Check out the Cheating Culture website and report on an article on cheating currently in the news: www.cheatingculture.com.
3. Obtain a copy of the Pontifical Council for Justice and Peace's, *Compendium of the Social Doctrine of the Church,* Libreria Editrice Vaticana (Washington, D.C.: United States Conference of Catholic Bishops, 2005). Do one of the following:
   a. Read Chapter 6 on "Human Work."
      • Write a paragraph on the dignity of human work. Cite the appropriate paragraphs to back up your observations.
      • List and briefly discuss some important rights of workers.
   b. Read Chapter 10 on "Safeguarding the Environment." List ten principles of how humans should be good stewards of God's earth. Cite the relevant paragraphs of where you got the principles.
4. View and take notes on a PowerPoint presentation of an "Overview of Catholic Social Teaching." You can access this presentation at the Office of Social Justice of the Diocese of St. Paul and Minneapolis link for Catholic Educators: www.osjsprm.org/teachers_tool box.aspx.
5. Visit the Social Agenda website: www.thesocialagen da.com. It contains "the central statements of the Roman Pontiffs from a range of texts, including papal encyclicals, apostolic letters, and Conciliar documents, on matters relating to politics, economics, and culture." Using the quotes given, prepare a one-page report on one of the following themes of Catholic social justice:
   a. Solidarity
   b. Subsidiarity
   c. Participation
   d. The common good
   e. Charity and the preferential option for the poor

Summary Points

◆ The Seventh, Eighth, and Tenth Commandments are all related to the cardinal virtue of justice.

◆ The Seventh Commandment requires us to respect the goods of others and respect God's good earth by exercising the virtues of justice and love.

◆ The Tenth Commandment uproots from our heart covetousness, which is at the root of theft, robbery, and fraud.

◆ The Eighth Commandment requires us to be just toward our neighbor in the area of truth.

◆ The cardinal and moral virtue of justice requires us to render to God and our neighbors what is due them by right. *Commutative justice* regulates relationships of exchange. *Distributive justice* is the justice of sharing, seeing to the fair distribution of the goods of creation that God intends for us all to use and share. *Legal justice* governs what individuals owe society as a whole. *Social justice* applies the Gospel message of Jesus Christ to the structures, systems, and laws of society in order to protect the dignity of persons and guarantee the rights of individuals.

◆ Four important themes of Catholic social justice teaching are: (1) profit cannot be the only norm and sole goal of economic activity; (2) the economy exists to serve people; people do not exist to serve the economy; (3) richer nations must work hard for international solidarity; (4) we must imitate Jesus by having a special love for the poor.

◆ *Solidarity* is the virtue of social charity or friendship that requires us to share our material wealth as well as our spiritual goods with others.

◆ Politicians have the chief responsibility to order society and the state in a just way. The state must grant freedom of religion and recognize the unique contribution of the Church to add its faith-based insights on the dignity of humans to the discourse about what makes up a just society.

◆ No matter how just a society is, there will always be the need to practice charity because human beings always needs love. There are always suffering, lonely, and poor people who need to benefit from charity.

◆ The Seventh Commandment outlaws any kind of theft, that is, taking someone else's property against his or her will. It requires us to make reparation for anything stolen.

◆ The Seventh Commandment requires us to adhere to the principle of the "universal destination of goods," that is, to recognize that God gave the use of creation to *all* people.

◆ The Seventh Commandment outlaws anything that leads to enslaving people, to their being bought, sold, or exchanged as merchandise. People have dignity and are persons made in God's image, not objects to be treated as things.

◆ The Tenth Commandment outlaws *greed*, the desire to accumulate unlimited goods; *avarice*, which is the passionate desire for riches and the power that comes from them; and *envy*, sadness over another person's possessions and the inordinate desire to get them for oneself, even using unjust means.

◆ Jesus requires "poverty of spirit," detachment from earthly riches that pass away. We gain this type of poverty by seeking God's Kingdom and righteousness above all.

◆ The Eighth Commandment enjoins us to be persons of truth, to reflect God, who is Truth, to walk in the way of Jesus, who is the way, the truth, and the life.

◆ The Eighth Commandment outlaws perjury (lying under oath), rash judgment, detraction, calumny, encouraging others to do evil, boasting and bragging, the use of irony that mocks others, and lying.

- Lying is speaking a falsehood with the intention to deceive. The moral evaluation of the seriousness of a lie includes the nature of the truth distorted, the circumstances, the intentions of the liar, and the harm suffered by the victims of the lie.

- The communications media have a serious obligation, for the sake of the common good, to communicate information honestly. The Golden Rule would be a superb standard for those in the media to follow.

- Government officials have a serious obligation to defend and safeguard the just and free flow of information, to enact laws that protect citizens' rights to a good name and to privacy, and to protect public morality from pornography, propaganda, and the like.

PRAYER REFLECTION

"Shine Through Me"[8]

Dear Jesus, help me to spread Your Fragrance everywhere I go.
Penetrate and possess my whole being so utterly
that all my life may only be a radiance of Yours.
Shine through me and be so in me,
that every soul I come in contact with
may feel Your Presence in my soul:
let them look up and see no longer me—but only Jesus.

—St. John Neuman

Where would you like the road of your life to eventually lead?

List five things you have to do right now to get on the road that will lead you to eternal happiness. Pick one of these things and resolve to put it into concrete action in the next week. Continue thereafter with the other four things.

NOTES

1. Pontifical Council for Justice and Peace, *Compendium of the Social Doctrine of the Church*, Libreria Editrice Vaticana (Washington, D.C.: United States Conference of Catholic Bishops, 2005), No. 63, 28.
2. Ibid. No. 172, 75.
3. Encyclical Letter *Deus Caritas Est* of the Supreme Pontiff Benedict XVI to the Bishops, Priests, and Deacons, Men and Women Religious, and All the Lay Faithful on Christian Love (Liberia Editrice Vaticana, 2005), No. 28 <www.vatican.va/holy_father/benedict_xvi/encyclicals/documents/hf_ben-xvi_enc_20051225_deus-caritas-est_en.html> (24 April 2006).
4. Adapted from "Baby Jesus' Ride in the Red Wagon" in *3 Minutes a Day*, vol. 33 (New York: The Christophers, 1998), December 26.
5. Adapted from "Teen Advice: What You Oughta Know About . . . Lies/Lying" <http://teenadvice.about.com/library/bl10thingslies.htm> (24 April 2006).
6. Surveys cited by Gay Jervy, "Cheating—'But Everybody's Doing It,'" *Reader's Digest*, March 2006, 124.
7. Ibid. 124–125.
8. Catholic Online, "Shine Through Me," <www.catholic.org/prayers/prayer.php?p=145> (12 March 2006).

CATHOLIC HANDBOOK
—For Faith

A. Beliefs

APOSTLES' CREED

I believe in God, the Father almighty,
Creator of heaven and earth.

I believe in Jesus Christ, his only son, our Lord.
He was conceived by the power of the Holy Spirit,
and born of the Virgin Mary.
He suffered under Pontius Pilate,
was crucified, died, and was buried.
He descended into hell.
On the third day he rose again.
He ascended into heaven,
and is seated at the right hand of the Father.
He will come again to judge the living and the dead.

I believe in the Holy Spirit,
the holy catholic Church,
the communion of saints,
the forgiveness of sins,
the resurrection of the body,
and the life everlasting. Amen.

NICENE CREED

We believe in one God,
    the Father, the Almighty,
    maker of heaven and earth,
    of all that is seen and unseen.
We believe in one Lord, Jesus Christ,
    the only Son of God,
    eternally begotten of the Father,
    God from God, Light from Light,
    true God from true God,
    begotten, not made, one in Being with the
        Father.
    Through him all things were made.
    For us men and for our salvation
        he came down from heaven:
by the power of the Holy Spirit
    he was born of the Virgin Mary, and became
        man.
For our sake he was crucified under Pontius
        Pilate;

he suffered, died, and was buried.
On the third day he rose again in fulfillment
    of the Scriptures;
he ascended into heaven and is seated at
    the right hand of the Father.
He will come again in glory to judge the
        living and the dead,
    and his kingdom will have no end.
We believe in the Holy Spirit, the Lord, the giver of
        life,
    who proceeds from the Father and the Son.
    With the Father and the Son he is worshiped
        and glorified.
He has spoken through the Prophets.
We believe in one holy catholic and apostolic
        Church.
We acknowledge one baptism for the forgiveness of
        sins.
We look for the resurrection of the dead,
    and the life of the world to come. Amen.

GIFTS OF THE HOLY SPIRIT

1. Wisdom	5. Knowledge
2. Understanding	6. Piety
3. Counsel	7. Fear of the Lord
4. Fortitude	

FRUITS OF THE HOLY SPIRIT

1. Charity	7. Generosity
2. Joy	8. Gentleness
3. Peace	9. Faithfulness
4. Patience	10. Modesty
5. Kindness	11. Self-control
6. Goodness	12. Chastity

THE SYMBOL OF CHALCEDON

Following therefore the holy Fathers, we unanimously teach to confess one and the same Son, our

Lord Jesus Christ, the same perfect in divinity and perfect in humanity, the same truly God and truly man composed of rational soul and body, the same one in being *(homoousios)* with the Father as to the divinity and one in being with us as to the humanity, like unto us in all things but sin (cf. Heb 4:15). The same was begotten from the Father before the ages as to the divinity and in the later days for us and our salvation was born as to his humanity from Mary the Virgin Mother of God.

We confess that one and the same Lord Jesus Christ, the only-begotten Son, must be acknowledged in two natures, without confusion or change, without division or separation. The distinction between the natures was never abolished by their union but rather the character proper to each of the two natures was preserved as they came together in one person *(prosôpon)* and one hypostasis. He is not split or divided into two persons, but he is one and the same only-begotten, God the Word, the Lord Jesus Christ, as formerly the prophets and later Jesus Christ himself have taught us about him and as has been handed down to us by the Symbol of the Fathers.

From the General Council of Chalcedon (451)

B. God and Jesus Christ

ATTRIBUTES OF GOD

Saint Thomas Aquinas named nine attributes that tell us some things about God's nature. They are:

1. **God is eternal.** He has no beginning and no end. Or, to put it another way, God always was, always is, and always will be.

2. **God is unique.** God is the designer of a one and only world. Even the people he creates are one of a kind.

3. **God is infinite and omnipotent.** This reminds us of a lesson we learned early in life: God sees everything. There are no limits to God. Omnipotence is a word that refers to God's supreme power and authority over all of creation.

4. **God is omnipresent.** God is not limited to space. He is everywhere. You can never be away from God.

5. **God contains all things.** All of creation is under God's care and jurisdiction.

6. **God is immutable.** God does not evolve. God does not change. God is the same God now as he always was and always will be.

7. **God is pure spirit.** Though God has been described with human attributes, God is not a material creation. God's image cannot be made. God is a pure spirit who cannot be divided into parts. God is simple, but complex.

8. **God is alive.** We believe in a living God, a God who acts in the lives of people. Most concretely, he came to this world in the incarnate form of Jesus Christ.

9. **God is holy.** God is pure goodness. God is pure love.

THE HOLY TRINITY

The Trinity is the mystery of one God in three persons—Father, Son, and Holy Spirit. The mystery is impossible for human minds to understand. Some of the Church dogmas, or beliefs, can help:

★ **The Trinity is One.** There are not three Gods, but one God in three persons. Each one of them—Father, Son, and Holy Spirit—is God whole and entire.

★ **The three persons are distinct from one another.** For example, the Father is not the Son, nor is the Son the Holy Spirit. Rather, the Father is Creator, the Son is begotten of the Father, and the Holy Spirit proceeds from the Father and Son.

★ **The divine persons are related to one another.** Though they are related to one another, the three persons have one nature or substance.

St. John Damascus used two analogies to describe the doctrine of the Blessed Trinity.

Think of the Father as a root,
of the Son as a branch,
and of the Spirit as a fruit,
for the substance of these is one.

The Father is a sun
with the Son as rays
and the Holy Spirit as heat.

Read the *Catechism of the Catholic Church* (232–260) on the Holy Trinity.

FAITH IN ONE GOD

There are several implications for those who love God and believe in him with their entire heart and soul (see CCC 222–227):

★ It means knowing God's greatness and majesty.

★ It means living in thanksgiving.

★ It means knowing the unity and dignity of all people.

★ It means making good use of created things.

★ It means trusting God in every circumstance.

FAMOUS QUOTATIONS ABOUT JESUS CHRIST

Meekness was the method Jesus used with the Apostles. He put up with their ignorance and roughness and even their infidelity. He treated sinners with a kindness and affection that caused some to be shocked, others to be scandalized, and still others to gain hope in God's mercy. Thus he bade us to be gentle and humble of heart.

St. John Bosco

Christ with me, Christ before me
Christ behind me, Christ in me,
Christ beneath me, Christ above me,
Christ on my right, Christ on my left,
Christ where I lie, Christ where I sit,
Christ where I arise,
Christ in the heart of everyone who thinks of
    me,
Christ in the mouth of everyone who speaks of
    me,
Christ in every eye that sees me,
Christ in every ear that hears me,
Salvation is of the Lord,
Salvation is of Christ,
May your salvation, Lord, be ever
    with us.

from the breastplate of St. Patrick

Oh, if all were to know how beautiful Jesus is, how amiable he is! They would all die of love.

St. Gemma Galgani

About Jesus Christ and the Church, I simply know they're just one thing, and we should not complicate the matter.

St. Joan of Arc

Our Lord does not come down from heaven every day to lie in a golden ciborium. He comes to find another heaven which is infinitely dearer to him—the heaven of our souls.

St. Thérèse of Lisieux

JUDAISM'S BELIEF IN ONE GOD

Like Catholics, Jews are monotheistic, that is, they believe in one God. Jews believe that God reveals himself in the Torah, through the prophets, in the life of the Jewish people, and through the history of the Jews. The key event of Jewish history is the Exodus, when God freed the Jewish nation from slavery in Egypt. This pivotal event is recounted every year during the seven-day festival known as Passover, celebrated around the time of Easter.

Jews believe that the covenant God established with Abraham and the Sinai covenant require Israel to adore and serve God always, and to observe his Law. In turn, they believe God will remain faithful to them and treat the members of the Jewish nation as special.

Jews believe that God is eternal, almighty, all-knowing, present everywhere, and loving of his creation. In prayer, God is addressed as *Adonai* (Lord). Jews use God's name respectfully and avoid saying the name revealed to Moses—Yahweh—because it is so holy. Jewish faith is summed up in a prayer pious Jews recite every day, the *Shema*:

Hear, O Israel! The LORD is our God, the LORD alone! Therefore, you shall love the LORD, your God, with all your heart, and with all your soul, and with all your strength. (Dt 6:4–5)

Jews differ on how God will fulfill his covenant with them, how God's Kingdom will be established, and on the nature of the final judgment. For example, some Jews believe the concept of a Messiah refers to an individual person; others think of it in terms of the community of God's people or the development of historical events; still others believe God himself will intervene directly into human history.

The Catholic Church encourages utmost respect for the Jewish faith. For example, at the Second Vatican Council, Church fathers wrote:

This sacred Synod . . . recalls the spiritual bond linking the people of the New Covenant with Abraham's stock. . . .

The Church, therefore, cannot forget that she received the revelation of the Old Testament through the people whom God in his inexpressible mercy deigned to establish the Ancient Covenant. . . .

The Church recalls too that from the Jewish people sprang the apostles, her foundation stones and pillars, as well as most of the early disciples who proclaimed Christ to the world. . . .

The Jews still remain most dear to God because of their fathers, for He does not repent of the gifts He makes nor of the calls He issues. (*Declaration on the Relationship of the Church to Non-Christian Religions,* No. 4)

C. Scripture and Tradition

CANON OF THE BIBLE

There are seventy-three books in the canon of the Bible, that is, the official list of books the Church accepts as divinely inspired writings: forty-six Old Testament books and twenty-seven New Testament books. Protestant Bibles do not include seven Old Testament books on its list (1 and 2 Maccabees, Judith, Tobit, Baruch, Sirach, and the Wisdom of Solomon). Why the difference? Catholics rely on the version of the Bible that the earliest Christians used, the *Septuagint.* This was the first Greek translation of the Hebrew Scriptures, begun in the third century BC. Protestants, on the other hand, rely on an official list of Hebrew Scriptures compiled in the Holy Land by Jewish scholars at the end of the first century AD.

Today, most Protestant Bibles print the disputed books in a separate section at the back of the Bible called the *Apocrypha*.

The twenty-seven books of the New Testament are divided into three categories: the gospels, the letters written to local Christian communities or individuals, and the letters intended for the entire Church. The heart of the New Testament, in fact all of Scripture, is the gospels. The New Testament is central to our knowledge of Jesus Christ. He is the focus of all Scripture.

There are forty-six books in the Old Testament canon. The Old Testament is the foundation for God's self-revelation in Christ. Christians honor the Old Testament as God's word. It contains the writings of prophets and other inspired authors who recorded God's teaching to the Chosen People and his interaction in their history. For example, the Old Testament recounts how God delivered the Jews from Egypt (the Exodus), led them to the Promised Land, formed them into a nation under his care, and taught them in knowledge and worship.

The stories, prayers, sacred histories, and other writings of the Old Testament reveal what God is like and tell much about human nature, too. In brief, the Chosen People sinned repeatedly by turning their backs on their loving God; they were weak and easily tempted away from God. Yahweh, on the other hand, *always* remained faithful. He promised to send a Messiah to humanity.

Listed below are the categories and books of the Old Testament and the New Testament:

THE OLD TESTAMENT

The Pentateuch

Genesis	Gn
Exodus	Ex
Leviticus	Lv
Numbers	Nm
Deuteronomy	Dt

The Historical Books

Joshua	Jos
Judges	Jgs
Ruth	Ru
1 Samuel	1 Sm
2 Samuel	2 Sm
1 Kings	1 Kgs
2 Kings	2 Kgs
1 Chronicles	1 Chr
2 Chronicles	2 Chr
Ezra	Ezr
Nehemiah	Neh
Tobit	Tb
Judith	Jdt
Esther	Est
1 Maccabees	1 Mc
2 Maccabees	2 Mc

The Wisdom Books

Job	Jb
Psalms	Ps(s)
Proverbs	Prv
Ecclesiastes	Eccl
Song of Songs	Sg
Wisdom	Wis
Sirach	Sir

The Prophetic Books

Isaiah	Is
Jeremiah	Jer
Lamentations	Lam
Baruch	Bar
Ezekiel	Ez
Daniel	Dn
Hosea	Hos
Joel	Jl
Amos	Am
Obadiah	Ob
Jonah	Jon
Micah	Mi
Nahum	Na
Habakkuk	Hb
Zephaniah	Zep
Haggai	Hg
Zechariah	Zec
Malachi	Mal

THE NEW TESTAMENT

The Gospels

Matthew	Mt
Mark	Mk
Luke	Lk
John	Jn
Acts of the Apostles	Acts

The New Testament Letters

Romans	Rom
1 Corinthians	1 Cor
2 Corinthians	2 Cor
Galatians	Gal
Ephesians	Eph
Philippians	Phil
Colossians	Col
1 Thessalonians	1 Thes
2 Thessalonians	2 Thes
1 Timothy	1 Tm
2 Timothy	2 Tm
Titus	Ti
Philemon	Phlm
Hebrews	Heb

The Catholic Letters

James	Jas
1 Peter	1 Pt
2 Peter	2 Pt
1 John	1 Jn
2 John	2 Jn
3 John	3 Jn
Jude	Jude
Revelation	Rv

HOW TO LOCATE A SCRIPTURE PASSAGE

Example: 2 Tm 3:16–17

1. ***Determine the name of the book.***

   The abbreviation "2 Tm" stands for the second book of Timothy.

2. ***Determine whether the book is in the Old Testament or New Testament.***

   The second book of Timothy is one of the Catholic letters in the New Testament.

3. ***Locate the chapter where the passage occurs.***

   The first number before the colon—"3"—indicates the chapter. Chapters in the Bible are set off by the larger numbers that divide a book.

4. ***Locate the verses of the passage.***

   The numbers after the colon indicate the verses referred to—in this case, verses 16 and 17 of chapter 3.

5. ***Read the passage.***

   For example: "All Scripture is inspired by God and is useful for teaching, for refutation, for correction, and for training in righteousness, so that one who belongs to God may be competent, equipped for every good work."

Timeline On Church History

ca. 50
The Council of Jerusalem
(Gentiles can be admitted to the Church)

ca. 64 or 67
Peter and Paul
are martyred
in Rome

ca. 70
The Jewish Temple
in Jerusalem
is destroyed

381
First Council of Constantinople
(Nicene Creed expanded;
divine nature of Holy Spirit defined)

ca. 30–33 AD
Pentecost

311
Emperor Constantine
ends persecution of
Christians

ca. 6–4 BC
Jesus is born

ca. 100
Death of St. John the Evangelist;
apostolic era ends

313
Edict of Milan
(political act of tolerating Christians)

ca. 64
Persecutions of
Christians begin under
Roman emperor Nero

325
Council of Nicea
(Arian heresy refuted;
divinity of Christ defended; Nicene Creed composed)

1545
Council of Trent begins (lasts until 1563),
which advances the Catholic Reformation

1054
Final schism between the Eastern
and Western churches occurs, which remains today

1533
King Henry VIII is excommunicated,
leading to the start of the Anglican Church

1517
Martin Luther posts ninety-five theses
beginning the Protestant Reformation

1170
St. Thomas Becket murdered
in Canterbury Cathedral

1215
St. Dominic founds
Dominican order
of preachers

1431
St. Joan of Arc
is executed

1209
St. Francis of Assisi founds
Franciscan order

1378
The Great Schism in the Church
begins (lasts until 1417), with the
pope residing in France and two
or three men claiming to be pope

1073
Pope St. Gregory VII
begins Church
reforms

1095
Pope Urban III calls first Crusade
to free Holy Land from Muslims

1540
St. Ignatius of Loyola founds Society of Jesus (Jesuits)
to assist in reform of the Church

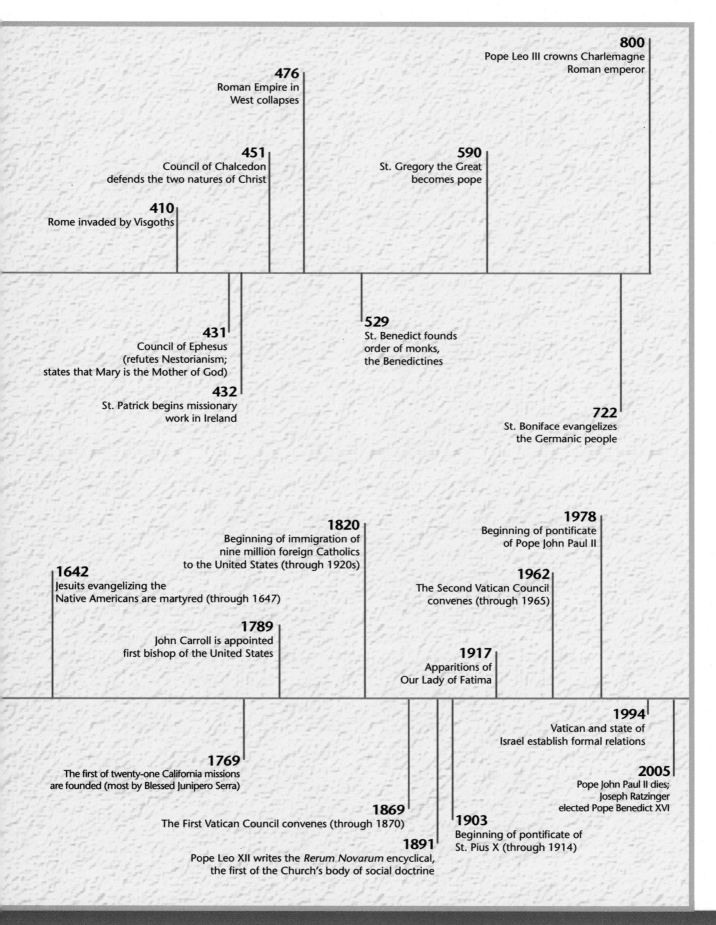

800
Pope Leo III crowns Charlemagne
Roman emperor

476
Roman Empire in
West collapses

451
Council of Chalcedon
defends the two natures of Christ

590
St. Gregory the Great
becomes pope

410
Rome invaded by Visgoths

431
Council of Ephesus
(refutes Nestorianism;
states that Mary is the Mother of God)

529
St. Benedict founds
order of monks,
the Benedictines

432
St. Patrick begins missionary
work in Ireland

722
St. Boniface evangelizes
the Germanic people

1820
Beginning of immigration of
nine million foreign Catholics
to the United States (through 1920s)

1978
Beginning of pontificate
of Pope John Paul II

1642
Jesuits evangelizing the
Native Americans are martyred (through 1647)

1962
The Second Vatican Council
convenes (through 1965)

1789
John Carroll is appointed
first bishop of the United States

1917
Apparitions of
Our Lady of Fatima

1994
Vatican and state of
Israel establish formal relations

1769
The first of twenty-one California missions
are founded (most by Blessed Junipero Serra)

2005
Pope John Paul II dies;
Joseph Ratzinger
elected Pope Benedict XVI

1869
The First Vatican Council convenes (through 1870)

1903
Beginning of pontificate of
St. Pius X (through 1914)

1891
Pope Leo XII writes the *Rerum Novarum* encyclical,
the first of the Church's body of social doctrine

D. Church

MARKS OF THE CHURCH

1. ***The Church is one.*** The Church remains one because of its source: the unity in the Trinity of the Father, Son, and Spirit in one God. The Church's unity can never be broken and lost because this foundation is itself unbreakable.

2. ***The Church is holy.*** The Church is holy because Jesus, the founder of the Church, is holy and he joined the Church to himself as his body and gave the Church the gift of the Holy Spirit. Together, Christ and the Church make up the "whole Christ" (*Christus totus* in Latin).

3. ***The Church is catholic.*** The Church is catholic ("universal" or "for everyone") in two ways. First, it is catholic because Christ is present in the Church in the fullness of his body, with the fullness of the means of salvation, the fullness of faith, sacraments, and the ordained ministry that comes from the Apostles. The Church is also catholic because it takes its message of salvation to all people.

4. ***The Church is apostolic.*** The Church's apostolic mission comes from Jesus: "Go, therefore, and make disciples of all nations" (Mt 28:19). The Church remains apostolic because it still teaches the same things the apostles taught. Also, the Church is led by leaders who are successors to the apostles and who help to guide us until Jesus returns.

THE POPE

The bishop of Rome has carried the title "pope" since the ninth century. Pope means "papa" or "father." Saint Peter was the first bishop of Rome and, hence, the first pope. He was commissioned directly by Jesus:

> And so I say to you, you are Peter, and upon this rock I will build my church, and the gates of the netherworld shall not prevail against it. I will give you the keys to the kingdom of heaven. Whatever you bind on earth shall be bound in heaven; and whatever you loose on earth shall be loosed in heaven. (Mt 16:18–19)

Because Peter was the first bishop of Rome, the succeeding bishops of Rome have had primacy in the Church. The entire succession of popes since Saint Peter can be traced directly to the apostle.

The pope is in communion with the bishops of the world as part of the Magisterium, which is the Church's teaching authority. The pope can also define doctrine in faith or morals for the Church. When he does so, he is infallible and cannot be in error.

The pope is elected by the College of Cardinals by a two-thirds majority vote in secret balloting. Cardinals under the age of eighty are eligible to vote. If the necessary majority is not achieved, the ballots are burned in a small stove inside the council chambers along with straw that makes dark smoke. The sign of dark smoke announces to the crowds waiting outside Saint Peter's Basilica that a new pope has not been chosen. When a new pope has been voted in with the necessary majority, the ballots are burned without the straw, producing white smoke, signifying the election of a pope.

RECENT POPES

Since 1900 and through the pontificate of Pope Benedict XVI, there were ten Popes. Pope John Paul II was the first non-Italian pope since Dutchman Pope Adrian VI (1522–1523). The popes since the twentieth century through Pope Benedict XVI with their original names, place of origin, and years as pope are as follows:

- ★ Pope Leo XIII (Giocchino Pecci): Carpineto, Italy, February 20, 1878–July 20, 1903.
- ★ Pope Saint Pius X (Giuseppe Sarto): Riese, Italy, August 4, 1903–August 20, 1914.
- ★ Pope Benedict XV (Giacomo della Chiesa): Genoa, Italy, September 3, 1914–January 22, 1922.
- ★ Pope Pius XI (Achille Ratti): Desio, Italy, February 6, 1922–February 10, 1939.
- ★ Pope Pius XII (Eugenio Pacelli): Rome, Italy, March 2, 1939–October 9, 1958.
- ★ Pope John XXIII (Angelo Giuseppe Roncalli): Sotto il Monte, Italy, October 28, 1958–June 3, 1963.
- ★ Pope Paul VI (Giovanni Battista Montini): Concessio, Italy, June 21, 1963–August 6, 1978.
- ★ Pope John Paul I (Albino Luciani): Forno di Canale, Italy, August 26, 1978–September 28, 1978.

either Latin Fathers (West) or Greek Fathers (East). Among the greatest Fathers of the Church are:

Latin Fathers	Greek Fathers
St. Ambrose	St. John Chrysostom
St. Augustine	St. Basil the Great
St. Jerome	St. Gregory of Nazianzen
St. Gregory the Great	St. Athanasius

DOCTORS OF THE CHURCH

The Doctors of the Church are men and women honored by the Church for their writings, preaching, and holiness. Originally the Doctors of the Church were considered to be Church Fathers Augustine, Ambrose, Jerome, and Gregory the Great, but others were added over the centuries. Saint Teresa of Avila was the first woman Doctor (1970). Saint Catherine of Siena was named a Doctor of the Church the same year. The list of Doctors of the Church:

★ Pope John Paul II (Karol Wojtyla): Wadowice, Poland, October 16, 1978–April 2, 2005.
★ Pope Benedict XVI (Joseph Ratzinger): Marktl am Inn, Germany, April 19, 2005–present.

FATHERS OF THE CHURCH

Church Fathers, or Fathers of the Church, is a traditional title that was given to theologians of the first eight centuries whose teachings made a lasting mark on the Church. The Church Fathers developed a significant amount of doctrine that has great authority in the Church. The Church Fathers are named as

Name	Life Span	Designation
St. Athanasius	296–373	1568 by Pius V
St. Ephraem the Syrian	306–373	1920 by Benedict XV
St. Hilary of Poitiers	315–367	1851 by Pius IX
St. Cyril of Jerusalem	315–386	1882 by Leo XIII
St. Gregory of Nazianzus	325–389	1568 by Pius V
St. Basil the Great	329–379	1568 by Pius V
St. Ambrose	339–397	1295 by Boniface VIII
St. John Chrysostom	347–407	1568 by Pius V
St. Jerome	347–419	1295 by Boniface XIII
St. Augustine	354–430	1295 by Boniface XIII
St. Cyril of Alexandria	376–444	1882 by Leo XIII
St. Peter Chrysologous	400–450	1729 by Benedict XIII
St. Leo the Great	400–461	1754 by Benedict XIV
St. Gregory the Great	540–604	1295 by Boniface XIII
St. Isidore of Seville	560–636	1722 by Innocent XIII
St. John of Damascus	645–749	1890 by Leo XIII
St. Bede the Venerable	672–735	1899 by Leo XIII
St. Peter Damian	1007–1072	1828 by Leo XII
St. Anselm	1033–1109	1720 by Clement XI
St. Bernard of Clairvaux	1090–1153	1830 by Pius VIII
St. Anthony of Padua	1195–1231	1946 by Pius XII
St. Albert the Great	1206–1280	1931 by Pius XI
St. Bonaventure	1221–1274	1588 by Sixtus V
St. Thomas Aquinas	1226–1274	1567 by Pius V
St. Catherine of Siena	1347–1380	1970 by Paul VI
St. Teresa of Avila	1515–1582	1970 by Paul VI
St. Peter Canisius	1521–1597	1925 by Pius XI
St. John of the Cross	1542–1591	1926 by Pius XI
St. Robert Bellarmine	1542–1621	1931 by Pius XI
St. Lawrence of Brindisi	1559–1619	1959 by John XXIII
St. Francis de Sales	1567–1622	1871 by Pius IX
St. Alphonsus Ligouri	1696–1787	1871 by Pius IX
St. Thérèse of Lisieux	1873–1897	1997 by John Paul II

The Apostles and Their Emblems

 SAINT ANDREW
Tradition holds that Andrew was crucified on a bent cross, called a *saltire*.

 SAINT BARTHOLOMEW
Bartholomew was flayed alive before being crucified. He was then beheaded.

 SAINT JAMES THE GREATER
James the Greater, the brother of John, was beheaded by Herod Agrippa. It is the only death of an apostle mentioned in Scripture (Acts 12:2). The shell indicates James's missionary work by sea in Spain. The sword is of martyrdom.

 SAINT JAMES THE LESS
James the Less is traditionally known as the first bishop of Jerusalem. The saw for his emblem is connected with the tradition of his body being sawed into pieces after he was pushed from the pinnacle of the Temple.

 SAINT JOHN THE EVANGELIST
John was the first bishop of Ephesus. He is the only apostle believed to have died a natural death, in spite of many attempts to murder him by his enemies. One attempt included his miraculous survival of drinking a poisoned drink.

 SAINT JUDE
Some traditions have Jude and Saint Peter martyred together. It is thought that he traveled throughout the Roman Empire with Peter.

 SAINT MATTHEW
Matthew's shield depicts three purses, reflecting his original occupation as tax collector.

 SAINT MATTHIAS
Matthias was the apostle chosen by lot to replace Judas. Tradition holds that Matthias was stoned to death and then beheaded with an ax.

 SAINT PETER
Simon Peter was the brother of Andrew. The first bishop of Rome, Peter was crucified under Nero, asking to be hung upside down because he felt unworthy to die as Jesus did. The keys represent Jesus' giving Peter the keys to the kingdom of heaven.

 SAINT PHILIP
Philip may have been bound to a cross and stoned to death. The two loaves of bread at the side of the cross refer to Philip's comment to Jesus about the possibility of feeding the multitudes of people (Jn 6:7).

 SAINT SIMON
The book with fish depicts Simon as a "fisher of men" who preached the gospel. He was also known as Simon the Zealot.

 SAINT THOMAS
Thomas is thought to have been a missionary in India, where he is thought to have built a church. Hence, the carpenter's square. He may have died by arrows and stones. It is thought that he then had a lance run through his body.

Ecumenical Councils

An ecumenical council is a worldwide assembly of bishops under direction of the pope. There have been twenty-one ecumenical councils, the most recent being the Second Vatican Council (1962–1965). A complete list of the Church's ecumenical councils with the years each met:

Nicaea I	325
Constantinople I	381
Ephesus	431
Chalcedon	451
Constantinople II	553
Constantinople III	680
Nicaea II	787
Constantiople IV	869–870
Lateran I	1123
Lateran II	1139
Lateran III	1179
Lateran IV	1215
Lyons I	1245
Lyons II	1274
Vienne	1311–1312
Constance	1414–1418
Florence	1431–1445
Lateran V	1512–1517
Trent	1545–1563
Vatican Council I	1869–1870
Vatican Council II	1962–1965

E. Morality

The Ten Commandments

The Ten Commandments are a main source for Christian morality. The Ten Commandments were revealed by God to Moses. Jesus himself acknowledged them. He told the rich young man, "If you wish to enter into the life, keep the commandments" (Mt 19:17). Since the time of Saint Augustine (fourth century AD), the Ten Commandments have been used as a source for teaching baptismal candidates.

I.	I, the Lord am your God: you shall not have other gods besides me.
II.	You shall not take the name of the Lord, your God, in vain.
III.	Remember to keep holy the Sabbath day.
IV.	Honor your father and your mother.
V.	You shall not kill.
VI.	You shall not commit adultery.
VII.	You shall not steal.
VIII.	You shall not bear false witness against your neighbor.
IX.	You shall not covet your neighbor's wife.
X.	You shall not covet your neighbor's goods.

The Beatitudes

The word *beatitude* means "happiness." Jesus preached the Beatitudes in his Sermon on the Mount. They are:

Blessed are the poor in spirit, for theirs is the kingdom of God.

Blessed are they who mourn, for they will be comforted.

Blessed are the meek, for they will inherit the land.

Blessed are they who hunger and thirst for righteousness, for they will be satisfied.

Blessed are the merciful, for they will be shown mercy.

Blessed are the clean of heart, for they will see God.

Blessed are the peacemakers, for they will be called children of God.

Blessed are they who are persecuted for the sake of righteousness, for theirs is the kingdom of heaven.

Cardinal Virtues

Virtues—habits that help in leading a moral life—that are acquired by human effort are known as moral or human virtues. Four of these are called the cardinal virtues because they form the hinge that connects all the others. They are:

★ Prudence   ★ Fortitude

★ Justice   ★ Temperance

THEOLOGICAL VIRTUES

The theological virtues are the foundation for moral life. They are related directly to God.

- ★ Faith
- ★ Hope
- ★ Love

CORPORAL (BODILY) WORKS OF MERCY

- ★ Feed the hungry.
- ★ Give drink to the thirsty.
- ★ Clothe the naked.
- ★ Visit the imprisoned.
- ★ Shelter the homeless.
- ★ Visit the sick.
- ★ Bury the dead.

SPIRITUAL WORKS OF MERCY

- ★ Counsel the doubtful.
- ★ Instruct the ignorant.
- ★ Admonish sinners.
- ★ Comfort the afflicted.
- ★ Forgive offenses.
- ★ Bear wrongs patiently.
- ★ Pray for the living and the dead.

PRECEPTS OF THE CHURCH

1. You shall attend Mass on Sundays and on holy days of obligation and rest from servile labor.
2. You shall confess your sins once a year.
3. You shall receive the Sacrament of Eucharist at least during the Easter season.
4. You shall observe the days of fasting and abstinence established by the Church.
5. You shall help to provide for the needs of the Church.

CATHOLIC SOCIAL TEACHING: MAJOR THEMES

The 1998 document *Sharing Catholic Social Teaching: Challenges and Directions—Reflections of the U.S. Catholic Bishops* highlighted seven principles of the Church's social teaching. They are:

1. Life and dignity of the human person
2. Call to family, community, and participation
3. Rights and responsibilities
4. Option for the poor and vulnerable
5. The dignity of work and the rights of workers
6. Solidarity
7. Care for God's creation

SIN

Sin is an offense against God.

Mortal sin is the most serious kind of sin. Mortal sin destroys or kills a person's relationship with God. To be a mortal sin, three conditions must exist:

- ★ The moral object must be of grave or serious matter. Grave matter is specified in the Ten Commandments (e.g., do not kill, do not commit adultery, do not steal, etc.).
- ★ The person must have full knowledge of the gravity of the sinful action.
- ★ The person must completely consent to the action. It must be a personal choice.

Venial sin is less serious sin. Examples of venial sins are petty jealousy, disobedience, and "borrowing" a small amount of money from a parent without the intention of repaying it. Venial sins, when unrepented, can lead a person to commit mortal sins.

Vices are bad habits linked to sins. The seven capital vices are pride, avarice, envy, wrath, lust, gluttony, and sloth.

F. Liturgy & Sacraments

CHURCH YEAR

The cycle of seasons and feasts that Catholics celebrate is called the Church Year or Liturgical Year. The Church Year is divided into six main parts: Advent, Christmas, Lent, Triduum, Easter, and Ordinary Time.

HOLY DAYS OF OBLIGATION IN THE UNITED STATES

★ Immaculate Conception of Mary
   December 8

★ Christmas
   December 25

★ Solemnity of Mary, Mother of God
   January 1

★ Ascension of the Lord
   Forty days after Easter

★ Assumption of Mary
   August 15

★ All Saints Day
   November 1

THE SEVEN SACRAMENTS

1. Baptism
2. Confirmation
3. Eucharist
4. Penance and Reconciliation
5. Anointing of the Sick
6. Holy Orders
7. Matrimony

HOW TO GO TO CONFESSION

1. Spend some time examining your conscience. Consider your actions and attitudes in each area of your life (e.g., faith, family, school/work, social life, relationships). Ask yourself, "Is this area of my life pleasing to God? What needs to be reconciled with God? with others? with myself?"

2. Sincerely tell God that you are sorry for your sins. Ask God for forgiveness and for the grace you will need to change what needs changing in your life. Promise God that you will try to live according to his will for you.

3. Approach the area for confession. Wait an appropriate distance until it is your turn.

4. Make the Sign of the Cross with the priest. He may say: "May God, who has enlightened every heart, help you to know your sins and trust his mercy." You reply: "Amen."

5. Confess your sins to the priest. Simply and directly talk to him about the areas of sinfulness in your life that need God's healing touch.

6. The priest will ask you to pray an act of contrition. Pray an Act of Contrition you have committed to memory. Or, say something in your own words, like: "Dear God, I am sorry for my sins. I ask for your forgiveness and I promise to do better in the future."

7. The priest will talk to you about your life, encourage you to be more faithful to God in the future, and help you decide what to do to make up for your sins—your penance.

8. The priest will then extend his hands over your head and pray the Church's official prayer of absolution:

   God, the Father of mercies, through the death and resurrection of his Son, has reconciled the world to himself and sent the Holy Spirit among us for the forgiveness of sins; through the ministry of the Church may God give you pardon and peace, and I absolve you from your sins in the name of the Father, and of the Son, and of the Holy Spirit.

   You respond: "Amen."

9. The priest will wish you peace. Thank him and leave.

10. Go to a quiet place in the church and pray your prayer of penance. Then spend some time quietly thanking God for the gift of forgiveness.

ORDER OF MASS

There are two main parts of the Mass, the Liturgy of the Word and the Liturgy of the Eucharist. The complete order of Mass:

The Introductory Rites

The Entrance
Greeting of the Altar and of the People Gathered
The Act of Penitence
The Kyrie Eleison
The Gloria
The Collect (Opening Prayer)

The Liturgy of the Word

Silence
The Biblical Readings (the reading of the Gospel is the high point of the Liturgy of the Word)
The Responsorial Psalm
The Homily
The Profession of Faith (Creed)
The Prayer of the Faithful

The Liturgy of the Eucharist

The Preparation of the Gifts
The Prayer over the Offerings
The Eucharistic Prayer
The Communion Rite
The Lord's Prayer
The Rite of Peace
The Fraction (Breaking of the Bread)
Communion
Prayer after Communion

The Concluding Rites

COMMUNION REGULATIONS

To receive Holy Communion properly, a person must be in the state of grace (free from mortal sin), have the right intention (only for the purpose of pleasing God), and observe the Communion fast.

The fast means that a person may not eat anything or drink any liquid (other than water) one hour before the reception of Communion. There are exceptions made to this fast only for the sick and aged.

THREE DEGREES OF THE SACRAMENT OF ORDERS

There are three degrees of the Sacrament of Holy Orders: the ministries of bishop, priest, and deacon.

The bishop receives the fullness of the Sacrament of Orders. He is the successor to the apostles. When he celebrates the sacraments, the bishop is given the grace to act in the person of Christ who is the head of the body of the Church.

Priests are ordained as co-workers of the bishop. They, too, are configured to Christ so that they may act in his person during the Sacraments of Eucharist, Baptism, and the Anointing of the Sick. They may bless marriages in the name of Christ and, under the authority of the bishop, share in Christ's ministry of forgiveness in the Sacrament of Penance and Reconciliation.

Deacons are ordained for service and are configured to Christ the servant. Deacons are ordained to help and serve the priests and bishops in their work. While bishops and priests are configured to Christ to act as the head of Christ's body, deacons are configured to Christ in order to serve as he served. Deacons may baptize, preach the Gospel and homily, and bless marriages.

SACRAMENTALS

"Sacramentals are prayers and sometimes actions or things that resemble the sacraments and signify spiritual effects which are obtained through the intercession of the Church. Sacramentals do not confer grace the way the sacraments do, but by the Church's prayer, they prepare us to receive grace and dispose us to cooperate with it" (*CCC*, 1670). Examples of sacramentals include:

★ *Actions* (blessings; genuflections; the Sign of the Cross; church processions)

★ *Objects* (candles; holy water; statues and icons; blessed ashes; blessed palms; rosaries; relics; incense; vestments; scapulars, church building; religious medals)

★ *Places* (the Holy Land, Rome, Fatima, Lourdes, and other places of pilgrimage; chapels; retreat centers)

★ *Prayers* (short prayers we say throughout the day; grace before meals)

★ *Sacred Time* (holy days; feast days; special days of prayer, fasting, and abstinence)

G. Mary and the Saints

MOTHER OF GOD

Mary, the mother of Jesus, is the closest human to cooperate with her Son's work of redemption. For this reason, the Church holds her in a special place. Of her many titles, the most significant is that she is the Mother of God.

The Church teaches several truths about Mary.

First, she was conceived immaculately. This means from the very first moment of her existence, she was without sin and "full of grace." This belief is called the Immaculate Conception. The feast of the Immaculate Conception is celebrated on December 8.

Second, Mary was ever-virgin. She was a virgin before, in, and after the birth of Jesus. As his mother, she cared for him in infancy and raised him to adulthood with the help of her husband, Joseph. She witnessed Jesus' preaching and ministry, was at the foot of his cross at his crucifixion, and present with the apostles as they awaited the coming of the Holy Spirit at Pentecost.

Third, at the time of her death, Mary was assumed body and soul into heaven. This dogma was proclaimed as a matter of faith by Pope Pius XII in 1950. The feast of the Assumption is celebrated on August 15.

The Church has always been devoted to the Blessed Virgin. This devotion is different from that given to God—Father, Son, and Holy Spirit. Rather, the Church is devoted to Mary as her first disciple, the Queen of all Saints, and her own Mother. Quoting the fathers of the Second Vatican Council:

> In the meantime the Mother of Jesus, in the glory which she possesses in body and soul in heaven, is the image and the beginning of the Church as it is to be perfected in the world to come. Likewise she shines forth on earth, until the day of the Lord shall come, a sign of certain hope and comfort to the pilgrim People of God. (*Lumen Gentium*, 68)

MARIAN FEASTS THROUGHOUT THE YEAR

January 1	Solemnity of Mary, Mother of God
March 25	Annunciation of the Lord
May 31	Visitation
August 15	Assumption
August 22	Queenship of Mary
September 8	Birth of Mary
September 15	Our Lady of Sorrows
October 7	Our Lady of the Rosary
November 21	Presentation of Mary
December 8	Immaculate Conception
December 12	Our Lady of Guadalupe

CANONIZATION OF SAINTS

Saints are those who are in glory with God in heaven. *Canonization* refers to a solemn declaration by the Pope that a person who either died a martyr or who lived an exemplary Christian life is in heaven and may be honored and imitated by all Christians. The canonization process first involves a process of beatification that includes a thorough investigation of the person's life and certification of miracles that can be attributed to the candidate's intercession.

The first official canonization of the universal Church on record was Saint Ulrich of Augsburg by Pope John XV in 993.

Some non-Catholics criticize Catholics for "praying to saints." Catholics *honor* saints for their holy lives, but we do not pray to them as if they were God. We ask the saints to pray with us and for us as part of the Church in glory. We can ask them to do this because we know that their lives have been spent in close communion with God. We also ask the saints for their friendship so that we can follow the example they have left for us.

PATRON SAINTS

A patron is a saint who is designated for places (nations, regions, dioceses) or organizations. Many saints have also become patrons of jobs, professional groups, and intercessors for special needs. Listed below are patron saints for several nations and some special patrons:

Patrons of Places

Americas	Our Lady of Guadalupe, St. Rose of Lima
Argentina	Our Lady of Lujan
Australia	Our Lady Help of Christians
Canada	St. Joseph, St. Anne
China	St. Joseph
England	St. George
Finland	St. Henry
France	Our Lady of the Assumption, St. Joan of Arc, St. Thérèse of Lisieux
Germany	St. Boniface
India	Our Lady of the Assumption
Ireland	St. Patrick, St. Brigid, St. Columba
Italy	St. Francis of Assisi, St. Catherine of Siena
Japan	St. Peter
Mexico	Our Lady of Guadalupe
New Zealand	Our Lady Help of Christians
Poland	St. Casmir, St. Stanislaus, Our Lady of Czestochowa
Russia	St. Andrew, St. Nicholas of Myra, St. Thérèse of Lisieux
Scotland	St. Andrew, St. Columba
Spain	St. James, St. Teresa of Avila
United States	Immaculate Conception

Special Patrons

Accountants	St. Matthew
Actors	St. Genesius
Animals	St. Francis of Assisi
Athletes	St. Sebastian
Beggars	St. Martin of Tours
Boy Scouts	St. George
Dentists	St. Apollonia
Farmers	St. Isidore
Grocers	St. Michael
Journalists	St. Francis de Sales
Maids	St. Zita
Motorcyclists	Our Lady of Grace
Painters	St. Luke
Pawnbrokers	St. Nicholas
Police Officers	St. Michael
Politicians	St. Thomas More
Priests	St. John Vianney
Scientists	St. Albert
Skaters	St. Lydwina of Schiedam
Tailors	St. Homobonus
Teachers	St. Gregory the Great, St. John Baptist de la Salle
Wine Merchants	St. Amand

H. Devotions

THE MYSTERIES OF THE ROSARY

Joyful Mysteries
1. The Annunciation
2. The Visitation
3. The Nativity
4. The Presentation in the Temple
5. The Finding of Jesus in the Temple

Mysteries of Light
1. Jesus' Baptism in the Jordan River
2. Jesus' Self-manifestation at the Wedding of Cana
3. The Proclamation of the Kingdom of God and Jesus' Call to Conversion
4. The Transfiguration
5. The Institution of the Eucharist at the Last Supper

Sorrowful Mysteries
1. The Agony in the Garden
2. The Scourging at the Pillar
3. The Crowning with Thorns
4. The Carrying of the Cross
5. The Crucifixion

Glorious Mysteries
1. The Resurrection
2. The Ascension
3. The Descent of the Holy Spirit
4. The Assumption of Mary
5. The Crowning of Mary as the Queen of Heaven and Earth

HOW TO PRAY THE ROSARY

Opening
1. Begin on the crucifix and pray the Apostles' Creed.
2. On the first bead, pray the Our Father.
3. On the next three beads, pray the Hail Mary. (Some people meditate on the virtues of faith, hope, and charity on these beads.)
4. On the fifth bead, pray the Glory Be.

The Body

Each decade (set of ten beads) is organized as follows:
1. On the larger bead that comes before each set of ten, announce the mystery to be prayed (see above) and pray one Our Father.
2. On each of the ten smaller beads, pray one Hail Mary while meditating on the mystery.
3. Pray one Glory Be at the end of the decade. (There is no bead for the Glory Be.)

Conclusion

Pray the following prayer at the end of the rosary:

Hail, Holy Queen

Hail, holy Queen, Mother of Mercy,
our life, our sweetness, and our hope.
To thee do we cry,
poor banished children of Eve.
To thee do we send up our sighs,
mourning and weeping in this valley of
tears.
Turn then, most gracious advocate,
thine eyes of mercy toward us;
and after this our exile,
show unto us the blessed fruit of thy womb,
Jesus.

O clement, O loving, O sweet Virgin Mary.
Pray for us, O holy Mother of God,
that we may be made worthy of the promises
of Christ.
Amen.

STATIONS OF THE CROSS

The Stations of the Cross is a devotion and also a sacramental. (A sacramental is a sacred object, blessing, or devotion.) The Stations of the Cross are individual pictures or symbols hung on the interior walls of most Catholic churches depicting fourteen steps along Jesus' way of the cross. Praying the stations means meditating on each of the following scenes:

1. Jesus is condemned to death.
2. Jesus takes up his cross.
3. Jesus falls the first time.
4. Jesus meets his mother.
5. Simon of Cyrene helps Jesus carry his cross.
6. Veronica wipes the face of Jesus.
7. Jesus falls the second time.
8. Jesus consoles the women of Jerusalem.
9. Jesus falls the third time.
10. Jesus is stripped of his garments.
11. Jesus is nailed to the cross.
12. Jesus dies on the cross.
13. Jesus is taken down from the cross.
14. Jesus is laid in the tomb.

Some churches also include a fifteenth station, the resurrection of the Lord.

NOVENAS

The novena consists of the recitation of certain prayers over a period of nine days. The symbolism of nine days refers to the time Mary and the apostles spent in prayer between Jesus' ascension into heaven and Pentecost.

Many novenas are dedicated to Mary or to a saint with the faith and hope that she or he will intercede for the one making the novena. Novenas to Saint Jude, Saint Anthony, Our Lady of Perpetual Help, and Our Lady of Lourdes remain popular in the Church today.

LITURGY OF THE HOURS

The Liturgy of the Hours is part of the official, public prayer of the Church. Along with the celebration of the sacraments, the recitation of the Liturgy of the Hours, or Divine Office (office means "duty" or "obligation"), allows for constant praise and thanksgiving to God throughout the day and night.

The Liturgy of the Hours consists of five major divisions:

1. An hour of readings
2. Morning praises
3. Midday prayers
4. Vespers (evening prayers)
5. Compline (a short night prayer)

Scriptural prayer, especially the psalms, is at the heart of the Liturgy of the Hours. Each day follows a separate pattern of prayer with themes closely tied in with the liturgical year and feasts of the saints.

THE DIVINE PRAISES

These praises are traditionally recited after the benediction of the Blessed Sacrament.

Blessed be God.
Blessed be his holy name.
Blessed be Jesus Christ, true God and
    true man.
Blessed be the name of Jesus.
Blessed be his most Sacred Heart.
Blessed be his most Precious Blood.
Blessed be Jesus in the most holy sacrament
    of the altar.
Blessed be the Holy Spirit, the Paraclete.
Blessed be the great Mother of God, Mary
    most holy.
Blessed be her holy and Immaculate
    Conception.
Blessed be her glorious Assumption.
Blessed be the name of Mary, Virgin and
    Mother.
Blessed be Saint Joseph, her most chaste
    spouse.
Blessed be God in his angels and his saints.

I. Prayers

SIGN OF THE CROSS

In the name of the Father,
and of the Son,
and of the Holy Spirit. Amen.

OUR FATHER

Our Father
who art in heaven,
hallowed be thy name.
Thy kingdom come;
thy will be done on earth as it is in heaven.
Give us this day our daily bread
and forgive us our trespasses
as we forgive those who trespass against us.
And lead us not into temptation,
but deliver us from evil.
Amen.

GLORY BE

Glory be to the Father
and to the Son
and to the Holy Spirit,
as it was in the beginning,
is now,
and ever shall be,
world without end. Amen.

HAIL MARY

Hail Mary, full of grace,
the Lord is with thee.
Blessed art thou among women
and blessed is the fruit of thy womb, Jesus.
Holy Mary, Mother of God,
pray for us sinners now
and at the hour of our death. Amen.

MEMORARE

Remember, O most gracious Virgin Mary,
that never was it known
that anyone who fled to your protection,
implored your help,
or sought your intercession was left unaided.
Inspired by this confidence,
I fly unto you,
O virgin of virgins, my mother,
To you I come, before you I stand,
sinful and sorrowful.
O Mother of the Word incarnate,
despise not my petitions,
but in your mercy hear and answer me.
    Amen.

HAIL, HOLY QUEEN

Hail, holy Queen, Mother of Mercy,
our life, our sweetness and our hope!
To you do we cry,
    poor banished children of Eve;
to you do we send up our sighs,
    mourning and weeping in this valley of
        tears.
Turn then, O most gracious advocate,
your eyes of mercy toward us,
and after this exile,
show us the blessed fruit of your womb,
    Jesus.
O clement, O loving, O sweet Virgin Mary.
V. Pray for us, O holy mother of God.
R. that we may be made worthy of the promises of
Christ. Amen.

THE ANGELUS

V. The angel spoke God's message to Mary.
R. And she conceived by the Holy Spirit.
    Hail Mary . . .
V. Behold the handmaid of the Lord.
R. May it be done unto me according to your word.
    Hail Mary . . .
V. And the Word was made flesh.
R. And dwelled among us.
    Hail Mary . . .
V. Pray for us, O holy mother of God.

R. That we may be made worthy of the promises of
Christ.
    Let us pray: We beseech you, O Lord, to pour
out your grace into our hearts. By the message of an angel we have learned of the
incarnation of Christ, your son; lead us by his
passion and cross, to the glory of the resurrection. Through the same Christ our Lord.
Amen.

REGINA CAELI

Queen of heaven, rejoice, alleluia.
The Son you merited to bear, alleluia,
has risen as he said, alleluia.
Pray to God for us, alleluia.
V. Rejoice and be glad, O Virgin Mary, alleluia.
R. For the Lord has truly risen, alleluia.
    Let us pray.
God of life, you have given joy to the world
by the resurrection of your son, our Lord
Jesus Christ. Through the prayers of his
mother, the Virgin Mary, bring us to the happiness of eternal life. We ask this through
Christ our Lord. Amen.

GRACE AT MEALS
Before Meals

Bless us, O Lord,
and these your gifts,
which we are about to receive from your
    bounty,
through Christ our Lord. Amen.

After Meals

We give you thanks, almighty God,
for these and all the gifts
which we have received
from your goodness
through Christ our Lord. Amen.

GUARDIAN ANGEL PRAYER

Angel of God, my guardian dear, to whom
God's love entrust me here, ever this day be
at my side, to light and guard, to rule and
guide. Amen.

Prayer for the Faithful Departed

Eternal rest grant unto them, O Lord.

R: And let perpetual light shine upon them.

May their souls and the souls of all faithful departed,

through the mercy of God, rest in peace.

R: Amen.

Morning Offering

O Jesus, through the immaculate heart of Mary, I offer you my prayers, works, joys, and sufferings of this day in union with the holy sacrifice of the Mass throughout the world. I offer them for all the intentions of your Sacred Heart: the salvation of souls, reparation for sin, the reunion of all Christians. I offer them for the intentions of our bishops and all members of the apostleship of prayer and in particular for those recommended by your Holy Father this month. Amen.

Act of Faith

O God,
I firmly believe all the truths that you have revealed
and that you teach us through your Church,
for you are truth itself
and can neither deceive nor be deceived.
Amen.

Act of Hope

O God,
I hope with complete trust that you will give me,
through the merits of Jesus Christ, all necessary grace in this world
and everlasting life in the world to come,
for this is what you have promised
and you always keep your promises.
Amen.

Act of Love

O my God, I love you above all things, with my whole heart and soul, because you are all good and worthy of all my love. I love my neighbor as myself for the love of you. I forgive all who have injured me, and I ask pardon of all whom I have injured. Amen.

Prayer for Peace

Lord, make me an instrument of your peace.
Where there is hatred, let me sow love;
where there is injury, pardon;
where there is doubt, faith;
where there is despair, hope;
where there is darkness, light;
where there is sadness, joy.
O Divine Master,
grant that I may not seek so much to be consoled as to console;
to be understood, as to understand,
to be loved, as to love.
For it is in giving that we receive,
it is in pardoning that we are pardoned,
and it is in dying that we are born to eternal life.

St. Francis of Assisi

Glossary

abortion—The deliberate killing of unborn human life by means of medical or surgical procedures. Direct abortion is seriously wrong because it is an unjustified attack on human life.

absolution—The statement by which a priest, speaking as the official minister of Christ's Church, declares forgiveness of sins to a repentant sinner in the Sacrament of Reconciliation. The formula of absolution reads: "I absolve you from your sins; in the name of the Father, and of the Son, and of the Holy Spirit. Amen."

abstinence—The moral virtue that tempers one's appetite or desire for food, drink, sex, or other pleasurable experiences, such as the use of tobacco and drugs.

adultery—Sexual intercourse between a man and woman who are married to other people. (Or intercourse between an unmarried person and a married person.)

apostolic orders—Religious orders that stress apostolic works like caring for the downtrodden and sick, teaching, or preaching. Apostolic congregations for women include the Sisters of Charity, Franciscan Sisters, Sisters of Mercy, and Dominican Sisters. Apostolic orders for men include the Society of Jesus (the Jesuits), Franciscans, Salesians, Holy Cross, Christian Brothers, and Dominicans.

apostasy—The total rejection of Jesus Christ (and the Christian faith) by a baptized Christian.

assisted suicide—The intentional assistance of any dying or suffering person in taking his or her own life.

beatitude—An attitude guiding us to follow Jesus more closely in order to achieve holiness and happiness.

blasphemy—Hateful, defiant, reproachful thoughts, words, or acts against God, Jesus, his Church, the saints, or holy things.

calumny—Lying about others so people will make false judgments about them.

canon law—The full body of officially established rules governing the Catholic Church, which was last revised in 1983.

capital sins—Moral vices that give rise to many other failures to love. They are pride, avarice, lust, anger, gluttony, envy, and sloth.

cardinal virtues—The four hinge virtues that support moral living: prudence, or "right reason in action," concerning the best way to live morally; justice, or giving God and each person his or her due by right; fortitude, or courage to persist in living a Christian life; and temperance, or moderation in controlling our desires for physical pleasures.

charisms—Special gifts the Holy Spirit gives to individual Christians to build up the Church.

chastity—The moral virtue that helps one control sexual drive and expression in a way compatible to his or her state in life.

circumstances—The conditions or facts attending an event and having some bearing on it. Circumstances can increase or decrease the moral goodness or evil of an action.

complaisance—Pleasing others so they can carry out your wishes.

common good—"Sum total of social conditions that allow people, either as groups or as individuals, to reach their fulfillment more fully and more easily" (*Pastoral Constitution of the Church in the Modern World*, 26).

concupiscence—An inclination toward evil caused by Original Sin. More specifically, in Christian theology, it means "the rebellion of the 'flesh' against the spirit" (*CCC*, 2515).

conscience—A practical judgment of reason that helps a person decide the goodness or sinfulness of an action or attitude. It is the subjective norm of morality we must form properly and then follow.

contemplative orders—Religious orders that put a focus on living a life centered on the celebration of prayer, rather than on active ministry. Contemplative orders of men include the Benedictines, Trappists, and Carmelites. Contemplative orders for women include the Benedictines, the Poor Clares, Carmelites, and Trappistines.

contrition—Heartfelt sorrow and aversion for sins committed along with the intention to sin no more.

covenant—the strongest possible pledge and agreement between two parties.

determinism—The philosophy that holds that every event, action, and decision results from something independent of the human will.

detraction—Revealing a person's faults and failings to someone who did not previously know about them and who had no need or right to know about them.

dignity—The quality of being worthy of esteem or respect. Every human person has worth and value because each person is made in God's image.

discernment—A decision-making process that attends to the implications and consequences of an action or choice.

discipleship—The mandate of all baptized Christians to follow Jesus and participate in his role as priest, prophet, and king.

divorce—The dissolution of the marriage contract.

divination—Attempts to unveil what God wants hidden by calling up demonic powers, consulting horoscopes; the stars, or mediums; palm reading, etc.

euthanasia—Direct or active euthanasia is any "action or omission which of itself and by intention causes death, with the purpose of eliminating all suffering" (*Gospel of Life*, 65). Direct euthanasia is always wrong despite one's good intentions.

evangelical counsels—Vows taken to poverty, chastity, and obedience in order to live the Gospel more fully. The evangelical counsels were typically embraced by those in religious life.

fecundity—The ability to produce offspring, a gift proper to marriage, which can allow a husband and wife to participate with God in the creation of new life.

fidelity—Marital faithfulness between husbands and wives that requires reserving all sexual activity and affection for each other and also asks couples to be loyal to each other through good times and bad.

fornication—Sexual intercourse engaged in by an unmarried male and female.

fortitude—"The moral virtue that ensures firmness in difficulties and constancy in the pursuit of the good" (*CCC*, 1808).

free unions—Extended relationships where couples refuse to have their commitment formalized or sanctioned by law.

free will—"The power, rooted in reason and will [that enables a person], to perform deliberate actions on one's own responsibility" (*CCC*, 1731).

freedom—"The power, rooted in reason and will, . . . to perform deliberate actions on one's own responsibility" (*CCC*, 1731).

fruits of the Holy Spirit—Described as the firstfruits of eternal glory, they are charity, joy, peace, patience, kindness, goodness, generosity, gentleness, faithfulness, modesty, self-control, and chastity.

gifts of the Holy Spirit—God-given abilities that help us live a Christian life with God's help. Jesus promised and bestows these gifts through the Holy Spirit, especially in the Sacrament of Confirmation. The seven gifts are wisdom, understanding, knowledge, counsel (right judgment), fortitude, piety (reverence), and fear of the Lord (wonder and awe).

grace—A free and unearned favor from God, infused into our souls at Baptism, that adopts us into God's family and helps us to live as his children.

heresy—Outright denial by a baptized person of some essential truth about God and faith that we must believe.

humanism—A belief that deifies humanity and human potential to the exclusion of any belief in or reliance on God.

idolatry—The worship of false gods.

imputable—Ascribed, attributed, or definitely linked to a specific accountable person or entity.

incest—Sexual intimacy between relatives or in-laws.

incredulity—A mental disposition that either neglects revealed truth or willfully refuses to assent to it.

infertility—The physical incapacity of a female or male to cooperate with God's creative power in conceiving a child.

inherent—Inborn or inherited, something that does not need to be earned or acquired.

intention—The aim or objective of a course of action.

justification—The Holy Spirit's grace that cleanses us from our sins through faith in Jesus Christ and baptism. Justification makes us right with God.

Kingdom of God (or reign of God)—God's peace, justice, and love that was proclaimed by Jesus and inaugurated in his life, death, and resurrection. It refers to the process of God reconciling and renewing all things through his Son, to the fact of his will being done on earth as it is in heaven. The process has begun with Jesus and will be perfectly completed at the end of time.

law—"An ordinance of reason for the common good, promulgated by the one who is in charge of the community" (St. Thomas Aquinas in *CCC*, 1976).

Magisterium—The official teaching authority of the Church. The Lord bestowed the right and power to teach in his name on Peter and the apostles and their successors, that is, the pope and the college of bishops.

martyr—A witness ready to suffer and even die for truth and virtue; martyrdom is the ultimate act of fortitude.

masturbation—The deliberate stimulation of the genitals to obtain solitary sexual pleasure. It is contrary to the virtue of chastity.

materialism—A belief that the physical, material world is the only reality, and that spiritual existence, values, and faith are illusions.

means—A method, course of action, or instrument by which something can be accomplished.

metanoia—Greek term for repentance, a turning away from sin with the intention of living a Christian life.

modesty—The virtue of temperance applies to how a person speaks, dresses, and conducts himself or herself. Related to the virtue of purity, modesty protects the intimate center of a person by refusing to unveil what should remain hidden.

morality—Knowledge based on human experience, reason, and God's revelation that discovers what we ought to be and what we ought to do to live fully human lives.

moral object—The moral content of an action that suggests whether the action is directed toward the true good.

mortal sin—Personal sin that involves serious matter, sufficient reflection, and full consent of the will. It results in total rejection of God and alienation from him.

natural law—The reasoned participation of humans in God's eternal law that reveals what God intends us to do and avoid according to his wise and loving plan.

nihilism—A philosophy that denies there's any meaning in existence or in religious beliefs. Nihilists maintain that the only thing that comes after life is nothingness, annihilation.

Original Sin—The consequence of the sin of our first parents; the hereditary stain with which human beings are born because of our origins or descent from Adam and Eve.

Paschal Mystery—God's love and salvation revealed through the life, passion, death, resurrection, and glorification (ascension) of Jesus Christ. The sacraments, especially the Eucharist, celebrate this great mystery of God's love.

perjury—False witness under oath.

personal sin—A failure to love God above everything and our neighbor as ourselves.

polygamy—The practice of having more than one spouse.

precepts of the Church—The minimal obligations for members in good standing of the Catholic faith community.

prudence—The moral virtue that inclines us to lead good, ethical, and moral lives of action; "right reason in action," as St. Thomas Aquinas put it.

Reconciliation—A sacrament of healing, also known as Penance or Confession, through which Christ extends his forgiveness to sinners.

repentance—From the Greek word *metanoia*, it means change of mind or change of heart. A key aspect of following Jesus is to turn from our sins and embrace the way of the cross.

sacrilege—Profane or unworthy treatment of the sacraments; other liturgical actions; and persons, places, and things consecrated to God.

self-esteem—A sense of happiness and contentment about who you are as a human being. People with self-esteem consciously appreciate their own worth and importance, as if viewed in the eyes of God.

schism—Refusal to submit to the pope's authority or remain in union with members of the Catholic Church.

simony—The buying or selling of spiritual goods.

sobriety—Moderation or abstinence from alcoholic beverages or the use of drugs.

social justice—The form of justice that applies the gospel message of Jesus Christ to the structures, systems, and laws of society in order to protect the dignity of persons and guarantee the rights of individuals.

social sin—A cycle of sin, violence, and injustice caused by individual sins.

solidarity—The Christian virtue of social charity and friendship.

subsidiarity—The principle of Catholic social teaching that holds that a higher unit of society should not do what a lower unit can do as well (or better).

temperance—The virtue that regulates our attraction to pleasure and helps us use God's created goods in a balanced way.

theological virtues—Three important virtues bestowed on us at baptism that relate us to God: faith, or belief in and personal knowledge of God; hope, or trust in God's salvation and his bestowal of the graces needed to attain it; and charity, or love of God and love of neighbor as one loves oneself.

venial sin—Personal sin that weakens but does not kill our relationship with God.

vice—A bad habit, such as laziness, that inclines us to choose the evil rather than the good.

virtues—"Firm attitudes, stable dispositions, habitual perfections of intellect and will that govern our actions, order our passions, and guide our conduct according to reason and faith" (*CCC*, 1804).

voluntary doubt—The decision to ignore or a refusal to believe what God has revealed or what the Church teaches.

Index

Environment, 246
Envy, 143, 156, 247
Eternal life, 13–14, 96
Eucharist, 101, 273; and first commandment, 175; and Mass, 182; and sacrilege, 177; and Sabbath, 181; and sin, 145
Euthanasia, 56, 156, 205; and fourth commandment, 193
Evangelical counsels, 87, 116
Evil: and character formation, 16; intrinsic, 51; and Lord's Prayer, 111; as sin, 39
External freedom, 57

F

Faith, 16–17, 112, 167, 170–71
Faithfulness, 10
Family, 193
Fasting, 88
Fate, and freedom, 73
Father Kolbe Missionaries of the Immaculata, 116
Fear, 17; and freedom, 78
Fear of the Lord, 10, 75
Fecundity, 219
Feelings. *See* Emotion
Female. *See* Sexes; Sexuality
Fidelity, 219
Fifth Commandment, 198–208
First Commandment, 170–78
Flattery, 250
Forgiveness, 105–6; and Lord's Prayer, 111; and moral life, 19; of others, 104; of sin, 145, 149–50, 158–59
Fornication, 226–27
Fortitude, 17, 132–34; as gift of Spirit, 10; and Oscar Romero, 135
Fourth Commandment, 193–97
Francis, James Allen, 99
Franciscans, 115
Franciscan Sisters, 115
Francis de Sales, St., 20, 114
Frankl, Viktor, 42
Freedom, 19, 72–73, 75; abuses against, 77–78; gift of, 35–36; and grace, 78; of humans, 9; and law, 87; and morality, 11; of religion, 175
Free unions, 221
Free will, 34–35
Freud, Sigmund, 123
Fruit of the Spirit, 10

G

Gambling, 246
Generosity, 10
Gentleness, 10
Giovanni, Nikki, 26
Gluttony, 143
God: attributes of, 259; as Creator, 28–29; as Father, 33, 39, 40, 64, 110; love for, 35; love of, 100, 146, 166, 173–74, 190; and morality, 11; name of, 179; righteousness of, 103; and virtues, 16; worship of, 170
God's call. *See* Vocation
God's Word, 12–14. *See also* Scripture
Golden Rule, 107–9, 126
Goodness, 10; of creation, 31
Good Samaritan (parable of), 101
Good works, 106–7
Gospel: and law, 87; and liturgy of the Word, 101; and moral life, 13
Gossiping, 144
Grace, 39–40, 112–13; and beatitudes, 96; and freedom, 78; and merit, 113–14; and moral life, 106; and prudence, 48
Greed, 143, 145, 155, 247
Guilt, 73

H

Habit, 78. *See also* Vice; Virtue
Happiness, 8; and beatitudes, 96–98; and conscience, 122; and merit, 113; and moral life, 12–14

Hatred, 144, 174
Health, 206
Hell, 154
Hemingway, Ernest, 8, 123
Heresy, 171
Hermits, 115
Holiness: and Beatitudes, 96–98; growth in, 112; and merit, 113–14; and moral life, 114
Holmes, Oliver Wendell, 216
Holy Communion. *See* Eucharist
Holy Days, 87, 88
Holy Family Institute, 116
Holy Orders, 175
Holy Spirit: and discipleship, 115; and freedom, 77; fruits of, 10, 258; gift of, 39–40, 100; graces of, 8, 258; help of, 11; and justification, 112; and Magisterium, 61–62; and moral life, 12, 64; sin against, 158
Homosexuality, 229–30
Honesty, 16, 34, 144, 239–40, 249–53; and conscience, 58, 125
Honor, 193–95
Hope, 16, 17, 112, 167, 172
Humanism, 177
Humanity, 30–31; fall of, 31, 39; gift of, 19; and moral life, 26–27; nature of, 9–11, 33–35, 38; and place in creation, 29
Human reason, 81
Hypocrisy, 249

I

Idolatry, 176
Ignatius of Loyola, St., 66
Ignorance, 77
Image of God, 28, 29–30, 216; and freedom, 73
Immaculata Movement, 41
Immigration, 109
Imputable, 79
Inadvertence, 77
Incest, 221
Incredulity, 171
Indifference, 174
Infallibility, of Magisterium, 61–62
Infertility, 220
Ingratitude, 174
Inordinate attachments, 78
Intellect: and conscience, 126; and freedom, 77; and moral life, 19, 34; use of, 50, 51
Intelligence, 11
Intention, 52–54

J

Jesuits. *See* Society of Jesus
Jesus Christ, 260–61; and Beatitudes, 96; as brother, 33; death of, 77, 201; and discipleship, 115; and forgiveness, 150; friends of, 40; as fulfillment of law, 105–6; on good works, 106–7; and hope, 171; imitating, 19; and merit, 114; and moral law, 84; and moral life, 10, 12; as moral norm, 98; moral teachings of, 61–62; name of, 179; as new Moses, 102; and the poor, 244; poverty of, 14; and prayer, 63–64; as savior, 39–40, 145, 146–47, 149–50; and sin, 149–50; teaching of, 99–101; union with, 81–82; and virtue, 78. *See also* Paschal Mystery
John Chrysostom, St., 245
John Damascus, St., 260
John Paul II, Pope, 33, 41, 52
Johnson, Samuel, 8
Joy, 10
Judaism, 261
Judgment: and conscience, 124; of others, 107
Justice, 17, 238, 240–43; and fourth commandment, 193–95. *See also* Social justice
Justification: definition of, 112; of moral action, 50–56

Respect: and eighth commandment, 250; and fourth commandment, 193–95; and human dignity, 33; and justice, 240; for life, 203; and moral life, 40; for others, 26, 60–62; and sexuality, 218

Responsibility: and circumstances, 55; and conscience, 123; and freedom, 72–73, 79–80; to God, 11; of humans, 9; and moral life, 35; for ourselves, 26–27

Revelation, 9

Righteousness: of God, 103; and love, 108–9

Robert Bellarmine, St., 106

Robinson, Jackie, 197

Romero, Oscar, 135

Roosevelt, Eleanor, 189

Rosary, 275–76

S

Sabbath, 181

Sacraments, 272–74; and faith, 170–71; and grace, 113. *See also particular Sacraments*

Sacrifice: and first commandment, 175; and love, 174

Sacrilege, 177

Saints, 274–75

Salesians, 115

Salvation, 39–40

Same-sex unions, 30. *See also* Homosexuality

Sanctifying grace, 112–13

Sankara, Thomas, 227

Savior, 39–40, 145, 146–47, 149–50

Schism, 171

Scripture, 81, 261–63; and moral law, 83–84; and natural law, 85; reading of, 170

Second Commandment, 179–80

Second Vatican Council: on conscience, 124; on freedom, 73

Secular institutes, 116

Self-control, as fruit of the Spirit, 10

Self-esteem, 189, 190–91

Self-interest, 126

Selfishness, 155

Self-love. *See* Self-esteem

Sermon on the Mount, 87, 102–11, 247; and Beatitudes, 96–98; on divorce, 216; and moral life, 13; and swearing, 180

Seventh Commandment, 245–46; and Justice, 240

Sex: abuses of, 223, 226–30; goodness of, 216–18; premarital, 59; purpose of, 219

Sexes, 30–31

Sexuality, 59, 105, 216–18; and creation, 30; and obscenity, 180; and Ten Commandments, 218

Sexually transmitted diseases, 59, 223

Shakespeare, William, 249

Shoplifting, 15

Sin, 39, 141–51, 271; as abuse of freedom, 77; and alienation, 148; Bible on, 146–48; capital, 143; confession of, 87–88; and faith, 171; and first commandment, 175; forgiveness of, 158–59. *See also particular types of sin*

Sincerity, 129–31

Sinners, 142

Sisters of Charity, 115

Sisters of Mercy, 115

Sixth Commandment, 218–30

Slavery, 35

Sloth, 143

Smoking, 58–59

Sobriety, 206–7

Social justice, 240, 241; Church teaching on, 243–44, 271

Social sin, 155–56

Society of Jesus, 115

Solidarity, 37

Sorcery, 177

Soul, 30, 33

Southwell, Robert, 49

Spiritism, 177

Stations of the Cross, 276

Stealing, 127, 245–46; as intrinsic evil, 51

Stewardship, 42

Subsidiarity, 37

Suffering, 39

Suicide, 205

Superstition, 177

Swearing, 105, 180

Swope, Herbert Bayard, 26

T

Temperance, 17; and chastity, 206–7, 223; and modesty, 224

Temptation, 17, 152, 153; and faith, 171; and fortitude, 133; and Lord's Prayer, 111

Ten Commandments, 15, 52, 270; and happiness, 98; and love, 168–69; and moral object, 51; and mortal sin, 153; and natural law, 85; and old law, 86. *See also particular commandments*

Tenth Commandment, 247–48; and justice, 240

Teresa of Avila, 39

Teresa of Calcutta, 35, 103

Terrorism, 56, 109, 145; and fifth commandment, 200, 202, 203

Theological virtues, 16–17, 167, 271; and first commandment, 170–75

Thérèse of Lisieux, 64

Third Commandment, 181–82

Third Orders, 116

Thomas à Kempis, 122

Thomas Aquinas, St., 80; on law, 83, 87; on love, 173; on prudence, 17, 48

Tolstoy, Leo, 79

Torture, 56

Tradition, 81, 261–65; and Ten Commandments, 169

Trappists, 115

Trinity, 29, 259–60; and love, 35; and moral law, 83; as society, 38

Trust, 106–7

Truth: and conscience, 125; and moral life, 34

Truth-telling, 16

Twain, Mark, 84, 249

U

Understanding, 10

V

Values, 81

Vendetta, 105

Venial sin, 155, 271

Vianney, John, St., 40, 251

Vice: and conscience, 125–26; and sin, 151, 271; and venial sin, 155

Violence, 105, 106

Virtue, 15, 16, 270–71; and conscience, 125–26; how to grow in, 78; perfection of, 10; and sin, 151; and venial sin, 155. *See also* Cardinal virtues; Theological virtues

Vocation, 38, 124

Vow, 175

Vulgarity, 180

W

War, 199–201

Widows, 115

Wisdom, 10

Worry, 107

Worship, 181

Z

Zaharias, Babe Didrikson, 134

Catechism of the Catholic Church Index

Scripture Index